Lecture Notes in Computer Scienc

Karin Coninx Kris Luyten
Kevin A. Schneider (Eds.)

Task Models and Diagrams for Users Interface Design

5th International Workshop, TAMODIA 2006
Hasselt, Belgium, October 23-24, 2006
Revised Papers

Volume Editors

Karin Coninx
Hasselt University
Wetenschapspark 2
3590 Diepenbeek, Belgium
E-mail: karin.coninx@uhasselt.be

Kris Luyten
Hasselt University
Wetenschapspark 2
3590 Diepenbeek, Belgium
E-mail: kris.luyten@uhasselt.be

Kevin A. Schneider
University of Saskatchewan
Saskatoon SK S7N 5C9, Canada
E-mail: kas@cs.usask.ca

Library of Congress Control Number: 2007920036

CR Subject Classification (1998): H.5.2, H.5, D.2, D.3, F.3, I.6, K.6

LNCS Sublibrary: SL 2 – Programming and Software Engineering

ISSN 0302-9743
ISBN-10 3-540-70815-4 Springer Berlin Heidelberg New York
ISBN-13 978-3-540-70815-5 Springer Berlin Heidelberg New York

Springer is a part of Springer Science+Business Media

springer.com

Printed in Germany

Typesetting: Camera-ready by author, data conversion by Scientific Publishing Services, Chennai, India
Printed on acid-free paper SPIN: 12018130 06/3142 5 4 3 2 1 0

Preface

We are proud to present the TAMODIA 2006 proceedings. In 2006, the TAMODIA workshop celebrated its fifth anniversary. TAMODIA is an obscure acronym that stands for *TAsk MOdels and DIAgrams for user interface design.* The first edition of TAMODIA was organized in Bucharest (Romania) by Costin Pribeanu and Jean Vanderdonckt. The fact that five years later the TAMODIA series of workshops still continues successfully proves the importance of this research area for the human–computer interaction community! The first workshop aimed at examining how multiple forms of task expressions can significantly increase or decrease the quality of user interface design. This is still the scope of the current edition; we tried to assemble papers that discuss how the complexity of HCI design and development can be managed with tasks, models and diagrams. Much like the previous editions, the selection of papers from the 2006 edition reflects the broad scope of this field, which cannot be labeled with a single title or term.

The invited paper is by Joëlle Coutaz and discusses meta-user interfaces for ambient spaces. Finding appropriate ways to design and develop user interfaces for interactive spaces is becoming an important challenge for the creation of future usable applications. This exciting work gives a good feel of the new type of user interfaces and the required new approaches we are evolving toward when we want to realize the vision of ambient intelligent environments and create systems that can be used and controlled by the end-users.

From the papers included in these proceedings, we can clearly see both fields, HCI and software engineering, moving toward each other. Techniques from software engineering are becoming more popular and tuned for HCI design and development. Requirements engineering, model-driven engineering, model-based design and patterns are already familiar in both fields, but differ in notations and approaches. Established notations such as UML and Petrinets are helping us link models used in both fields and integrate approaches. In all papers, the end-user is never forgotten, and the user tasks and context that need to be supported play a central role.

October 2006

Kris Luyten
Belgium

Organization

Workshop Chair

Karin Coninx (Hasselt University, Belgium)

Program Co-chairs

Kris Luyten (Hasselt University, Belgium)
Kevin A. Schneider (University of Saskatchewan, Canada)

Local Organization

Ingrid Konings (Hasselt University, Belgium)
Frederik Winters (Hasselt University, Belgium)
Jo Vermeulen (Hasselt University, Belgium)

Review Committee

Alan Dix, Lancaster University, UK
Peter Forbrig, University of Rostock, Germany
Fabio Paternò, ISTI-CNR, Italy
Philippe Palanque, Université Toulouse 3 (Paul Sabatier), France
Gerrit C. Van der Veer, Vrije Universiteit Amsterdam, The Netherlands
Rémi Bastide, Université Toulouse 1, France
Gaëlle Calvary, University of Grenoble I, France
Quentin Limbourg, Catholic University of Louvain, Belgium
Nuno Jardim Nunes, University of Madeira, Portugal
Costin Pribeanu, ICI Bucuresti, Romania
Matthias Rauterberg, Eindhoven University of Technology, The Netherlands
Anke Dittmar, University of Rostock, Germany
Dave Roberts, Usability Competency Centre, IBM, UK
Ahmed Seffah, Concordia University, Canada
Pavel Slavík, Czech Technical University in Prague, Czech Republic
Karin Coninx, Hasselt University, Belgium
Marco Antonio Alba Winckler, Université Paul Sabatier, France
Corina Sas, Lancaster University, UK
Christian Stary, University of Linz, Austria
Birgit Bomsdorf, University of Hagen, Germany
Carmen Santoro, ISTI-CNR, Italy
Maria-Dolores Lozano, Universidad de Castilla-La Mancha, Spain
Regina Bernhaupt, University of Salzburg, Austria
Erik G. Nilsson, Sinteff, Norway
Mieke Massink, ISTI-CNR, Italy

Kris Luyten, Hasselt University, Belgium
Victor M. López Jaquero, University of Castilla-La Mancha, Spain
Elizabeth Furtado, UNIFOR, Brasil
Peter J. Wild, University of Bath, UK
Zeljko Obrenovic, Centrum voor Wiskunde en Informatica, The Netherlands

Table of Contents

Invited Paper

Tool Support

Model-Based Interface Development

User Interface Patterns

Bridging the Gap: Driven by Models

Task-Centered Design

Multi-modal User Interfaces

Reflections on Tasks and Activities in Modeling

Context and Plasticity

Meta-User Interfaces for Ambient Spaces

Joëlle Coutaz

Université Joseph Fourier, LIG,
385 rue de la Bibliothèque, BP 53, 38041 Grenoble Cedex 9, France
joelle.Coutaz@imag.fr

Abstract. In this article, we propose the concept of meta-User Interface (meta-UI) as the set of functions (along with their user interfaces) that are necessary and sufficient to control and evaluate the state of interactive ambient spaces. This set is *meta-*, since it serves as an umbrella beyond the domain-dependent services that support human activities in an ambient interactive space. They are *User Interface*-oriented since their role is to help users to control and evaluate the state of this space. We present a dimension space to classify, compare, and contrast disparate research efforts in the area of meta-UI's. We then exploit the generative power of our design space to suggest directions for future research.

Keywords: Ubiquitous computing, ambient interactive spaces, design space, taxonomy, meta-UI, GUI desktop.

1 Introduction

The capacity for users to control and evaluate system state is fundamental to Computer-Human Interaction [33]. This principle, promoted in the early 1980's by cognitive psychologists and human factors specialists, has actually been applied twenty years earlier by computer scientists who introduced the concept of Job Control Language (JCL). JCL, used for batch processing, has been progressively replaced with the Unix Shell followed by graphical desktops. With the emergence of ambient computing, users are not limited to the system and applications of a single computer. Instead, ambient computing embraces a model in which users, services, and resources discover other users, services and resources, and integrate them into an ambient interactive space.

An *ambient interactive space* is a dynamic assembly of physical entities coupled with computational and communicational entities to support human activities. An ambient interactive space can be as simple as a workstation or a PDA connected to the services of the Internet, or as complex as a computational ecosystem that evolves to adapt to the context of use. Augmented rooms such as FAME [29], iRoom [25], i-LAND [40] and Dynamo [24], are early examples of interactive spaces where users meet in a dedicated place to collaborate. With Jigsaw, users can create domestic services by assembling augmented objects [38]. Coupling two tranSticks makes it possible to extend a local interactive space to that of a distant machine [1]. An ambient interactive space can also be viewed as a computational aura that follows users as they move from place to place [16].

K. Coninx, K. Luyten, and K.A. Schneider (Eds.): TAMODIA 2006, LNCS 4385, pp. 1–15, 2007.

These examples show that, with ambient computing, we are shifting from the control of systems and applications confined to a single workstation to that of a dynamic interactive space where the boundaries between the physical and the digital worlds are progressively disappearing. As a result, the pre-packaged well-understood solutions provided by shells and desktops are not sufficient [5], and many interaction techniques are being developed for ambient computing, although on a case-per-case basis. This ad-hoc approach is adequate for local exploration, but may not provide sufficient insights to the problem.

In this article, we propose the concept of meta-UI (meta-User Interface) to denote a kind of interactive system that allows users to control, mould and understand their interactive ambient spaces. In the following section, we define the notion of meta-UI and propose a taxonomic space to understand its nature more precisely. Then, using this space, we classify, compare, and contrast disparate research efforts in the area of meta-UI's to suggest directions for future research.

2 Definition and Taxonomy

A *meta-UI* is an interactive system whose set of functions is necessary and sufficient to control and evaluate the state of an interactive ambient space. This set is *meta-* because it serves as an umbrella *beyond* the domain-dependent services that support human activities in this space. It is *UI*-oriented because its role is to allow users to control and evaluate the state of the ambient interactive space. In the context of this article, a meta-UI *is not* an abstract model, nor a language description, whose transformation/interpretation would produce a concrete effective UI. It is an over-arching interactive system whose role is to ambient computing what desktops and shells are to conventional workstations.

As shown in Fig. 1, a meta-UI is characterized by its *functional coverage* in terms of *services* and *object types*. In turn, the services and objects are invoked and referenced by the way of an *interaction technique* (or UI) that provides users with some *level of control*. An interaction technique is a language (possibly *extensible*) characterized by the *representation* (vocabulary) used to denote objects and functions as well as by the way users construct sentences (including how they select/*designate* objects and functions). Given the role of a meta-UI, the elements of the interaction technique of the meta-UI cohabit with the UI's of the domain-dependent services that it governs. The last dimension of our taxonomy, the *integration level*, expresses this relationship.

Functional coverage, interaction technique, and quality, are typical issues to be addressed when analyzing and designing an interactive system. We have refined these issues for the particular case of meta-UI's into a set of dimensions that are discussed next in more detail.

2.1 Object Types

Objects involved in the services of a meta-UI may be *digital*, *mixed-by-design* and/or *mixed-by-construction*. Applications and files are typical examples of digital objects

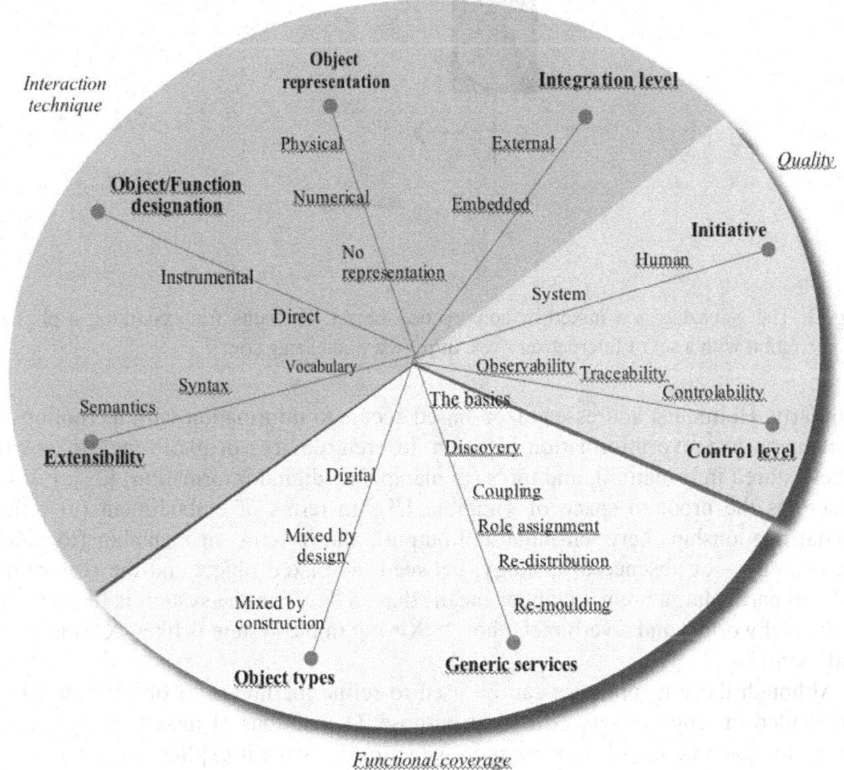

Fig. 1. Dimension space for meta-UI's

manipulated through the services of a meta-UI. Interactors such as windows, pointers, menus and forms, are other examples of digital objects. They are the conceptual units of windowing systems, which, according to our definition, are part of a conventional meta-UI.

A *mixed-by-design object* is an entity that results from the coupling, *by the designer*, of physical entities with digital services. A PDA and a mobile phone are mixed-by-design objects: the assembly of physical components with digital parts has been performed by designers beforehand.

A *mixed-by-construction object* is a mixed object that results from the coupling, *by the end-user*, of physical entities with digital service in order for that object to fulfill its *raison d'être*. For example, to function as a pointing device, the physical object that holds in the hand (called the mouse) must be coupled with the system mouse driver by the end-user. Similarly, the plastic rabbit shown in Fig. 2 must be coupled by the end-user to an Internet service (such as time of the day or weather forecast) to serve as a communicating object.

The distinction between pure digital objects and mixed reality objects is now well understood. For mixed objects, the situation is still unclear. For example, Fitzmaurice's taxonomy applies to a particular type of phicons – the bricks [15].

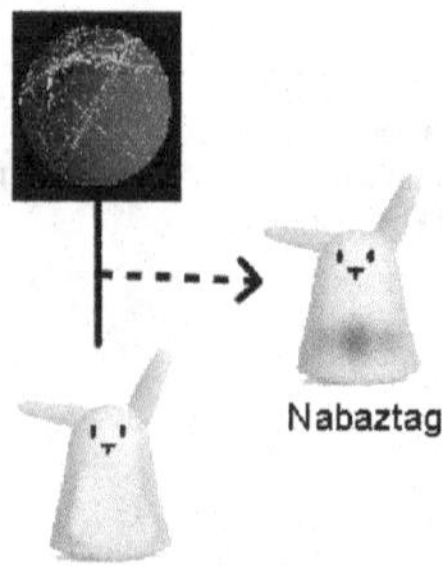

Fig. 2. The Nabaztag is a mixed-by-construction object. It results from coupling a physical plastic rabbit with a set of Internet services. http://www.nabaztag.com

Similarly, Holmquist addresses token-based access to information with the notions of containers (to move information between different devices or platforms), tokens (to access stored information), and tools (to manipulate digital information) [23]. Fishkin structures the problem space of Tangible UI's in terms of embodiment (to reflect spatial relationships between input and output), and in terms of metaphor (to reflect the analogy – or absence of analogy, between the mixed object and the real world) [14]. In particular, a noun metaphor means that an "<X> in the system is like an <X> in the real world", and a verb metaphor, "<X>-ing in the system is like <X>-ing in the real world."

Although these taxonomies can be used to refine the notion of object types, they are limited in scope or serve different purpose. Our notions of mixed-by-design and mixed-by-construction objects are more generic and make it explicit the capacity (or incapacity) for end-users to mould their own interactive space.

2.2 Generic Services

Back in the 1960's, JCL provided end-users with generic services to control jobs execution and to perform files management. In the early 1980's, the Xerox Star introduced additional generic functions such as find, cut and paste, undo and redo. Starting/stopping the execution of a service, moving and renaming files, cutting and pasting data, as well as finding, are the *basics* of conventional meta-UI's. They are conceptually valid in ambient computing, but they need to be extended and refined.

In particular, the notion of finding can be extended with that of *objects discovery*. Objects discovery is key to building a sound mental model of the boundary and of the state of ambient spaces. For example, the Speakeasy browser allows users to explore lists of objects that satisfy some specified search criteria (such as location, object types, availability, etc.) [32].

Because users are not simply consumers, but the designers and architects of their own interactive space, because the system must manage resource allocation dynamically, *coupling objects* becomes key. Coupling is the act of binding objects so that they can operate together to provide a new set of functions that these objects are unable to provide individually [11]. Two ConnecTables can be dynamically coupled by approaching them close to each other to enlarge the screen real estate [41]. With DataTiles, users obtain new services by configuring tagged transparent tiles on a flat panel display [37]. The analysis presented in [11] shows that coupling raises a large number of research issues.

Objects discovery allows users (and the system) to be aware of the objects that can be coupled. By coupling objects, users (and the system) build new constructs whose components play a set of roles (or functions). In conventional computing, roles are generally predefined. Typically, the screen of a laptop plays the role of an interaction resource, and this role is immutable by design. In ambient computing, where serendipity is paramount, *assigning roles to objects* becomes crucial. For example, in the Olympic Café scenario illustrated in Fig. 3, Bob and Jane uses spoons and lumps of sugar to denote the streets and buildings of the city they are planning together [10]. Bob couples a spoon with the table by laying it down on the table. The system can then discover the presence of the spoon and assigns it the role of interaction resource. (The spoon coupled with the system objects tracker and identifier is a mixed-by-construction object.) Then, by uttering the sentence "this spoon is Street Michel-Ange" while pointing at the spoon, Bob couples the interaction resource with a particular digital object known by the system as Street Michel-Ange. By doing so, Bob assigns the role of token[1] to the spoon.

Fig. 3. Bob and Jane use physical objects on the table to illustrate their ideas for the layout of the city they are planning together

One particular role of interest in UI design, is that of input and output interaction resource. In conventional computing, these resources are connected to a single computer. In ambient computing, the platform is a dynamic cluster composed (by the way of coupling) of multiple interconnected computing devices whose interaction resources, all together, form an *habitat* for UI components. Instead of being *centralized*, user interfaces may now be *distributed* across the interaction resources of the cluster.

UI re-distribution, i.e. the application of *objects re-distribution* to UI components, denotes the re-allocation of the UI components of the interactive space to different interaction resources. For example, the Sedan-Bouillon Web site shown in Fig. 4, whose UI is centralized on a single PC screen, is re-distributed in Fig. 5 across the interaction resources of the PC and the PDA. Objects re-distribution and objects coupling may require object re-moulding.

[1] Token, as in Holmquist's taxonomy [23].

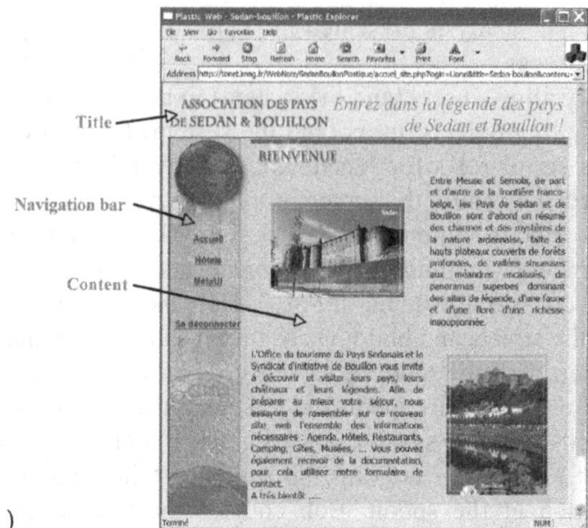

Fig. 4. The Sedan-Bouillon Web site when centralized on a PC

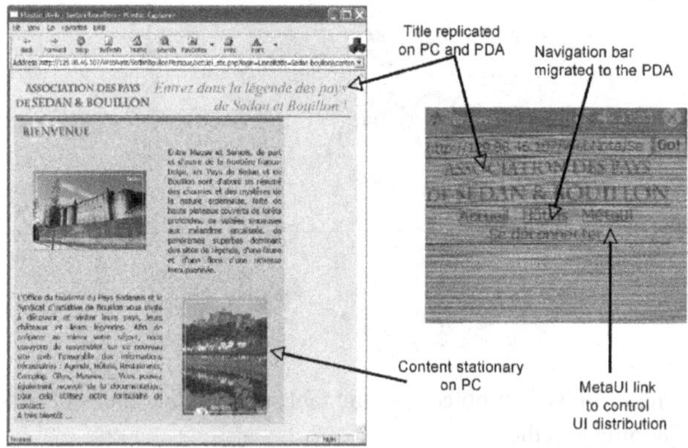

Fig. 5. The UI of the Sedan-Bouillon Web site when distributed across the resources of the PC and the PDA

Object re-moulding is to reshape objects without distorting their role. Applied to user interface components, *UI re-moulding* denotes the reconfiguration of the user interface that is perceivable to the user and that results from transformations applied to the source user interface. UI transformations include: *suppression* of the UI components that become irrelevant in the new context of use; *insertion* of new UI components to provide access to new services relevant in the new context of use, *reorganization* of UI components by revisiting their spatial layout and/or their temporal dependency. Reorganization may result from the suppression and/or insertion of UI components.

Re-moulding may result in using different modalities, or in exploiting multimodality differently. For example, because of the lack of computing power, the synergistic-complementarity [12] of the source multimodal UI (as in the example of

Fig. 3) may be transformed into an alternate-complementarity, or complementarity itself may disappear.

UI re-moulding is *intra-modal* when the source UI components that need to be changed are retargeted within the same modality. Note that if the source user interface is multimodal, then, the target UI is multimodal as well: intra-modal remoulding does not provoke any loss in the modalities set. UI re-moulding is *inter-modal* when the source UI components that need to be changed are retargeted into a different modality. Inter-modal retargeting may engender a modality loss or a modality gain. Thus, a source multimodal UI may be retargeted into a mono-modal UI and conversely, a mono-modal UI may be transformed into a multimodal UI. UI Re-moulding is *multi-modal* when it uses a combination of intra- and inter-modal transformations. For example, Teresa supports multi-modal re-moulding between graphics and vocal modalities [6]. As for inter-modal re-moulding, multi-modal re-moulding may result in a modality loss or in a modality gain.

All of the services provided by a meta-UI are executed under some level of human/system control.

2.3 Control

As for any interactive system, the services of a meta-UI may be executed on the system *initiative* and/or user's *initiative*. In the example of Fig. 3, the system takes the initiative to discover and couple the spoon with the table. May be, Bob did not mean this. Initiative owning relates to implicit and explicit interaction which, in turn, relies on an appropriate model of context of use [10]. Context modeling as well as the balance between implicit and explicit interaction are still open issues.

Once a meta-UI service is launched, what kind of control does the user have? At minimum, *observability* should be supported, i.e. users should be able to evaluate the internal state of the service from its current perceivable representation. The next step is *traceability* by which users can observe the evolution of the service over time, but they cannot modify this evolution. With *controllability*, users can observe, trace, and intervene on the evolution of the meta-UI service. As shown in Fig. 6, Sedan-Bouillon users can decide where to re-distribute the UI components of the web site.

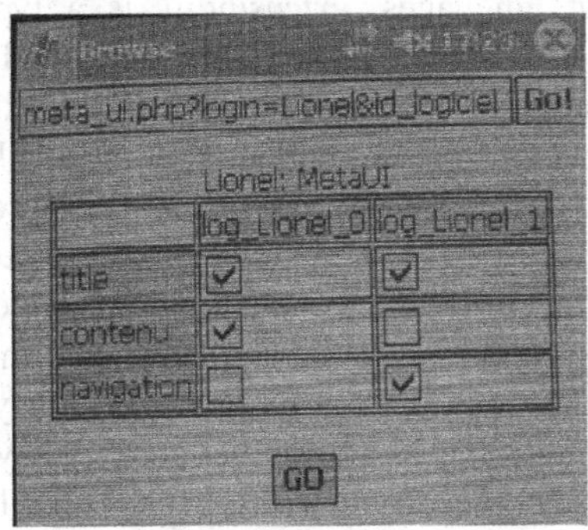

Fig. 6. This form allows users to specify the re-distribution of the UI components of the Sedan-Bouillon web site

Accessing a particular service of a meta-UI and controlling its execution is supported by the way of an interaction technique.

2.4 Interaction Technique

In the context of this article, the term interaction technique denotes the user interface of the meta-UI. It is the set of sentences (i.e. the language) built from vocabulary elements assembled according to some predefined syntax, and whose semantics is expressed in terms of the generic services of the meta-UI.

Objects that can be involved in a meta-UI service are denoted by vocabulary elements. Some objects may be denoted by a representative which, in turn, may be *numerical* of *physical*. Others have *no representative*. They belong to the vocabulary. In the Olympic café scenario, a spoon is a physical representation of a street. It is not the street of the real world. Alternatively, in GUI geographical systems, real-world streets are represented numerically as lines in graphical maps. When coupling a mouse with its driver by plugging its connector into a USB port, the physical object mouse is part of the sentence. It is not represented. Coupling Hinckley's tablets is performed by bringing them in contact [20]. The tablets are not represented. The absence of representative may apply to digital objects as well: when moving a window, one acts on the window per se, not on a representative. Jigsaw, based on the noun metaphor, uses jigsaw pieces to represent objects and services for domestic environments [38]. Jigsaw pieces may be numerical or physical.

The elaboration of a sentence, which requires objects and functions designation, may be *direct* by acting on vocabulary elements, or indirect by the way of *instruments*. In turn, instruments may be physical or digital with various levels of indirection [4]. Moving a window with a finger is direct, whereas, moving it by the way of a pen is instrumental (the pen acts as a physical instrument). Alternatively, moving a window with a mouse is instrumental with one additional level of indirection: the window is not moved by the mouse, but by a pointer, a digital representative of the mouse. By assembling Jigsaw pieces, users can build sentences like "if someone rings the bell, take a picture and send it to my PDA". Selecting physical pieces is direct whereas selecting numerical pieces is instrumental.

When reasoning about languages, *extensibility* is a typical issue to consider. Applied to our domain, is it possible for users to extend the *vocabulary* of the interaction technique, change its *syntax*, and from there, extend its *semantics*, thus create new meta-UI services? In an unbound domain like ambient computing, extensibility seems unavoidable, but the risk of introducing additional complexity is high. In conventional desktops, most users build simple sentences such as 'move this window here" or "cancel this process". Simple programs are elaborated by the way of macros. From end-user programming, we are now entering the area of end-user development. Although end-users are not programmers, they want to program their interactive space without meaning it. This is yet another key challenge that systems like Jigsaw, iCAP, and many others try to address (Cf. Table 1).

Given that a meta-UI provides users with the means to govern the domain-specific services of an interactive ambient space, how do its UI elements relate with that of the domain-specific services? What are they *level of integration*? We propose two approaches to this question: all or parts of the UI components of the meta-UI are *embedded* with (or weaved into) the UI components of the domain-dependent services. Collapse-to-zoom [3] and "Attach me, detach me, Assemble me" use the weaving approach [18]. Fig. 7 shows another example.

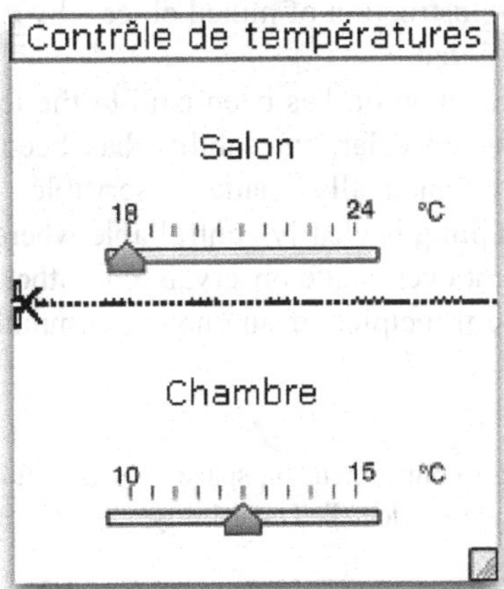

Fig. 7. The scissors icon, which allows users to cut the window into two pieces, denotes a meta-UI service whose UI is weaved into the UI of domain-dependent services (here, controlling the heat level of two rooms in a domestic environment)

Alternatively, UI components of the meta-UI services are not mixed with the UI components of the domain-dependent services. They are *external*. As shown in Fig. 6, Sedan-Bouillon users specify the re-distribution of the UI components of the web site using a dedicated form. Actually, a mix of weaving and external sounds reasonable. For example, in Sedan-bouillon, access to the re-distribution service is embedded in the navigation bar of the web site (see the "meta-UI" link in Fig. 4), whereas the specification of the re-distribution is external.

3 Analysis

Tables 1 and 2 synthesize research efforts we have selected for their relevance to the area of meta-UI. Although we have used a subset of our dimension space, the tables call for the following preliminary remarks.

In terms of functional coverage and human control:

- None of the systems proposes the full set of meta-UI services. In particular, role assignment is ignored (which means that it is hard-coded into the systems), and re-moulding is rarely supported. On the other hand, discovery and coupling are rather well represented. In addition, if discovery is supported, coupling is available as well: objects that can be discovered call naturally for their assembly. If coupling is available, re-distribution is generally supported, but, as in Put-That-There, the opposite is not necessarily true. In this case, the ambient space permits re-configuration but only for a predefined set of objects.

- Almost all meta-UI's of our list manipulate pure digital objects, and most of them include mixed-by-design objects (that is objects assembled by designers). The construction of mixed objects by end-users is emerging, but still under-represented.
- So far, very little attention has been paid to the level of control left to the human actor. In particular, traceability has been systematically ignored. Discovery is systematically made observable, and, to a less extent, controllable. Coupling is clearly controllable whereas re-moulding is out of human control, not even made observable. In other words, system designers tend to adopt the principles of autonomic computing, rejecting the human from the loop.

Table 1. Meta-UI's according to our dimension space. (Legend: E denotes the existence of the service, O = Observability of the service, T=Traceability, C=Controllability).

	Discovery				Coupling				Redistribution				Remoulding			
	E	O	T	C	E	O	T	C	E	O	T	C	E	O	T	C
Aris [7]	X	X			X				X	X	X	X				
a CAPella [13]	X	X														
DongleRelate [26	X	X		X	X	X		X								
MigreXML [30]	X	X			X				X	X	X	X	X			
AmbientDesk [1	X	X			X	X		X	X	X		X				
SpeakEasy [32]	X	X		X	X				X			X	X			
Jigsaw [38]	X	X			X	X		X								
E-Gadget [27]	X	X			X	X		X								
iCAP [39]	X	X		X												
Lego Logo [28]					X	X		X								
Bope [34]					X			X	X			X				
MightyMouse [9	X	X			X				X			X				
Dynamo [24]	X	X			X	X		X	X	X		X				
Peebles [31]	X				X				X	X		X				
PutThatThere[19									X			X				
iStuff [2]	X				X											
Icrafter [35]	X	X		X												
Collapse [3]									X			X				
AttachMe [18]					X			X	X			X				
Stitching [21]					X			X	X	X	X	X				
DataTiles [37]					X	X		X								
Triangles [17]					X	X		X								
Hinckley [22]					X	X		X	X	X		X	X			
SyncTap [36]					X			X								
tranSticks [1]					X			X								

Table 2. Meta-UI's according to our dimension space (contd.)

	Object Types			Representation			Integration level	
	Mixed-by-Construct	**Mixed-by-design**	**Digital**	**No-Repr.**	**Digital Repr.**	**Physical Repr.**	**Embedded**	**External**
Aris		X	X		X			X
a CAPella	X	X	X		X			X
DongleRelate		X			X			X
MigreXML		X	X		X			X
AmbientDes		X	X	X	X			X
SpeakEasy		X	X		X			X
Jigsaw	X	X	X		X	X		X
E-Gadget	X	X			X			X
iCAP	X	X	X		X			X
Lego Logo	X	X				X		X
Bope		X	X		X	X		X
MightyMous		X	X		X			X
Dynamo		X	X		X			X
Peebles		X	X		X			X
PutThatTh			X	X	X			X
iStuff	X	X		X				X
Icrafter		X	X		X			X
Collapse			X	X			X	
AttachMe			X	X			X	
Stitching			X	X	X			X
DataTiles			X		X	X		X
Triangles		X	X		X	X		X
Hinckley		X	X	X				X
SyncTap		X	X	X	X			X
tranSticks		X	X			X		X

In terms of interaction technique:

- Most systems use a mix of two styles of representation: on one hand, digital with physical representations, on the other hand, digital representation and absence of representation. Only two systems cover all three modes: a CAPella and ICAP. Interestingly, the absence of representation is progressively emerging, but then the objects to be manipulated must be closely co-located with the user.
- The UI of the meta-UI's of our list is almost always external, rarely embedded, and never uses a mix of embedded and external. Embedding the UI the meta-UI potentially increases a feeling of continuity at a risk, however, to overload the UI of the domain-dependent services. Not surprising then that observability is not well supported. For example, in Collapse-to-zoom, which allows users to collapse areas of web pages deemed irrelevant, the existence of the service for re-moulding is not observable. An external UI that is not observable has even

less chance to be discovered. For example, Stitching [21], based on synchronous gestures [22], allows users to call upon two meta-UI services in one single gesture: using a stylus as an instrument, two tablets can be coupled, and at the same time, the UI components of the domain-dependent services can be re-distributed across the tablets. The interaction trajectory is very efficient, feedback is provided as the gesture is accomplished (re-moulding is both traceable and controllable), but the availability of coupling is not observable.

4 Conclusion: Directions for Future Research

The frenetic development of ambient interactive systems has entailed the creation of many sorts of end-user tools for controlling and shaping their interactive spaces. In this article, we propose the concept of meta-UI as a unifying umbrella along with a taxonomy to structure the problem space and to identify directions for future research.

Using our taxonomy, the analysis of the state of the art shows that we need to re-think the "basics" (find, cut&paste, etc.) in the light of multi-scale interactive spaces; The integration (embedded-ness) of the meta-UI with domain-dependent services has not been addressed explicitly, and services like role assignment and coupling have been overlooked [11]. Models and mechanisms are currently being developed for re-moulding and re-distribution under the umbrella of plastic UI's and context-aware adaptive UI's. But we should be very careful at considering the level of control left to end-users. We all agree that the Human should be kept in the loop, but the temptation is high for "systemers" to develop autonomic systems just for the sake of the scientific challenge.

Based on these observations, we have designed a prototype meta-UI that supports the discovery and coupling of mixed-by-design objects (PDA's and PC), as well as UI re-distribution. The integration of the UI of this meta-UI uses a combination of embedded-ness and externality using objects ownership as a driving principle: the user interface of the meta-UI services that act on the UI components of the domain-specific services are embedded (e.g., splitting and duplicating informational content) whereas the user interface of the meta-UI services that manipulate objects that are domain-independent (e.g., coupling PDA's and PC's) is external. For UI re-distribution, which allows end-users to re-allocate domain-dependent UI components to domain-independent objects such as PDA's and PC's, we use a mix of embedded and external approaches to bridge the gap between the system infrastructure and the application domain.

This early experience also demonstrates the difficulty to empower end-users with the appropriate programming mechanisms. End-user programming has been around for nearly twenty years. Graphical notations and programming by demonstration, all have shown limitations over textual programming. Combining expressive power and simplicity is yet another challenge to address for ambient interactive spaces.

Acknowlegments. This work is supported partly by the EMODE ITEA project (if04046), and partly by the SIMILAR network of excellence (http://www.similar.cc), the European research task force creating human-machine interfaces similar to human-human communication (FP6-2002-IST1-507609). Our thanks to Anne Roudaut, Xavier Alvaro, Jean-Sébastien Sottet, and Lionel Balme for the early implementation of the CESAME meta-UI prototype.

References

1. Ayatsuka, Y., and Rekimoto, J. tranSticks: Physically Manipulatable Virtual Connections. In *Proceedings of the SIGCHI conference on Human factors in computing systems* (CHI 2005), ACM Press, New York, NY, 2005, 251-260.
2. Ballagas, R., Ringel, M., Stone, M., and Brochers, J. iStuff: A Physical User Interface Toolkit for Ubiquitous Computing Environments. In *Proceedings of the SIGCHI conference on Human factors in computing systems (CHI 2003),* ACM Press, New York, NY, 2003, 537-544.
3. Baudisch, P., Xie, X., Wang, C., and Ma, W.Y. Collapse-to-zoom: Viewing Web Pages on Small Screen Devices by Interactively Removing Irrelevant Content. In *Proceedings of User Interface Software and Technology (UIST 2004)*, Technotes, ACM Press, New York, NY, 2004, 91-94.
4. Beaudouin-Lafon, M. Instrumental Interaction: An Interaction Model for Designing Post-WIMP User Interfaces. In *Proceedings of the SIGCHI conference on Human factors in computing systems (CHI 2000),* ACM Press, New York, NY, 2000, 446-453.
5. Bellotti V., Back M., Edwards K., Grinter R., Henderson A., and Lopes C. Making Sense of Sensing Systems: Five Questions for Designers and Researchers. In *Proceedings of the SIGCHI conference on Human factors in computing systems (CHI 2002),* ACM Press, New York, NY, 2002, 415–422.
6. Berti, S., and Paternò, F. Migratory multimodal interfaces in multidevice environments. In *Proc. International Conference on Multimodal Interfaces (ICMI 2005)*, ACM Publ., 2005, 92-99.
7. Biehl, J.T, and Bailey, B.P. ARIS: An interface for application Relocation in an interactive space. *In Proceedings GI 2004, Canadian Human-Computer Communications Society,* 2004, 107-116.
8. Block, F., Schmidt, A., Villar, N., and Gellersen, H.W. Towards a Playful User Interface for Home Entertainment Systems. In *Proceedings of European Symposium on Ambient Intelligence (EUSAI 2004)* (Eindhoven, Netherlands), Springer, 2004, 207-217.
9. Booth, K.S., Ficher, B.D., Lin, C.J.R., and Argue, R. The « mighty Mouse » Multi-Screen Collaboration Tool. *Proceedings of User Interface Software and Technology (UIST 2002),* ACM Press, New York, NY, 2002, 209-212.
10. Coutaz, J., Crowley, J. , Dobson, S., and Garlan, D. Context is Key, *Communications of the ACM,* ACM Publ., 48(3), March 2005, 49-53.
11. Coutaz, J., Borkowski, S., and Barralon, N. Coupling Interaction Resources: an Analytical Model. In *Proceedings of European Symposium on Ambient Intelligence (EUSAI 2005) (Grenoble, France)*, 183-188.
12. Coutaz, J., Nigay, L., Salber, D., Blandford, A., May, J. and Young, R. Four Easy Pieces for Assessing the Usability of Multimodal Interaction: The CARE properties. In *Proceedings of the INTERACT'95 conference (Interact'95) (Lillehammer, Norway)*, S. A. Arnesen & D. Gilmore Eds., Chapman&Hall Publ., June 1995, 115-120.

13. Dey, A., Hamid, R., Beckmann, C., Li, Y., and Hsu, D. a CAPpella: Programming by Demonstration of Context-Aware Applications. In *Proceedings of the SIGCHI conference on Human factors in computing systems (CHI 2004) (Vienne, Austria),* ACM Press, New York, NY, 2004, 33-40.
14. Fishkin, K.P., A taxonomy for and analysis of tangible interfaces. *Journal of Personal and Ubiquitous Computing*. Springer Verlag, 2004, 8: 347–358.
15. Fitzmaurice, G., Ishii, H., and Buxton, W. Bricks: Laying the foundations for graspable user interfaces. In *Proceedings of the SIGCHI conference on Human factors in computing systems (CHI 95),* ACM Press, New York, NY, 1995, 432-449.
16. Garlan, D., Siewiorek, D., Smailagic, A. and Steenkiste, P. Project Aura: Towards Distraction-Free Pervasive Computing. *IEEE Pervasive Computing*. Volume 21, Number 2, April-June, 2002, 22-31.
17. Gorbet, G.M., Orth, M., and Ishii, H. Triangles: Tangible Interface for Manipulation and Exploration of Digital Information Topography. *In Proceedings of the SIGCHI conference on Human factors in computing systems (CHI 98) (Los Angeles, USA),* ACM Press, New York, NY, 1998, 49-56.
18. Grolaux, D., Vanderdonckt, J., and Van Roy, P. Attach Me, Detach Me, Assemble Me Like You Work. In *Proceedings of 10th IFIP TC 13 Int. Conf. on Human-Computer Interaction Interact'2005 (Rome, Italy),* 2005, 198-212.
19. Harada, S., Hwang, J., Lee, B., and Stone, M. "Put-That-There": What, Where, How? Integrating Speech and gesture in Interactive Workspace. In *Proc. International Conference on Computer Graphics and Interactive Techniques,* 262–270.
20. Hinckley, K., Pierce, J., Sinclair, M., and Horvitz, E. Sensing Techniques for Mobile Interaction. In *Proceedings of User Interface Software and Technology (UIST 2000)*, ACM Press, New York, NY, 2000, 91-100.
21. Hinckley, K., Ramos, G., Guimbretiere, F., Baudisch, and P., Smith, M. Stitching: Pen Gesture that Span multiple Displays. In *Proceedings of Advanced Visualization of Information (AVI 2004) (Gallipoli, Italy)*, ACM Press, New York, NY, 2004, 23-31.
22. Hinckley, K. Synchronous gestures for multiple persons and computers. In *Proceedings of User Interface Software and Technology (UIST 2003) (Vancouver, Canada)*, ACM Press, New York, NY, 2003, 149-158.
23. Holmquist, L.E, Redström, J., and Ljungstrand, P. Token-Based Access to Digital Information. *Lecture Notes in Computer Science 1707,* 1999, 234–245.
24. Izadi, S., Brignull, H., Rodden, T., Rogers, Y., and Underwood, M. Dynamo: a public interactive surface supporting the cooperative sharing and exchange of media. *Proceedings of User Interface Software and Technology (UIST 2003) (Vancouver, Canada)*, ACM Press, New York, NY, 2003, 159-168.
25. Johanson B., Fox A., and Winograd T. The Interactive Workspace Project: Experiences with Ubiquitous Computing Rooms. *IEEE Pervasive Computing Magazine 1(2)*, April-June 2002.
26. Kortuem, G., Kray, C., and Gellersen, H. Sensing and Visualizing Spatial Relations of Mobile Devices. In *Proceedings of User Interface Software and Technology (UIST 2005)*, ACM Press, New York, NY, 2005, 93-102.
27. Markopoulos, P., Mavrommati, I., and Kameas, A. End-User Configuration of Ambient Intelligent Environments: Feasibility from a User Perspective. In *Proceedings of European Symposium on Ambient Intelligence (EUSAI 2004)* (Eindhoven, Netherlands), Springer, 2004, 243-254.
28. McNerney, T.S. From turtles to Tangible Programming Bricks: explorations in physical language design. *Journal of Personal and Ubiquitous Computing,* 8(5), 2004, 326-337.

29. Metze, F., Gieselmann, P., Holzapfel, H., Kluge, T., Rogina, I., Waibel, A., Wölfel, M., Crowley, J., Reignier, P.,Vaufreydaz, D., Bérard, F., Cohen, B., Coutaz, J., Arranz, V., Bertran, M., and Rodriguez, H. The FAME Interactive Space. *2nd Joint Workshop on Multimodal Interaction and Related Machine Learning Algorithms (MLMI) (Edinburgh, UK)*, July 2005.
30. Molina, J.P., Vanderdonckt, J., López, P.G, Caballero, F., and Pérez· M. Rapig Prototying of distributed user interfaces, In *Proceedings of Computer-Aided Design of User Interfaces (CADUI'06)*, 2006.
31. Myers, B. Mobile Devices for Control. In *Proceedings of the 4th International Symposium on Mobile Human-Computer Interaction (MobileHCI 02),* Springer-Verlag, 2002, 1-8.
32. Newman, M.W., Sedivy, J.Z., Neuwirth, C.M., Edwards, W.K., Hong, J.I., Izadi, S., Marcelo, K., and Smith, T.F. Designing for Serendipity: Supporting End-User Configuration of Ubiquitous Computing Environments. In *Proceedings of Designing Interactive Systems (DIS 2002) (London UK),* ACM Press, New York, NY, 2002, 147-156.
33. Norman, D.A., and Draper, S.W. *User Centered System Design: New Perspectives on Human-Computer Interaction.* Erlbaum Associates, Hillsdale, NJ, 1986.
34. Pering, T., Ballagas, R., and Want, R. Spontaneous marriages of Mobile Devices and Interactive Spaces. *Communications of the ACM,* Volume 48, Issue 9, (Sep. 2005), 53 – 59.
35. Ponnekanti, S.R., Lee, B., Fox, A., Hanrahan, P., and Winograd, T. ICrafter: A Service Framework for Ubiquitous Computing Environments. In *Proceedings of Ubiquitous Computing Conference (Ubicomp 01).* Springer-Verlag, Lecture Notes in Computer Science, vol. 2201, 2001, 56-75.
36. Rekimoto, J., Ayatsuka, Y., and Kohno, M. SyncTap: An Interaction Technique for Mobile Networking. In *Proceedings of the 5th International Symposium on Mobile Human-Computer Interaction (MobileHCI 03),* Springer-Verlag, 2003, 104-115.
37. Rekimoto, J., Ullmer, B., and Oba, H. DataTiles: A Modular Platform for Mixed Physical and Graphical Interactions. In *Proceedings of the SIGCHI conference on Human factors in computing systems (CHI 2001) (Seattle USA),* ACM Press, New York, NY, 2001, 269-276.
38. Rodden, T., Crabtree, A., Hemmings, T., Koleva, B., Humble, J., Akesson, K.P., and Hansson, P. Configuring the Ubiquitous Home. In *Proceedings of the 2004 ACM Symposium on Designing Interactive Systems (DIS 04) (Cambridge, Massachusetts),* ACM Press, 2004.
39. Sohn, T.Y., and Dey, A.K. iCAP: An Informal Tool for Interactive Prototyping of Context-Aware Applications. In *Proceedings of the International Conference on Pervasive Computing 2006 (Pervasive 2006) (Dublin, Ireland),* May 2006, 974–975.
40. Streitz N., Tandler P., Müller-Tomfelde C., and Konomi S. Roomware: Towards the Next Generation of Human-Computer Interaction based on an Integrated Design of Real and Virtual Worlds. *In Human-Computer Interaction in the New Millenium,* Carroll J. (Ed.), Addison-Wesley, 2001, 553-578
41. Tandler, P., Prante, T., Müller-Tomfelde, C., Streitz, N., and Steinmetz, R. ConnecTables: Dynamic Coupling of Displays for the Flexible Creation of Shared Workspaces. In *Proceedings of User Interface Software and Technology (UIST 2001) (Orlando USA),* ACM Press, New York, NY, 2001, 11-20.

Tool Support for Handling Mapping Rules from Domain to Task Models

Costin Pribeanu

National Institute for Research and Development in Informatics
Bd. Mare al Averescu No. 8-10, 011455 Bucure ti, Romania
pribeanu@ici.ro

Abstract. The success of model-based approaches to user interface design depends on the ability to solve the mapping problem as well as on the availability of tools able to reduce the effort of establishing and maintaining of links between models throughout the development life cycle. In this paper a tool supporting a small set of mapping rules is presented. The tool enables the designer to produce task model fragments at operational level based on the patterns of mapping between task and domain models. The task model fragments are generated in XML format and can be further loaded in task modeling tools like CTTE or Teresa.

1 Introduction

The explosion of mobile and embedded systems is challenging the development of interactive systems able to run in different contexts of use. The model-based approach could be seen as a progressive derivation of user interface components from representations expressing relations between users, tasks, domain, environment, and technology. The strength of this approach relies on the separation of various models which are capturing the context variations. In turn, the generative power of these abstractions relies mainly on the mappings between models.

The mapping problem has been defined in [10] as a key problem for the gradual transformation of models from abstract to concrete level as well as for the mapping between different models on the same level of abstraction. Previous work in this area highlights various concerns: preserving consistency between models along the progression from one model to another [3], elaboration of graceful degradation rules for multi-target user interfaces [4], development of a description language and tools supporting the specification transitions [6] as well as elaboration of a reference framework for adaptation [1].

In the unifying reference framework for multi-target user interfaces defined by Calgary et al [1], ontological models are used to produce both archetypal models for various contexts of use and observed models guiding the adaptation process. Ontological models are grouped into three categories: domain (concepts and tasks), context (user, platform and environment) and adaptation (evolution and transition). Archetypal models are driving the design process along the development life cycle.

K. Coninx, K. Luyten, and K.A. Schneider (Eds.): TAMODIA 2006, LNCS 4385, pp. 16–23, 2007.

As such, they serve as a basis to produce representations that support the progressive derivation of the user interface (UI).

The objective of this work is to present a small set of mapping rules between task and domain models and a tool supporting the automate derivation of task model fragments from the domain model. The tool enables the designer to integrate domain modeling results (object, attributes and relationships) into task models that are developed by using the Concur Task Tree (CTT) notation [7].

According to the ISO standard 9126-4:2004 [5], the context of use includes users, tasks, platform and environment. In this paper, we will focus on the design process in order to investigate mappings between domain and task representations at archetypal level (i.e. depending on a given target). Hence, in the afore mentioned framework this mapping takes place at the domain model level (concepts and tasks).

The rest of this paper is organized as follows. In section 2, we will briefly describe our task modelling framework and some general mapping rules between domain, task and presentation models. Then we will describe a tool supporting a set of rules that are covering a significant effort in a task-based design of user interfaces. The paper ends with conclusion in section 4.

2 The Task-Based Design Framework

A problem with the mapping between models is that a detailed representation of model components is required. This means that we need to consider at least three aspects when exploring the mapping space:

(a) the model type (e.g. domain, task, presentation, and platform);
(b) the hierarchical structure of each model (e.g. dialog unit, interaction object), and
(c) the progression level along the development life cycle.

The last two dimensions seem to be neglected in existing approaches since up to now, only interface models have defined transitions from abstract to final representations. The problems are mainly located in the task and domain models since it is not clear how they relate each-other and which are the transitions they have to undergo in order to effectively support the design process.

Our model-based design framework is focusing on the relations between three models: task, domain and presentation. The purpose of modeling is to derive as much as possible from the user interface based on the mappings between the components of these models.

The domain model is capturing representations of functions, domain objects (entities), relationships between domain objects and domain object attributes.

We identified three layers which are relevant in the task modeling for user interface design:

- A functional layer that results from mapping application functions onto user tasks, corresponding to business goals (such as client data management or order data management). This layers enable the analyst to incorporate results of the requirement specification into the task model.

- A planning layer that results from the decomposition of functional tasks up to the level of unit tasks [2, 9], having a clear relevance for the user (such as adding a new client or updating the client address). This layer shows how the user is planning to accomplish the goal by dividing tasks in subtasks and giving a temporal order of execution.
- An operational layer that results from the decomposition of unit tasks up to the level of basic tasks. This layer shows how a user is actually accomplishing a goal with a given technology. A basic task has been defined in [9] as the lowest level task that is using a single interaction object, or a single external object or serves a communicational goal.

The basic element in the presentation is the abstract interaction object (AIO). We distinguish between information control AIOs (such as text boxes, check boxes or lists) and function control AIOs (such as buttons or menus). The user interface is structured into dialog units featuring various AIO configurations. The user is manipulating AIOs to change something in the domain model: objects, attributes and relationships between objects.

Fig. 1 is illustrating various kinds of patterns of mapping that occur in and between task, domain and presentation models. By mappings we understand transformations between different models as well as transformations within a model from one level of abstraction to another.

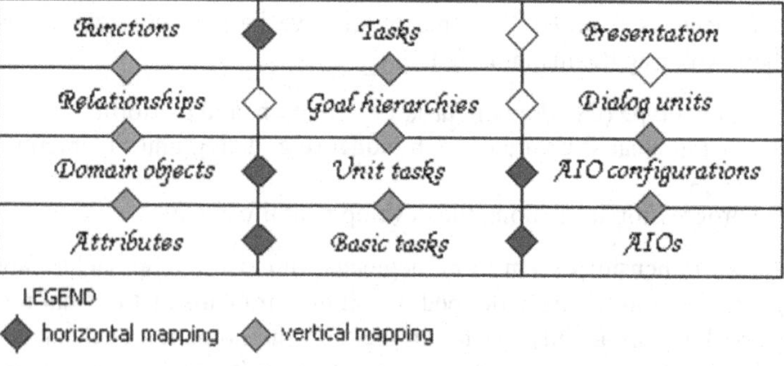

Fig. 1. Domain-task-presentation mappings

The framework shows two types of mapping:

- Horizontal mappings between models at the same level of abstraction.
- Vertical mappings within the hierarchical structure of each model.

In this paper we will focus on mapping rules that apply to the lower levels of task and domain models, i.e. the mapping of domain objects and attributes onto unit tasks and basic tasks.

In order to illustrate our approach to task modeling we will take an example: an application for data management in a trade company. The target task is the recording of new orders. In Fig. 2, a task model representation using the CTT notation is given.

Tasks on the first decomposition level are corresponding to the business goals of the application: management of clients, products and orders. Each of them is further decomposed in tasks that correspond to the high level functions of the applications that support these goals. Typical for the functional layer is the use of "order independency" temporal operator (|=|).

The task "New order" is a leaf in the functional layer and is further decomposed in the planning layer up to the level of unit tasks. For the sake of simplicity and legibility of the representation, only the decomposition of the target task "New order" is shown in Fig. 2. The planning layer is a goal hierarchy that shows tasks goals with a clear relevance to the user, independent from a given technology.

Unit tasks are further decomposed up to the level of basic tasks. Again, for the sake of legibility, only the task "New product" has been decomposed up to the level of basic tasks.

In [9] it was shown that the operational task model suggests the first level of aggregation of abstract interaction objects into AIO groups. Interaction object groups, which have one or more information control AIO (for example, a text box or a list box) and one function control AIO (sometimes two, but the user could choose only one of them at a given time – for example buttons OK vs. Cancel) provide with a first level of structuring the interface. As such, they can be used as basic building blocks for the presentation model in a task-based design.

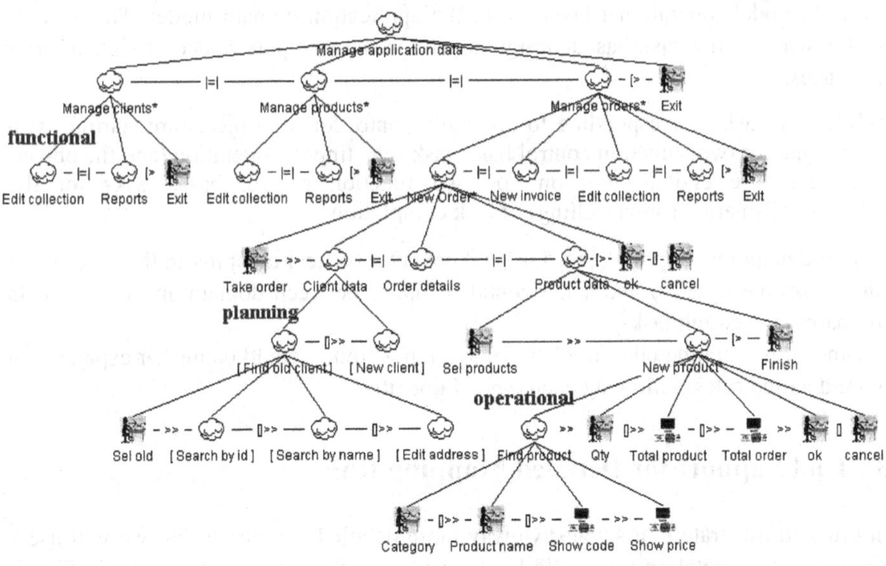

Fig. 2. An example illustrating the layered task modeling approach

The goal of an information control basic task is the manipulation of a domain object attribute (such as display or edit). The mapping rule described below is well known in the model based design of user interfaces and has been widely used in early model-based approaches to user interface design.

MR1. Information control basic tasks in the task model are mapped onto domain object attributes in the domain model and abstract interaction objects in the presentation model. Attribute names are mapped onto AIO labels.

The goal of a function control basic task is to trigger a transaction changing some attribute values in the domain model or to present them in the interface. Each basic task in this category is using a function control AIO. (Function control is sometimes termed as action control and the focus is on low level functions or commands provided by the user interface).

MR2. Function control basic tasks in the task model are mapped onto available commands on the target platform and abstract interaction objects (AIO) in the presentation model

Mapping rules MR1 and MR2 are the lowest level of horizontal mappings illustrated in Figure 1 on the last row of the table.

The operations performed on domain objects (such as display, new, update or delete) are mapped onto unit tasks. In Figure 2, the first basic task has an enabling role for the unit task. Usually, the task name is a concatenation of the enabling basic task name denoting the operation and the domain object name.

This task structure is a typical task pattern for data entry tasks carried on in a separate dialog unit and suggests a composition rule for this category of unit tasks. The mapping rule described below makes it possible the derivation of a great part of the task model (operational layer) from the application domain model. This is very useful when using task-based design tools for the computer-aided design of user interfaces.

MR3. Unit tasks corresponding to operations onto domain objects are starting with one (or two) function control basic task selecting the operation (and the object) and are ending with one or two function control basic tasks for the confirmation (or cancelling) of task completion

In the mapping diagram (Fig. 1), MR3 covers a vertical mapping in the task model (unit tasks-basic tasks) and a horizontal mapping between domain and task models (domain objects-unit tasks).

Since this mapping takes the form of a composition, it could be further expanded in more detailed rules, following each type of operation.

3 Tool Support for Detailed Mapping Rules

In order to illustrate in a suggestive way more detailed mapping rules, we will use a simplified task notation that could be mapped onto the CTT notation, like in Fig. 3.

○ unit task	■ info control	● function control	□ display
abstraction	interaction	interaction	application

Fig. 3. A simplified task notation and the correspondence with the CTTE graphical notation

Unit tasks are mapped onto abstract tasks in CTT. There are three types of basic tasks: two for information control (interactive and display only) and one for function control.

We identified five detailed mapping rules by applying MR3 to five operations performed onto domain objects. Each mapping rule is expressed bellow as a task pattern having a prefixed part, a sequence of information control basic tasks and a post fixed part. In three cases (b, c and d), a task for selecting the target object is needed before selecting the command.

Table 1. Detailed mapping rules

(a) add new object 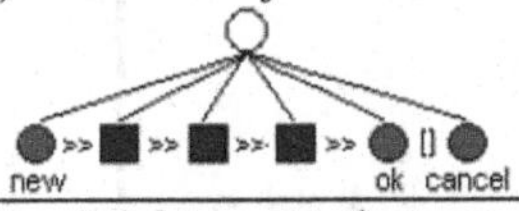 new ok cancel	The user selects the "new" command and the object attributes are displayed with their default values and available for data entry. The user can confirm or cancel the transaction.
(b) edit object attributes 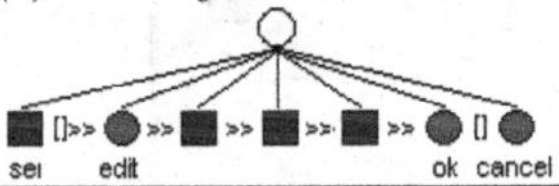 sel edit ok cancel	The user selects the object to be modified and then selects the "edit" command. The object attributes are displayed and available for data entry. The user can confirm or cancel the transaction.
(c) delete object 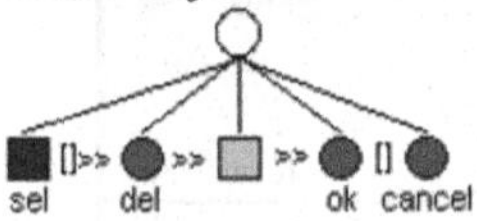 sel del ok cancel	The user selects the object to be deleted and then selects the "delete" command. A shield message is displayed so the user could check once again if (s) he really wants to perform. The user can confirm or cancel the transaction.
(d) display object attributes 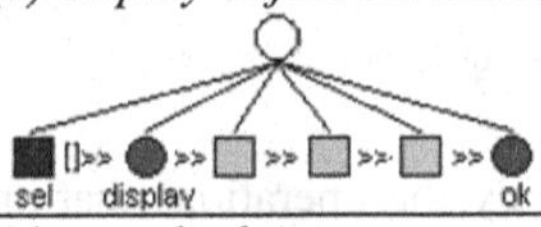 sel display ok	The user selects the object to be displayed and then selects the "display" command. The object attributes are displayed until the user confirm the visualization
(e) search object 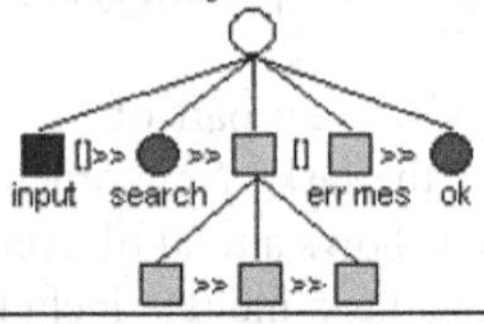 input search err mes ok	The user inputs the search key (attribute) and then selects the "search" command. If the search succeeds, then object attributes are displayed. Otherwise, an error message is displayed.

The process of computer-aided generation of full decomposition for unit tasks is illustrated in Fig. 4. The designer selects the object and the object attributes that are relevant for the context of use. Then (s) he checks on the operations to be performed onto it. In the case of a search operation, (s) he will also select the search key attribute. The generated unit tasks are shown in the lower left list box.

The designer can choose all the operations or only those that are relevant for the context of use. Moreover, (s)he can select only attributes that are relevant for the target context of use.

For example, according to the functional layer in Fig. 2, in the context of client data management, all operations on domain objects and all object attributes are

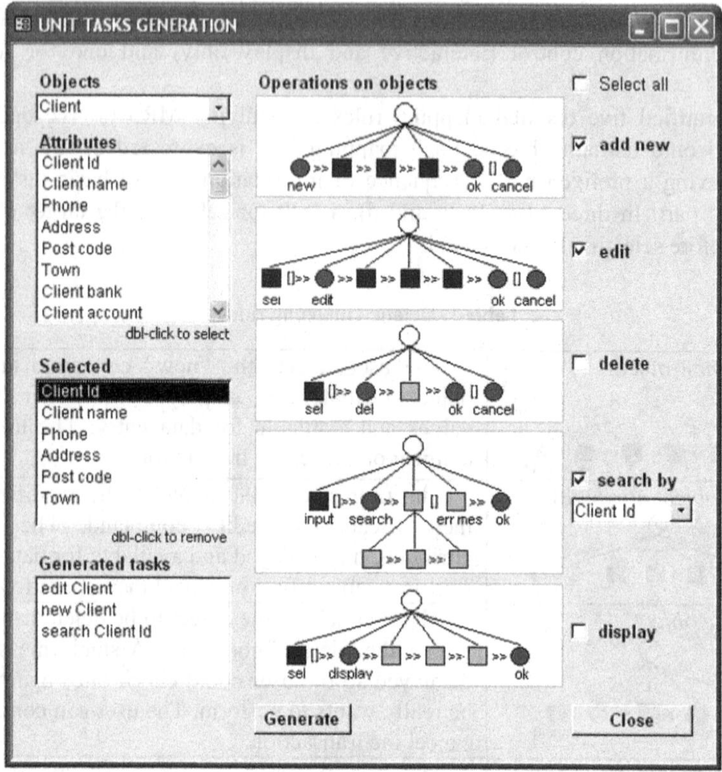

Fig. 4. Tool supporting mappings from domain to task model

needed while in the context of recording a new order, only the operations that are checked in Fig. 4 are selected. On another hand, the "search object" pattern is applied twice in this case (search by id and search by name).

This tool makes it possible to automate the derivation of a great part of the task model from the domain model. For example, in the case of the task "New order" in Figure 2, the task model statistics provided by the CTTE tool shows a total of over 40 tasks for which the designer should manually specify the task model, including temporal relations (operators), attributes and objects for each task.

In some situations, a manual post processing might be needed for the task model fragment generated by the tool. For example, the enabling basic task might not be needed, if the unit task is implicitly enabled. An example is the case of iterative tasks that are implicitly started and explicitly stopped, like in the case of "New product" in Fig. 2. The user ends the iteration by selecting the "Finish" command.

The unit tasks are generated in XML format and are loaded in the CTTE tool [7] with the "Load CTT as XML" function. The generation process is producing a full specification (task attributes and interaction objects) according to the specification of domain object attributes in the domain model (a time consuming work if manually introduced with the CTT editor).

4 Conclusion and Future Work

In our task-based approach, the task model is gradually developed from functional to planning and operational levels. In this paper we presented a tool supporting a small set of patterns of mapping between task and domain models at operational level. Further work is needed to extend these detailed mapping rules and to explore the mappings between goal hierarchies in the task model and relationships between domain objects in the domain model.

The mapping rules are preserving the consistency between domain, task and presentation models and make it possible the computer aided design of user interface. In this respect, the specification of domain objects is automatically transformed into a XML specification of unit tasks following the composition rules. Then the generated tasks could be loaded in Teresa [8] or other tool supporting the computer-aided generation of the presentation. Since task variations play an important role when migrating from a target context of use to another, the computer aided generation of (an important part of) contextualized task models is a key facility for designers.

Acknowledgement

This tool has been developed during a scientific visit at ISTI-CNR Pisa. We gratefully acknowledge the support of SIMILAR NoE under FP6-507609 project.

References

1. Calvary, G., Coutaz, J., Thevenin, D., Limbourg, Q, Bouillon, L., & Vanderdonckt, J.: A unifying reference framework for multi-target user interfaces. *Interacting with Computers, Vol. 15/3*, Elsevier. (2003) 289-308.
2. Card, S. K., Moran, T. P. and Newell, A.: The psychology of human-computer interaction. Lawrence Erlbaum Associates. (1983).
3. Clerckx, T., Luyten, K. & Coninx, C.: The mapping problem back and forth: Customizing dynamic models while preserving consistency. Proc. of Tamodia 2004 (2004) 99-104.
4. Florins, M. & Vanderdonckt, J.: Graceful degradation of user interfaces as a design method for multiplatform systems. Proceedings of IUI'2004. ACM Press (2004) 140-147
5. ISO DIS 9126-4:2001 Software Engineering - *Software product quality. Part 4: Quality in Use Metrics*
6. Limbourg, Q. & Vanderdonckt, J.: Addressing the mapping problem in user interface design with USIXML. Proc. of Tamodia 2004 (2004) 155-164.
7. Paternò, F., Mancini, C., Meniconi, S.: ConcurTaskTree: a Diagrammatic Notation for Specifying Task Models. In: Proceedings of IFIP TC 13 Int. Conf. on Human-Computer Interaction (Syndey, June 1997). Chapman & Hall, London (1997), 362–369
8. Paternò, F. , Santoro, C. :One Model, Many Interfaces. Proceedings of CADUI'2002, Kluwer. 143-154.
9. Pribeanu, C. & J. Vanderdonckt (2002) Exploring Design Heuristics for User Interface Derivation from Task and Domain Models. Proceedings of CADUI'2002, Kluwer,103-110.
10. Puerta, A.R. & Einsesnstein: J. Towards a general computational framework for model-based interface development systems. Proceedings of IUI'99 (5-8 January 1999). ACM Press. (1999). 171-178.

Towards Visual Analysis of Usability Test Logs Using Task Models

Ivo Malý and Pavel Slavík

Czech Technical University in Prague, Karlovo Namesti 13,
121 35 Prague 2, Czech Republic
{malyi1, slavik}@fel.cvut.cz

Abstract. In this paper we discuss techniques on how task models can enhance visualization of the usability test log. Evaluation of the usability tests is a traditional method in user centered design. It is a part of the methodology for design of usable products. We developed a tool for visualization of usability logs that uses the hierarchical structure of the task models to group and visualize observers' annotations. This way of visualization is very natural and allows investigation of the test dynamics and comparison of participant's behavior in various parts of the test. We also describe methods of visualization of multiple logs that allow for comparison of the test results between participants. For that purpose we present a new visualization method based on alignment of the visual representations of tasks, where binding between the task model and the log visualization is used. Finally, we present an evaluation of our tool on two usability tests, which were conducted in our laboratory and we discuss observed findings.

Keywords: Task model, Usability testing, Usability log visualization, Annotations visualization.

1 Introduction

Design and implementation of user interfaces has been supported for a long time by many tools that are used in all stages of the interface design and implementation. Usability testing has a well developed methodology and it is a widely accepted technique in the process of the UI design.

With the growing complexity of applications the complexity of the UI is also increasing. This situation creates obstacles for evaluation of the UI developed. The standard methods used now cannot provide enough information either to the observer or to the UI designer. The problem is that the information is in general rather complex and traditional approaches have reached their limits. In this paper we will describe a new approach that will help the observer to get a quick overview of particular information that is contained in the logs of a usability test. Moreover it allows for evaluating several usability tests in parallel.

This new approach will allow the observers to process much more results obtained in the usability tests and thus increase the productivity and quality in this specific phase of the UI design.

K. Coninx, K. Luyten, and K.A. Schneider (Eds.): TAMODIA 2006, LNCS 4385, pp. 24–38, 2007.

1.1 Usability Testing

There are many methods of how usability tests can be executed. An overview of these methods can be found in [14]. Basically, a part of the user interface is selected for usability testing and then the real user characteristics are defined. After that, the task list is written. This list characterizes typical or important user tasks that in general represent typical user activities. Participants who correspond to the real user characteristics, are one by one asked to go through the tasks. Their actions and comments are recorded using video, audio, observer annotations and sometimes also mouse and keyboard events. The data are then processed and results are found. An advantage of the usability test is that the tested system needs not to be finished. The usability test is also useful in early phases of application development, when only mock-ups or prototypes are available.

HCI studies and techniques, which are proposed in [11] and in [6], show that it is better to focus on individual subjective opinions. These qualitative usability tests have the same potential for discovering the most important usability issues as quantitative usability tests have. Therefore, we typically test from 3 to 10 participants which is the usual number of participants [6].

1.2 Test Results Evaluation

Results of participant observation can vary. In most cases, the result of a usability test session is an observer log where all participant actions are stored. This log, an example of which is in Figure 1, is an accompanying document to video (or audio) recordings where participant activities were recorded during the test. In general, during usability testing, observers collect a lot of data. The most important data in the log are observer annotations, which the observer writes down - typically as text annotations, usually connected with a video through common time stamps. Observer annotations are important, because they help in getting an overview of video and audio recordings after the test is finished. These video recordings are usually long, but important moments or sequences are usually short and each participant has problems in different periods of time. It takes the observer a long time to get an overview of the data, to see what exactly happened and if there are some connections to different events. This is all quite complicated and usually incorporates browsing annotations and audio/video recordings. Moreover it is quite complicated to look for similar behavior or usage patterns between participants.

Therefore, supporting tools were developed to help observers recall each session. These tools used video recording to help the observer to have an overview of recorded session data. The tools also help write annotations and optionally collect events like mouse clicks and keyboard events. One such tool was proposed in [1] where an advanced environment has been shown. Sessions were recorded using a VHC recorder, events and observer annotations were logged and linked with the video using timestamps. Today, most supporting tools share the same idea. They use digital video and audio recording, which helps them to easily navigate through the video. Annotations are more precisely linked with the video, because they use the same timer as the video recorder. Nowadays, software like Morae [9] or Observer [12] offers similar capability, but using digital technology.

time	text	task
0:06:30	start	1
0:06:43	play tutorial	
0:06:45	going through tutorial	
0:10:08	make a call - direct	
0:10:08	didn't start speech recognition	
0:10:19	Selecting contact	
0:10:27	Making call	
0:10:32	Didn't start speech recognition	
0:10:50	Adding new contact	
0:10:56	"Add a new number" - wrongly recognised as "Dial number"	
0:11:02	Still continues with entering the number	

Fig. 1. Example of typical annotation file

Unfortunately, even when annotations link to the video, they are usually not able to show the test structure. As said before, during the usability test participants go through the task list and try to complete the tasks. These tasks could be divided into several subtasks if desirable. Generally, the task list can be presented as a hierarchical structure. That is a problem, because it is quite complicated for an observer to have an overview of recorded data with respect to tasks.

So if we want to support such a feature we have to define a structured form of the log and tasks. We will show further that the XML format is suitable both for a hierarchical task list and the observer log storage. This structure plays an important role in further processing of this information.

1.3 Task Models and Usability Testing

Usability testing (or at least the majority of usability test methodologies) is based on a concrete set of tasks. This set of tasks represents the tasks which are significant in the way the users use the developed software. The participant gets the task description in a textual form (task list). Such a form is suitable for testing but it may be rather unwieldy for the observer during the test design process and also during the evaluation process. A more sophisticated way of task list representation can be used. If we want to navigate through the observation results we need to build a hierarchical structure of the test tasks. Moreover, the task hierarchy is similar to the task model of the tested software. Therefore we can use task model tools already developed or even use the task models themselves. The task models represent tasks that the user or an application should do to accomplish the task. Sometimes the task model is developed as too detailed for a usability test. In this case, we usually can omit the deeper levels of the hierarchy. With a defined structure of tasks list we can do a visual analysis of the test data.

1.4 Visual Analysis of Usability Test Results

Visualization of various data has gained popularity in the last few decades. Using this approach, a larger amount of data could be better analyzed by means of some information visualization technique. In the case of usability testing, there are many tools [9], [12] that support the conducting of a usability test. They also offer some visualization to overview the collected data. But none of them allow the observer to compare data between participants. What the observers misses by standard visualization tools used in the field of usability testing is the lack of tools allowing the observers to get information about the dynamics of the usability test performed.

This sort of information might also be useful and convenient for the observer. Therefore our tool will focus on presentation of the test annotation data with respect to the task list, commonly represented by the task model and the task time, which can show more clearly the task dynamics. We also want to focus on comparison between participants, where the task dynamics and usage patterns can be examined.

2 Related Work

To formally describe the tasks performed by participants during the usability testing we should use some appropriate formalism. For our purposes the task model approach will be very suitable. Task modeling is a means for modeling tasks in general – we will concentrate on the task models use for our particular purpose: task modeling in a usability testing environment.

There are many methods used to represent the task model. We will focus on a visual representation of the task model and have chosen task model ConcurTaskTree (CTT), see Figure 2, proposed by Paternò in [13]. CTT is represented by a tree, where each node represents one of four task categories: Abstract, Application, User and Interaction. The tree structure goes from the top (abstract tasks) to the bottom (concrete tasks) and the tasks are organized from the left to the right corresponding with the time flow. The flow of tasks on the same level is also supported with relationships.

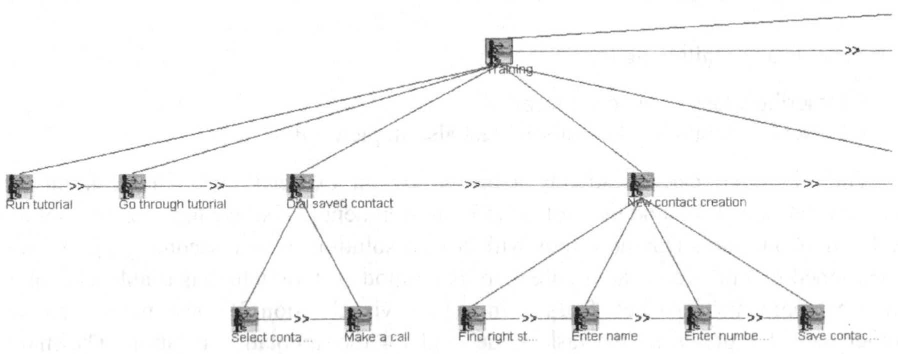

Fig. 2. Concur Task Tree (CTT)

There are several papers where this CTT is used as a background for usability testing. Paternò in [8] proposes using a CTT in remote usability testing. Remote usability testing is a method where the observers do not observe a participant's behavior directly, but observe only the results of the test. The results are the logs recorded as a sequence of mouse clicks and keystrokes connected to the particular task. The logs show which windows the participant opened and which actions the participant performed. For remote usability, the task model can be very detailed. Each list of the CTT is equivalent to a single participant action. We want to show that task model is suitable also for qualitative usability tests.

A similar approach is proposed in [3]. This paper is also focused on development of user interfaces using CTT. Here we can see a more subtle tool for remote usability testing. Papers [7] and [15] propose how the task model can be used for UI design, which leads to more usable software. In [17] we can see how CTT is used for modeling of a usability test task list in the case of a usability test of visualization techniques.

The most interesting approach is proposed in [5]. There it is shown how the annotations and events can be visualized to help observers get an overview of the usability test results. Annotations are transformed into timelines which are separated by annotation category into 4 levels. This approach for presenting time dependent information is natural and easily understandable and we will use a similar one in our work. On the other hand there are also some drawbacks. The first is that there is probably no systematic task representation so it is more complicated to separate each task. The second drawback is that in one time you can observe only annotations from one participant. Removing these two drawbacks will significantly help the observer in viewing the dynamics of the test and will help them to find similar usage patterns of the tested persons.

The observer from Noldus [12] is a commercial application, which uses events in timelines similar to [5], but still does not offer task model visualization and visualization of more than one participant in parallel.

3 Why to Design a New Tool

Our goal is a tool allowing us to:

- Describe a task in pictorial form
- Present dynamics of the usability test also in pictorial form

The first goal can be already achieved by an external tool. The task model representation is CTT and the tool is CTT Environment [2] but we have to incorporate CTT into our tool. Our new tool will be the solution of our second goal. As we mentioned in a previous paragraph, there is no modern tool, which is usable as a base for development of our new features in test log visualization. We also need to create other tools for preparing the task model and for the annotation creation. The main features of our tool are proposed in the following sections.

3.1 Easy-to-Use Visualization

While conducting a usability study, there are several steps that precede the test with participants. These steps are quite demanding and they take substantial time, before the test itself is carried out. One of the duties is to prepare a task list. In many cases this task list is abstract and straightforward. The CTT model can be produced only for the test or it can be developed beforehand during software development. Preparing the task list using the CTT Environment is not much more complicated than using any other tool.

During the usability test with participant, the observer usually uses a certain kind of logger tool, which creates annotations with timestamps, task numbers and sometimes also annotation categories. In our tool the amount of collected information will be the same, so the interface will not be more complicated.

After conducting the test, some tools require some post-processing to allow for the visualization of data. Our tool will be able to visualize results immediately without any additional post-processing.

3.2 Standardized Task Organization

The CTT model will be used for task representation. It offers more advanced functions which are not used now, but there are no constraints that should reduce functions of our tool in the future.

An example of a task described in pictorial form (CCT) is given in Figure 2. Here we can see the structure of the task. When the dynamic course of the test is taken into account, we can easily identify in which part of the test the participant is in currently.

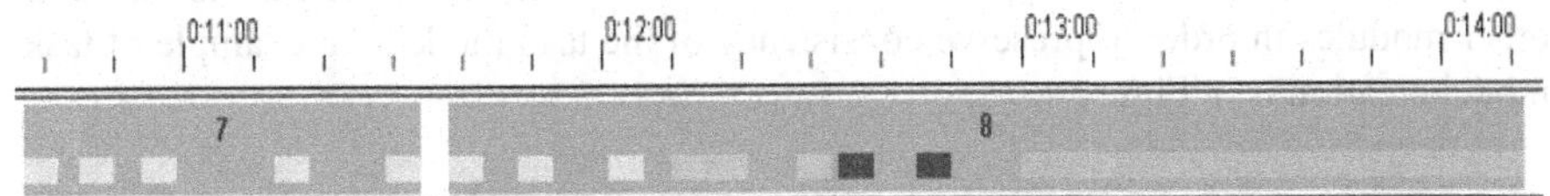

Fig. 3. Timeline detail

3.3 Quick Overview of Test Dynamics

The result of interpretation of the log is available in the form of a timeline – see Figure 3. The textual form of a log (provided in the structural form – XML) is automatically transformed into a horizontal line (time line) where individual subtasks can be easily recognized including the information about the time needed and the problems encountered in some particular tasks. These problematic parts are marked using colored rectangles (also called glyphs) that correspond to the annotations. Timelines or a similar visualization of time dependent data is very natural to understand and to interpret. Our new tool will show annotations in a similar way to ensure quick and easy overview of the test results. It will help the observer to find important points, where the participant behaved unexpectedly.

3.4 Comparison Between Participants

Normally the observer has to make conclusions only from the data obtained by one participant. Our tool will offer a comparison with other participants and the observer can have additional information. In addition, data transformation can be used to reveal new information hidden in classical test observations. Observers can better search for similar behavior, correlations between certain errors etc. Observers can also view dynamic aspects of the test like dependency of task execution length on number of mistakes or occurrence of same errors between participants.

4 Our New Tool

Our tool consists of several modules, which together support full usability test activities. The Task Model module is used for preparing task models. The Annotation Logging module is used for creating annotations during the test and the Visualization module visualizes collected logs.

4.1 Task Model Module

The task model is prepared by a specific Task Model module. This module was created as a simple tool for preparing task models in XML form. Currently, it only consists of a simple tree structure editor. It can also parse the CTT XML files, which were prepared by the CTT Environment. During our previous tests we found that the typical usability task list is nearly sequential and not very complicated and therefore it is possible to represent it simply with a tree. This tree representation is also used in other modules in order to preserve consistency of the task model. An example of task model creation is in Figure 4.

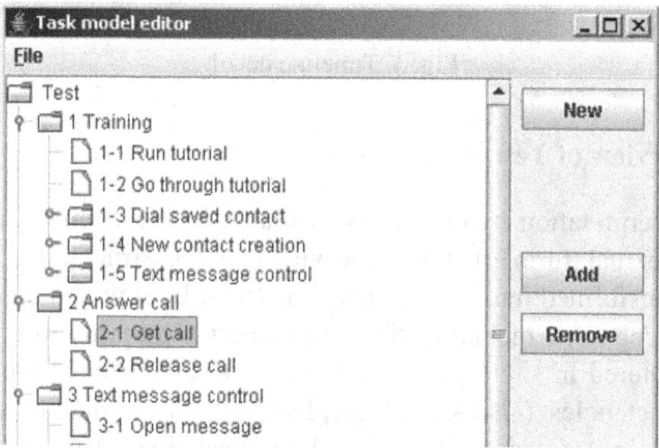

Fig. 4. Task Model module

4.2 Annotation Logging Module

The Annotation Logging module is very similar to other annotation logging tools. The difference is that we help the observer to get oriented in the test by giving him the task model of the test at his disposal. The task model is represented in the same way (task tree) as in the Task Model module. Annotations are logged as a single row in a table. Each annotation has several attributes used during the visualization. Attributes are:

- Start time of the annotation
- Duration of annotated action
- Category of annotation
- Task
- Annotation text

Logs are stored in XML files. We assume that we can also use logs from other logging tools as input into the visualization module. These other annotating tools can use more sophisticated means of data collection.

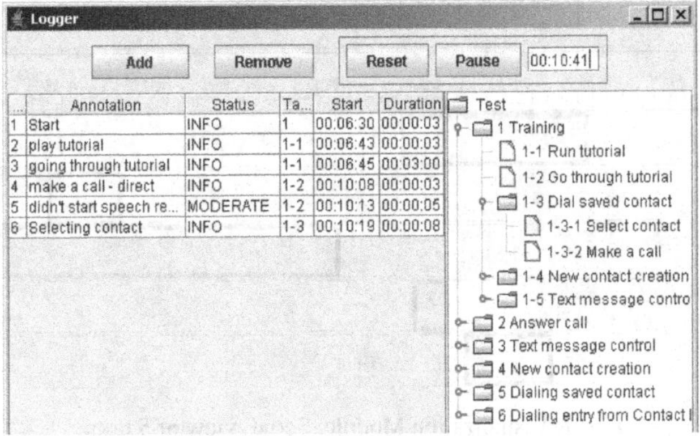

Fig. 5. Annotation Logging module

4.3 Visualization Module

The Visualization module is the main part of our work and it contains most of the new features. An example of visualization is given in Figures 6, 7 and 8. In the next paragraphs we explain our realization of the features introduced.

Quick and easy overview of test

For each participant one timeline is created. Each timeline contains all the information from the test. The length of the time line represents duration of the participants test. The timeline is divided into several parts, each representing one task. Tasks are recognized by a number which stands in the middle of the task rectangle above the annotation line. Each timeline visualizes 2 levels of the task model hierarchy. The first level is coded into the big blue rectangles in the background which enclose all annotations from the task. The second level is visualized by task lines of annotations inside the blue first level task rectangle. If there are no subtasks of a task at level 1, then all annotations are in a single line (compare Figures 6 and 7). Figure 6 is an example of one timeline with linking between timeline and tasks. Here we can see the structure of task 4 and the corresponding structure of the time line related to this task. By means of this feature the observer has a possibility to establish in any phase of the usability test, correspondence between visual representation of the task (usability test

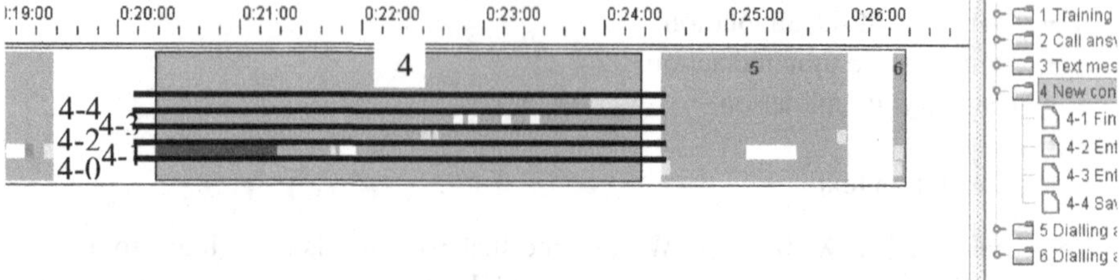

Fig. 6. Binding between task model and task in timeline

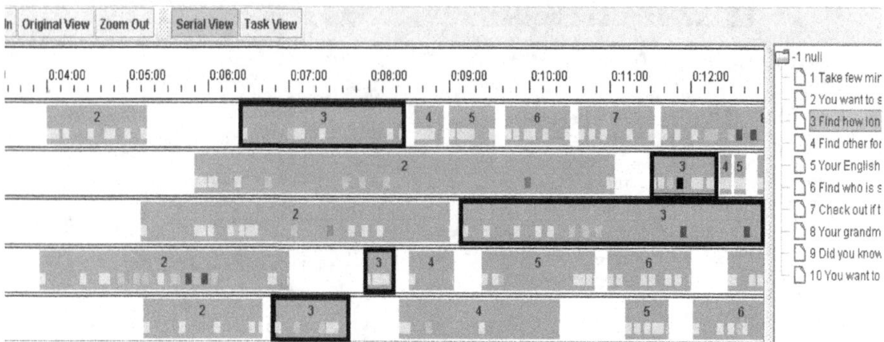

Fig. 7. Visualization Module, Serial view of 5 tests

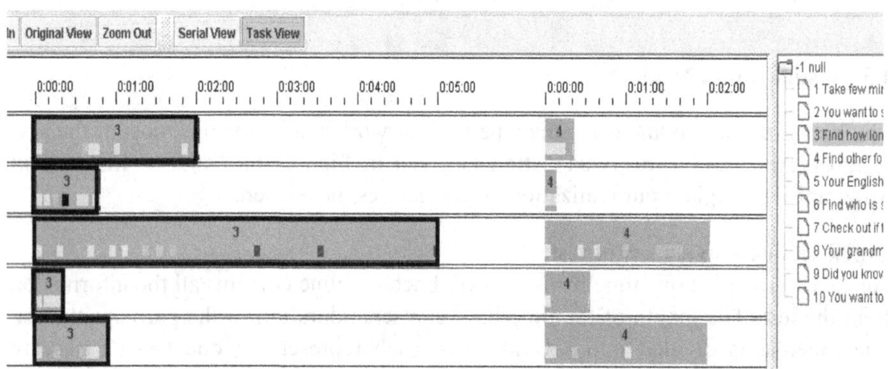

Fig. 8. Visualization Module, Task aligned view of 5 tests

in general) and visual representation of a log (time line). When more participants are visualized, each one is represented by his own timeline.

Each annotation is represented by a rectangle inside the task line. The width of annotation represents duration of annotation action. Annotations can be divided into several categories. Each category is represented by a different color. It is up to the observer as to which categories he creates and which color will be assigned to each category. Using the color as the main information carrier is encouraged in [18].

Currently, annotation text is presented as a tooltip, which appears after moving the mouse over the annotation.

An overview of the whole test is useful for picking up critical or interesting moments. After identification of these moments observers usually go into details. For that purpose our tool offers zooming functionality.

Comparison between participants based on task models
Our tool allows for showing of more than one participant results simultaneously. This functionality can be used for searching for similar participant's behavior. Thanks to usage of the task model, we can clearly differentiate between the tasks, because each of them is represented by its own rectangle. To support this feature even more, we present the task highlighting and task alignment.

Task highlighting is a border highlighting of the task rectangle, while we select the task in the task model. An example can be seen in Figures 6 and 7. Here we can see timelines with annotations divided by the task structure. On the right is the task model, which corresponds with the selected task in the timeline. Because the task model and the task visualization use the same data model, it is possible to highlight the task both by clicking on the task label in the task tree and by clicking on the task rectangle in the timeline. The color of annotation represents the annotation category. For further orientation in the test the timescale is provided at the top of the module. Highlighting helps in browsing data in the serial view.

When we want to align tasks by the task start, we use the task aligned mode, which is presented in Figure 8. Layout of components is the same as in the serial view. This visualization mode aligns a selected task so that for all participants this selected task starts at the same time (see task 3 in Figure 8). This feature allows the observer to analyze each task for all participants more in depth, because they need not search for the task by each participant. Typically, the participants spend different time with the tasks (as seen in Figure 7) and thus the tasks are naturally not aligned in the timeline.

Arrangement of collected data
During the usability test, participants sometimes do not follow the task model. Sometimes it happens accidentally, sometimes it is for research reasons. In comparative studies the observer tests usually two or more types of user interfaces and tries to find out which user interface is better and why. Then the selected user interface is used in the future development. For that type of usability test the observers sometimes use one group of participants. To avoid bias, participants are divided into two groups. One group performs the tasks using the first and then the second user interface, while the second group does tasks using the interfaces in reverse order.

The annotations are visualized sequentially as they are logged. The observer can analyze the test results in two ways. One way is to view the behavior of each group of participants separately. A second way is to view results from both groups of participants together but the task sequence for each participant will be different and task numbers in timelines will not be sequential. Nevertheless the correspondence of timeline segments and tasks in the task model is preserved by highlights.

Visualizing dynamics of a test

Dynamics of the data can be inspected in detail, either inside one participant log or through several participants. To be able to understand the behaviour in depth, annotation text of each annotation is available as a mouse tool tip, visible when the mouse is over the annotation. When combining views, the observer can see both important events related to tasks and surroundings of the important event.

5 Evaluation

In order to evaluate the principles of our tool we used it for evaluation of usability test of our university web site and also for evaluation of a car phone tool.

- **University website.** Tested web site was in late development lifecycle phase, almost in beta testing. Our goal was to observe main participants problem, while doing typical tasks using only tested site content. Content of the site were dynamic pages.
- **Car phone tool.** This tool was a prototype of an integrated car telephone, which could be controlled by voice or by the buttons on the steering wheel.

5.1 Tests Execution

The tests were conducted at our usability laboratory. This laboratory consists of two rooms. One room is allocated for observers, designers or programmers and other technical staff. The second room is the participant room. In our case, the test moderator was not in the participant room but he was in the observer room. The participant had only the task list and computer as in real life. There was also audio connection between observer and participant rooms.

For both tests we selected groups of 5 students. For the web site test their characteristic is only one which is more than 2 years at our university. This ensures that participants know about their school duties and they already have experience in using university web pages. For the car phone test the participants were required to speak English fluently as the test setting was based on the use of English.

5.2 Task Model

There were several tasks, see Table 1 and Table 2. The task models where little more complex, so we present only top level tasks.

The structure of the task model had a maximum of 3 levels. This is usual in usability tests. When testing complex user interfaces, there is usually more than one way to achieve the goal of the task. When testing a simple user interface, it is not possible to decompose a task to more subtasks.

5.3 Test Logging (Annotation)

For logging, we used a set of annotation categories. They are introduced in Table 3.

Table 1. Web site task list (top level)

1.	Take few minutes to get familiar with new web pages
2.	You want to spend one study period at University abroad. Find information about Socrates/Erasmus program and find Confirmation of Socrates/Erasmus study period document.
3.	Find how long is standard Engineer study program.
4.	Find other forms of study at our University.
5.	Your English speaking colleague wants to know, how much the scholarship for courses in English is.
6.	Find student senator in University senate.
7.	Check out if there is not new type of student ID card. If so, find pros and cons of this new ID card.
8.	Your grandmother wants to study U3V. Find guarantee of U3V at Faculty of Architecture.
9.	Did you know that there are post-study courses? Try to find some information about post-study language courses.
10.	You want to find contact to one of your former teacher, because you want start new student project under his lead.

Table 2. Car phone task list (top levels)

1.	Go through tutorial
1-1.	Answer call
1-2.	Read text message
1-3.	Add new contact
1-4.	Dial saved contact
1-5.	Dial entry from Contact list
2.	Drive a car
2-1.	Answer call
2-2.	Read text message
2-3.	Add new contact
2-4.	Dial saved contact
2-5.	Dial entry from Contact list

Category Info is used for observer's comments about participant behavior. It is mostly used to help the observer get context during deeper exploration of a selected part of the test task.

Categories Minor problem and Major problem represent situations where the participant had problems with the user interface. Category Minor problem is used

Table 3. Annotations and colors

Annotation category	Color
Info	Yellow
Minor problem	Pink
Major problem	Red
Interesting event	Green
Help	Gray
Program	Black
Break	Light gray
Comment	Orange

when participant is only slowed down but after a while he was able to recover from misunderstanding the user interface. Category Major problem is used when the participant cannot recover.

Category Interesting event is for a situation which is somehow interesting for the observer. Category Comment is for participant comments on the user interface.

Category Program indicates program failure or unwanted restart of the test environment. Category Break indicates when participant wants to have a break in the test.

Category Help indicates that participant got help from the moderator of the test.

5.4 Test Results Visualization and Evaluation

University website

Observers got an overview of the test, and they could compare behavior of all 5 participants together. Observers easily identified several problematic parts of the test. Some of them were expected but we also tried to find new outcomes from our tool.

Using the task aligned view we found, that in task 3 some participants were confused on whether to use Information for students or Information for incomers. We found this information quickly, because annotations about first user actions were at the beginning of each task. The ratio of usage was 3:2.

Comparison of selected results from task 8 revealed that each participant went the same wrong way and wanted to enter local department pages. Comparison of tasks also showed that 9 out of 10 tasks were easy and could be accomplished in one minute, but usually 2-3 participants had difficulties with task completion.

Task alignment showed that participants spent a lot of time on 2 or 3 tasks, but went quickly through the rest of the test. This information was a little bit hidden using one user log visualization.

Car phone test

The Car phone test showed other advantages of our tool. The test started with a tutorial where the participants were taught to handle the car phone mainly by voice and without driving the car simulator. Then the participants were given similar tasks as in the tutorial but they were asked also to drive a car simulator using a steering wheel (see Table 2). Therefore we were able to compare the same task from the tutorial and from the car driving part. We found some common problems, like forgetting to start the speech recognition tool. We also observed the correlation between the task duration in the tutorial and the task duration in the car driving part.

6 Conclusion

In this paper we presented an extension to the classical methods of evaluation of usability testing logs. We showed how the task model can be used to define a structure in tasks in the usability test. We also presented how this structure could be incorporated into the usability log during task observation. Furthermore, we presented new concepts of the task log visualization, which extended the timelines to show the task models hierarchy, supported navigation in annotations and allowed the comparison of more participants simultaneously. We also presented a way of task aligned visualization based on the task model, which was useful for comparing logs between more participants. In the last section we presented usability tests, where our tool was used. We could observe the results of all participants simultaneously and we could look for correlations between groups of tasks, using the task aligned view (see Chapter 5.4). We were also able to identify several findings that would not be so easy to find in traditional ways. The pictorial form of information presented was very easy to understand and to interpret. In such a way the observer gets the type of information not easily obtained from the test log in a traditional format.

7 Future Work

Although our tool supports evaluation of the usability test, there is room for further development in many aspects. One of these is in the way that annotations and especially annotation categories are logged. It is known that annotations are usually logged after the participant performs an action. This time drift is small and nearly constant, and hardly should be omitted. But the annotation category, which is sometimes more important, should be logged more quickly and should be permanently presented. This should especially help when two levels of hierarchy are presented in the timeline.

The second aspect is the filtering of annotations. Some annotations such as program failure or a similar disturbance sometimes occur and they have a bad impact on the dynamics of the test and therefore they should be removed from the visualization.

Some changes can be done also to the timelines and annotations. It is usual that events that last only a few seconds (usually automatically collected data) are more important than events that last longer. Sometimes it is important to know also the duration of subtasks. Therefore new techniques for visualization of events will be developed.

Acknowledgments. This work has been supported by the grant MSM 6840770014.

References

1. Badre, A. N., Hudson, S. E., and Santos, P. J. 1994. Synchronizing video and event logs for usability studies. In Proceedings of the Workshop on Advanced Visual interfaces (Bari, Italy, June 01 - 04, 1994). M. F. Costabile, T. Catarci, S. Levialdi, and G. Santucci, Eds. AVI '94. ACM Press, New York, NY, 222-224.
2. CTT Environment: http://giove.cnuce.cnr.it/ctte.html
3. Forbrig, P., Buchholz, G., Dittmar, A., Wolff, A., and Reichart, D. Model-Based Software Development and Usability Testing. In Proceedings of INTERACT 2005 Workshop (Rome, Italy, September 13, 2005)
4. Guzdial, M., Santos, P., Badre, A., Hudson, S., and Gray, M. Analyzing and Visualizing Log Files: A Computational Science of Usability. GVU Center TR GIT-GVU-94-8, Georgia Institute of Technology, 1994.
5. Harrison, B.L., Owen, R. and Baecker, R.M. (1994). Timelines: An Interactive System for the Collection of Visualization of Temporal Data. In Proc. of Graphics Interface'94. Toronto: Canadian Info. Proc. Society, 141-148
6. Jakob Nielsen's Alertbox, March 19, 2000: Why You Only Need to Test With 5 Users
7. Klug, T. and Kangasharju, J. 2005. Executable task models. In Proceedings of the 4th international Workshop on Task Models and Diagrams (Gdansk, Poland, September 26 - 27, 2005). TAMODIA '05, vol. 127. ACM Press, New York, NY, 119-122.
8. Lecerof, A. and Paternò, F. 1998. Automatic Support for Usability Evaluation. IEEE Trans. Softw. Eng. 24, 10 (Oct. 1998), 863-888.
9. Morae: http://www.techsmith.com
10. Mori, G., Paternò, F., Santoro, C. (2002). CTTE: Support for Developing and Analyzing Task Models for Interactive System Design. IEEE Transactions on Software Engineering, pp. 797-813, August 2002 (Vol. 28, No. 8).
11. Nielsen, J. Usability Engineering, Morgan Kaufmann, 1994
12. Noldus Observer: http://www.noldus.com
13. Paternò, F. Model-Based Design and Evaluation of Interactive Applications. Springer, 2000
14. Rubin, J. Handbook of Usability Testing, John Wiley and Sons, New York, 1994
15. Sousa, K. and Furtado, E. 2005. From usability tasks to usable user interfaces. In Proceedings of the 4th international Workshop on Task Models and Diagrams (Gdansk, Poland, September 26 - 27, 2005). TAMODIA '05, vol. 127. ACM Press, New York, NY, 103-110.
16. Spence, R. Information visualization, ACM Press, Addison Wesley, 2000
17. Winckler, M. A., Palanque, P., and Freitas, C. M. 2004. Tasks and scenario-based evaluation of information visualization techniques. In Proceedings of the 3rd Annual Conference on Task Models and Diagrams (Prague, Czech Republic, November 15 - 16, 2004). TAMODIA '04, vol. 86. ACM Press, New York, NY, 165-172.
18. Yost, B. and North, C. 2005. Single complex glyphs versus multiple simple glyphs. In CHI '05 Extended Abstracts on Human Factors in Computing Systems (Portland, OR, USA, April 02 - 07, 2005). CHI '05. ACM Press, New York, NY, 1889-18

Dialog Modeling for Multiple Devices and Multiple Interaction Modalities*

Robbie Schaefer[1], Steffen Bleul[2], and Wolfgang Mueller[1]

[1] Paderborn University/C-LAB, Fürstenallee 11, 33102 Paderborn, Germany
[2] Kassel University, Willhelmshöher Allee 73, 34121 Kassel, Germany

Abstract. Today a large variety of mobile interaction devices such as PDAs and mobile phones enforce the development of a wide range of user interfaces for each platform. The complexity even grows, when multiple interaction devices are used to perform the same task and when different modalities have to be supported. We introduce a new dialog model for the abstraction of concrete user interfaces with a separate advanced control layer for the integration of different modalities. In this context, we present the Dialog and Interface Specification Language (DISL), which comes with a proof-of-concept implementation.

1 Introduction

Today's computing devices have reached such small sizes and low power consumption that Weiser's vision of Ubiquitous Computing [1] has become a reality. However, this brings up big challenges for user interface development, as computing technology can only disappear, when the user is able to interact as naturally and intuitively as possible. Therefore, we need the appropriate user interface for the individual user communicating with a specific device under the consideration of the current situation.

Situations mainly imply varying user location, context of use, and different interaction alternatives, which can all be captured by dynamic profiles. As the combination of general ubiquitous computing concepts with situation dependent provision of multimodal user interfaces requires some system intelligence, this is also referred to as Ambient Intelligence (AmI) [2].

In principle, we can identify two approaches to implement AmI scenarios. Either small mobile devices can be applied just as an intelligent universal remote control, such as given in the Pebbles project [3], or they can establish real multimodal interaction with the different embedded devices of the environment. In the first case, PDAs or mobile phones can be easily used as most users already have such devices available at hand. For the second case, any available input or output device with respective modalities can be used. However, this additionally requires an advanced infrastructure as given by W3C's Multimodal

* Parts of the work presented here have been funded by the EU within the 6th Framework Program project UBISEC and by the German Research Foundation (DFG) within the project ADDO.

K. Coninx, K. Luyten, and K.A. Schneider (Eds.): TAMODIA 2006, LNCS 4385, pp. 39–53, 2007.

Interaction (MMI) Framework [4]. Since those environments can be considered as highly dynamical, the provision of the platform-specific user interfaces only is by far not sufficient to support all possible kinds of devices and modalities in the context of different situations. To overcome this, model-based approaches were introduced to develop user interfaces that can be provided and adapted on the fly, e.g., [5,6].

Following this tradition, we propose the Multimodal Interface Presentation and Interaction Model (MIPIM), which consists of a dialog model for the design of user interfaces that abstract from concrete modalities and from control features processing events from different modalities or devices as well as multimodal presentations. For the description of such dialogs, we developed the Dialog and Interface Specification Language (DISL), which is an extended subset of the User Interface Markup Language (UIML) [7].

In the next section, we motivate our work on a specialized dialog model and our modeling language. After the discussion of current efforts in the domain of user interface modeling for multiple devices and modalities, we present our dialog model with its control features in detail. Before concluding this paper, we show how a model can be implemented by the means of the DISL language and finally illustrate how it embeds into a Service-Oriented Architecture for multimodal interaction.

2 Implications for Multimodal Dialogs

Providing user interfaces for a wide range of devices with different capabilities in varying contexts implies several requirements, which had to be considered for the definition of our dialog model and the corresponding user interface dialog description language. The most important ones are summarized as follows.

A user should not be limited to use one device for a specific task but more likely should have the choice between different devices (e.g., PCs, PDA, mobile phone) as well as between different modalities (e.g., voice/audio, GUI). In addition, different contexts may require different user interfaces. Therefore, the user interface should be adaptable on the fly, instead of having just one preconfigured for each possible device or situation. When external tools do the adaptation, the interface description should be simple enough to support automated transformation.

Scalability directly evolves from the fact that all kinds of devices have to be supported and each user interface should be renderable on small devices with limited presentation and interaction capabilities but also on much richer devices. Since user interfaces developed for limited devices are not very appealing on less limited devices, they should become more attractive for and better adaptable to other devices or device classes, respectively.

Related to the scalability issue is also the requirement for reusability, since it is more efficient to have small generic components, which work for limited devices and can later also be reused as parts of a library for other more complex appliances.

While through adaptation of a user interface description, different target modalities and devices can be addressed, this does not solve the problem of dealing with multiple interaction modalities on probably different devices at the same time. Therefore, the synchronization of different systems and modalities should be supported.

The user interface modeling process should be as easy and intuitive as possible for the designer. Therefore, it is a long-term goal to come up with a suitable dialog-modeling tool. However, as a first step, the development of a dialog modeling language support should be sufficient; modeling tools can then be built on top of these language constructs later on. For developing a user interface description language, existing standards and common practices that proofed to be viable should be used as far as possible while the description itself should be easy and straightforward.

Since a goal of this work is to specifically address mobile and embedded limited devices, we should carefully consider limited resources like network bandwidth and device memory.

With the possibility of limited networks comes also the problem, that a user interface cannot be synchronized with the backend logic at any event. Therefore an asynchronous model should be supported in order to ensure UI-responsiveness under less perfect circumstances.

The development of user interfaces is not to be seen as an isolated and pure application specific task. Since we have to deal with many different devices and modalities, which are selected in specific situations, a user interface server and the renderers have to be embedded in a larger framework, providing context sensitivity and adaptation.

3 Related Works

In the last years, different groups proposed model-based approaches for development of user interfaces in multi device environments. For example [5], discusses how model-based techniques can be applied to support the development of user interfaces for mobile computers. Much research has been conducted to use task modeling for the user interface generation, as given in [6] and more recently in [8]. Common to all high-level modeling approaches is that they have to be further refined to lower levels of abstraction, especially to dialog and presentation models. With USIXML [9], a transformational approach for multiple levels of abstraction has been established, while our approach mainly focuses on the lower levels in order to support easy modifications of the user interfaces during all development cycles including the support of automated adaptations.

While in [8] also a dialog model is provided, which is automatically generated from the task description, our approach differs in the description of multiple state transitions, the support for small footprint devices, and a reduced server communication.

In order to meet the discussed requirements, one aim is to create a user interface/dialog description language, which allows advanced dialog models for multimodal and multi device interaction, supporting even most limited and mobile devices. One major prerequisite is the separation of structure, presentation, and behavior. The User Interface Markup Language (UIML) [7] provides such a separation of concerns and can serve as a basis for our purposes. However, the behavioral part of UIML in its current form does not give sufficient means to implement a powerful dialog model based on state machines with parallel transitions.

The strength of UIML, its concept of a meta-language, is yet a drawback for our purpose since UIML provides a too tight mapping to the target platform by using dedicated vocabularies, which limits is flexibility. However, in order to support arbitrary target devices and modalities we need to be more generic, so to say modality- and device-agnostic. Otherwise, the user interface would have to be remodeled for every new platform, although this task is already partly supported through UIML's separation of concerns.

CUIML [10] eliminates the drawback of UIMLs tight mapping by introducing generic components, which allows multimodal interaction. However, the control model of CUIMLs Discrete Finite Automat is limited when defining more complex user interfaces. The same problem also holds for several other widely used languages as Xforms [11] or WML [12], which take a straightforward simple DFA-approach.

In contrast to the previous listed languages, we wanted to introduce more powerful control models that allow modeling parallel state transitions in order to reduce the modeling complexity and to arrive at more concise model descriptions. Examples for such approaches can be found with Petri Nets [13], Dialogue-Nets [14], the Dialogue Specification Notation (DSN) [15], or State Charts [16], probably most prominently used for modeling system behaviors in the Unified Modeling Language (UML).

In order to assess the support of multiple modalities with our dialog model, several attributes can be observed as the CARE properties (Complementary, Assignment, Redundancy and Equivalence) [17] or in the TYCOON framework [18]: Equivalence, Specialization, Redundancy, Complementary and Transfer. In this publication, we follow for the sake of brevity the more simple definition of the multimodal interaction framework (MMI) [4] where a distinction between supplementary and complementary modality is made: Supplementary means that for one interaction one modality is used, as if it were the only available modality. However, after the completion of an interaction, a different modality can be applied. Complementary stands for the combined use of modalities to support general user interaction, e.g., visual feedback with voice output or simple hand gestures with voice input. Note that for this example capturing text by a motion sensing device would be less adequate.

Since UIML already provides an event-based control model, we tried to extend this by concepts from the previously cited works. Before going into those details, we outline the dialog and control model with support for multiple modalities and devices in the next section first.

4 Dialog Model

In our work, we focus on the dialog and control model. The separation of the dialog model from the control layer is helpful to support adaptation and to provide individual renderers for different end-devices, as well as transformations to other user interface description languages. The designer could provide an interface description, based on our dialog model directly or with help of dedicated design tools. On the other hand, high-level modeling techniques can be used to generate a dialog description from, e.g., task models. Together with adaptation mechanisms – as for example compared in [19] – integration of this work into other frameworks e.g. USIXML or targets as those described in section 3 seems to be feasible.

Figure 1 gives an overview of our dialog model, which is divided into three components for interaction, dialog flow, and presentation. Since our model aims for multimodality, user interaction is received by the Multimodal Interaction component. This component accepts input in different modalities and triggers the behavior resolver, which in turn starts generating the resulting UI that will be presented by the Multimodal Interface Presentation component for the activated modalities. Here, the dialog flow specification plays a central role. It is basically comparable to the UIML model with a separation between structure and style and the specification of the dialog behavior. However, the specification of the dialog behavior takes a different approach, based on more powerful state machines, while the control model of UIML is event-based without capturing user interface or system states. Therefore, we also introduce the Behavior Resolver Model to evaluate the dialog behavior.

Our dialog flow specification provides a set of interfaces that can be activated and deactivated at runtime, which is also captured by our modeling language.

In order to meet with the requirements of adaptability, scalability, reusability and multimodality, our design imposes the use of basic generic (modality independent) widgets, which can be broadly used allowing simple but sufficiently efficient means for interaction representation. Generic widgets are described in more detail in [20]. They are partly inspired by the notion of abstract

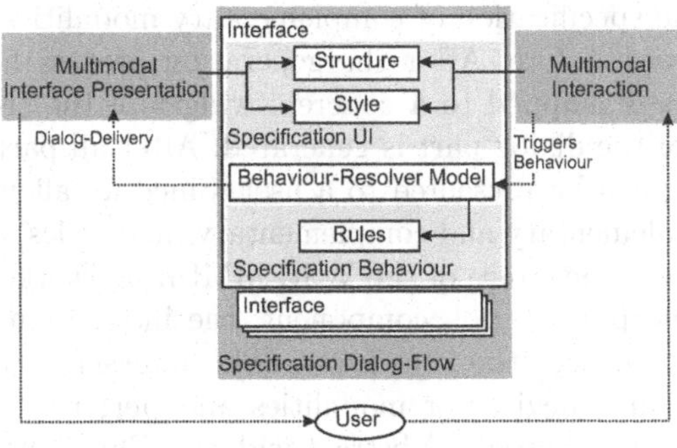

Fig. 1. Structure of the MIPIM dialog model

interaction objects (AIOs) [22] ant the development of a generic UIML vocabulary in [21].

For each interface, a structure of generic widgets as defined in [20], together with their style has to be specified. Using generic widgets allows the specification for devices with limited interaction and presentation capabilities, as they do not require any advanced device-specific properties. In fact these widgets are also modality-agnostic as they only provide basic operations like trigger, data input, and data output etc. Therefore, it does not matter which modality is applied as long as the operation itself is supported. For example, data input in a graphical user interface can be handled through a text input field whereas voice interfaces may listen for spoken phrases. On the other hand, a physical push-button does not support text-input at all, so this functionality should be delegated to a more adequate device. Interfaces can be used for re-usability of already realized specifications. For example, a sub-interface that implements a control for setting the preferred temperature of a heating system can be reused to set the volume in the context of a media player application.

The multimodal dialog flow is indicated by dashed lines in Figure 1. It is a cyclic process that:

1. generates the dialog
2. presents the multimodal dialog
3. waits for multimodal interaction
4. starts the evaluation of the dialog

The following paragraphs describe main components starting with the multimodal presentation and the interaction component. Finally, the behavior resolver control model is introduced.

4.1 Presentation and Interaction

The way in which generic interfaces are mapped to a concrete modality is specified in the interface presentation component as sketched in Figure 2. The part, which generates the actual dialog, is triggered by the behavior resolver and reads the generic dialog specification, consisting of structure and style. The device profiles and the specification of complementary modalities are imported in an initialization phase before. After the generation process has been started, each generic widget is mapped to a concrete widget in the specified modality and the structure of the dialog part is generated. After all parts are generated, the complete dialog can be presented to a user. Since we allow a synchronized presentation of supplementary and complementary modalities, our dialog model can be considered as an instance of the W3C MMI framework.

In contrast to the presentation component, the interaction component (see Figure 3) is used to collect the user input. The interaction manager collects input from all available devices or modalities and performs a reverse widget mapping from concrete widgets to abstract widgets. This is necessary, in order to retrieve properties or events and to assign them to specific properties of the generic widget. These properties are then passed to the behavior resolver, which

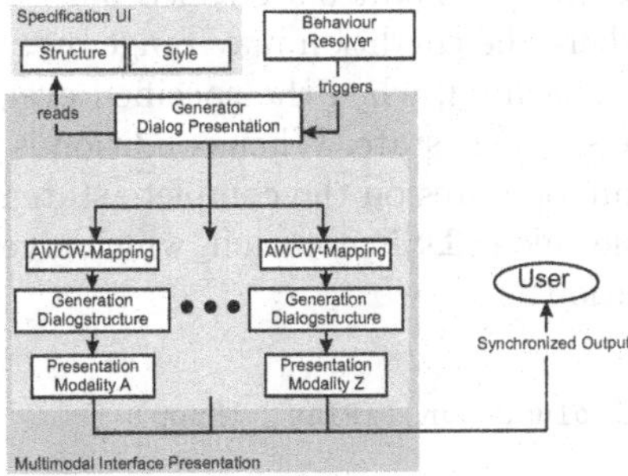

Fig. 2. The presentation component

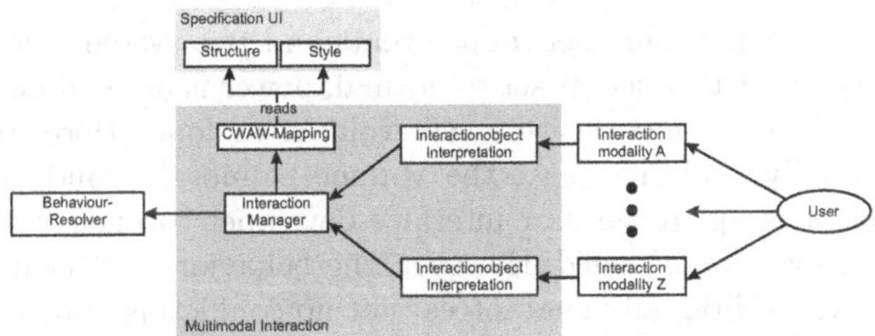

Fig. 3. The interaction component

has no information about the modalities used for the interaction, but knows how to react on the passed values. Therefore, we are able to consider interaction values in our model without needing the details from which modality or how the information is retrieved.

4.2 Dialog Notation

After the introduction of multimodal interaction and presentation, we focus on the main task, i.e., controlling the behavior of the dialog. As stated in the related works section, we address a dialog model with multiple state transitions. To support an easier integration into the UIML language, we tailored our model towards the textual DSN notation. DSN defines (user input) events, system states, and rules that fire transitions when a set of events and states are true. Note here, that the event-based model of the behavioral UIML part supports rules that define actions based on incoming events, but has no notion of system states. In the following, we will explain the notation in more detail and show how it is captured by the behavior resolver model in the next subsection.

We consider the state space of a user interface as a cross product of all properties, which can be triggered by user input or system events. In the DSN notation, the complexity is reduced by grouping states, which are mutually exclusive and assigned to the same input events, which are received from user, system, or interface objects, where groups of states are called flags. Rules consist of a condition and an action, where the condition may range over sets of states and sets of events. The action is executed, when the specified events occur and the user interface object is in the specified state. When condition is true a state transition is performed, which again operates on the complete state space. As an example, consider following simple rule in DSN notation, which gives a volume control for a music playing application.

```
USER INPUT EVENTS
switches (iVolumeUp, iVolumeDown, iPlay, iStop)
SYSTEM STATES
volume (#loud #normal #quiet)
power (#on #off)
RULES
#normal #on iVolumeUp --> #loud
```

That example defines four user input events and two system state spaces. It fires if the volume of the object is set to normal, power is on, and an iVolumeUp event appears. After firing, the rule sets volume to loud. Here, the grouped states are mutually exclusive, e.g., the volume cannot be loud and quiet at the same time. It is up to the user interface developer to make sure that only plausible transitions are specified. However, the behavior resolver model, which is described next, additionally guarantees that no conflicting states are possible at any time.

4.3 Behavior Resolver

Figure 4 shows the structure of the Behavior Resolver (BR) control model and how it combines with the MIPIM dialog model. Here, the BR control model is the central part, which is in charge of the evaluation of interaction events and the firing of transitions. Additionally, it refreshes structure and style of the dialog. Since after each Behavior Resolver call the dialog is updated, this model also supports direct manipulation.

The basic elements of this model are the content elements, which represent the complete dialog state at runtime. The control of the dialog is done by evaluating and modifying these elements. Content elements are divided into (render) properties, variables, system events, and rule states.

Render properties are used to describe style and content of each generic widget. For example, modifying the appropriate render property could modify the title of a widget. Note here, that it not part of the BR model to define how this widget is displayed. This is due to the presentation component of the dialog model.

In contrast to the render properties, variables are just used to store system state and are not linked to widgets. For example, the system states volume and power from the previous DSN example are captured in variables and thus can be retrieved for later evaluation, as well as for modification.

System events cover all kinds of events like user interaction events, internal events, such as the expiration of a timer, and other possible external events which

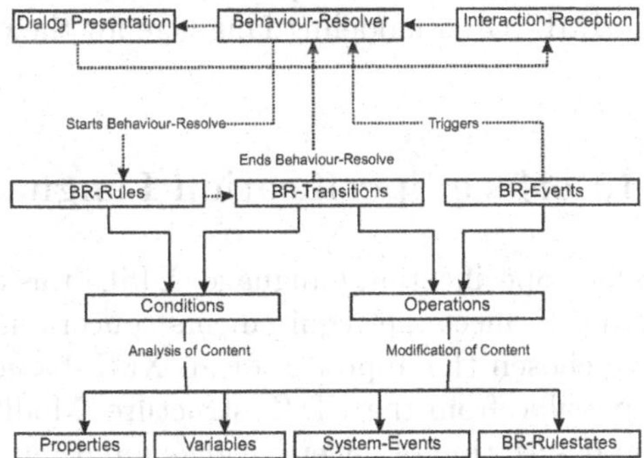

Fig. 4. The behavior resolver model

were not user initiated. In order to work with low bandwidth, the BR can be used in a fashion to limit the number of requests to the remote backend. Additionally, our BR model supports timed events, which may also occur periodically. This is of importance when a user interface has to provide continuously updated status information, for example, when synchronizing and displaying the current playing time of a track in a music player.

A rule fires a transition when an event occurs and certain rule states are true, where latter type of content elements corresponds to the DSN flags.

A complete cycle of the behavior resolver starts with evaluating the BR rules that consist of conditions, which are used to set the flags to true or false. If all required rules evaluate to true and required system events occurred, the transition fires, and modifies the system state through a set of operations. This also includes firing new events as some of them may be not externally triggered. Conditions provide more a more powerful computation than traditional DSN flags, as they not only provide Boolean operations but allow computation of arbitrary data.

Since a dialog (or dialog fragment) consists of several transitions, we have to define a behavior resolving cycle that ensures that all transitions are evaluated. This is implemented as follows: Before a transition is executed, all rules are evaluated. Then the first transition checks if the condition is true or not. If it evaluates to false, the next transition is processed without evaluating the rules again as content elements remained unmodified. In case of a true condition, the action section may modify the content elements[1]. Therefore, all rules have to be evaluated again before the next transition is checked. This ensures that a transition operates on the most recent dialog state. After having processed all transitions, some selected content elements are reset to a default state and the behavior resolver is ready to accept the next interaction.

[1] Note here that like in most other modeling/programming languages, the definition of deadlocks are due to the individual user and are not avoided by the language.

While this section presented the basic principles of the BR model, the next section introduces a UIML-based modeling language for the description of such dialogs.

5 Dialog and Interface Specification Language

The Dialog and Interface Specification Language (DISL) was defined in the context of MIPIM. In order to meet the requirements concerning adaptability and tool support, we have chosen the approach of an XML-based language, which inherits as much as possible from the UIML structure. Modifications to UIML mainly concerned the description of generic widgets and improvements the behavioral section by concepts of our BR control model. Generic widgets are introduced in order to separate the presentation from structure and behavior, i.e., mainly to separate user- and device-specific properties and modalities from a modality- independent presentation. For the ease of definition, we introduced the generic widgets as elements of the language and discarded the UIML-peers section but the generic widgets could also be defined as a UIML vocabulary instead.

The global DISL structure consists of an optional head element for meta information and a collection of templates and interfaces from which one interface is considered to be active at one time. Interfaces are used to describe the dialog structure, style, and behavior, whereas templates only describe structure and style in order to be reusable by other dialog components. In [23] we extended DISL for a more rigorous reusability through an object-oriented approach that also allows the reuse of behavior, which can be regarded to as a method for user interface object development.

Except for the introduction of generic widgets, DISL resembles in the definition of structure and style to UIML. For our requirements, we had to introduce major modifications to UIML's behavioral part however, which are explained with the volume control example from the previous section. The corresponding behavioral section in DISL looks as follows:

```
<behavior>
  <variable id="Volume"
    internal="no" type="integer">
    128
  </variable>
  <variable id="incVolumeValue"
    internal="no" type="integer">
    20
  </variable>
  ...
  <rule id="IncVolume">
    <condition>
      <equal>
        <property-content
           generic-widget="IncVolume"
           id="selected">yes
        </property-content>
      </equal>
    </condition>
  </rule>
  <transition>
    <if-true rule-id="IncVolume"/>
    <action>
      <statement assignment="add">
        <variable-content id="Volume"/>
        <variable-content
                  id="incVolumeValue"/>
      </statement>
      <statement>
        <property-content id="visible"
          generic-widget="Apply">yes
        </property-content>
      </statement>
      ...
    </action>
  </transition>
</behavior>
```

First, variables for the current volume and a value for increasing the volume are assigned. The rule "IncVolume" implements the condition that evaluates to true, if the widget "IncVolume" is selected. When all conditions of each rule are evaluated, we have to decide which transitions will be fired. This has to be determined for each transition with true conditions in the if-true tag, after which the set of statements is executed in the action part. In the above example, "incVolumeValue" increases the current volume and additional statements update the user interface, e.g., setting a "yes" and "cancel" control.

6 Architecture and Application

As a first step, we have implemented a client-server-based architecture with DISL transformation tools and a DISL renderer for a Java2 Micro Edition enabled mobile phone (see [20]). The idea of the architecture is to have a user interface server, where a mobile device can download a DISL UI description given by abstract widgets, which are rendered on the mobile device. The server can also connect to remote applications, which can be controlled by DISL.

For a proof-of-concept, we implemented an interactive music player remote control for a Siemens M55 mobile phone. The mobile phone contacts the UI server and retrieves the DISL description. In fact, to be more precise, it downloads the serialized format S-DISL (introduced in [20]), a compressed ASCII version of DISL for low bandwidth transmission in order to meet the limited network requirement. The abstract widgets are bound to individual modalities and rendered. In case that the remote application has to be controlled, the action part sends an according http request to the UI server, which in turn triggers the remote application. In the case of our music player, the remote application additionally synchronizes the track time with the user interface.

To support multimodal interaction, we explored a Service-Oriented Architecture (SOA) as shown in Figure 5. Before discussing this architecture, we first show how interaction events are captured for processing and presentation objects are later mapped to output devices.

As already introduced, our Dialog Model is generic with respect to interaction channels and presentation channels. Our central component for interaction is the Interaction Manager (cf. figure 3); for presentation, it is the Dialog Generator (cf. figure 2). The Interaction Manager receives interaction objects. For example, the interaction object of a keyboard is text or a function key, the interaction object of a motion sensor device includes movement information, e.g., up, down, left or right direction. The description of interaction objects is XML-based and the Interaction Manager is able to handle the receival of interaction objects by mapping its contents to generic widgets. For example, either the upward movement of the gesture device or a function key on the keyboard can trigger an action. Furthermore, speech input or keyboard text input may be mapped to the text property of a text widget. As the Interaction Manager can handle such

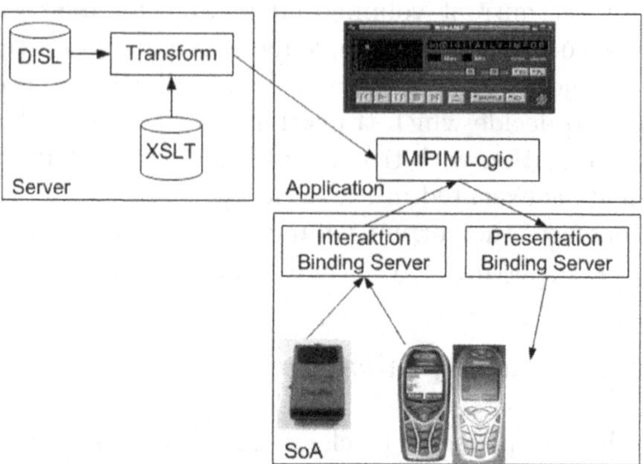

Fig. 5. architecture

interaction objects, the source of the interaction objects is generic. A definition is given by the following example.

```
<interactionobject name="soapboxmovement"
    class="gestureinteraction">
  <property name="movement">left</property>
</interactionobject>
```

An interaction object has a unique name and a class. The class "gestureinteraction" identifies the interaction object as a gesture-based interaction and the Interaction Manager can process the interaction object when it has a plugin for gesture-based interaction. The gesture-based plugin implements the property "movement", for instance, and mapping to the UI widget, e.g. triggering a button for skipping back one title in the playlist.

The Dialog Generator is similar to the Interaction Manager. It processes style and structure information to generate a presentation in a given modality. For example, it generates graphical output and speech output but is generic with respect to available output channels. The Dialog generator produces XML-based presentation objects like the following:

```
<presentationobjects name="spoken"
  class="speechoutput">
  <property name="say">Starting playback</property>
</presentationobject>
```

That presentation object has a unique identifier "spoken" and is an instance of the output class "speechoutput". Any output channel, e.g., a text-to-speech engine, which can process that presentation object, will generate a spoken output of the property "say". In the above case, the output "Starting playback" is synthesized.

Although both components can produce objects for a set of modalities they are unconscious with respect to available input and output devices. We have implemented a central server for automatic interaction reception and presentation delivery in a Service-Oriented Architecture as given in Figure 5. The Interaction Binding Server is a central server where input devices can register itself and their classes of interaction objects. For example, a gesture-based device registers its "gestureinteraction" class and sends the interaction objects to the server afterwards. Additionally, an output device may register itself at the Presentation Binding Server. Then, both servers can forward interaction objects from any input devices and distribute presentation objects among all output devices.

The MIPIM logic registers itself at both servers. After registration the Interaction Binding Server forwards interaction objects to the application's Interaction manager and the Dialog Generator's presentation objects to any of the registered output device. Therefore, this architecture is open to be tailored to any multi-modal environment, even when environment changes occur (e.g. introduction of further interaction devices).

7 Conclusions and Future Work

In this paper, we presented a dialog model for support of multi-modal and multi-device interaction by separating multimodal interaction and presentation components from our control model, the Behavior Resolver Model. One major result is the language DISL, which allows the specification of user interfaces with our dialog model.

Our prototype implementation, based on a Web-based user interface server and a textual renderer for mobile phones demonstrates the efficiency of our dialog and control model for limited devices. To support multimodal interaction environments, we also have implemented a Java RMI Interaction Binding Server and a self-registering motion sensing device, which provides gesture interaction objects.

In reflection of the requirements in section 2, we can conclude that adaptation is supported through an easy transcode-able XML-based UI-description language with generic widgets that are modality independent and also contribute to the issues of scalability and reusability. Network limitations are addressed by a compressed format of DISL to reduce traffic, as well as through measures to implement an asynchronous model. With the aid of adaptation mechanisms that go beyond this work, integration into other frameworks is in principle possible.

Remaining points to improve are more sophisticated means for the synchronization of different modalities, e.g. support of the CARE properties and improved tool support, while the latter issue can be resolved when results of this work can be integrated into existing tools.

Further work will consider automatic binding of our Interaction Manager to available input devices and the Dialog Generator to available output devices, which is achieved by integrating results from the ADDO project [24], that introduces semantic service discovery for functional [25] and QoS dependent [26] properties of services. As our input and output devices are implemented as services we hope to achieve fully automatic binding of these devices with semantic service discovery, which contributes to context aware computing. Especially mobile devices can benefit from this approach, as they can only use devices that offer specific QoS abilities, e.g., specific bandwidth for individual interaction objects.

References

1. Weiser, M.: The Computer for the 21st Century, in Scientific American 265(3), pp. 94-104, 1991.
2. Aarts, E.: Technological Issues in Ambient Intelligence, Aarts, E., and Marzano, S. (Eds.), in The New Everyday – Views on Ambient Intelligence. 010 Publishers, Rotterdam, The Netherlands, pp. 12-17, 2003.
3. Nichols, J., Myers, B. A., Higgins, M., Hughes, J., Harris, T. K., Rosenfeld, R., and Pignol, M.: Generating remote control interfaces for complex appliances, in CHI Letters: ACM Symposium on User Interface Software and Technology, UIST02, 2002.
4. Larson, J. A., Raman. T. V., Ragget, D., Bodell, M., Johnston, M., Kumar, S., Potter, S., and Waters, K.: W3C Multimodal Interaction Framework, W3CNote, 2003.
5. Eisenstein, J., Vanderdonckt, J., and Puerta A.: Applying Model-Based Techniques to the Development of UIs for Mobile Computers, in Proceedings of Intelligent User Interfaces Conference (IUI2001), 2001.
6. Paternò, F., and Santoro, C.: One Model, Many Interfaces, in Proceedings Fourth International Conference on Computer Aided Design of User Interfaces (CADUI 2002), Kluwer Academic, 2002.
7. Abrams, M., and Phanouriou, C., Batongbacal, A. L., Williams S. M, and Shuster, J. E.: UIML: an appliance-independent XML user interface language, in Computer Networks 31, Elsevier Science, 1999.
8. Clerckx, T., Luyten, K., and Coninx, K.: Generating Context-Sensitive Multiple Device Interfaces From Design, in Proceedings Fifth International Conference on Computer Aided Design of User Interfaces (CADUI 2004), Kluwer Academic, 2004.
9. Limbourg, Q., Vanderdonckt, J., Michotte, B., Bouillon, L., and Lopez-Jaquero, V.: USIXML: A Language Supporting Multi-path Development of User Interfaces. in Bastide, R., Palanque, P. and Roth, J. (Eds.), Engineering Human Computer Interaction and Interactive Systems, LNCS, 3425, pp. 200 - 220, Springer, 2005.
10. Sandor, C. and Reicher, T.: CUIML: A language for generating multimodal human-computer interfaces, in Proceedings of the European UIML Conference, 2001.
11. Boyer, J. M., Landwehr, D., Merrick, R., Raman, T. V., Dubinko, M., and Klotz Jr., L. L.: XForms 1.0 (Second Edition), W3C Recommendation, 2006.
12. Open Mobile Alliance: Wireless Markup Language Version 2.0, Wireless Application Protocol, WAP-238-WML-20010911-a, 2001.
13. Roché, P., d'Ausbourg, B., and Durrieu, G.: Deriving a Formal Model from UIL Description in order to Verify and Test its Behavior, in Duke, D. J., and Puerta, A. R. (eds.), Proceedings of 6th Int. Eurographics Workshop on Design, Specification, Verification of Interactive Systems DSV-IS99, Springer, 1999.
14. Janssen, C.: Dialogue Nets for the Description of Dialogue Flows in Graphical Interactive Systems, in Proceedings of Software Ergonomie 93, Bremen, 1993.

15. Curry, M. B., and Monk, A. F.: Dialogue Modelling of Graphical User Interfaces with a Production System, in Behaviour and Information Technology 14 (1), pp. 41-55, 1995.
16. Harel, D.: State Charts: A Visual Formalism for Complex Systems, in Science of Computer Programming 8, 1987.
17. Coutaz, J., Nigay, L., Salber, D., Blandford A., May, J., and Young, R. M.: Four easy pieces for assessing the usability of multimodal interaction: The care properties, in Arnesen S. A., and Gilmore, D. (Eds.), Proceedings of the INTERACT'95 conference, pp. 115-120, Chapman & Hall, 1995.
18. Martin, J. C.: TYCOON: Theoretical Framework and Software Tools for Multimodal Interfaces, in John Lee (Ed.), Intelligence and Multimodality in Multimedia interfaces, AAAI Press, 1998.
19. Plomp, J., Schaefer, R., and Mueller, W.: Comparing Transcoding Tools for Use with a Generic User Interface Format, in Proceedings of Extreme Markup Languages, 2002.
20. Bleul, S., Schaefer, R., and Mueller, W.: Multimodal Dialog Description for Mobile Devices, in Luyten, K., Abrams, M., Vanderdonckt, J., and Limbourg, Q. (Eds.) Developing User Interfaces with XML: Advances on User Interface Description Languages, Satellite Workshop of Advanced Visual Interfaces (AVI), 2004.
21. Plomp, J., and Mayora-Ibarra, O.: A generic widget vocabulary for the generation of graphical and speech-driven user interfaces, in International Journal of Speech Technology 5(1), pp, 39-47, 2002.
22. Vanderdonckt, J., and Bodart, F.: Encapsulating Knowledge For Intelligent Automatic Interaction Objects Selection in ACM Conference on Human Aspects in Computing Systems, INTERCHI'93, 1993.
23. Schaefer, R., and Bleul, S.: Towards Object Oriented, UIML-Based Interface Descriptions For Mobile Devices, in Calvary G., Pribeanu, C., Santucci, G., and Vanderdonckt, J. (Eds.) Computer-Aided Design of User Interfaces V, Proceedings of 6th Int. Conf. on Computer-Aided Design of User Interfaces CADUI'2006 Information Systems Series, Springer, pp. 15-26, 2006.
24. Automatic Service Brokering in Service oriented Architectures, Project Homepage, URL: http://www.vs.uni-kassel.de/research/addo/
25. Jaeger, M. C., et al.: Ranked Matching for Service Descriptions using OWL-S, in Kommunikation in verteilten Systemen (KiVS 2005), Informatik Aktuell, Springer Press, pp. 91-102, 2005.
26. Bleul, S., and Geihs, K.: Automatic Quality-Aware Service Discovery and Matching, in 13th HP OpenView University Association (HP-OVUA) workshop, 2006.

Model-Based Support for Specifying eService eGovernment Applications

Florence Pontico, Christelle Farenc, and Marco Winckler

LIIHS-IRIT, Université Paul Sabatier
118 Route de Narbonne, 31062 Toulouse, France
{Florence.Pontico, Christelle.Farenc, Marco.Winckler}@irit.fr

Abstract. Model-based approaches are a suitable alternative to cope with the increasing complexity of eServices made available in the last years by eGovernment applications. However, up to now, only a few studies have investigated which are the requirements for notations and tools devoted to support eService modeling. The main goal of this paper is to make a state of knowledge on the specification of user activity and processes in eGovernment eServices. Our results advocated for a hybrid approach for modeling combining task models and process models.

Keywords: Model-Driven Engineering, task modeling, workflow, eServices, eGovernment.

1 Introduction

eServices technologies have become very popular in the last years and have been the origins for a milestone of application domains such as eCommerce [1], eAdministration/eGovernment [2], scientific workflows [3] and so on. eServices deal with high level modeling of web-based applications contrary to web services that treat software architecture. According to the application domain, the development of eServices is submitted to several constraints. First of all, the growing of their complexity raises the number of data sources to take into account in the process. In addition, the development process requires cooperative work between several agents who have different (and even competitive) backgrounds and interests. Coordination of all the actors involved at every step of the design process becomes really critical.

In the past few years, the Software Engineering community has devoted a lot of work on Model-Driven Engineering (MDE) approaches. The basis of MDE is to treat the various models that are developed in the course of software development as the main assets of the software life cycle, and to provide tools and techniques to manipulate, transform or combine ("weave") these models in order to ultimately generate the final application code. Following the initial impulse of the OMG[1] towards Model-Driven Architecture (MDA), several advanced tools and environments have been developed to support MDE: meta-modeling environments that enable one

[1] Object Management Group http://www.omg.org/ (last visit on 6 December 2006).

K. Coninx, K. Luyten, and K.A. Schneider (Eds.): TAMODIA 2006, LNCS 4385, pp. 54–67, 2007.

to properly define and manipulate models, model-transformation languages that allow for instance to generate code from models, model-weaving languages that allow to reconcile models that describe different facets of the system under design, etc. This multi model based design approach seems to be much appropriated to the complexity of eService application design case in which several viewpoints have to be provided.

However, before to start "weaving" models it is important to understand requirements and concepts from the application domain and how they are treated by currently available notations. Thus, the main goal of this paper is to make a state of knowledge of modeling notations and tools that can be employed to specify eServices. In particular, we are mainly concerned by eGovernment applications using eServices technologies.

2 Requirements for Administrative eProcedures Specification

Government agencies are increasingly moving towards providing web support for their administrative procedures. This can be at a very local level (e.g. registration to after-school programs) or at a nationwide scale (e.g. electronic tax payment). In any case, the Web is used as a mean to support administrative procedures (e.g. administrative eProcedures) which is mandated by the government. eProcedures are subject to very strict requirements (e.g. need for procedures simplification, French regulation of 25 May 2001) in terms of security, accessibility, usability, etc. Such applications must ensure the security of information exchange (e.g. authentication of users, date and time, secure transfer of data, etc.), provide an efficient notification system helping all users (i.e. citizens and organizations) to monitor the progress of the process, provide flexible support to complex business rules (which might change according to new regulations and laws), support data exchange among several databases and legacy systems, and last (but not least) be accessible and usable for a large public of users.

The government agency that contracts the development of such a web-based system must have means to formally assess that these requirements are met. On the other hand, the software company that develops the system needs strong software engineering support for developing such demanding software in a cost-efficient way.

2.1 Several Categories of Users as Beneficiaries

Several categories of agents are involved in the development of an administrative eProcedure: **domain experts** and **developers** of the application (including graphical designers etc.). Following a user-centered design process, two main categories of users are concerned: **administrative agents** (who might belong to different administrative agencies or different departments) and **citizens** (who must be considered as the primary group of end users).

The domain expert is the person who is responsible for the definition of the administrative procedure, considering his legal competencies and his complete knowledge of the administrative domain. For example, he is able to check if the eProcedure is in accordance with the current regulation. End users of the administrative eProcedure (claimants as well as administrative agents) will also benefit from a correct specification of the administrative eProcedure.

Providing different viewpoints is mandatory in order to attend the diverse population of actors participating in the process. The granularity of information made available must be adapted to different interests for each person involved in the process. For example, the domain expert would have a view at glance on the process, in terms of scheduling of steps in the procedure administrative. However, domain experts might not be concerned on the details about user activities on the user interface. As soon as the interface elements are considered, the developers are the only ones who really take an advantage of such as detailed descriptions of user activity. Administrative eProcedures have then to provide stable and useful functionalities, that is the application has to conform to the legal definition of the administrative procedure. It also has to ensure the security of user transactions on the application as well as the storage of personal data. In terms of ethical requirements, universal usability and accessibility are major requirements for application made available for a wide and diverse community of end users (i.e. citizens).

2.2 Requirements for Notations When Specifying eProcedures

In order to model administrative eProcedures, the relationship between information concerning the organization, user tasks, workflow process and data issued from the application domain must be combined in a seamless way. Figure 1 presents a case study for the task "evaluate a submission" using a scientific conference review system according to an information system perspective. This example is similar to many of currently available eProcedures in terms of coordination of activities, responsibilities and resources. It lacks the critical aspect of the administrative procedures and of the data handled in such context but it has the advantage of not requiring much explanation to be understood. The elements presented by Figure 1 should be taken into account for the specification of an administrative eProcedure. Hereafter we detailed requirements for modeling and spread them among different categories.

User-centered description of the activity. Many user requirements can be expressed in terms of users' goals and user's strategies to reach such goals. A suitable alternative for describing user activity is to decompose tasks into sub tasks and give some support to take into account user choices. For example, to evaluate a submission, a reviewer reads the paper, accepts (or not) the paper, and fills in eventual comments and decision explanation on the review report.

Intervention of several users in an activity. Different configurations can be found when several users are involved in the same work and among them coordination and cooperation, the two that most correspond to what is found in the administrative domain: *coordination* looks to inform each unit or part of the whole as to how and when it must act whereas *cooperation* is acting together, in a coordinated way, in order to reach a common goal or for the enjoyment of the joint activity. For example, the meta-reviewer *is in charge of* taking a final decision *according to* individual decisions of each reviewer *in order to* participate to the building of the conference program.

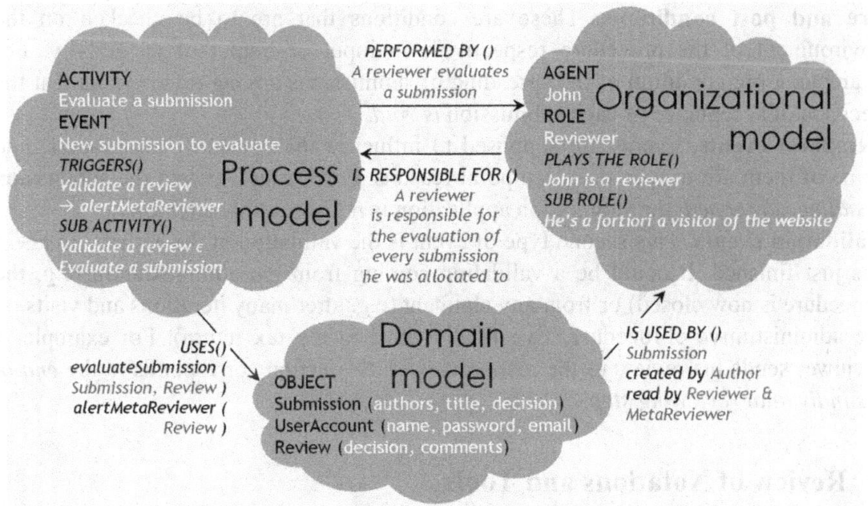

Fig. 1. Case study for reviewing process

Role definition. A user involved in an administrative procedure holds a particular role that is a set of activities he is allowed to fulfill, a set of data he is allowed to access, and whatever may define his competencies and responsibilities towards the success of the procedure. For example, the agent who holds the meta-reviewer role *is the one allowed to* take a final decision about the acceptance of a submission he was allocated to; he is also allowed to read the review reports and the submission itself.

Use of a resource. Data describing current user status (e.g. civil status, number of children), concrete documents (e.g. forms, identity papers) as well as eventual tools (e.g. scanner, software to access the list of stolen vehicles) have to appear in the specification of the procedure they are involved in as they have an impact on the way it is fulfilled. For example, *chat software* could be used to organize debate among reviewers and the meta-reviewer around the decision of acceptance of a paper.

Timing conditions. Some of the constraints that influence and define the specification of an administrative procedure are about temporal conditions such as conditions on duration. For example, a reviewer has a delay of *three weeks* to write and communicate his review report to the meta-reviewer. This is a requirement for easy instantiation of administrative eProcedures.

Causality conditions. During a procedure execution, an activity can enable a second activity, or interrupt it. This kind of sequencing is filed here under the category "causality conditions" and can be illustrated with the following example: the publication of the call for papers *enables* the submission of articles.

Logical conditions. These conditions deal with the logical scheduling of activities such as sequence, parallelism, concurrency, alternative, and loop on an activity and so on. For example, *while* authors are submitting their papers, anyone can apply for being reviewer which has to be specified as two looping activities (iterations are here possible until a fixed deadline) being accessible in parallel. This is a requirement for flexible activity modeling.

Pre and post conditions. These are conditions that are to be checked on the environment of the procedure respectively in input or output of an activity. For example, a pre condition of the spreading of submissions among reviewers is that the decision of acceptance of each submission *is void.*
Temporal events. Events are supposed to influence the course of the process, and some of them are triggered for temporal reasons. For example, when the submission *deadline is reached*, the submission application is not accessible anymore.
Validation events. This second type of event is the validation of the activity an agent has just finished. It could be a validation coming from the administration (e.g. the procedure is now closed) or from any claimant (e.g. after many iterations and visits on the administrative eProcedure, I've finally finished my tax return). For example, a reviewer sends his review to the meta-reviewer: this action corresponds to the *end of his individual reviewing step.*

3 Review of Notations and Tools

As this work focuses on the specification of administrative eProcedures that is an early position in the design process, application models and more generally implementation notations won't be treated here.

As we can see in the Figure 1, user activity is dispatched at different places and it requires information issued from the organization model, the process model and the domain model. In our example, submitted papers are evaluated by several reviewers. Notice that the task "Evaluate a submission" is represented only through the relationships between actors. This way of representing user tasks can be easily justified from an information systems point of view but it poses a big problem to understand user activity on the system, especially when actors must cooperate to perform a single activity (e.g. support paper discussion among reviewers and the meta-reviewer). So, this review is centered on task modeling, as the user point of view is needed in the administrative eProcedure specification, but also on process modeling that help describe a functional and scheduling centered point of view in the administrative eProcedure specification. A particular interest will be given to the methods that try and mix the two kind of modeling.

3.1 Task Models

A task can be defined as a goal together with the ordered set of tasks and actions that would satisfy it in the appropriate context (e.g. with the help of a given computerized application) [4]. A task model is basically used to describe the tasks the end user (here procedure claimants and administrative clerks) has to perform. Several research domains integrate task-related concepts and viewpoints, and among them ethnography, cognitive psychology or human computer interaction (HCI). Each one has its own objectives and interests in this process but generally task models make for better understanding of end-users' logic of utilization, and therefore help improving the usability during the design phase. Task models can also support usability evaluation after the application has been set up. Here are some task modeling methods whose inventors have different backgrounds and interests (e.g. human factors for TKS [5] or computing science for CTT [6]), which outlines the wide range of uses of task modeling.

GOMS (Goals Operators Methods Selectors) [7] decomposes tasks until they reach a level that can be evaluated in terms of execution time performance on the basis of the cognitive model of the end user. Existing systems can be evaluated this way or, at least compared in terms of execution performance time. Several tools supporting GOMS have been developed, and among them ***QGOMS*** [8] that allows performance calculus on GOMS models.

MAD (Méthode Analytique de Description des tâches) [9] task analysis notation is the description of task details, such as pre- and post-conditions, initial and final states, task types, priorities and interrupt abilities. Based on MAD and on other famous task models (GTA [10], DIANE+ [11] and CTT [6]), N-MDA (Noyau du Modèle de Description de l'Activité) formalism was published [12] as well as an associated tool ***K-MADe*** [13]. The aim of this new version is to add formality to the description of the task environment by ensuring coherence and non ambiguity in the semantic of domain objects.

TKS (Task Knowledge Structure) [5] is another historically important task modeling method. It describes the knowledge involved in the planning and fulfillment of a task, including objects belonging to the environment as well as information recorded in the user's memory. ***Adept*** [14] tool was developed to support the automated generation of the interface of an application on the basis of a TKS task model and a user model. TKS team currently works on TICKS project whose aim is to develop a task modeling approach based on TKS and ICS (Interacting Cognitive Subsystems) [15] to permit the modeling of multitasking and collaborative work tasks from both psychological and social perspectives [16]. As this extension on multitasking doesn't concern directly administrative eProcedures specification, we will only study here the TKS task modeling method.

DIANE+ [11] provides a link to an OPAC data model that is responsible for the basic management of the data, whereas the task model refers to the data only in terms of its involvement in the task realization and its importance in the automated generation of the interface. ***TAMOT*** [17] is a tool supporting the DIANE+ formalism. It aims to support quick edition of tasks, top-down and bottom-up approaches to task modeling. Unfortunately, the pertinent link between DIANE+ and the data is not available in Tamot. The model is then reduced to a hierarchical representation of the task.

CTT (Concur Task Trees) [6] provides a hierarchical decomposition of an individual or collaborative task, including system tasks as well as user tasks and interactive ones. This computer-inclusive task modeling aims to generate part of the application or to check if the task model and the other models of the application are coherent. This notation is editable and analyzable thanks to the ***CTTe*** tool (Concur Task Trees editor) [18], which generates scenarios which are useful for task analysis and simulation of the use of the application.

3.2 Process Models

In the literature, the terms "process" and "workflow modeling" are sometimes mixed up to talk about the sequence of activities (manual as well as automated) to fulfill in order to reach a goal. The process model actually includes the workflow model according to the WfMC definitions [19]:

- Workflow refers to "*the automation of a business process, in whole or part, during which documents, information or tasks are passed from one participant to another for action, according to a set of procedural rules*";
- Process definition refers to "*the computerized representation of a process that includes the manual definition and workflow definition.*"

However, one of these terms is often used for the other, in particular because workflow designers are willing to include human activities in their models and not only automated activities. Many viewpoints exist on a process going from a control flow on the execution of a sequence of activities (e.g. YAWL [20]), to service exchanges between agents (e.g. Cooperative Objects [21]). Other modeling methods, such as StateCharts [22], are multi purpose modeling methods that can, among other things, model processes. Hereafter we present a sample of the most important process modeling methods.

StateCharts' [22] original aim is to describe the behavior and states changes of an object in reaction to events. The considered object can be the whole environment of the procedure, with a final state to be reached to satisfy the goal. Therefore, StateCharts can be used as a process modeling method to decompose the process as a hierarchical state machine, with a starting point and an ending one, as well as constraints held by transitions that are triggered by events. ***Statemate*** [23] is the tool supporting Harel's StateCharts graphic modeling, simulation, code generation, documentation generation, and test plan definition.

Cooperative Objects [21] formalism is an Object Oriented design language based on colored Petri nets that helps modeling a system at different levels of abstraction. The system is represented as a set of concurrent objects that cooperate according to predefined ways in order to complete services. It can be seen as a process modeling method to help designing Office Information Systems. A tool supports Cooperative Objects as well as their extension for interaction specification (ICO): ***PetShop*** [24].

UML diagrams [25] (structure and behavior diagrams) allow the modeling of data and data treatment, which also allows process specification. Early in design, **activity** diagrams are variations of state machines that describe the flow of activities: the performance of an activity (called 'action' if atomic) is represented by a state. Objects can appear on the flow with some of their attributes modified by the process. Furthermore, activities can be partitioned into groups (e.g. grouped along the person responsible for the activity) called 'swim lanes' because of their graphical notation. UML diagrams appear in web engineering methods such as UWE or OO-H that use activity diagrams to describe the process and provide link from it to the domain and navigation models [26]. Many tools are available for the support of UML artifacts creation, some of them providing further design support and even some generation of the application. This latest category obviously requires the development of several UML diagram types. Among them, there is ***ArgoUML***[2].

[2] http://argouml.tigris.org/ (6 December 2006).

APM (Action Port Model) [27] is a flexible workflow modeling language. Modeling can be done at several levels of abstraction which enables the use of the language throughout the design lifecycle and for a wide range of persons involved in it. In APM, a cooperative activity is viewed as a common framework in which several agents are involved and use shared resources. No support is provided for APM modeling method for the moment.

YAWL (Yet Another Workflow Language) [20] is a control flow modeling method based on high level Petri nets. Additions were made to Petri nets notation to satisfy the requirements raised by the specification of workflow patterns [28] that were developed to permit an in-depth evaluation and comparison of existing workflow modeling methods. An editor as well as a ***YAWL model simulator*** is available on the Web[3].

BPMN[4] (Business Process Modeling Notation) provides a common exchange framework for all the actors involved in the design and implementation process. It aims to have a standard position among all the business process modeling methods developed. Among the numerous existing tools that support BPMN, ***Intalio*** is an open source one and is available on the Web[5].

3.3 Methods Trying to Bridge the Gap

Task modeling and process modeling were originated from clearly different backgrounds, respectively human factors and work organization. However, in cases such as an administrative eProcedure, the system to model is an interactive support for cooperative work between several agents. When describing the cooperative work supported by such a system, cooperative task models and process models get closer even if they don't have the same purpose (modeling respectively the users' activities and the scheduling of activities to fulfill to reach a common goal).

Boundaries between task and process models are thus not that clear, and the concepts devoted to each of them often interleave in the description of an application. To illustrate this fuzzy frontier, let's notice that YAWL workflow modeling notation decomposes the goal to reach into 'activities' which is typically a concept belonging to task modeling and human factors jargon ('step' or 'phase' would have been more appropriated).

Researches are led about bridging the gap between task and process (mainly workflow in fact) modeling during the design of an application.

Traetteberg [29] claims that in a development process, task modeling is a more precise description of each step of the workflow model. A set of notations is provided to support this designing method (**DiaMODL, RML and TaskMODL**) strongly inspired by APM [27] process modeling notation that views a cooperative activity as a common framework in which several agents are involved and use shared resources. No tool supports the method yet, although some prototypes have been developed to help editing models, and to evaluate the feasibility of developing such models. Some information about those prototypes can be found in [30] (Chapter 8.3 "Tools and implementations", p.174).

---

[3] http://sourceforge.net/projects/yawl/ (6 December 2006, beta version).

[4] http://www.bpmn.org/ (6 December 2006).

[5] http://bpms.intalio.com/ (6 December 2006).

GTA [10] is a framework to support Groupware Task Analysis. Besides the hierarchical decomposition into sub tasks, tasks are described in relation with events, objects, roles and agents belonging to their environment. ***Euterpe*** [31] is a task analysis tool that supports the GTA notation. It helps to build task trees, object hierarchies and other important concepts such as events and roles. Templates allow detailed information to be specified and multimedia can be attached to concepts to clarify their nature.

AGATA framework [32] executes a CTT collaborative task model on the server side, to provide the appropriate functions to the user who is connected to the application. There, the CTT collaborative task model monitors the scheduling of the procedure by allocating to each user the tasks he has to realize in order to get ahead with satisfying the goal.

Winckler et al. [33] provides a way to weave CTT task models of each role by using the navigation model described with **SWC** [34]. State Web Charts navigation modeling method is based on StateCharts formalism and supported by an edition and simulation tool called ***SWCEditor*** [35]. Several viewpoints on the application are provided by each individual task model, and they are linked together and to the application by the navigation model.

4 Specification Requirements for the Notations

Here is a summary of what is currently possible to represent with the modeling notations exposed in the former section. Each criterion presented in the first section as required for administrative eProcedures specification is evaluated and represented in the Table 1 as follows:

✓ Direct support is provided by the method.

~ A workaround is possible to specify the element, or a cumber-some support is provided.

× No support is provided to specify this element.

Role definition is generally described as the set of tasks the considered role is allowed to realize. However, role concepts have to do with work allocation and global procedure fulfillment, which belongs to process' viewpoint. Role definition is sometimes cumbersome even in process modeling methods, as it is a partial role definition, according to how roles are treated in the method. For example, for CTT, a role is a task eventually composed of alternative subtasks which actually means "the role is allowed to realize this set of tasks". This is not properly a role definition in the organizational domain, but it is sufficient to specify a role in a CTT model.

The presence of "timing condition" – such as the expression of duration – in a task model is only relevant in the case of performance evaluation task models such as GOMS. Otherwise, this kind of specification should rather appear in the process model as information on the sequencing of activities to accomplish the procedure.

Temporal events appear in task modeling methods as well as in process modeling: it eventually influences the course of the process and thus the course of the activity of a user involved in the process. However, when an event carries a semantic, such as an informational message (validation event), it is supposed to appear in the process modeling. For example, a reviewer evaluates a submission, and it takes him a few iterations on the website as the decision to take is not obvious. Finally, he decides to send this version of the report to the meta-reviewer. This final action is a task. The fact that this action is a "validation event" that is going to trigger the following activity in the procedure belongs to what is relevant in the process' viewpoint.

Table 1. Existing modeling methods coverage of administrative eProcedures specification requirements

	Task					Process						Both			
	GOMS	N-MDA	TKS	DIANE+	CTT	StateCharts	Cooperative Objects	UML Activity diagrams	APM	YAWL	BPMN	DiaMODL, RML and TaskMODL	GTA	AGATA	SWC and CTT
User centered description of activities	✓	✓	✓	✓	✓	~	~	~	~	~	~	~	✓	✓	✓
Intervention of several users	×	×	✓	×	✓	~	✓	✓	✓	✓	✓	✓	✓	✓	✓
Role definition	×	×	~	×	~	×	~	~	✓	~	✓	~	✓	✓	~
Use of a resource	×	×	✓	~	~	~	✓	✓	✓	✓	✓	✓	✓	✓	~
Timing conditions	✓	×	×	×	×	✓	✓	✓	✓	✓	✓	✓	~	×	✓
Causal conditions	✓	✓	✓	✓	✓	✓	✓	✓	✓	✓	✓	✓	~	✓	✓
Logical conditions	✓	✓	~	✓	✓	✓	✓	✓	✓	✓	✓	✓	~	✓	✓
Pre and post conditions	×	✓	✓	✓	✓	✓	✓	✓	✓	✓	✓	✓	~	✓	✓
Temporal event	✓	✓	✓	✓	✓	✓	✓	✓	✓	✓	✓	✓	✓	✓	✓
Validation event	×	×	✓	×	×	×	×	✓	✓	×	✓	✓	✓	×	×

5 Requirements for the Tools

Software tools are a major requirement to support model-based design. It may help editing models and provide additional functionalities as well: syntax verification (e.g. “each state must have an input transition at least”); higher properties checking (e.g. “each activity has to be reachable by one user at least”). The tool should also cover the data and resources of the environment and some links should be provided from the models edited to these concrete data. Concerning further functionalities, models simulation functionality is highly appreciated to detect errors and check the execution of scenarios. The system model integration may be appropriated if part or whole of it aims to be generated automatically from the specification realized with the tool. Table 2 shows the evaluation of the existing modeling tools according to the features required to specify administration eProcedures. The legend is the same as in the method evaluation grid (i.e. Table 1).

It is worthy noting that none of the task or process modeling tools exposed in this grid generates the final and usable application (e.g. Intalio – BPMN tool – generates BPEL code to be integrated in the application for workflow management). However, in some cases tasks models can be loosely coupled with the system through scenarios [36].

Table 2. Existing modeling tools coverage of administrative eProcedures specification requirements

	TASK					PROCESS						BOTH			
	QGOMS	K-MADe	Adept	Tamot	CTTe	StateMate	PetShop	ArgoUML	*No tool for APM*	YAWL editor	Intalio	*No tool for DiaMODL, etc.*	Euterpe	AGATA framework	SWCe and CTTe
Edition	✓	✓	✓	✓	✓	✓	✓	✓		✓	✓		✓	✓	✓
Syntax verification	✓	✓	✓	✓	✓	✓	✓	✓		✓	✓		✓	✓	✓
High level properties checking	×	×	✓	×	×	~	~	×		×	✓		✓	×	~
Coverage of the data	×	✓	✓	×	✓	✓	✓	✓		✓	✓		✓	✓	✓
Simulation	✓	✓	×	×	✓	✓	✓	~		✓	✓		×	✓	✓
Automated generation of part of the application	×	×	~	×	✓	×	×	~		✓	✓		×	✓	×

6 Discussion

A view at glance can reveal several similarities between task models and workflow models. Task and process modeling methods are suitable to model different aspects of administrative eProcedures applications since they cover several important issues of administrative eProcedures such as systematic decomposition of procedures in more manageable activities, the dynamics of electronic procedures (e.g. activities orchestration and temporal relationships), collaboration between individuals, relationships with information from the application domain (e.g. physical documents and information required to pursue with the procedure) and so on. In particular, cooperative task models might look very similar to workflow models with respect to the dynamics of the process and the representation of the collaboration between the agents.

However, the approach for modeling with workflow notations is often centered on the design and implementation of the procedures. Workflow models such as BPMN cover a huge set of concepts including the notion of activities, agents, temporal events, and so on which are also represent by task models. However, workflow models produced in that way are devoted to be executable views of the process. Doing so, they cannot be exploited to analyze the activity of agents involved in a given process because the user interaction is scattered throughout the process. The analysis of the user activity presents many advantages to measure usability, task workload and even improve the user interaction.

In all the modeling notations investigated, system developers and/or human-factor experts have been the main focus of model-driven approaches. Some work is still required to make notations used by model-based approaches more comprehensible by stakeholders such as domain experts involved in the development of eProcedures. We suggest that more appropriate notations and tools could facilitate the analysis of requirements with domain experts in very early phases of the development process. In some cases they can even extend their participation in the design process. For example, domain experts and regulators could provide detailed specification of the workflow process without having to take care of how the final application will be implemented.

The development of administrative eProcedures applications requires a multi-layered perspective for modeling. Following a top down approach, for instance, it will require an overall description of the process (using a process modelling notation), then a description of user activities performed in such a process, and the details of the user interaction with the final applications.

Many of the requirements discussed in this paper are not specific of eGovernment applications, but rather they are shared by other kinds of eService applications. What makes eGovernment an interesting application domain for our investigation is the evident need for combined user-centered design methods and model-based approached. User-centered design methods are required to accommodate both end-users (e.g. administrative agents and citizens) and stakeholders (e.g. domain experts, regulators, designers, etc.) views about the system, tasks and administrative processes. On its turn, model-based approach is required to cope with the increasing complexity of eServices made available in the last years by eGovernment applications.

7 Conclusion and Future Work

On one hand, the present study leads us to conclude the need for more investigation on the methodological issues to support the design of eProcedures. User-centered approach is critical to support the development of usable administrative eProcedures at every step of the life cycle. In order to optimize and improve the interaction with administrative eProcedures applications, appropriate views should be provided according to the step of development. After having surveyed the currently available notations, it seems that this goal cannot be reached by just one approach for modeling and better results are reached when task models and process models are associated throughout the development process.

On the other hand, the present study shows that currently available notations are not enough to cope with requirements for modeling eProcedures. Again, better coverage of requirements is obtained by approaches associating task and process models. A Model Driven Architecture (MDA) can provide a framework infrastructure for weaving these models. However, first of all, it is necessary to establish a common ontology of concepts covered by task models and process models.

Concerning task models, Q. Limbourg et al. [37] has already defined the mapping of task modeling notations. However, this work should be extended to support mapping between task models and process models.

Our future work concerns the definition of a meta-model description of the concepts presented by task models and process models. Among the potential advantages of such a model based approach for specifying administrative eProcedures, we can mention a uniform model mapping allowing the creation of appropriate views of tasks and processes according to the diversity of users and to the diversity of their needs.

Acknowledgments. Research sponsored by Genigraph (http://www.genigraph.fr), Genitech Group.

References

1. Babin, G., Crainic, T. G., Gendreau, M., and al., "Towards Electronic Marketplaces: A Progress Report" *ICECR-4,* Dallas, Texas, USA, 2001.
2. Tambouris, E., Spanos, E., and Kavadias, G., "An integrated platform for realising online one-stop government (eGOV)" IST technical report, Oct 2002.
3. Ailamaki, A., Ioannidis, Y. E., and Livny, M., "Scientific Workflow Management by Database Management" *10th International Conference on Scientific and Statistical Database Management,* Capri, Italy, 1998.
4. Storrs, G., "The notion of task in Human Computer Interaction" *HCI,* Huddersfield, UK, 1995.
5. Johnson, P. *Human computer interaction: psychology, task analysis and software engineering*, Berkshire, UK: McGRAW-HILL Book Company Europe, 1992.
6. Paternó, F., Santoro, C., and Tahmassebi, S., "Formal models for cooperative tasks: concepts and an application for en-route air traffic control" *DSV-IS,* Abingdon, UK, 1998.
7. Card, S. K., Newell, A., and Moran, T. P. *The Psychology of Human-Computer Interaction*, Mahwah, NJ, USA: Lawrence Erlbaum Associates, Inc., 1983.
8. Beard, D. V., Smith, D. K., and Denelsbeck, K. M., "QGOMS: A direct-manipulation tool for simple GOMS models" *CHI,* Vancouver, Canada, 1996.
9. Pierret-Golbreich, C., Delouis, I., and Scapin, D., "Un outil d'acquisition et de représentation des tâches orienté objet" INRIA Rocquencourt, Le Chesnay, France, 1989.
10. Van der Veer, G. C., Van Welie, M., and Chisalita, C., "Introduction to Groupware Task Analysis" *TAMODIA,* Bucharest, Romania, 2002.
11. Tarby, J.-C. and Barthet, M.-F., "The DIANE+ method" *CADUI,* Namur, Belgium, 1996.
12. Lucquiaud, V., Sémantique et outil pour la modélisation des tâches utilisateur : N-MDA, 2005. PhD thesis, Université de Poitiers, France.
13. Baron, M., Lucquiaud, V., Autard, D., and Scapin, D., "K-MADe : un environnement pour le noyau du modèle de description de l'activité" *IHM'06,* Montréal, Canada, 2006.
14. Johnson, P., Wilson, S., Markopoulos, P., and Pycock, J., "ADEPT - Advanced Design Environment for Prototyping with Task Models" *INTERCHI'93,* Amsterdam, The Netherlands, 1993.
15. Barnard, P. J. and Teasdale, J. D., Interacting Cognitive Subsystems: A systemic approach to cognitive-affective interaction and change. *Cognition and Emotion*, no.5, pp.1-39, 1991.
16. Wild, P. J., Johnson, P., and Johnson, H., "Towards a composite modeling approach for multitasking" *TAMODIA,* Prague, Czeck Republic, 2004.
17. Lu, S., Paris, C., and Linden, K. V., "Tamot: Towards a Flexible Task Modeling Tool" *Human Factor Conference,* Melbourne, Victoria, Australia, 2002.

18. Mori, G., Paternó, F., and Santoro, C., CTTe: support for developing and analyzing task models for interactive system design *IEEE Transactions on software engineering*, vol. 28, pp. 797-813, 2002.
19. WfMC, "WfMC Terminology and Glossary" 1999.
20. Van Der Aalst, W. M. P. and Ter Hofstede, A. H. M., "YAWL: Yet Another Workflow Language" Queensland University of Technology, Brisbane, Australia, 2002.
21. Bastide, R., Objets Coopératifs : Un formalisme pour la modélisation des systèmes concurrents. 1992. PhD thesis, Université Toulouse 1, France.
22. Harel, D., Statecharts: A visual Formalism for complex systems *Science of Computer Programming*, vol. 8, no. 3, pp. 231-274, 1987.
23. Harel, D. and Naamad, A., The STATEMATE semantics of statecharts *ACM TOSEM*, vol. 5, pp. 293-333, 1996.
24. Bastide, R., Palanque, P., and Navarre, D., "A Model Based Tool for Interactive Prototyping of Highly Interactive Applications" *CHI'2002,* Minneapolis, USA, 2002.
25. Rumbaugh, J., Booch, G., and Jacobson, I. *The Unified Modelling Language Reference Manual*, Reading, Massachusetts, USA: Addison Wesley, Inc., 1999.
26. Koch, N., Kraus, A., Cachero, C., and Meliá, S., "Modeling Web Business Processes with OO-H and UWE" *IWWOST'03,* Oviedo, Spain, July 2003.
27. Carlsen, S., "Action Port Model: a mixed paradigm concepttual workflow modeling language" *3rd IFCIS,* NYC, New York, USA, 1998.
28. Van der Aalst, W., ter Hofstede, A., Kiepuszewski, B., and Barros, A. B., Workflow patterns *Distributed and Parallel Databases*, vol. 14, pp. 5-51, 2003.
29. Traetteberg, H., "Modeling work: workflow and task modelling," *CADUI,* Louvain-la-Neuve, Belgium, 1999.
30. Traetteberg, H., Model-based user interface design: Computer and Information Science, 2002, PhD thesis, NTNU University, Trondheim, Norway.
31. Van Welie, M. and Van der Veer, G., "Euterpe: tool support for analyzing cooperative environments" *9th European Conference on Cognitive Ergonomics,* Limerick, Ireland, 1998.
32. Bruno, A., Paternó, F., and Santoro, C., "Supporting interactive workflow systems through graphical web interfaces and interactive simulators," *TAMODIA,* Gdansk, Poland, 2005.
33. Winckler, M., Farenc, C., Barboni, E., and Pontico, F., "Modélisation orientée tâche de la navigation d'une application web : catalogue des thèses de l'AFIHM," *IHM'05,* Toulouse, France, 2005.
34. Winckler, M. and Palanque, P., "StateWebCharts: a formal description technique dedicated to navigation modelling of Web applications," *DSV-IS,* Madera, Portugal, 2003.
35. Winckler, M., Barboni, E., Farenc, C., and Palanque, P., "SWCEditor: a model-based tool for interactive modelling of web navigation," *CADUI,* Madera Island, Portugal, 2004.
36. Navarre, D., Palanque, P., Bastide, R., Paterno, F., and Santoro, C., "A tool suite for integrating task and system models through scenarios," *DSV-IS,* Glasgow, Scotland, 2001.
37. Limbourg, Q., Pribeanu, C., and Vanderdonckt, J., "Towards Uniformed Task Models in a Model-Based Approach," *DSV-IS,* Glasgow, Scotland, 2001.

A Model-Based Approach to Develop Interactive System Using IMML

Jair C. Leite

Federal University of Rio Grande do Norte
Campus Universitário – Natal – RN – Brazil
jair@ufrnet.br, jaircleite@acm.org

Abstract. Software engineering and human-computer interaction communities use methods, techniques and tools that are not easily integrated. Our work argues that the development process could be improved by providing the designer with models, languages and tools that provides a seamless integration of software engineering and human-computer interaction approaches. In order to achieve this goal we have developed a language the Interactive Message Modeling Language (IMML) to support the development of interactive systems. This paper presents and discusses the concepts and models that are the foundation of IMML. We also compare our process with traditional task-based perspectives.

Keywords: Model-based User Interface Development, Semiotic Enginnering, User Interface Description Languages, XML-based User Interface Languages.

1 Introduction

Software engineering and human-computer interaction communities have approached the development of interactive systems differently. They use methods, techniques and tools that are not easily integrated. The gap between both processes is an important hassle to developers. For instance, it is difficult construct a functional specification or a software architecture from task models, scenarios and user interface prototypes. It is also difficult to generate a user interface prototype directly from software engineering specification. The generation of system's software architecture is also difficult considering just the functional specification. Information about the interaction model and user interface objects has an important impact in the final software architecture model. The IFIP working group on User Interface Engineering has organized several activities to discuss how to bridge the SE and HCI communities. Several important results have been achieved in the first years, but much more still need to done (see http://www.se-hci.org).

Our work argues that the design process could be improved by providing the designer with models, languages and tools that provides a seamless integration of software engineering and human-computer interaction approaches. In order to achieve this goal we have developed a language to support the development of interactive systems. Our language is the Interactive Message Modeling Language (IMML). IMML is an XML-based language to the specification of and interactive system.

K. Coninx, K. Luyten, and K.A. Schneider (Eds.): TAMODIA 2006, LNCS 4385, pp. 68–81, 2007.

IMML is composed of models that allow the designer to specify different aspects of an interactive system. It is also a vocabulary for reasoning about both the functional, interactive and communicative purposes of the UI elements. Each model describes the functional, interaction and communication concepts of the intended user interface.

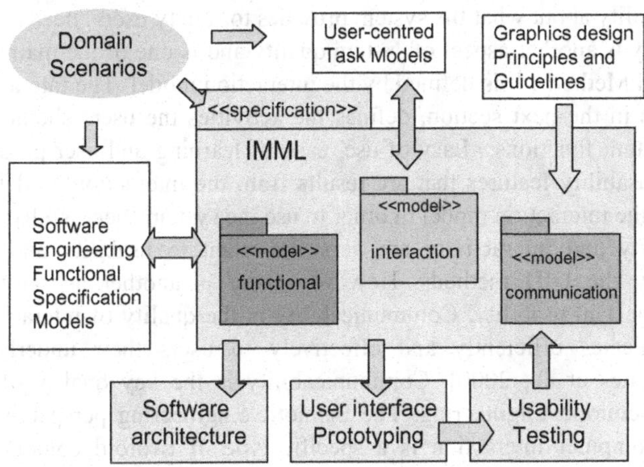

Fig. 1. A development process using IMML

In order to understand the role of IMML in a development process, figure 1 shows an overview how it is related with different development methods and techniques. We use techniques from. The IMML models can be construct from different requirements methods and techniques from software engineering and human-computer interaction. The models can be directly derived from domain scenarios or other informal requirements techniques. A functional model can also be derived from traditional model-based functional specification. An interaction model can also be derived from task models.

The IMML was designed with some important requirements in mind. The IMML is a XML language to allow expressive power, flexibility and computation. The motivation behind IMML is motivated by the semiotic engineering theory of HCI that provides a new perspective that reviews the role of the designer and the system [de Souza, 2005]. It also reveals important limitations in design process.

Our approach also follows the model-based paradigm but it uses a particular set of models based on the semiotic engineering perspective. It can be easily integrated with software engineering specification models, language and tools and with task-oriented ones. The models also allow separation of concerns and they can be used to reason about the interactive system.

This paper presents and discusses the concepts and models that are the foundation of IMML. We also compare our process with traditional task-based perspectives. This is the goal of the second section. The third section presents the IMML using a simple example. The last section presents our conclusions.

2 The Models Behind Our Approach

Functionality is one of the main concerns of Software Engineering Methods. Software functional specification should define the functions the system should offer to the users. The result is a functional model describing the domain information and the domain functions that process domain information[1]. Hence, the functionality is the system quality about what the system provides to satisfy users' needs.

Interactivity is another aspect of system quality and is one of the main concerns in User Centered Methods. It is defined by the interaction model. The interaction model, as we discuss in the next section, defines the activities the users should perform to command system functions. Easy of use, easy of learning and user productivity are some of the usability features that are results from the interaction model. The users should know the interaction model in order to use the system successfully.

Functionality and interactivity are very important to usability and are always considered by the UID methods. However, there is another aspect that has an important impact in usability. Communicability is the quality of interactive systems that communicates efficiently and effectively to users their underlying design intentions [Prates et al., 2000]. Communicability is the key quality of interactive systems for Semiotic Engineering. The Semiotic Engineering perspective considers that human-computer interaction is a specific type of twofold computer-mediated metacommunication in which computer systems designers send systems users a one-shot message. The message tells the users how to communicate with the system in order to accomplish a certain range of effects [de Souza, 2005].

Based on this theoretical perspective, we consider that the User Interface is the message that tells the users what to do (the functional model) and how to use the system (the interaction model). In order to communicate effectively, the designer should construct this message using the most appropriate signs.

These distinctions have the benefits to allow the separation of concepts, roles and concerns in the development process. The goals of our models are to emphasize and to integrate the functionality, interactivity and communicabilty aspects.

2.1 The Functional, Interaction and Communication Models

In the Semiotic Engineering approach, a UI conceptual model is about how the designer could communicate with the user. Our model considers that a UI has three main components: the functional model, the interaction model and the communication model.

The functional model describes the domain functions provided by the system. Each application function modifies the state of the system. The system state is defined by the properties and relationships of domain objects. For instance, a file system is a domain object composed by other domain objects such as directories and files. Directories are related with by the "contain" relationship. Directories contain files and other directories. Files and directories have names, size and date properties.

---

[1] We have used the term domain model in previous papers, but due to some misinterpretation we prefer the term functional to denote the functional aspects of the system.

Create, delete, move, copy and rename are examples of domain functions that modify the properties and relationships of files and directories.

The interaction model describes the activities the user should perform to command domain functions in order to achieve his/her goals. An interaction model is described using the concepts of task, command and basic interaction. A task is composed of commands and a command is composed of basic interactions in a hierarchy way. The composition is done using sequence, repeat, select, combine and join operators. This model has a very important role in our approach and we will describe it in details in the next section.

The UI Communication model has three basic components: the Display Medium, the User Interface Signs and the Interaction Tools. The Display Medium is the physical medium where all interface signs are conveyed. The interaction activity happens through it. In most computer system, the display medium is usually the computer screen, but it could be also a speaker. The Interaction Tool refers to any mechanism that can be used to perform actions using the interface signs in the display medium. Mouse devices, light-pens and keyboard are examples of the interaction tool.

UI Signs are the widgets, icons, words, menus, dialog boxes, wizards and all interface elements that can convey messages. UI signs convey designer's message to users and are also a medium to the interaction activity. In the most design tools the designer has a repertory of interface sign-types to create the concrete user interface message. There are some basic types of UI Signs: Task Environment, Command Panel, Domain object area and Information Display. These types are used to provide a refined mapping to actual user interface signs. The widgets provided in most design

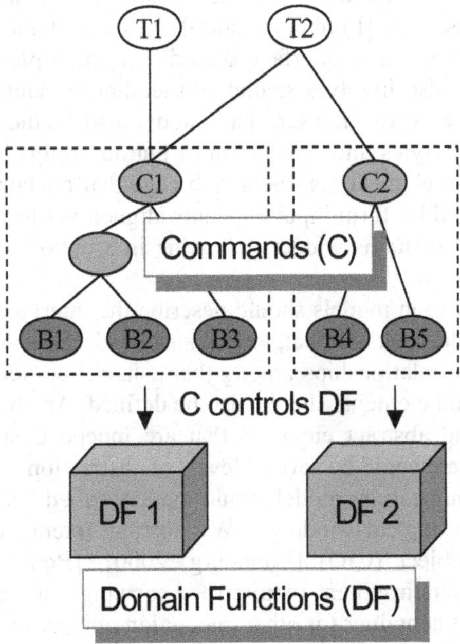

Fig. 2. The relationship between functional and interaction models

tools may be classified as one of these types. It is possible to extend them to more concrete UI Models.

The UI Signs are used to define the UI Communication Model. The communication model defines the role of the basic UI Sign types and the rules that govern the way they could be arranged to compose the UI message.

The interaction model and functional model are related with the communication model. We discuss this relationship more deeply in the next section. The IMML is the language based on these models to describe the UI. We present the IMML in a later section.

2.2 The Relationship Between Functional and Interaction Models

Functional model describes the domain objects and the functions that manipulate them. Each object is describe by a set of attributes and could be related to other objects. The functions modify objects attributes and relationships – the system state. The functional model is a specification of the system functionality and we are adopting a model-based approach to functionality specification.

Our approach integrates functional and interaction models associating one or more commands to a domain function. A command is the set of activities the user should perform to order the system to control the execution of a function. For each domain function there is at least one command. A command should not control more than one function. If a user wants the system to execute two functions, he/she should perform a task composed of two commands to control the two functions.

The relatitionship between Interaction and Communication Models.

The communication model describes the visual, haptic, and auditory elements provided by a UI to its users [Limbourg, 2000]. It is a declarative description of the external representation of a user interface according to multiple channels of use. The communication model also involves spatial and temporal relationships defining how the elements are presented to the user. This model also includes static presentation attributes, such as font styles and orientation of button groups [Bouillon, 2002]. For example, a presentation element may be a web page that contains frames. A specific frame may be composed by form input elements aligned vertically. Another example may be a window that contains widgets. Clicking in a button widget makes another window to appear.

Concrete communication models should describe the interface using elements of a specific interaction style, look and feel, toolkit and UI platform (window manager and system hardware). The relationships among them should be defined more precisely. Details of representation elements should also be defined. An abstract communication model is defined using abstract elements that are independent of a specific style, toolkit or platform. There could be several levels of abstraction.

An abstract communication model could be described using the concepts of presentation unit (PU), logical window (LW), abstract interaction object (AIO) and concrete interaction object (CIO) [Limbourg, 2000], [Bouillon, 2002]. PU is a complete presentation environment required for carrying out a particular interactive task. A LW is a logical container for other interaction objects as a physical window, a dialog box or a panel. Each PU can be composed by one or many LWs, which should be organized in space and time. An AIO consists of an abstraction of all CIOs from both presentation and behavioral viewpoints that is independent of any given computing platform. A CIO is a real object that belongs to the UI world that any user can see (e.g., text, image, animation) or manipulate such as a check box.

Our approach provides an abstract communication model that is composed by abstract elements, the User Interface Signs that are similar to these ones. Even a communication model is very close to the user interface model as defined in the previous section. In our UI model a presentation unit is the display medium, a logical window may be a task environment, a display area or a command panel. The abstract interaction objects are UI signs such as text box, buttons, menus, etc.

In our approach, the communication model is integrated with the interaction model considering that each presentation element is a medium or environment for the user to perform activities. We are rooted in the Semiotic Engineering perspective that considers that the design should communicate the functional and interaction model through the user interface. In this perspective the communicative purpose is fundamental. Each element in the communication model has a communicative function. The communication model provides the language that the designer uses to communicate with the users. For instance, an abstract interaction object is an element to the user to perform a basic interaction. A text box is an UI Sign that should communicate that the users could enter some data.

The communicative function of the communication model has the role to provide both the *feedforward* that informs what the users could do and how they could interact and the *feedback* that informs the results of what were done by the user. The communication of the dialog level of the interaction model should inform what the user should do to perform the basic actions of a command according with its rules. The communication of the task level should inform what the available commands are and how the users could use them to compose more the abstract tasks.

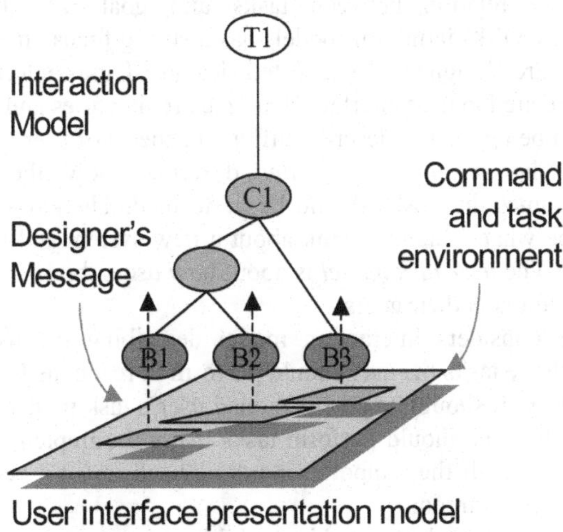

Fig. 3. The relationship between interaction and Communication models

2.3 Task and Dialog Models as Different Abstraction in Interaction Model

Our work assumes that task and dialog models are modeling the user-system interaction at different levels of abstraction. In this section, we consider how task and dialog models are considered in the literature (especially those from the model-based tradition) and then we discuss why they could be considered different views of the interaction model.

Task models are logical descriptions of the activities to be performed in reaching user's goals. They have shown to be useful for designing, analysing and evaluating interactive software applications. Task models have their origins in the sixties with HTA [Allen, 1969].

The basic idea is to describe the set of activities structured in different levels. Latter, based on psychology models, the GOMS approach provides a language to describe tasks in terms of goals and operators (cognitive, perceptive and motor) [Card, Moran and Newell, 1983]. Methods are sequences of subgoals and operators used to structure the description of how to reach a given goal. The selection rules indicate when to use a method instead of another one. A limitation of GOMS approaches is that it considers only sequential tasks and error-free behaviour.

UAN (User Action Notation) has been another successful approach that is also structured in a hierarchy [Hartson, 1992]. It allows describing the dynamic behaviour of a GUI.

CTT (ConcurTaskTrees) is inspired by UAN to supports hierarchical specifications and provide a graphical representation of the hierarchical structure [Paterno, 1997]. It also uses operators (based in LOTOS) to express the temporal relationships among tasks at the same abstraction level. CTT provides a rich set of operators to describe enabling, concurrency, disabling, interruption and optionality.

One common aspect of all these approaches is the logical hierarchical structure. HTA focus on the relation between tasks and goals and hierarchical task decomposition. The GOMS family of models has a strong focus on evaluation of task performance. CTT are designed to supported design of user interfaces. It is more formal and can be related to user interface dialogue architectures and languages.

Task models can be applied to describe different aspects of user-system interaction [Paterno, 2000]. The *system task model* describes how the current system implementation assumes that tasks should be performed. The *envisioned task model* attempts to describe what designers think about a new system and how users should interact with them. The *user task model* is about how users think that tasks should be performed in order to reach their goals.

Our perspective considers interaction model describing the user's tasks. It is concerned only with the tasks the user should perform to reach his/her goals, using the specified functionality. It should be an envisioned user's task model at design time or the model of how the user should perform tasks using the implemented system. So, we do not need to have all the temporal operators used in CTT because concurrent user's action is not very common.

The term *dialog model* has been used in model based approaches to define the way in which the user can interact with the presentation through the various interaction devices [Limbourg, 2000]. It represents the actions that a user may initiate via the presentation elements and the reactions that the application communicates via elements user interface elements. It usually contains some specification of the input that the user interface enables and of the output that the system may convey through the user interface.

Dialog model could be seen as a low-level and solution-oriented description of the user-system interaction. Traetteberg considers that to describe the system-user behaviour, three main user interface design perspectives could be considered: the task/domain perspective, the abstract dialog perspective and the concrete interaction perspective [Traetteberg, 2003]. The task/domain perspective describes the behavior in a problem-oriented perspective, while the latter two is more solution-oriented. Abstract dialog modeling is concerned with dataflow, activation and sequencing, while concrete interaction focuses on the relation to input and output devices, e.g. windows, widgets and mice. Traetteberg considers that these perspectives can be partly integrated in one modeling language.

The perspective that task and dialog models are at different levels of abstraction can also be explained by the concepts of upper and lower level taks, and of unit and basic tasks [Pribeanu and Vanderdonckt, 2002]. Upper levels in task decomposition show how users are planning task performance by decomposing a task in sub-tasks. They describe ordering preference for each task, expressing what the user really wants to do. The leaves in the upper level task hierachy are unit tasks (considered by [Card, Moran and Newell, 1993] as the lower level tasks which the user really wants to perform). Pribeanu and Vanderdonckt consider that in this modeling context, unit tasks are defined as the lowest level tasks which is device independent. In our work, we consider this level as the task level of the interaction model.

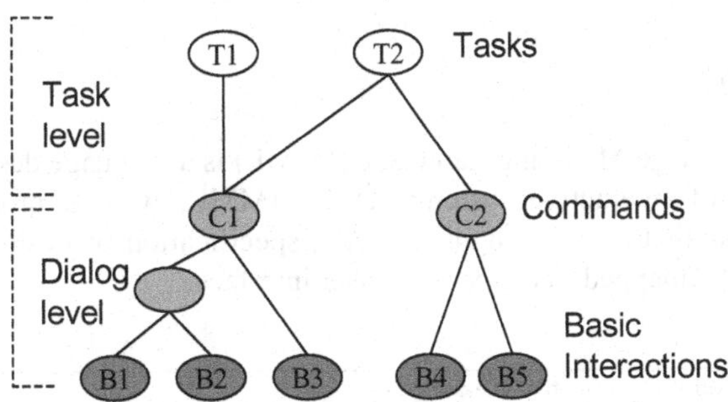

Fig. 4. The task and dialog levels of the interaction model

In this level, Pribeanu and Vanderdonckt consider that the basic tasks describe a structure that depends on the technology by which the goal is operationalized. They are obtained by decomposing *unit tasks*. The authors cite [Tauber, 1990] that defines the basic task as a task for which the system provides with one single command or unit of delegation.

In our model (and also in IMML) we consider these activities as part of the dialog model. Unit tasks are the commands the application provides to the user. We go further and use the concept of *simple task* [Payne, 1986] to refer to the leaves of a lower level basic task hierarchy. A basic task of the lower level part of the task hierachy (the dialog model in our approach) has a unit task (a command in IMML) as a root and a simple task as leaves (the basic interactions in IMML).

All these concepts are the basis of our approach. We consider that interaction model is a hierachy of the activities the user has to perform to use a computer application (user's tasks). At the higher level we have the task model describing the several ways the user could do to achieve his/her goals. It is about cognitive tasks. The user has different ways to compose tasks using the commands provided by the system. However, these possibilities should be compatible with the natural way the user performs tasks in his/her domain of activities.

At the lower level, the dialog model is the set of commands provided by the software the user should know. Each command determines the lower level tasks (or activities) the user should perform using the UI devices. The command defines the rules to delegate the execution of a function by the system. They are composed of basic actions performed using an interaction device.

The names interaction, task and dialog models are not very important to our approach. However, the distinction between tasks, commands and basic interaction are crucial. Tasks are the activities the user perfoms composing commands provided by the system. They are abstract activities at the upper level and are not imposed by the system. Commands are the activities the user performs following the rules defined by the system.

The benefit of integrating task and dialog is that we use the same modeling language and the same operators to structure tasks and commands. Tasks are composed by structuring commands using operators such as sequence, repeat and select. Commands are also composed using the same operators.

3 The IMML

The Interactive Message Modeling Language (IMML) is a language designed to allow the specification of interactive systems. Using IMML, we are proposing a sign production process that uses a language to the specification of designer's intended meaning that can be mapped in elements of user interface.

```
<imml application="Application name">
    <functional-model>
    ... specification of the functional model
    </functional-model>

    <interaction-model>
    ... specification of the interaction model
    </interaction-model>

    <communication-model>
    ... specification of the communication model
    </communication-model>
</imml>
```

Fig. 5. The specification of the models in IMML

IMML provides constructs to define the functional, interaction and communication models. It is also based on the theoretical foundations of semiotic engineering that considers that the system is the result of designer's decision about (1) what he/she thinks are the users' needs and (2) how the users want to interact to the system.

IMML is a markup language based on the XML standard. It provides a structured way to express the semantic model and it is flexible to allow extensions. These features are very important to express the structure of our model, which reflect our vision of an interactive system.

The role of IMML models is to provide types of semantic units (semantic types) about all these aspects. These semantic types can be associated with user interface objects (e.g., widgets) that are types of expressive units (expressive types).

A template of the basic form of an IMML specification is described in figure 5. This structure reflects the main models that ground the IMML approach.

The specification of domain objects in IMML describes a name and a basic type. There are pre-defined types of domain objects but new ones can be defined. The balance of a bank account number is a domain object that can be represented by a "number" type.

A domain object can also be composed of other domain objects. Composition of domain objects is also possible using the <item> element. For instance, a bank account is a domain object composed of other domain objects such as user's name and account number.

```
<domain-object name="Date" type="date" />
<domain-object name="Balance" type="number" />
<domain-object name="Monthly balance"
    type="composed-object">
  <item domain-object="Date" />
  <item domain-object="Balance" />
</domain-object>
```

Fig. 6. An example of a domain object in IMML

In figure 6 there is also a fragment of the specification of a domain object for a bank account balance, which is compose of a date and a balance.

Domain functions refer to application function that modifies the state of the system. The states are the properties, relationships among domain objects and states of domain functions. Deposit and withdraw are domain functions that change the state of a bank account balance. Figure 7 shows an example of a function to withdraw money from a bank account.

As we can see in figure 7, the specification of a domain function has several elements. The input and output operands are domain objects that are, respectively, the input and output of the functions. The pre-conditions and post-conditions are natural language statements that specify the conditions before and after the execution. This follows model-based approach to software engineering functional specification.

The domain function also allows the specification of a finite state machine using the state element and the control elements to describe the transitions between the states. In the example depicted in figure 7, there is only a main state: processing. Initial and final are default states and do not need to be specified. The controls should allow the user to start, stop, pause or resume the execution of some function. The start control indicates where the execution begins. A control is triggered by some external event that is specified in the interaction model.

All these constructs were designed to allow a seamless mapping between software engineering specification models and IMML.

```
<domain-function name="Withdraw">
  <input-operands>
    <item domain-object="Account Number" />
    <item domain-object="PIN" />
    <item domain-object="Value" />
  </input-operands>
  <output-operands>
    <item domain-object="Balance" />
  </output-operands>
  <pre-condition>
    The account number and PIN must be valid
    and the account should have a balance
    greater or equal then the value.
  </pre-condition>
  <post-condition>
    The balance is subtracted by the
    value withdrawn.
  </post-condition>
  <states>
    <state name="initial" />
    <state name="Processing" />
    <state name="final" />
  </states>
  <controls>
    <control name="Start" from-state="initial"
      to-state="Processing" />
    <control automatic="yes"
      from-state="Processing" to-state="final" />
  </controls>
</domain-function>
```

Fig. 7. The specification of a domain function

The specification of interaction model in IMML has the elements presented in the example in figure 8. It shows a function command to get a monthly balance. The designer wants the user to select between to do all basic interactions to complete the command or to quit (go direction="away"). If the user selects to complete the command, he/she needs to do it in a sequence of steps for entering all the input operands (account number, PIN, value, month or dates) and then he/she can activate the start control of the monthly balance domain function.

A task that encompasses the command "get a monthly balance", "see the function result" and "perform withdraw" is specified in figure 9. It means that the designer thinks that this is a task that user performs frequently and he wants to communicate it explicitly.

A frame is a composite sign to organize the presentation of other user interface elements. It is used to fit the contained elements with the communication medium (computer screen). This means that user interface elements can be organized in one frame if the screen size is big enough or in a sequence of frames if the screen size is small. The frame element has attributes to specify how its internal element are organized (orientation and align). The transition from one frame to another one is specified by a go element. An example of a frame is in figure 10.

```
  <function-command name="Get a monthly balance" domain-function="Monthly
balances">
    <select>
      <sequence>
       <enter-information domain-object="Account Number" />
       <enter-information domain-object="PIN" />
       <enter-information
            domain-object="Value" />
       <select>
         <join>
           <perceive-information>
             Select the month
           </perceive-information>
           <enter-information
               domain-object="Month" />
         </join>
         <join>
           <perceive-information>
             Enter a start date and end date:
           </perceive-information>
           <enter-information
               domain-object="StartDate" />
           <enter-information
               domain-object="EndDate" />
         </join>
       </select>
       <activate control="Start" />
      </sequence>
      <go direction="away" />
    </select>
  </function-command>
```

Fig. 8. The IMML specification of the command function to “get monthly balance”

```
  <task name="Withdraw after get a monthly balance">
    <sequence>
      <do function-command="get monthly balance" />
      <do function-result="Monthly balance" />
      <do function-command="Withdraw" />
    </sequence>
  </task>
```

Fig. 9. The IMML specification of a task

A command panel is a composite sign and it is associated with a command function. It contains frames and interaction signs to allow the user to perform all actions needed to command a domain function. In a final user interface, a command panel can be a dialog box or an HTML form. The command-panel element also has

```
<frame name="topFrame" title="mainFrame"
    orientation="horizontal" align="left">
  <push-button label="Balance"
    show="frameBalance" />
  <push-button label="Monthly"
    show="frameMonthly" />
  <push-button label="Payments" show="framePay" />
  <push-button label="Get balance and pay"
    show="frameBalanceAndPay" />
</frame>
```

Fig. 10. The IMML specification of frame

```
<command-panel function-command="Balance"
   name="frameBalance"
   orientation="vertical" align="left">
  <edit-box label=" Enter your account number"
    domain-object="Account number" />
  <edit-box label="Enter your PIN"
    domain-object="PIN" />
  <group orientation="horizontal" align="center">
    <push-button label="Balance" control="Start"
      transition="ShowBalance"
      target="bottomFrame" />
    <push-button label="Quit" hide="this" />
  </group>
</command-panel>
```

Fig. 11. A command panel in IMML

attributes to specify how its internal elements are organized (orientation and align). Figure 11 shows a description of a command panel in IMML.

4 Conclusion

Our work contributes to interactive system development by providing a first step in developing a set of tools to integrate SE and HCI methods and techniques. The first step is the IMML, a language that is in the heart of a visual development environment. It is a language to the specification of the functional, interaction and communicative aspects of an application. Our approach has many things in common with other model-based ones. However, we think it is a thought-provoking approach providing a new perspective to user interface design. The main difference is that the IMML statements are not system activities but designer's message to user's action. IMML helps to integrate functional, task, dialog and presentation models, emphasizing the communicability aspects of interactive systems without losing control of the interactivity and functionality. We expected that putting functionality, interactivity and communicability specification in the same formalism enhance designer productivity and system usability.

In a near future, designers do not need to specify a user interface directly in IMML. Visual IMML is an extension of the Unified Modelling Language (UML) that was constructed using the requirements for an UML profile. Visual IMML is not a visual programming language. It is a visual specification language that provides a graphical vocabulary (the UML stereotypes) to construct an abstract description of a user interface according to the theoretical foundations of IMML.

Visual IMML has stereotypes and diagrams to every element in IMML. Following the UML concepts, the visual elements are organizes in packages. Visual IMML represents the interaction model as a tree structure following the hierarchical nature of tasks, commands and basic interactions in IMML.

Since IMML allows the UI specification in an abstract level it is possible muli-platform development. We are developing a tool that use the IMML as an abstraction and device independent specification of a UI to multiple target platforms. We have developed a software tool that analyses an IMML specification and translates to DHTML code. DHTML stands for Dynamic Hypertext Mark-up Language and encompass the standard technologies to Browser-Based User Interface in Web System. The technologies are HTML, JavaScript, Document Object Model (DOM) and Cascading Style Sheets (CSS). A compiler from IMML to Java is under construction.

References

1. Bouillon, L.; Vanderdonckt, J. and Souchon, N. Recovering Alternative Presentation Models of a Web Page with VAQUITA. Proceedings of CADUI'2002, pp. 311-322, 2002.
2. Card, S., Moran, T., Newell, A., The Psychology of Human-Computer Interaction, Lawrence Erlbaum, Hillsdale, 1983.
3. de Souza, C. The Semiotic Engineering of Human-Computer Interaction. MIT Press, 2005.
4. Hartson R., Gray P., Temporal Aspects of Tasks in the User Action Notation, Human Computer Interaction, Vol.7, pp.1-45, 1992.
5. Limbourg, Q., Vanderdonckt, J., and Souchon N. The Task-Dialog and Task-Presentation Mapping Problem: Some Preliminary Results. Proceedings of DSV-IS 2000.
6. Paternò, F., Mancini, C., Meniconi, S. ConcurTaskTrees: A Diagrammatic Notation for Specifying Task Models. Proceedings of Interact '97, Chapman & Hall (1997) 362-369.
7. Paternò, F. Model-Based Design and Evaluation of Interactive Applications. Springer-Verlag, 2000.
8. Payne, S., Green, T., Task-Actions Grammars: A Model of the Mental Representation of Task Languages, Human-Computer Interaction, 2, pp.93-133, 1986.
9. Prates, R.O.; de Souza, C.S; Barbosa, S.D.J. (2000) A Method for Evaluating the Communicability of User Interfaces. ACM interactions, Jan-Feb 2000. pp 31-38.
10. Puerta, A. and Eisenstein, J. Towards a general computational framework for model-based interface development systems, Proceedings of the 4th international conference on Intelligent user interfaces, ACM Press, 171—178, 1999.
11. Tauber, M.J., ETAG: Extended Task Action Grammar - a language for the description of the user's task language, in D. Diaper et al. (eds.), Proc. of Interact'90, Elsevier, Amsterdam, 1990.

PIM Tool: Support for Pattern-Driven and Model-Based UI Development

Frank Radeke[1,2], Peter Forbrig[1], Ahmed Seffah[2], and Daniel Sinnig[2]

[1] University of Rostock, Software Engineering Group, Institute of Computer Science, Albert-Einstein-Str. 21, 18059 Rostock, Germany
{pforbrig, frank.radeke}@informatik.uni-rostock.de
[2] Concordia University, Human-Centered Software Engineering Group, Department of Computer Science and Engineering, 1455 de Maisonneuve Blvd West, Montreal, QC, Canada, H3G 1M8
seffah@cse.concordia.ca, dsinnig@encs.concordia.ca

Abstract. Model-based approaches describe the process of creating UI models and transforming them to build a concrete UI. Developers specify interactive systems on a more abstract and conceptual level instead of dealing with low level implementation. However, specifying the various models is a complex and time consuming task. Pattern-based approaches encapsulate frequently used solutions in form of building blocks that developers may combine to create a user interface model. Thus they enforce reuse and readability and reduce complexity. In this paper we present a comprehensive framework that unites model-based and pattern-driven approaches. We introduce the "Patterns In Modelling" (PIM) tool, that implements this framework. We will demonstrate the functioning of the tool by using an illustrative example. We primarily focus on the creation of the task model and give a brief outlook how patterns will be applied to the other levels within the framework.

Keywords: User interface design, UI pattern, UI model.

1 Introduction

Software applications are becoming more and more complex. User interfaces are no exception of this rule. Additionally, with the increasing importance of other platforms besides the desktop PC, today's software applications must be developed in a way that they can be easily adapted to platforms like PDAs or Mobile Phones. Developing software on a more abstract and conceptual level can cope with these challenges. This idea is followed by many of the model-based approaches. Nevertheless, specifying the various models and linking them together is still a time consuming and complex task. Specifying the models while using frequently used solutions in form of patterns can reduce complexity and enhance reuse and readability.

Based on these ideas we introduce a pattern driven model-based framework, which allows the application of patterns as building blocks to the different UI models. Afterwards we will introduce the "Patterns In Modeling" (PIM) tool, which aims to support the user with the application of patterns to UI models. We will primarily

K. Coninx, K. Luyten, and K.A. Schneider (Eds.): TAMODIA 2006, LNCS 4385, pp. 82–96, 2007.

focus on the application of task patterns to task models since this step has been already fully implemented in the tool. Additionally we give an outlook on how to apply patterns to the other models of the approach. In doing so, we will use an illustrative example to motivate our approach. Finally we will exhibit future avenues for the development of the framework and the tool.

2 Related Work

There exist a couple of tools that support either model-based UI design or pattern-driven approaches. Figure 1 mentions some of them. The PIM tool, which is introduced in this paper, aims to combine both approaches into one tool and hence to bridge the gap between model-based development and pattern-driven design.

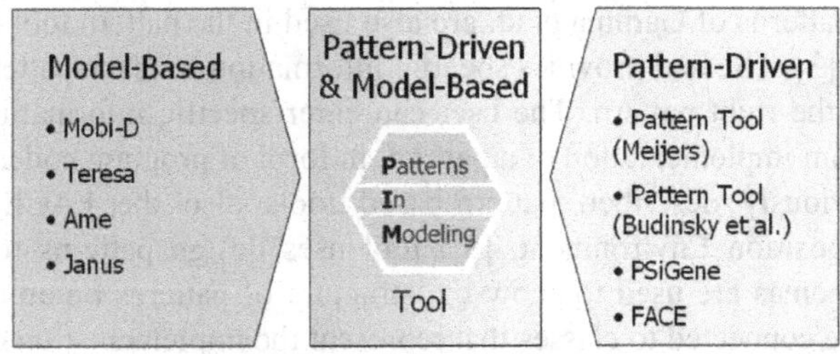

Fig. 1. PIM Tool – Bridging the gap between model-based and pattern-driven approaches

Key idea of model-based approaches is to specify the system on an abstract level using different models. Each model describes a specific aspect of the application.

MOBI-D (Model-Based Interface Designer, [10]) is a software environment for the design and development of user interfaces from declarative interface models. The MOBI-D system supports the user interface developer to design the user interface through specifying task, domain, user, dialog, and presentation models. Internally, the MIMIC modeling language is used to define the various models. MIMIC is the forerunner of XIML and supports the declaration of a so-called design model. This design model describes dynamic relationships between entities of the other declarative models.

TERESA is a semi-automatic environment developed to generate the concrete user interface for a specific type of platform based on the task model. It is composed of a number of steps allowing designers to start with an envisioned overall task model of a multiple user interface application [6] and then derive concrete user interfaces for multiple devices. In particular, TERESA distinguishes four main steps: First a single high level task model of a multi platform application is created. Based on this system task models for specific platforms are defined. The system task model is then used to obtain an abstract user interface, which is composed of a set of abstract interactors. Finally, the platform dependent UI is created by mapping the abstract interactors to platform specific interaction techniques.

The AME and JANUS systems both emphasize the automatic generation of the desired user interface from an extended object-oriented domain model. During this automatic generation process, both systems make use of different comprehensive knowledge bases. They do not include any other declarative models. Both systems generate user interface code for different target systems like C++ source code in order to link it with UI toolkits [11].

In pattern-based approaches frequently occurring solutions in form of patterns are used as building blocks to create the system. In the "Pattern Tool" [7] design patterns are regarded as coarse-grained blocks or fragments for UI design. Accordingly, the resulting system is represented by a hierarchical fragment model. The patterns within this approach are mainly based on the design patterns proposed by Gamma et al. [5] but not restricted to them. Patterns are instantiated by being cloned from a prototype. Sub-fragments of this resulting fragment are then replaced by customized sub-fragments according to the current context of use.

The design patterns of Gamma et al. are also used in the pattern tool introduced by Budinsky et al. [3]. The tool provides specific information for each pattern helping the user to choose the right pattern. The user can enter specific information in order to generate a custom implementation of a pattern, in form of program code.

As the previously described pattern-based tools also the FACE (Framework Adaptive Composition Environment, [8]) tool uses design patterns to develop the application. Schemas are used to show the structure of patterns on an abstract level. The schemas are connected to classes that represent the implementation of a pattern.

PSiGene [12] is a pattern-based component generator for applications in the domain of building simulation. Code templates, which are associated with each pattern, are used to generate the final application code. The user starts with the creation of a class model. Then predefined simulation patterns are assigned to the elements of the model.

3 Integrating Model-Based and Pattern-Driven Design

Design models provide a more abstract and conceptual view on software. Describing software through models on different conceptual levels can reduce complexity and distraction by low level implementation details. In the literature various models like task, domain, user, device, platform, application, presentation, dialog or navigation model are discussed [15]. In this paper we will concentrate on the following models:

- The task model is a hierarchical decomposition of tasks into sub-tasks until an atomic level is reached. The execution order of the task is defined by temporal relationships among peer tasks [15].
- The dialog model describes the human-computer interaction. It specifies when the user can invoke functions, when the user can select or specify inputs and when the computer can query information. Task and dialog model are closely related since tasks are assigned to different dialog states within the dialog model.

- The presentation model describes which UI elements appear in different dialog states of the dialog model. It consists of a hierarchical decomposition of the possible screen display into groups of interaction objects [10]. A relation between dialog and presentation model can be constructed through linking the abstract UI elements with the dialog states in which they appear.
- The layout model finally assigns style attributes like size, font or color to the abstract UI elements of the presentation model [13].

In model-based UI design the user interfaces are specified by creating and transforming UI models and linking them with each other (MBUID, e.g. [14]). The creation of the models and linking them together, however, is a tedious and time-consuming activity. Even for relative simple applications the models quickly become complex. Moreover, it lacks an advanced concept of reuse, besides copy-and-paste-reuse, of already modelled solutions [4]. We believe that patterns, which describe generic solutions to common problems in a specific context [5], can be employed to avoid these disadvantages. Additionally extending the model-based approach with patterns can enhance reuse, flexibility and readability.

Figure 2 integrates the ideas of the former paragraphs in a pattern-driven and model-based approach. The left side shows the task, dialog, presentation and layout model, and the mappings between these models. These models are considered as one integrated model, which is collectively referred to as UI multi model. The right side of figure 2 shows the UI patterns, which are employed to establish the UI multi model. A UI pattern contains one or more model fragments as visualized by the hexagons. If a pattern contains only a model fragment of one specific type we refer to this pattern as task pattern (e.g. TP1), dialog pattern (e.g. DP1), presentation pattern (e.g. PP1) or layout pattern (e.g. LP1), depending on the type of model fragment. Patterns that contain two or more model fragments are referred to as multi patterns (e.g. MP4). While multi patterns represent in general less abstract solutions, specific type patterns represent more abstract solutions, which can be employed in different contexts.

Task model fragments are used to describe task fragments, which frequently appear. They are used as building blocks for the gradual development of the task model. Dialog model fragments suggest how tasks should be grouped to dialog views and how transitions between dialog views should be defined. Presentation model fragments provide predefined sets of abstract UI elements in order to create the presentation model. Finally, layout model fragments can be used to assign certain predefined styles to the abstract UI elements in order to establish the layout model. Beside the model fragments the patterns may contain predefined mappings between the different model components.

Additionally it is possible to composite patterns using sub patterns. Thus, more abstract patterns can be used to create more specific UI patterns. Figure 3 visualizes such a pattern-sub-pattern relation. The task model fragment of pattern 1 is established using the task model fragments of pattern 2 and pattern 3. Moreover, pattern 1 uses pattern 3 as sub pattern to establish the dialog model fragment.

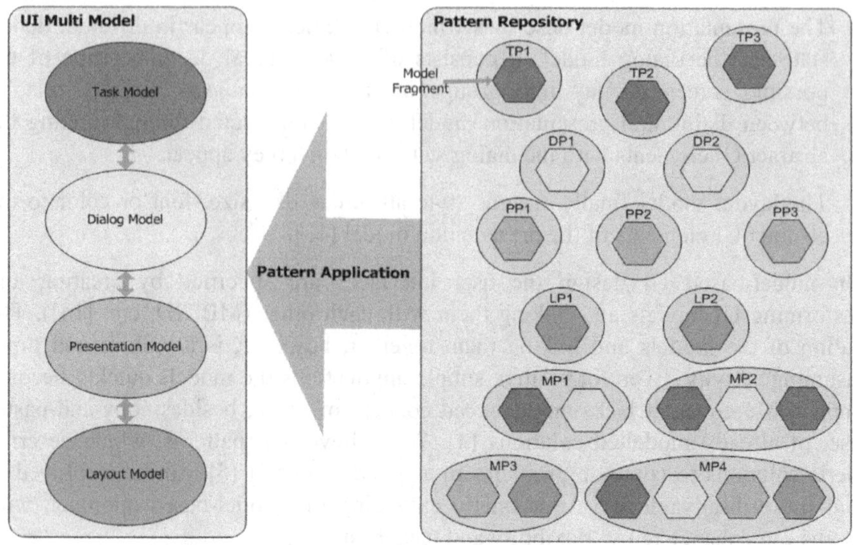

Fig. 2. Pattern-Driven and Model-Based Approach

In order to model the solution stated in the pattern in a generic and reusable fashion, patterns may contain variables and a flexible structure, which have to be adapted to the current context of use. This adaptation takes place during the process of pattern application as visualized by the arrow in figure 2. The pattern application process entails the steps: pattern selection, pattern instantiation and integration of the instantiated pattern into target models.

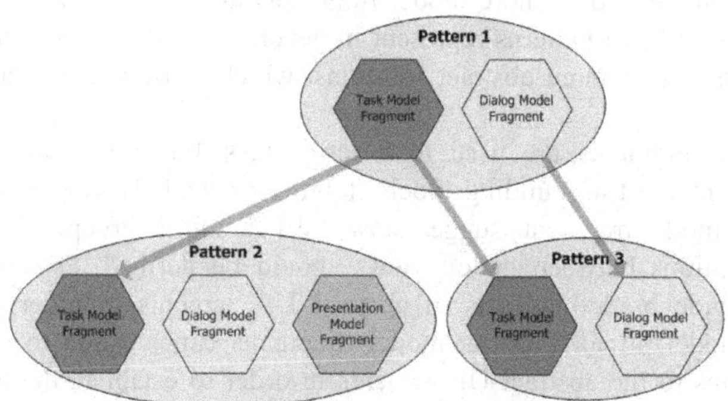

Fig. 3. Pattern-Sub-pattern relations

In the next section, we show how patterns are generally applied to the different UI models. Moreover, we will introduce a tool, which supports the user by applying patterns to the different models of our approach. Primarily we will focus on the task level, which is fully implemented in the tool.

4 PIM Tool: Support for Applying Patterns in Model Construction and Transformation

In the previous section, we introduced a pattern-driven model-based framework, which makes use of patterns to facilitate the creation of the UI multi model. Since patterns are abstract and generic solutions the need to be instantiated. Generally the process of pattern application consists of four steps.

1. *Identification*
   A subset M' of the target model M is identified. This subset will be replaced and extended by the instance of the pattern, which is selected in the next step.

2. *Selection*
   In this step an appropriate pattern is selected to be applied to M'.

3. *Instantiation*
   To apply the pattern to the model it needs to be instantiated. In this step the concrete structure of the pattern is defined and values are assigned to the variable parts of the pattern in order to adapt it to the current situation.

4. *Integration*
   The pattern instance is integrated into the target model. It is connected to the other parts of the model in order to create a seamless peace of design.

Handling these steps depends, to great extent, on the creativity and experience of the designer. At this point efficient tool support can assist the designer in selecting and applying appropriate patterns in order to make the design process more traceable and to increase its effectiveness. For this purpose we introduce the PIM (Patterns In Modeling) tool, which aims to support the user in applying patterns to models by following these steps. Figure 4 shows the user interface of the PIM tool.

The screen mainly consists of three views. (1) The model view, which allows the user to specify the target model (task, dialog, presentation, and layout). In the figure, the task-model label is marked by a bold border frame in order to indicate that the user is working on the task level of the integrated UI multi model. (2) The work view, which is responsible for displaying the selected model. For example, in figure 4 the work view shows the task model of a hotel management application. (3) The pattern view, which shows available patterns for the chosen target model. In this case the pattern view shows a set of task patterns.

In what follows we will use a brief example to illustrate how the tool works. Since currently only pattern application to the task level has been implemented in the tool, we will focus on the task pattern application and mention briefly how pattern application can be realized on the other levels of the approach as well.

4.1 Brief Example: A Desktop Radio Player

To illustrate the functioning of the PIM tool we will now describe a small example, in which we the task model of a simple Desktop Radio Player application is developed.

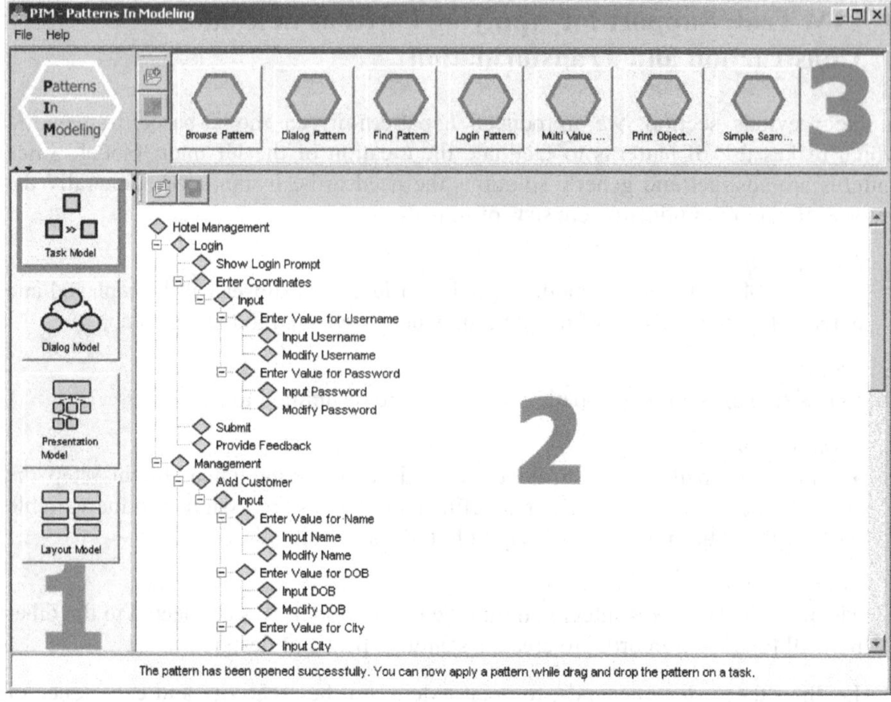

Fig. 4. User Interface of the PIM (Patterns In Modeling) Tool

Table 1 depicts the textual description of the use case capturing the main functionality of the envisioned application.

Following the process of pattern application parts of the task model that can be replaced and extended by task pattern instances are identified. Then appropriate task patterns are selected, instantiated and finally integrated into the original task model. In the following the entire process is described in more detail.

4.1.1 Identification

In order to get started a base model is needed, which can be extended by using pattern instances. Figure 5 shows a very basic task model, visualized in CTTE [9]. The task model entails only the basic task structure of the application. It describes that after logging in the user can search and select a radio station. According to his choice the application will then play music. Instead of refining these tasks now 'by hand' details will be added to the model by applying appropriate patterns. For example, after loading the task model into the PIM tool[1], the "Log In" task may be identified as subset M' of the original model to which a first pattern shall be applied.

---

[1] Currently the PIM tool accepts only XIML files as model specification. Therefore, in order to reuse the CTT task specification, we used the editor [17] to convert the CTT file to XIML.

Table 1. Brief example: Desktop Radio Player

Many programmers enjoy listening to music while they are working. If you have access to a broadband internet connection online radio stations offer a wide range of music. However, accessing internet, opening the right web pages, log in to the network and force through the web pages of the network in order to choose and listen to a radio station is an extensive business. Thus it would be a nice idea to have a small desktop application that allows logging in to an online radio network and afterwards to search through the radio stations, select a preferred station and that finally allows listening to this station.

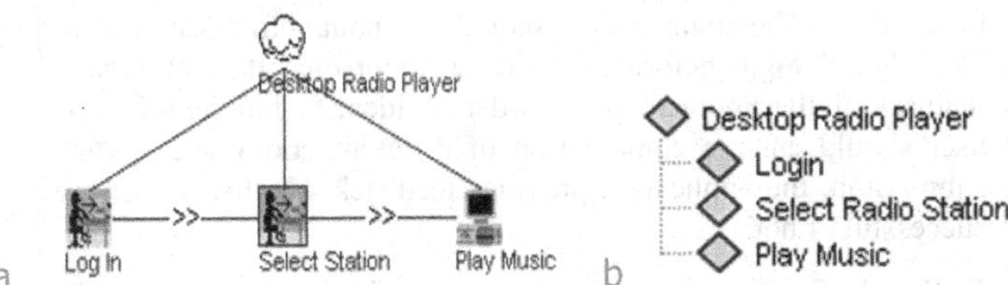

Fig. 5. The task model of the Desktop Radio Player in the CTTE tool (a) and after being loaded into the PIM tool (b)

4.1.2 Selection

Since the task model is selected as working level, the tool offers a set of task patterns that can be applied to the task model, as depicted in the pattern view of Figure 4. With a right mouse click on a task pattern the tool displays more detailed information. For example, table 2 shows the information, which is displayed for the "Log In" pattern.

The format of all patterns follows the uniform format that Alexander [1] proposed for his patterns. Internally the patterns are specified in a XML-based language called TPML (Task Pattern Mark up Language, [13]). As figure 6 shows each pattern specification contains a Name, Problem, Context, Solution, Rational, but also a Body element. Whereas the first five elements are primarily used to help the designer chose an appropriate pattern, the body element specifies the structure of the pattern.

In the PIM tool the "Log In" pattern is dragged and dropped onto the selected "Log In" task of the task model. As a result, the pattern application wizard is launched, which supports the designer performing the next step.

4.1.3 Instantiation

After identifying the "Log In" task as the sub-model M', and after choosing the "Log In" pattern the pattern application process needs to be started in order to create an instance of the chosen pattern. This step is necessary since patterns are generic solutions that have to be adapted to the current context.

The instantiation of a task pattern consists of two steps: (1) The structure of the resulting instance is specified. (2) Values to variable parts of the pattern are assigned.

Table 2. Information displayed for the "Log In" pattern

Problem: The user needs to identify him/herself in order to access secure or protected data and/or to perform authorized operations.
Context: The pattern is applicable if the application manages different types of users fulfilling different roles. The login process is also required if the application supports individual user modeling. An example is the individual customization of the appearance of the front end. In addition, the login feature is necessary if the user wants to create his/her own space, which makes it possible to have users enter that information once and use it again for future visits to the site.
Solution: By displaying a login dialog, the user can identify him/herself. The login dialog should be modal. In addition, the user should login before accessing any personal data or secure features of the application. In order to identify him/herself, the user should enter a combination of different coordinates. After submission, the application provides feedback whether login was successful or not.
Rational: By using the Login Pattern, the user can uniquely identify him/herself. Therefore the applications can provide customized views to the user and authorize the user to perform operations according to the user's role.

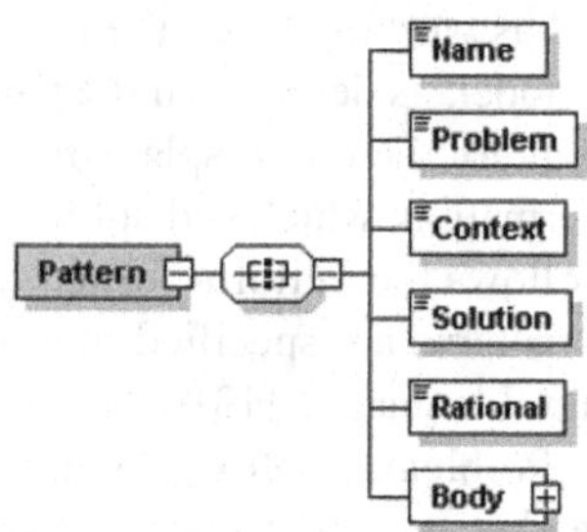

Fig. 6. Pattern structure

The first step includes the selection of optional parts of the pattern. In particular it has to be chosen whether they shall be included or not. Additionally, the number of executions for parts, which can be performed iteratively, has to be defined.

Figure 7 shows the pattern wizard that appears after the "Log In" pattern was dragged and dropped on the "Log In" task. It will guide the user through the pattern application process. The right pane shows the current state of the pattern instance during the whole process. As one can see the "Log In" pattern itself has a simple structure. It describes the "Log In" task as follows: First a login prompt is shown. Then the user enters and submits its coordinates for identification. Finally feedback is provided by the system. Since the "Log In" pattern contains no optional or iterative parts and also no variables the pattern application process immediately finishes after the user presses the next button in the wizard.

However, as portrayed in the right pane of figure 7 the "Log In" pattern makes use of the "Multi Value Input Form" pattern [2]. The "Multi Value Input Form" pattern is applicable when the user needs to enter a couple of related values. In the context of the "Log In" pattern it is used to enter the values that are necessary to identify the user. Therefore, after completing the process of pattern application for the "Log In" pattern the PIM tool identifies the sub-pattern and prompts the user whether he or she would like to instantiate the "Multi Value Input Form" pattern as well. Figure 8a shows the structure of the "Multi Value Input Form" pattern, which is displayed by the pattern wizard if the user confirms this prompt.

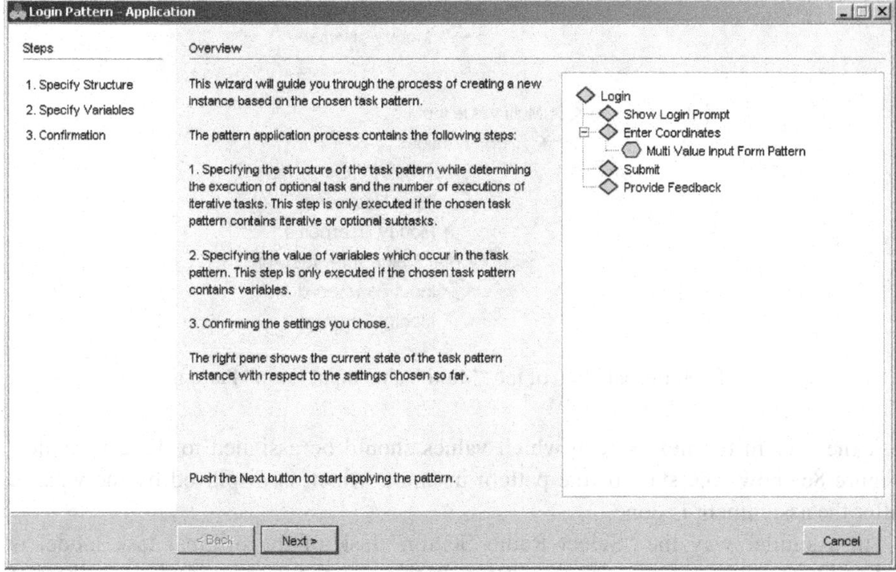

Fig. 7. Wizard for task pattern application to task models

A task icon with a star inside informs the user about the fact that the pattern contains a repetitive task for which the number of executions has to be determined. The number of repetitions depends on the number of values, which are entered within the form. Since it is used within the context of a log-in dialog, the user shall enter two values: 'username' and 'password'. Thus, the structure of the pattern instance in the next screen of the pattern wizard is modified in such a way that the "Enter Value for" task is performed two times. The pattern wizard allows the user to specify the structure of the current pattern instance while directly modifying the pattern instance in the pattern preview. The result is shown in figure 8b. Having a closer look at the obtained pattern instance, it is noticeable that each "Enter Value for" task contains a variable <name> to which a value has to be assigned. Thus, the pattern wizard will

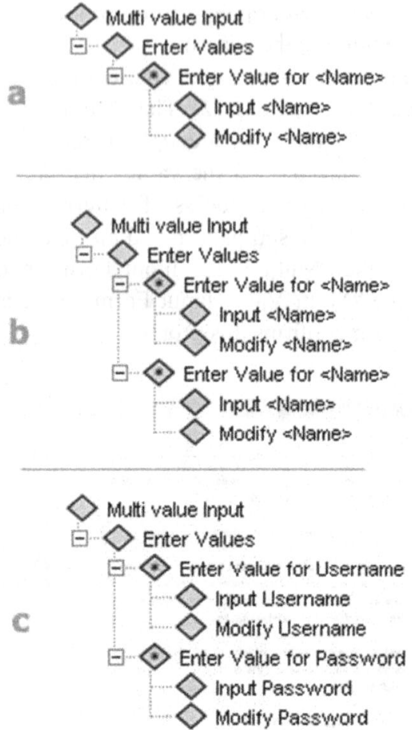

Fig. 8. Instantiation of the "Multi Value Input Form" Pattern

ask the user in the next screen which values should be assigned to these variables. Figure 8c shows the state of the pattern instance, which is displayed by the wizard, after the assignment is done.

In a similar way the "Select Radio Station" task of the original task model is refined by applying an appropriate pattern. In this task the user informs his- or herself about a set of available radio stations and finally chooses one. A suitable pattern for this purpose is the "Browse" task pattern which allows inspecting a set of objects. Figure 9a shows the structure of the "Browse" pattern prior the instantiation process. It contains a variable <object> that describes what kinds of objects are browsed. Since Radio Stations should be browsed the value 'Radio Stations' is assigned to this variable. As a result the pattern instance, which is displayed in figure 9b is received. As portrayed, the "Browse" pattern contains the "Print" pattern as a sub-pattern. It is used to display specific attributes of the browsed objects. Consequently the PIM tool offers a possibility to instantiate this pattern afterwards.

Figure 10a shows the structure of the "Print" pattern. It contains the repetitive task "Print <attribute>" for which the number of repetitions has to be determined. In our example two attributes of the browsed radio stations shall be displayed: The station name and the station genre. Thus it is defined that the "Print <attribute>" task is executed two times. Since the print task contains a variable declaration the value for

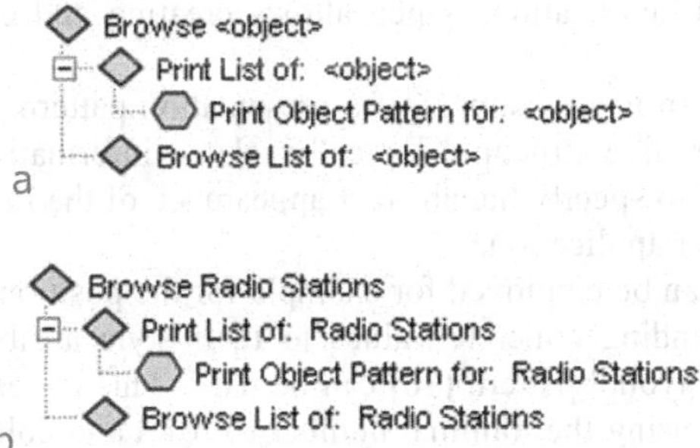

Fig. 9. Instantiation of the "Browse" Pattern

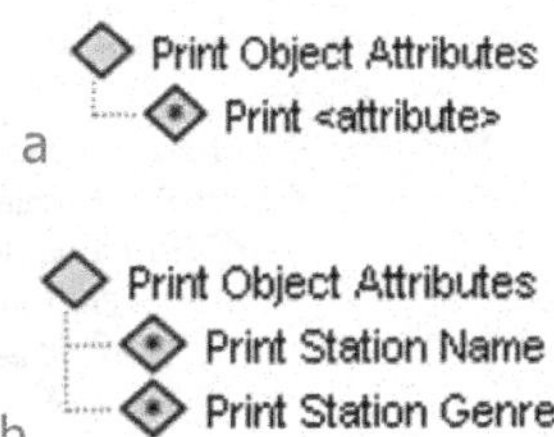

Fig. 10. Instantiation of the "Print" Pattern

the variable <attribute> has to be assigned twice. The instantiation of the "Print" pattern results in the task fragment, displayed in figure 10b.

4.1.4 Integration

Every time a pattern is instantiated as results an instance is received, whose structure and variable parts are adapted to the current context of use. In the last step of the pattern application process this instance has to be integrated into the target model. Therefore, as soon as the pattern wizard is finished, the PIM tool converts the pattern instance to the model format and integrates it into the target model by replacing the part that was selected in the first step.

Figure 11 shows once again the basic task model for the Desktop Radio Player and the resulting task model that was achieved with fewer efforts while making use of pre-defined solutions in form of patterns.

4.2 Outlook

In the future we will further extend the PIM tool so that it will be possible to apply patterns to all models involved in our approach. In the following we will briefly describe applicable patterns for the dialog, presentation and layout model.

A typical dialog pattern that can be applied to the dialog model is the "Recursive Activation" pattern [2]. This pattern is used when the user can activate several instances of a dialog view. It is applicable in many modern user interfaces. An example is an email application, which allows creating and editing several emails concurrently.

The “Form” pattern is an example of a presentation pattern. It is applicable when the user needs to provide structural logically related information to the application. Thus, it can be used to specify the abstract appearance of the log-in dialog within the Desktop Radio Player application.

Layout patterns can be employed for example for the positioning of the abstract UI elements and for binding concrete values to their style attributes. For the former purpose the “Grid Layout” pattern [16] can be used. This pattern aims to arrange all UI objects in a grid using the minimal number of rows and columns and making the cells as large as possible. An example for the latter purpose is the “House Style” pattern which provides an overall look–and-feel for the entire application.

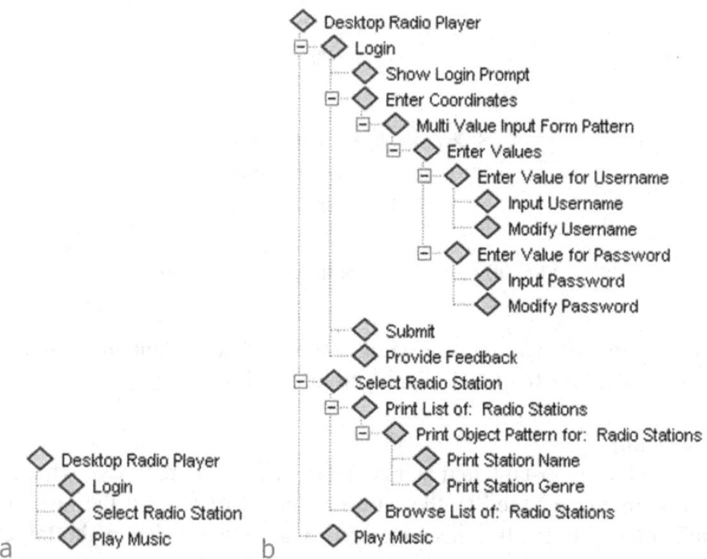

Fig. 11. Original (a) and resulting (b) task model for Desktop Radio Player Example

5 Conclusion

In this paper, we have introduced a novel tool that aims to bridge the gap between pattern-driven and model-based tools. Within the proposed underlying framework instances of patterns are used as building blocks for the creation of UI models and the mappings between them. Employing frequently used solutions in form of patterns reduces complexity and enhances reuse and readability. We demonstrated how the “Patterns In Modeling” (PIM) tool can support software developers in applying patterns to create the UI models. We used an illustrative example to show in detail how the application of task patterns to task models can be supported.

In order to apply patterns on all levels of the UI multi model the proposed framework needs to be formalized. This includes the examination of formal notations for the specification of UI models and the corresponding UI patterns. Presently there exists a multiplicity of UI description languages. Languages like UsiXML and XIML, which support the most common UI models, including the models mentioned in this paper, might be suitable for UI pattern specification as well. This requires extending their schemas to allow the specification of specific pattern features like variables and flexible structures.

References

[1] Alexander, C., S. Christopher, I. Sara, S. Murray, M. Jacobson, I. Fiksdahl-King and S. Angel (1977). *A Pattern Language*. New York, Oxford University Press.

[2] Breedvelt, I., F. Paternò and C. Severiins (1997). *Reusable Structures in Task Models*. In Proceedings of Design, Specification, Verification of Interactive Systems '97, Granada, Springer Verlag.

[3] Budinsky, F., M. Finnie, J. Vlissides and P. Yu (1996). Automatic Code Generation from Design Patterns. *IBM Systems Journal* Vol. 35(No. 2).

[4] Gaffar, A., D. Sinnig, A. Seffah and P. Forbrig (2004). *Modeling patterns for task models*. In Proceedings of ACM International Conference, Prague, Czech Republic.

[5] Gamma, E., R. Helm, R. Johnson and J. Vlissides (1995). *Design Patterns: Elements of Reusable Object-Oriented Software*. Boston, USA, Addison Wesley.

[6] Marucci, L., F. Paternó and C. Santoro (2003). Supporting Interactions with Multiple Platforms Through User and Task Models. *Multiple User Interfaces, Cross-Platform Applications and Context-Aware Interfaces*. London, Wiley: pp. 217-238 London, Wiley.

[7] Meijers, M. (1996). *Tool Support for Object-Oriented Design Patterns*. Master's Thesis in the Department of Computer Science. Utrecht, Netherlands, Utrecht University.

[8] Meijler, D., S. Demeyer and R. Engel (1997). *Making Design Patterns Explicit in FACE, A Framework Adaptive Composition Environment*. In Proceedings of 6th European Software Engineering Conference (ESEC '97), Springer-Verlag.

[9] Mori, G., F. Paternò and C. Santoro (2002). *CTTE: Support for Developing and Analyzing Task Models for Interactive System Design*. In Proceedings of IEEE Transactions on Software Engineering.

[10] Puerta, A. (1997). A Model-Based Interface Development Environment, IEEE Software. 14: pp. 41-47, IEEE Software.

[11] Schlungbaum, E. (1996). *Model-Based User Interface Software Tools - Current State of Declarative Models*. Technical Report 96-30, Graphics, Visualization and Usability Center Georgia Institute of Technology.

[12] Schütze, M., J. P. Riegel and G. Zimmermann (1999). PSiGene - A Pattern-Based Component Generator for Building Simulation. *Theory and Practice of Object Systems (TAPOS)* 5: pp. 83-95.

[13] Sinnig, D. (2004). *The Complicity of Patterns and Model-based UI Development*. Master's Thesis in the Department of Computer Science. Montreal, Canada, Concordia University.

[14] Trætteberg, H. (2001). *Model-based User Interface Design*. PhD Thesis in the Deptartment of Computer and Information Sciences. Trondheim, Norway, University of Science and Technology.

[15] Vanderdonckt, J., E. Furtado, J. Furtado and Q. Limbourh (2003). Multi-Model and Multi-Level Development of User Interfaces. *Multiple User Interfaces, Cross-Platform Applications and Context-Aware Interfaces*. London, Wiley: pp. 193-216 London, Wiley.
[16] Welie, M. (2006). *Patterns in Interaction Design*. http://www.welie.com/ July 2006
[17] Wolff, A., P. Forbrig, A. Dittmar and D. Reichart (2005). *Linking GUI Elements to Tasks - Supporting an Evolutionary Design Process.* In Proceedings of TAMODIA 2005, Gdansk, Poland.

Pattern-Based UI Design: Adding Rigor with User and Context Variables

Homa Javahery[1], Daniel Sinnig[1], Ahmed Seffah[1], Peter Forbrig[2], and T. Radhakrishnan[1]

[1] Department of Computer Science and Software Engineering, Concordia University
Montreal, QC, H3G 1M8, Canada
{h_javahe, d_sinnig, seffah, krishnan}@encs.concordia.ca
[2] Department of Computer Science University of Rostock
Albert-Einstein-Str.21, 18051, Rostock, Germany
pforbrig@informatik.uni-rostock.de

Abstract. In current practice, user interface development is often based on a vague and undocumented design process, relying solely on the designer's experience. This paper defines a pattern-based design process, which adds rigor to user interface design. The process is based on the notion of user variables to capture user requirements in a formal manner – based on discrete values that are amenable for tool support and automated analysis. Other context of use information is captured as context variables. Using these values as input, design patterns are selected to leverage best design practices directly into user interface development. Pattern-Oriented Design is then employed to derive a conceptual design, or early prototype, of the user interface. A case study with a Bioinformatics information site exemplifies the feasibility and applicability of this process.

Keywords: HCI patterns, pattern-oriented design, persona, user variables, design methodology, context.

1 Introduction

Over the last decade, the development of interactive applications, and consequently the user interface (UI), has become increasingly complex. Designers need to be aware of many different factors which influence UI design: (a) user analysis and their characteristics, (b) environmental constraints (such as platform and device characteristics), and (c) task analysis in the intended place of use. Collectively these are referred to as the context of use [1]. Since the UI development process has become highly context-sensitive, UI Design based on the intuition of the designer is no longer adequate. In order to cope with this multi-dimensional complexity, we need to add rigor to UI development. To attain this feat, we require processes that are systematic, traceable and practical for designers, but which also leave room for design creativity when appropriate.

In recent years, there have been considerable efforts to add rigor to UI development. One such approach is model-based UI development. The main idea

K. Coninx, K. Luyten, and K.A. Schneider (Eds.): TAMODIA 2006, LNCS 4385, pp. 97–108, 2007.

surrounding model-based approaches is to identify useful abstractions that highlight key aspects to be considered when designing interactive applications [2]. Central to all model-based approaches is that all aspects of a user interface design are represented using declarative models. In a model-based approach, the UI design is the process of creating and refining the user interface models at different levels of abstraction [3]. In other words, model-based design focuses on finding mappings between the various models [4]. Eventually, user interfaces are generated automatically or semi-automatically with the designer's interventions and decisions, from the model descriptions.

Model-based user interface development has been investigated and researched for more than a decade [5]. Even though its potential and advantages are considerable, none of the model-based frameworks have been adopted by the mainstream developer. Industry does not share the perspective of employing model-based techniques for UI development. On the contrary; industry is still led by RAD (Rapid Application Development) tools, IDE (Integrated Development Environments) and authoring tools (like Macromedia Dreamweaver or Macromedia Flash) [6]. The main problems of model-based UI development are the lack of tool support, the immaturity of the process that transforms one model into another for refinement, and the lack of technology which is capable of rendering usable user interfaces from the model descriptions [7].

Taking these arguments into consideration we investigate an alternative solution, which, similar to model-based UI development, abstracts important requirements and context properties. However, in contrast to model-based UI development where model transformations are the means for successive refinements, we employ patterns to derive a UI prototype. Our development framework is based on Pattern-Oriented Design (POD) as a driving force for developers [8]. Design patterns are proven solutions to common design problems, and have been successfully applied in many different domains [9, 10, 11]. In user interface design, patterns have been introduced as a medium to capture, disseminate and reuse proven design knowledge, and to facilitate the design of more usable systems [12, 13]. Patterns are presented in a specific format with defined attributes, and are applicable at different levels of abstraction. These levels include the user-task model, navigation model and presentation model for the concrete presentation of the user interface. Moreover, patterns are context-sensitive entities, which make them particularly attractive as a tool to facilitate UI design.

In this paper, we propose to add rigor to UI development by using a clearly defined process; based on a finite set of variables containing discrete values and best design practices captured as patterns. We will define a pattern-based design framework, which helps designers derive an early UI prototype, or conceptual design, from specified variables. These variables abstract important properties from the user and context of use. The resulting UI prototype is then used for stakeholder evaluations and early usability testing. Design flaws are detected at a very early stage within UI development and can be recovered with little effort. Finally the prototype serves as a basis for the actual implementation of the UI.

2 Pattern-Based User Interface Development

Interactive application development typically commences with the elicitation of user requirements by investigating the characteristics of the target user group, performing a detailed task analysis, and determining relevant platform constraints. In current practice, user requirements are often captured in narrative form with no standard representation. To make matters worse, there is no mature process which supports the systematic transformation of user requirements and context information into concrete design solutions. Typically, the design is reliant almost completely on the designer's previous experience.

Our intention is to narrow the current gap between user requirements and conceptual design. To be able to effectively design user interfaces, it is important to capture and represent user requirements and context information in a rigorous manner. This entails representing the user model in a more formal form, facilitating automated analysis and processing. Within our approach, we represent each user description, or persona [14], in the form of variables with discrete domains. Each representative user is characterized by the set of variable assignments. Additionally we establish qualified links between the personas and selected tasks of the user task model. These links are used to further tailor tasks of the user-task model to specific user groups. Examples of the qualifications used are: *Task preference*, *task frequency* and *preferred device*.

For the design phase, in order to foster the reuse of proven and valid design solutions, we employ Pattern-Oriented Design (POD) as our foremost design directive. Therefore, based on the collection of user and context variables, a set of applicable patterns is selected and Pattern-Oriented Design (POD) is carried out. POD consists of understanding when a pattern is applicable during the design process, how it can be used, as well as how and why it can or cannot be combined with other related patterns. An example outlining its use is presented in Section 2.3.

Figure 1 depicts our pattern-based UI development process. The process commences after requirements elicitation and hence assumes the existence of a task model and information about user characteristics. It comprises the following three major phases:

- **User and Context Abstraction:** Relevant information about representative users and context of use information are captured as discrete variables into a *requirements matrix*.
- **Pattern Selection:** The mapping module is rule-based, and maps the variables of the requirements matrix with pattern variables in order to extract a set of applicable patterns.
- **Pattern-Oriented Design:** The designer further filters the pattern set by choosing appropriate patterns. At this stage, the creativity and experience of the designer plays an important role. The patterns are then used within a pattern-oriented design process to derive the conceptual design of the user interface.

In what follows, we will discuss each of the three phases in greater detail.

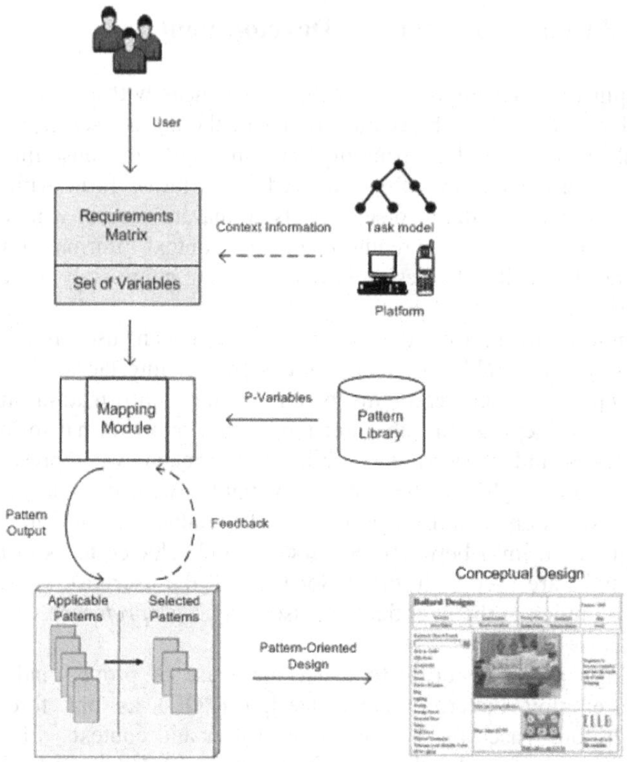

Fig. 1. The Pattern-Based UI Design Process

2.1 User and Context Abstraction

The first step of our pattern-based UI design process consists of abstracting important user properties from our persona descriptions [14]. In order to increase persona effectiveness as a technique, we develop our personas iteratively using ethnography, domain analysis and empirical evidence; we also extend them to include information about interaction behavior, user tasks and goals [15]. In current practice, user information is often captured in narrative form, with no standard representation. In order to make these requirements amenable for tool support and automated analysis, we represent them by a set of variables grouped into categories. In its current stage, our user variables are grouped into five basic categories; each of them containing about six variables, with one of five possible values. For example, the category *Knowledge and Experience* contains a variable 'System Experience' that can vary from novice to expert on a five-point scale. Another example is the category *Psychological Profile and Needs* which contains variables such as 'Initiative Taking' (proactive/reactive user) and 'Control' (amount of control a user needs while interacting with a system).

In addition, each persona is linked to a set of context variables. Selected higher-level user tasks, which are domain-dependent, and platform preferences, become important factors for later pattern selection. Examples of tasks relevant to our case study on a web-based application (see Section 3) are: 'Search database', 'Browse list', and 'Open Tool', with examples of their user-dependent properties being *Frequency of use*, *Importance* and *Duration*. Furthermore, platform preferences such as *Preferred Device* are included as context variables.

An important characteristic of our process is that task and device requirements are not universally valid across all categories of users. For example, for a novice user the *search* task may be less important than the *browse* task, since he/she may not be familiar with the search criteria. The advanced user however, may rate the search task as more important. In a similar manner the preferred device may vary between user groups. Currently we distinguish between three types of platforms: web, GUI, and mobile applications. We adopted this classification from [12] who uses a similar classification for his interaction design patterns.

The requirements matrix is a nested table, whose cells contain tuples as entries. Each row of the table represents a different persona. The persona properties are categorized into user and context variables. Variables and categories of variables can be ranked according to importance and impact, as determined by the designer. It is also important to note the task entries contain references to the corresponding node in the task model. These references will help the designer in the later stages of the process to select and apply the patterns appropriately. From a process-point of view, these references help in tracing task-related entries back to their origins in the task model.

The selected variables from personas are used as input for the next step of our process, which consists of selecting a set of applicable patterns. After the requirements matrix has been completed, the mapping module analyzes the information in order to select appropriate patterns. This step will be described in the next section.

2.2 Pattern Selection

Each pattern is associated with a set of variables (called P-variables). This set of P-variables captures the context of use of a pattern. Selected examples of P-variables are illustrated in Table 1, using the shortcut pattern as an example (Figure 2). The described representation of persona and patterns permits us to draw a relationship between the values described in the requirements matrix variables and P-variables.

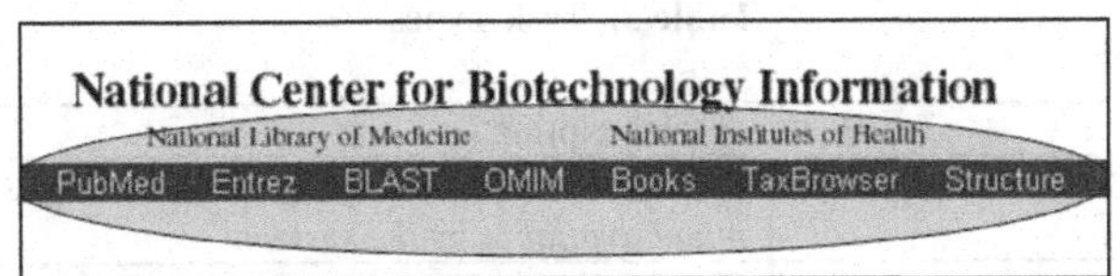

Fig. 2. Shortcut Pattern

Patterns are selected based on a mapping module, which takes user and context variables as input, and suggests various patterns as output to the designer. A library of patterns which is suitable for the domain should be used. In our case study, we used patterns that were appropriate for the web. The mapping of personas to patterns is rule-based, ensuring forward and backward traceability in the mapping. Such traceable output is essential for the evolution of the mapping module; if analyzed by expert designers, it may provide indications of errors in the mapping and can be used as a validation technique.

Table 1. Selected P-Variables of Shortcut Pattern [8]

P-Variables	**Values**
Application Experience	Expert
Supported Task(s)	Function_Selection
Usability Criteria	Guidance, Minimal Action

The rule-based engine of the mapping module is based on:

1. Direct mappings of certain user variables with patterns. Examples include patterns for certain user groups such as color-blind users, novice users, children, and users with disabilities.
2. Mappings based on more complex relationships between user variables, needs and design heuristics. This step is based on rules which link certain user needs with usability criteria [16] and design outcomes. For example, certain combinations of user variables (personality types, application experience and learning styles) are indicative of whether a certain persona requires more Guidance or Control, and this is captured in the pattern descriptions.
3. Filtering based on context variables. The persona descriptions make references to typical tasks of the user-task model. Here, particularly important information is the task type. As it turns out, some patterns are only applicable for a particular task type (i.e. *Advanced Search Pattern* and tasks of type *search*). The set of task types used in our case study is displayed in Table 2. As it turns out, the elicited task types cover a good portion of the possible user tasks encountered in web-based interactive applications.

The output of the mapping process is a set of patterns, linked with each persona. The designer must then use the appropriate patterns to build a UI prototype. Patterns include a textual description, as commonly found in current pattern libraries, and

Table 2. Task Types

Task Type	Description
`Function_Selection`	*The user selects one of the functionalities offered and made available by the system.*
`Data_Selection`	*The user is selecting and submitting a subset of the provided data.*
`Data_input`	*The user enters and submits data.*
`Access`	*The user requests access to a restricted area. The system provides the corresponding means.*
`Search`	*The user is searching for information. This step includes the system task of providing the means for entering the search criteria and the display of the search results.*
`Browse`	*The user is browsing through a list of information.*

relevancy data. The textual description provides insight on the pattern application and will influence the selection process. For instance, some patterns may not be used with others, and the designer may choose one of them over another based on that criteria. Relevancy data consists of the importance of each pattern for the given set of users.

2.3 Pattern-Oriented Design

When designers have a set of patterns, they tend to build a mental model representing the use of each pattern, its relationship with other patterns and its applicability in a given domain. For web application design, it is possible to follow four steps [8]: (1) choosing architectural patterns to describe the structure of the entire web site, (2) applying page manager patterns to establish a consistent physical and logical screen layout for each page, (3) employing information container patterns to "plug in" an information segment for each page, and (4) applying navigation support patterns to facilitate navigation in information spaces. Landay and Myers [17] and Welie [12] also propose to organize their Web pattern languages according to both the design process and UI structuring elements (such as navigation, page layout and basic dialog style).

In addition, to exploit relationships between patterns at a finer level of granularity , Zimmer [18] divided the relations between the patterns proposed in Gamma et al. [10] into 3 types: "X is similar to Y", "X uses Y", and "Variants of X uses Y". Based on [18, 19, 20], we define five types of relationships for composing UI design patterns: Similar, superordinate, subordinate, competitor, and neighboring. These will be discussed further in the next section.

3 Empirical Study

We applied our pattern-based development process during a three-year study which aimed to redesign an existing Bioinformatics web portal[1]. We wanted to evaluate whether the output of our process resulted in workable patterns, which could be used by designers to build a usable UI prototype, complying with the original requirements and context of use information.

We first conducted ethnographic studies and user interviews with an initial set of users of the site. We used these observations to understand the users, the bioinformatics problem domain, and user goals and preferences for the related tools. Based on this information, we carried out usability evaluations with a larger set of users. Participants included 16 bioinformatics users and five UI experts. Both psychometric and heuristic evaluations were used to collect relevant user, task and platform data. A brief summary of relevant findings will be presented here; further details about the study can be found in [21].

Our users were represented by two personas, with significantly different combinations of user and context variables (Table 3). Due to space constraints, the table only displays a subset of the variables used in our process. Differences were based predominantly on psychological profile, application experience, and task behavior. The platform variable was consistent, since none of our respondents indicated using the site on any other device other than a standard desktop or laptop, with a web browser.

[1] National Center for Biotechnology Information at http://www.ncbi.nlm.nih.gov.

Table 3. Subset of User and Context Variables

User Variables < *Application Exp., Usage Frequency…* >	**Context Variables** *<Task Name, Type, Frequency, Importance>*
Persona 1 <Novice, Medium…>	<Pubmed Search, Search, High, High>
	<Info. Gathering, Browse, High, High>
	<BLAST query, Complex (Data_Input, Search), Low, Medium>
	<Advanced Tool Use, Function_Selection, Low, Low>
Persona 2 <Expert, High…>	<BLAST query, Complex (Data_Input, Search), High, High>
	<Advanced Tool Use, Function_Selection, Med, Med>
	<Database Search, Search, Medium, High>
	<MyNCBI Access, Complex (Access, Function_Selection), Low, Medium>

Table 4. Pattern Selection based on Persona

Persona	**Design Pattern**	**Rationale for Mapper Logic**	**UI Expert Design Decision**
P1 (Novice)	On-Fly Description	Novice user is still unfamiliar with all menu options	Navigation menu (on left) has important site links with associated descriptions; these are useful for users that are less familiar with the site, but a hindrance for expert users (more scrolling). A solution is use of rollovers (on-fly descriptions) to help new users.
	Executive Summary	Novice user is still learning about application	General information about NCBI (what they do and their mandate) is interesting for novice users. For expert users, this clutters the site. An executive summary could solve this problem.
P2 (Expert)	Advanced Search	Expert user likes to limit searches	Simple search may be sufficient for novice users, but expert users often search against different parameters such as "limiting searches to specific species". An advanced search option could be useful for these users.
	Teaser Menu	Expert user likes to know recent updates	NCBI news is a good idea for expert users but will add additional content and scroll down for novice users. A good compromise is to replace it with a teaser menu, and place the content on another page.

Based on these variables, a number of patterns were suggested to UI designers. Table 4 illustrates examples of applicable patterns suggested by our process, which were then selected by UI designers. It is important to note that in our case study, due to both the nature of the application and the project requirements, UI designers focused heavily on the user variable "Application Experience", which had an impact on their pattern selection. The "Rationale for Mapper Logic" depicts the machine reasoning behind the choice. Note that this rationale is domain-independent. The column "UI Expert Design Decisions" explains why, from a domain-dependent point of view, the UI designer has deemed the suggested pattern as appropriate.

Finally, in order to construct the UI prototype, we used the POD approach to select and combine appropriate web patterns based on the desired task and user behavior. Patterns were combined based on the relationships introduced in the previous section:

1. **Similar** (X, Y) if and only if X and Y can be replaced by each other in a certain composition. This means that X and Y are patterns of the same category and they provide different solutions to the same problem in a similar context. For example, index browsing and menu bar patterns are similar. They both provide navigational support in the context of a medium size Web site. In our example, the index browsing pattern can be replaced by the menu bar pattern.
2. **Competitor** (X, Y) if X and Y cannot be used at the same time for designing the same artifact relationship that applies to two patterns of the same pattern category. Two patterns are competitors if and only if they are similar and interchangeable. For example, the Web convenient toolbar and menu bar patterns are competitors. The menu bar pattern can be used as a shortcut toolbar that allows a user to directly access a set of common services from any Web page. The convenient toolbar provides the same solution. In our design, we used the convenient toolbar and index browsing patterns and we have excluded the menu bar pattern.
3. **Super-ordinate** (X, Y) is a basic relationship to compose several patterns of different categories. A pattern X that is a super-ordinate of pattern Y means that Y is used as a building block to create X. An example is the home page pattern which is generally composed of several other patterns.
4. **Sub-ordinate** (X, Y) if and only if X is embeddable in Y. Y is also called super-ordinate of X. This relationship is important in the mapping process of POD. For example the Web convenient toolbar pattern is a sub-ordinate of the home page pattern.
5. **Neighboring** (X, Y) if X and Y belong to the same pattern category (family). For example, neighboring patterns may include the whole set of patterns to design a specific page such as a home page.

An improved design was carried out based on the selected patterns. All the web design patterns are well-known in the HCI community [8, 12, 13]. Figure 3 illustrates the navigational aspect of the UI redesign, and the combination of patterns that were used. The final design was tested with the original user sample and 11 new participants. The testing protocol included a comparative randomized study within initial groupings of the two personas, with task-based evaluation, structured questionnaires and open-ended interviews. Results indicated increased user satisfaction with the redesigned portal, and comments included less information overload, increased clarity and ease of navigation.

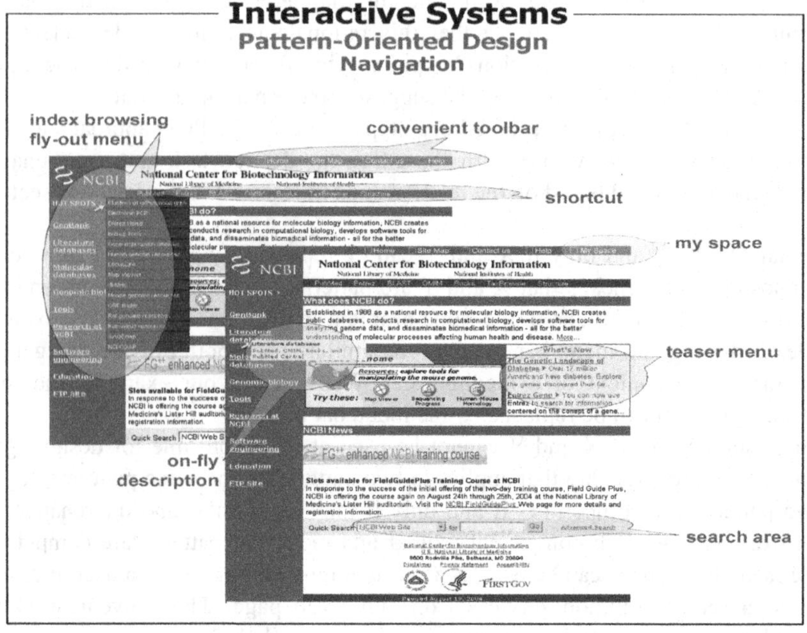

Fig. 3. Pattern oriented design of web portal

Moreover, we conducted ethnographic studies and workflow evaluations with UI designers. Ethnographic studies confirmed that our process follows closely with the mental model and the reasoning of experienced UI designers. Workflow evaluations indicated that our approach incorporates naturally with their UI design practices, with the majority of the UI experts (four out of five) finding an added-value when incorporating our process as a preliminary step in their pre-design or design activities.

4 Summary and Future Work

In this paper we proposed a pattern-based UI design process, with the goal of adding rigor and formalisms to UI development. A process, in general, is an organized set of activities, which transforms inputs to outputs. The input of our process is a set of variables, which abstracts user requirements and context information in a discrete manner. The output of the process is a set of patterns, which can be combined in a conceptual design or early prototype of the user interface. More precisely, a set of applicable patterns is extracted by the mapping module tool based on the variable input. These patterns are then used by the designer to derive the conceptual design of the UI.

Our approach shares similarities with model-based UI development, whose main idea is to identify useful abstractions highlighting the main aspects that should be considered when designing interactive applications. But, in contrast to model-based UI development, our process does not employ model transformations to generate the user interface. Instead, it employs best design practices and pattern-oriented design to derive a conceptual design of the user interface. By following such a "light-weight" approach we avoid most of the problems suffered by many model-based UI development approaches. These problems include the lack of tool support, the immaturity of the process that transforms one model into another, and the lack of technology that is capable of rendering usable user interfaces from model descriptions [7].

Our process can be seen as an "engineering compromise", which similar to model-based UI development, abstracts important requirements and context properties, but employs POD to derive a UI prototype. We strongly believe that such an approach is more feasible with today's technology and thus has greater chances to be adopted by the mainstream developer. Our process results in an early and inexpensive UI prototype based on best design practices. This can be especially useful for novice designers. A key element of our approach is the selection of appropriate patterns based on a discrete cross-mapping between pre-determined context factors. It is important to note that during pattern-oriented design, such abstracted information may be re-deployed by the UI designer when appropriate.

We carried out an initial case study to assess the applicability and feasibility of our approach. The resulting redesign of the Bioinformatics web portal proved to be an improvement in terms of usability and efficiency, compared to the original design. Furthermore, we investigated how our approach can be incorporated with current work practices of UI designers. Our results were promising, indicating that our process was an added value for a majority of the UI experts participating in the study.

We base our work on a finite set of user and context variables, each of them categorized, and consisting of a finite domain. In addition, our approach focuses on formalizing the parts of patterns that are most important for describing the context of use (such as user group, task information, and device), and which are suitable for discretization. The benefits are threefold: (1) We are able to abstract away from insignificant data noise and unneeded information, (2) We introduce a more systematic approach to UI design and additional guidance for the designer, and (3) We believe that such a discretization will also help us to document patterns in a more rigorous way and hence make them amenable for tool support. It is to be noted that our approach is highly dependent on the availability of pattern libraries. Many pattern libraries are still incomplete and are works-in-progress. Situations may occur where no suitable design patterns are available to the designer. In those cases, conventional techniques and methods such as contextual and participatory design still need to be employed. In addition, our current set of user and context variables are an initial set, and as pattern libraries expand, they will have to be refined.

The results presented in this paper are part of an ongoing research project. As of now, we have completed a proof-of-concept with the Bioinformatics portal and some preliminary validations, but are currently in the process of completing a more rigorous validation study. Future avenues aim at further refining and updating the user and context variables, as well as the mapping algorithm; with the goal of obtaining pattern suggestions that are more appropriate, and to facilitate the incorporation of newly-introduced design patterns.

References

1. Abi-Aad, R., Sinnig, D., Radhakrishnan, T., and Seffah, A.: CoU: Context of Use Model for User Interface Design. *Proceedings of HCI International 2003*, vol. 4, Greece, pp. 8 – 12, LEA, June 2003.
2. Marucci, L., Paternó, F., and Santoro, C..: Supporting Interactions with Multiple Platforms Through User and Task Models. *In: Seffah, A., Javahery, H. (eds.): Multiple User Interfaces, Cross-Platform Applications and Context-Aware Interfaces*, London, Wiley, pp. 217-238, 2003.
3. da Silva, P.: User Interface Declarative Models and Development Environments: A Survey. *Proceedings of DSV-IS 2000*, Springer, pp. 207–226, 2000.
4. Vanderdonckt, J., Limbourg, Q., and Florins, M.: Deriving the Navigational Structure of a User Interface. *Proceedings of INTERACT 2003*, Sept. 2003, Zuerich, IOS, pp. 455-462.
5. Szekely, P., Retrospective and Challenges for Model-Based Interface Development. *Proceedings of DSV-IS 1996*, Vienna, Austria, pp. 1 – 27.
6. Molina, P., and Trætteberg, H.: Analysis & Design of Model-based User Interfaces. *Proceedings of CADUI 2004*, 13.-16. Jan 2004, Funchal, Protugal, pp. 211-222.
7. Sinnig, D., Gaffar, A., Reichart, D., Forbrig, P., and Seffah, A.: Patterns in Model-based Engineering. *Proceedings of CADUI 2004 jointly organized with ACM-IUI 2004*, Funchal, Protugal, 13.-16. Jan., 2004, pp. 197 – 210.
8. Javahery, H., and Seffah, A.: A Model for Usability Pattern-Oriented Design. *Proceedings of TAMODIA 2002.*
9. Alexander, C., Ishikawa, S., and Silverstein, M.: *A Pattern Language: Towns, Buildings, Construction.* New York, Oxford University Press, 1977.
10. Gamma, E., Helm, R., Johnson, R., and Vlissides, J.: *Design Patterns: Elements of Object-Oriented Software.* Addison-Wesley, 1995.
11. Fowler, M.: *Patterns of Enterprise Application Architecture.* Addison-Wesley, 2003.
12. Welie, M.: Patterns in Interaction Design, [Internet]. *Available from <http://www.welie.com>* [Accessed February, 2006].
13. Tidwell, J.: UI Patterns and Techniques [Internet]. *Available from <http://time-tripper.com/uipatterns/index.php>* [Accessed February, 2006].
14. Cooper, A.: *The inmates are running the asylum. Indianapolis*, SAMS Publishing, 1999.
15. Pruitt, J., and Grudin, J.: Personas: practice and theory. *Proceedings of DUX 2003*, ACM Press, 2003.
16. Scapin, D.L. and Bastien, J.M.C.: Ergonomic criteria for evaluating the ergonomic quality of interactive systems, *Behaviour & Information Technology*, vol 16, no. 4/5, pp.220-231, 1997.
17. Landay, J. A., and Myers, B. A.: Sketching Interfaces: Toward More Human Interface Design. *IEEE Computer*, vol. 34 (3), 2001.
18. Zimmer, W.: *Relationships between design patterns. New York*, NY, ACM Press, 1995.
19. Duyne, D., Landay, J., and Hong, J.: *The Design of Sites*, Addison Wesley, 2002.
20. Yacoub, S., and Ammar, H.: *Composition of Design Patterns.* Addison Wesley Professional, Germany, 2003.
21. Javahery, H., Seffah, A., and Radhakrishnan, T.: Beyond power: making bioinformatics tools user-centered. *Communications of the ACM 47* (11), 2004.

Error Patterns: Systematic Investigation of Deviations in Task Models

Rémi Bastide[1] and Sandra Basnyat[2]

[1] LIIHS - IRIT - Université Toulouse 1, Toulouse, France
Remi.Bastide@irit.fr
[2] LIIHS - IRIT - Université Paul Sabatier, Toulouse, France
Sandra.Basnyat@irit.fr

Abstract. We propose a model-based approach to integrate human error analysis with task modelling, introducing the concept of *Error Pattern*. Error Patterns are prototypical deviations from abstract task models, expressed in a formal way by a model transformation. A collection of typical errors taken from the literature on human errors is described within our framework. The intent is that the human factors specialist will produce the task models taking an error-free perspective, producing small and useful task models. The specialist will then choose from the collection of error patterns, and selectively apply these patterns to parts of the original task model, thus producing a transformed model exhibiting erroneous user behaviour. This transformed task model can be used at various stages of the design process, to investigate the system's reaction to erroneous behaviour or to generate test sequences.

1 Introduction

Although task modelling is recognized as a useful part of the design process of interactive software, the construction of accurate task models is still a challenging task. There is no general consensus on the best level of detail to be used in task models, and in particular on the way human error should be considered in task modelling. Introducing error handling in task models usually results in an explosion of the complexity of the models, without any clear benefit, since the models become too complex to be readable.

We propose a model-based approach to integrate human error analysis with task modelling, introducing the concept of *Error Pattern*. Error Patterns are prototypical deviations from abstract task models, expressed in a formal way by a model transformation. The intended use of these error patterns is for a human factors specialist to first design the task models taking an error-free perspective, producing small and useful task models, and then to choose from the collection of error patterns to selectively apply them to parts of the original task model, thus producing a transformed, error-laden model exhibiting erroneous user behaviour.

K. Coninx, K. Luyten, and K.A. Schneider (Eds.): TAMODIA 2006, LNCS 4385, pp. 109–121, 2007.

In this paper, we propose using ConcurTaskTrees [1] (CTT) as the notation for task modelling, and we provide an ECore [2]-based metamodel of CTT to serve as the formal basis for model transformations. A collection of typical errors taken from the literature of human errors is described within our framework, and the model transformations are expressed using the Atlas transformation language (ATL [3]). We show how an error-free task model can be transformed into an error-laden one by incorporation of selected error patterns, using an example from the Air-Traffic Control (ATC) domain.

2 Related Work

The approach presented in this paper builds on previous work in the fields of task modelling, human errors and software engineering. The choice of CTT to serve as the language for task modelling in this work is motivated by the fact that it is a widely used notation, supported by a tool that allows for graphic edition and execution of the models. Although the metamodel of CTT has never been officially published as such by its originators, the construction of a metamodel for CTT is a fairly easy exercise, based on the published literature or even on the inspection the XML schema used by the CTTe tool to save the CTT models. An unofficial metamodel of CTT, described as an Entity-Relationship schema, has been proposed by Limbourg et al. [4].

Several theories of human error have been published, notably Rasmussen's early work on the SRK theory [5] where errors are classified as skill-based, rule-based or knowledge-based. Norman [6] also provided a classification of errors as slips and mistakes. Reason [7] described several failure modes and common mechanisms for human errors, summarized as the Generic Error Modelling System (GEMS). Hollnagel [8] introduced the notion of phenotype and genotype of errors, where the phenotype is the observable manifestation of errors, and the genotype the mental activity supposed to produce the observable phenomenon.

All this previous body of knowledge about human error has been processed and summarized in a usable form by Palanque and Basnyat [9], who introduce Human Error Reference Tables (HERT), where the various types of errors are classified, linked with the relevant literature and illustrated by examples. In the remainder of the paper we will use HERTs as the main reference to illustrate error patterns.

Earlier approaches to incorporate human error analysis with task modelling have been proposed. Paternó et al. [10, 11] propose the use of the HAZOP technique to analyse deviations in task models. Our goals are similar, but our approach relies on model-driven engineering techniques (metamodelling and model transformations) to provide a level of tool support that we feel better suited to modern Software Engineering practices.

The notion of *Error Pattern* proposed herein refers to the seminal work of Gamma et al. [12] who popularized the notion of *Design Pattern* as a higher-level reusable structure for software systems. A design pattern presents a piece of Software Engineering knowledge in a form that makes the recurring problem it solves easy to understand and to reuse while adapting it to the system under design. In the same vein, our goal is to present human errors in an easily communicable and processable form, that can be reused to investigate the potential hazardous effects human errors can have in task models.

The notion of *Task Pattern* has been explored by several authors [13,14] in order to provide support for the elicitation of recurring structures in task models. In this body of work, a domain-independent user task, that occurs in many software systems (such as "Search", for instance), is modelled as an abstract task model that can be easily reused and customized for inclusion in a domain-specific task description. Our notion of error pattern, while distinct from that of task pattern could be used in conjunction with this approach, either by applying error patterns to task patterns before they are instantiated in an domain-dependent task model, or directly to the final domain-specific task models built using task patterns.

3 Underlying Design Process

The approach proposed in this paper relies on several premises:

- Our work is geared for the design of a new interactive system (whether starting from an existing one or from scratch), rather than for the investigation of an existing system, where task modelling is merely used to faithfully describe and record the activity of users actually using the system.
- We assume a model-driven software development process, in the framework of an object-oriented methodology such as UML. Although we use UML notations (in particular OCL [15]) and object-oriented metamodels (ECore) to formally describe our approach, UML is not actually mandated for the design process itself. However, the whole approach makes much more sense if the task model is "just another model" in the design process (along with class models, StateCharts and the like), and if the development is carried out in a model-driven process, using model transformations and model weaving as much as is feasible. Our proposal would certainly not be of great benefit in an "agile" development process such as XP [16], where practitioners usually exhibit a general tendency to distrusting models in general.
- We assume a design process where task models are produced during the initial phases of development, mainly requirement gathering. In this usage of task modelling, task models are essentially useful to provide an abstract view of the user's activity, exploring their goals as well as the temporal and causal structure of their interactions with the system. In particular, we assume that the results of task analysis will be used as an input to the *Interaction Design* phase, where the user interface specialist will strive to design an interface that is best suited to the user task, while taking into account the limitations inherent to the target platform for the interactive system. Since task models are produced before the user interface is designed, they should be devoid of references to user interface specifics (such as "*The user clicks on the radio button*", for instance), but should instead express abstract user actions (such as "*The user selects from the available options*", that do not unduly constraint the forthcoming design of the user interface.

Considering these premises, we believe that task models should remain of manageable size, to better convey their intended meaning to the interaction designer. This precludes a very fine-grained level of detail, where every possible user error and the corresponding system reaction would be described. However we do not want to disregard user errors altogether, and to postpone error handling to the implementation phase, where the programmer would be responsible of caring for user errors without the high-level human-factor knowledge that is required.

Our work aims at finding an appropriate compromise between these two constraints: enabling the construction of simple and useful task models, while caring for human error at the right phase, i.e. during requirement gathering. When error-free task models are transformed by the injection of error patterns, the resulting error-laden task models can be used at several stages of the design process. During early stages, the error-laden models can be used to exercise early mockups or prototypes of the user interface to investigate how the system should best react to potential user errors. In the later stages, error scenarios can be used to test that the final software is error-tolerant, by using the CTTe tool to generate usage scenarios.

4 Error Patterns

We propose the notion of *error pattern* as a model of human errors, designed to be easily usable in a Model-Driven Engineering (MDE) framework. We first give a general, technology independent definition of error patterns, and then propose state-of-the-art technological notations that can be used to describe error patterns in a formal and machine-processable way.

Definition 1. *Error Pattern*

An *error pattern* is a formal description for a class of domain-independent user errors belonging to a structured classification of errors. An error pattern is defined by:

- A name, that allows to identify unambiguously the pattern,
- A text giving the informal description of the class of errors described by this pattern, illustrated by examples,
- References to the structured classification and relevant literature about the error,
- An error-free, abstract, domain independent task model fragment used to specify the structural context required for this error pattern to be used,
- An error-laden task model fragment showing the effect of the user error on the error free model.
- The error-free and error-laden models together can be substituted by a single *formal transformation* that states both the conditions for applications and the effects of the error pattern.

An task model is *error-free* if each scenario that can be generated from it allows the user's goal to be reached. Note that, for most authors, this is simply the definition of a task model in general: an intentional description of the causal structure of actions allowing the user's goal to be reached. When errors are introduced in a task model (thus making it an *error-laden* model), some generated scenarios can lead to a failure to reach the goal. It could be debated whether this can still be called a task model, since making errors is certainly not part of the user's goal. Regarding Hollnagel's approach [8], the error-free and error-laden models concern the error's *phenotype*, i.e. it's observable manifestations. The informal description is especially valuable to describe the error's genotype (psychological process that led to the error).

In this paper, we have made some technological choices for describing error patterns. We use CTT as the notation for task models. To allow for processing and transforming the error-free task models into error-laden ones, we need a precise metamodel of tasks, and a model transformation engine. We have chosen to use ECore [2] for the meta-metamodel notation, completed with OCL constraints [15] to express the metamodel of CTT, and ATL [3] as the model transformation language. We also use Human Error Reference Tables (HERT) from [9] as our reference and structured classification of human errors. These technical choices are motivated by the fact that these languages have good tool support, and are interoperable. With these choices, it is actually possible to edit CTT models (instances of the CTT metamodel presented here) and to transform them within the Eclipse environment that hosts them all.

It is perfectly possible to use the concept of error pattern with different technological choices. For instance, alternative models for tasks such as GTA [17]could be used in lieu of CTT, or another metamodeling language such as Entity-Relationships could replace ECore as Limbourg et al. did in [4]. A good combination of interoperable notations must however be preserved.

4.1 The ECore Metamodel of CTT

Our ECore metamodel of CTT is illustrated in Fig. 1. This metamodel does not include the notion of user and roles that is present in CTT, because it is not relevant here. The metamodel does not include either the notion of objects manipulated by the task, but the reason is different: we feel that this point deserves further work, in order to formally integrate the metamodel of CTT with metamodels of object-oriented notations such as UML. This will be a topic of further work for our approach.

ECore is a meta-metamodeling notation, basically a subset of UML class diagrams, albeit with a much tighter and properly defined semantics, precise to the point that a tree-based editor can be automatically generated from an ECore metamodel. The generated editor allows editing and saving models, i.e. instances of the metamodel. To illustrate how this metamodel of CTT can be instantiated to represent a CTT model, we provide in Fig. 3 the ECore model that corresponds to the CTT model in Fig. 2.

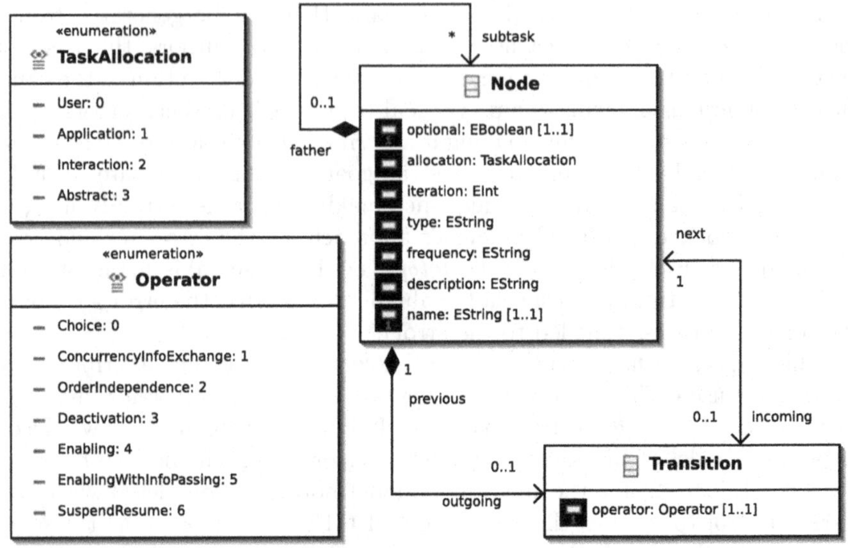

Fig. 1. The ECore metamodel of CTT

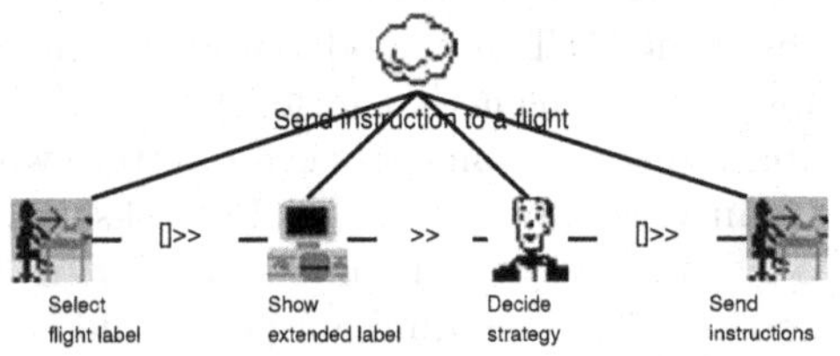

Fig. 2. CTT Model of an ATC task, from [10]

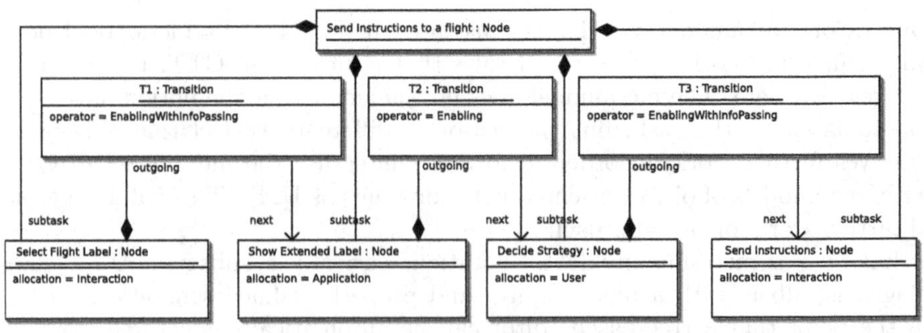

Fig. 3. The ECore model of Fig. 2

The CTT metamodel is designed to faithfully represent the structural features of a CTT model, which is tree of Nodes (a structure where each node except the root has exactly one father) where each level is structured as a list, all the nodes on one level being linearly connected by transitions that feature a temporal operator. This metamodel of CTT is similar in structure to the one presented in [4], differences in metamodeling language nonwithstanding. We have defined our metamodel so that the transformation rules are easy to express.

4.2 OCL Rules for the Metamodel

We need to ensure that our metamodel is both complete (all task models can be described with the metamodel) and consistent (only properly structured task

Listing 1.1. Additional OCL invariants for Fig. 1

```
context Node
  // Exactly one root : exactly one node with empty father
  inv: Node->collect(father->empty)->size = 1;
  // Connected nodes have the same father
  inv: not self.outgoing->empty implies
    self.father = self.outgoing.next.father;
 // Exactly one subtask without outgoing transition
  inv: not self.subtask->empty implies
    self.subtask->collect(outgoing->empty)->size = 1;
```

models can be described). The CTT metamodel proposed in [4] is complete, but inconsistent: for instance, it could represent a task with two roots, or a task where subtasks at one level are not connected. To be made consistent, it should have been completed by textual integrity constraints, but this was beyond the scope of that paper.

Our metamodel needs several additional constraints to be consistent: A task model has only one root, a node can only be connected to nodes at the same level, i.e. which have the same father, and at any level there is exactly one node without outgoing transition. These constraints are expressed formally in OCL [15] (and thus can automatically be checked by tools) in listing 1.1.

4.3 Example: Post-completion Error Pattern

Post-completion error [18] is a typical user interaction error used to describe when a user, after having reached an intermediary goal, omits a 'cleanup action' that is required to compensate for unnecessary side effects the previous actions might have produced on the state of the system. The omitted action can be considered as a *post-current goal* subtask, whose omission will jeopardize the ability for the user to reach future goals.

Table 1. Post-completion error pattern

Name	Post-Completion
Description	a post-completion error occurs when a user achieves her main goal but omits 'clean up' actions; examples include making copies on a photocopier but forgetting to retrieve the original, filling the car with fuel but failing to replace the fuel cap, and forgetting to take change with the goods from a vending machine.
References	see [18]. Classified in HERT as Skill-based / Inattention / Reduced intentionality [9]
Error-free	see Fig. 4(a)
Error-laden	see Fig. 4(b)

Error-free and error-laden abstract task models are often incomplete or generic, since different values for attributes of the metamodel can be allowed for the pattern to be applicable. Fig. 4(a) illustrates several graphical conventions we use to represent generic task models: we generally use the "cloud", by lack of a better symbol, to mean "any value allowed for attribute *allocation* [1]". We use "..." to mean that "any value allowed for the *operator* attribute", or we explicitly list the allowed values for this attribute. The barred computer symbol means "any value allowed for the *allocation* attribute except *Application*". All these constraints that complement the abstract task models should of course be expressed formally in order to make precise the necessary conditions for the pattern to be applicable. In our case, these constraints will be expressed as matching expressions in ATL transformation rules, that follow the same syntax as OCL expressions.

The above formal description of the *post-completion* error pattern can be paraphrased as follows : when a subtask is terminated by a non-optional, non-application cleanup task, triggered by an enabling operator, the post-completion error pattern is characterized by the user omitting to perform the cleanup task altogether. The rationale for this specification is that 1) if a subtask is optional, it's not an error to omit it, thus post-completion errors only concern non-optional tasks and 2) the cleanup task must be triggered by an enabling operator, since the previous subtasks must actually be accomplished before the cleanup operation is initiated.

The error-laden task in Fig. 4(b) is useful to make the error pattern more readable, but it is actually more useful to provide a formal transformation that produces the error-laden model as output when the error-free model is used as input. A transformation language such as ATL [3] is ideal for this operation. The ATL code for the transformation that defines the *post-completion* error pattern is given in listing 1.2.

[1] Refers to the allocation attribute in class Node of Fig. 1, stating whether it is a User, Application, Interaction or Abstract task.

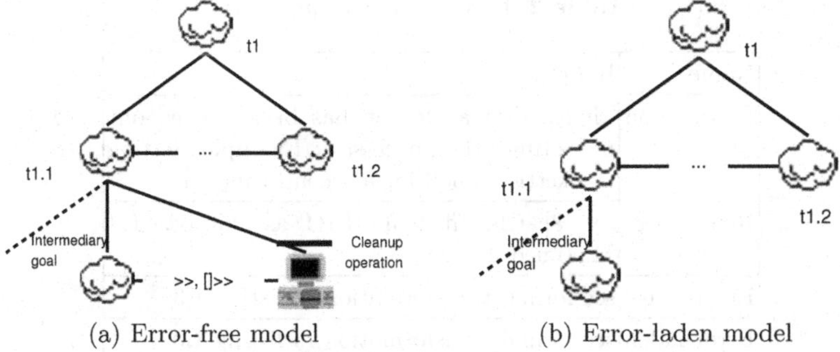

(a) Error-free model (b) Error-laden model

Fig. 4. Models for post-completion error

Listing 1.2. ATL code for the post-completion pattern

```
// Transforms a CTT node according to the post-completion
// error pattern
rule postCompletion {
 from errorFree : CTT!Node ( // Preconditions for applying
    let cleanup : Node = errorFree.subtask->last() in (
      // cleanup is the last subtask of the considered node
      // Additional conditions for the cleanup node
      cleanup.allocation != #Application and
             not cleanup.optional and
             Set(#Enabling, #EnablingWithInfoPassing)
                    ->include(cleanup.incoming.operator)
    )
 ) to errorLaden : CTT!Node ( // Transformed model
    // Remove last subtask
    errorLaden.subtask <- errorFree.subtask
             ->excluding(errorFree.subtask->last());
    // Remove last transition
    errorLaden.subtask->last().outgoing <- void;
 )
```

4.4 Example: Repetition Error Pattern

The repetition error [8] is formalized as an error pattern in table 2: This pattern is easy to express as a model transformation since the class *Node* in the CTT metamodel already contains the attribute *iteration* that states how many times a subtask should be repeated. In this case, the transformation merely increments the value of this attribute. The error-free node should not be optional, to ensure the repetition will actually occur.

Table 2. Repetition error pattern

Name	Repetition
Description	Means that an action has been carried out more times than necessary. Example: Setting the kettle to boil for a second time [7].
References	see [8]. Classified in HERT as Skill-based / Mistimed [9]
Error-free	see formal transformation in listing 1.3
Error-laden	see formal transformation in listing 1.3

Listing 1.3. ATL code for the repetition pattern

```
rule repetition  {
 from errorFree  : CTT!Node (
  not optional
 )
 to  errorLaden  : CTT!Node (
    repetition <- errorFree.repetition + 1;
 )
```

5 Applying the Patterns

Our error patterns are designed to put human factors knowledge about human errors in a form easily usable in a model-driven software development process. Errors patterns are put into use after an initial error-free task model has been built for the system under design. It is then the human factors specialist's task to investigate which errors are likely to occur at different locations in the task tree. The application of the corresponding error pattern will produce a transformed task model that exhibits this specific error.

The choice of technologies we have taken in this paper opens the way for various ways to automate the application of the error patterns to a given task model. The fact that error patterns are described by a model transformation is the key to enabling automation. With some help from software tools, the task analyst could for instance select one or several error patterns, and choose to apply them to a node in the task model under scrutiny. Using the precondition parts of the transformation rules, a software tool can automatically identify at which subnodes each error pattern can legally be applied (actually, this task is the chore of the transformation engine). The tool could systematically apply each pattern at each place where it is allowed, or perform some random choices. This process is very similar to the *fault injection* technique [19] which is frequently used in the field of safety critical software. A practical interest is that usage scenarios can be automatically computed from CTT task models (in our case, error-laden models), and one can further investigate how the system reacts to these

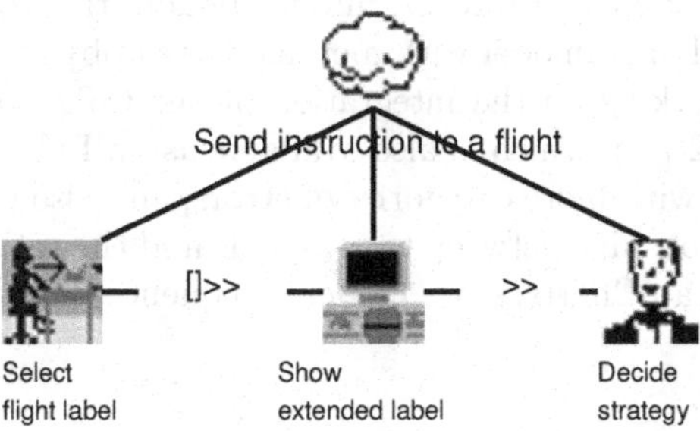

Fig. 5. The ATC task of Fig. 2 after application of the post-completion error pattern

error-laden scenarios. As it is the case for software design patterns, the choice of the error patterns to apply is ultimately a matter of craft and experience, and remains in the hands the task analysis specialist.

While inspecting the Air-Traffic Control task model of Fig.2, the human factors expert could foresee that there is a chance for a post-completion error to occur during the performance of this task. In this case, the *Decide strategy* subtask is considered as the intermediary goal reached by the air-traffic controller, while *Send instructions* is considered as the cleanup action. The analyst then applies the post-completion error pattern, thus producing the error-laden model illustrated in Fig.5. This transformed task model can then be used to investigate the system's response to this particular error: what happens if the air-traffic controller omits to send instructions to the pilot ? When is this detected by the system and what should the counter-measures be ?

6 Conclusion and Future Work

In this paper, we have proposed to notion of *error pattern*, and have given a definition of this concept in terms of formal model transformations. We are in the process of building a collection of these patterns by investigating the literature on human errors, basing our work on the HERT classification of [9]. These transformations rely on a metamodel of CTT expressed in ECore, which we believe to be a valuable asset in itself, since it can serve as the basis of different forms of manipulation of task models in a MDE framework.

In previous work [20], our team has investigated how CTT task models could be related to formal models of the system's behaviour based on Petri nets. However, this work predated the recent developments of model-driven engineering, and was performed using ad-hoc techniques, mainly at the source code level. We believe that MDE techniques operating at the metamodel level have the potential to bring significant benefits to this trend of research.

The error patterns described in this paper only deal with the temporal and causal structure of task models, since this is precisely what is covered by our metamodel. We want to investigate other categories of errors, that deal with the objects manipulated by the tasks (errors concerned by incorrect attribute values of the objects, for instance). However, in our opinion, this requires a formal integration of the CTT metamodel with metamodels of object-oriented notations. We are currently working on the integration of our CTT metamodel with the metamodel of UML2 [21], which is also available as an ECore metamodel. This will allow us to deal with more categories of errors, and also to investigate in detail the formal relationships between task models and the various system models present in UML2 (stateCharts, class models , sequence diagrams, etc.).

References

1. Mori, G., Paternò, F., Santoro, C.: Ctte: Support for developing and analyzing task models for interactive system design. IEEE Trans. Software Eng. **28**(8) (2002) 797–813
2. Budinsky, F., Brodsky, S.A., Merks, E.: Eclipse Modeling Framework. Pearson Education (2003)
3. Frédéric Jouault, Ivan Kurtev: Transforming Models with ATL. In Jean-Michel Bruel, ed.: Satellite Events at the MoDELS 2005 Conference. Volume 3844 of Lecture notes in computer science., Springer (January 2006) 128–138
4. Limbourg, Q., Pribeanu, C., Vanderdonckt, J.: Towards uniformed task models in a model-based approach. [22] 164–182
5. Rasmussen, J.: Skills, rules, knowledge; signals, signs and symbols; and other distinctions in human performance models. IEEE Transactions on Systems, Man, and Cybernetics **SMC-13**(3) (1983)
6. Norman, D.A.: The Design of Everyday Things. Doubleday, New York (1988)
7. Reason, J.: Human Error. Cambridge University Press, New York (1990)
8. Hollnagel, E.: The phenotype of erroneous actions. Int. J. Man-Mach. Stud. **39**(1) (1993) 1–32
9. Palanque, P., Basnyat, S.: Task Patterns For Taking Into Account In An Efficient And Systematic Way Both Standard And Erroneous User Behaviours. In Johnson, C., Palanque, P., eds.: IFIP 13.5 Working Conference on Human Error, Safety and Systems Development (HESSD), Toulouse, France, Kluwer Academic Publisher (august 22-27 2004) 109–130
10. Paternò, F., Santoro, C.: Preventing user errors by systematic analysis of deviations from the system task model. Int. J. Hum.-Comput. Stud. **56**(2) (2002) 225–245
11. Paternò, F., Santoro, C., Fields, R.: Analysing user deviations in interactive safety-critical applications. In Duke, D.J., Puerta, A.R., eds.: DSV-IS'99, Springer (1999) 189–204
12. Gamma, E., Helm, R., Johnson, R., Vlissides, J.: Design patterns: Abstraction and reuse of object-oriented design. Lecture Notes in Computer Science **707** (1993) 406–431
13. Breedvelt, I., Fabio Paternò, Sereriins, C.: Reusable structures in task models. In Harrison, M.D., Torres, J.C., eds.: DSVIS'97, Springer-verlag (1997) 251–265
14. Gaffar, A., Sinnig, D., Seffah, A., Forbrig, P.: Modeling patterns for task models. In: TAMODIA '04: Proceedings of the 3rd annual conference on Task models and diagrams, New York, NY, USA, ACM Press (2004) 99–104
15. Clark, T., Warmer, J., eds.: Object Modeling with the OCL, The Rationale behind the Object Constraint Language. In Clark, T., Warmer, J., eds.: Object Modeling with the OCL. Volume 2263 of Lecture Notes in Computer Science., Springer (2002)

16. Beck, K., Andres, C.: Extreme Programming Explained : Embrace Change (2nd Edition). Addison-Wesley Professional (November 2004)
17. van der Veer, G., Lenting, B., Bergevoet, B.: Gta: Groupware task analysis - modeling complexity. Acta Psychologica **91** (1996) 297–322
18. Paul Curzon, Ann Blandford: Formal Justification of a Design Rule for Avoiding Post-completion Errors. Technical report, Interaction Design Centre, School of Computing Science, Middlesex University (December 2003)
19. Hsueh, M.C., Tsai, T.K., Iyer, R.K.: Fault injection techniques and tools. IEEE Computer **30**(4) (1997) 75–82
20. Navarre, D., Palanque, P.A., Paternò, F., Santoro, C., Bastide, R.: A tool suite for integrating task and system models through scenarios. [22] 88–113
21. Unified Modeling Language (UML), version 2.0. Technical report, OMG, http://www.omg.org/technology/documents/formal/uml.htm (2005)
22. Johnson, C., ed.: Design, Specification and Verification of Interactive Systems'01, 8th International Workshop, Glasgow, Scotland, UK, June 13-15, 2001. In Johnson, C., ed.: DSV-IS'01. Volume 2220 of Lecture Notes in Computer Science., Springer (2001)

Using an Interaction-as-Conversation Diagram as a Glue Language for HCI Design Patterns on the Web

Ariane Moraes Bueno and Simone Diniz Junqueira Barbosa

Departamento de Informática, PUC-Rio
Rua Marquês de São Vicente, 225
Gávea, Rio de Janeiro, RJ, Brasil
+55 (21) 3527-1500 ext. 4353
{abueno,simone}@inf.puc-rio.br

Abstract. The benefits of using software design patterns have been widely reported. However, in order for user interface design patterns to achieve the same degree of success as software design patterns, it would be useful to document design pattern solutions using a representation language that can be readily transported into the definition or specification of the interactive solution. Moreover, patterns are fragmented, which may hinder the designers' global comprehension about their design decisions. In this paper, we present a small study that illustrates the use of an interaction modeling language called MoLIC as a glue language, which binds together the design pattern solutions and novel design constructs (for which there are no patterns defined) into forming a whole interactive solution.

1 Introduction

The software industry has long recognized the benefits of using design patterns, both in software engineering (SE) [8] and in human-computer interaction (HCI) [3,12,13,14]. In particular, we cite the benefits of documenting and capturing "design decisions, and the experience from past projects, to create a corporate memory of design knowledge" [3].

First proposed by Alexander in the multidisciplinary field of architecture [1], design patterns have followed slightly different paths in SE and HCI. In SE, design patterns present an emphasis on the representation of the solution in a way as to be reused in software specification. In HCI, however, the lack of unifying modeling languages and representations hinder the use of the solution as a concrete resource for HCI design specification.

Current user interface design patterns place an emphasis on the design of presentation units such as web pages and page elements. However, current user interface design patterns don't usually define how the web pages are related to each other and how navigation and interaction should take place.

There are at least two different levels of representation that must be dealt with during user interface design: the level of the (abstract or concrete) user interface itself, where most HCI design patterns are defined; and the interaction level, i.e., the definition of the user-system conversation and the processes that occur during

K. Coninx, K. Luyten, and K.A. Schneider (Eds.): TAMODIA 2006, LNCS 4385, pp. 122–136, 2007.

interaction, which should be revealed by elements that emerge at the user interface. This paper argues for the need to go beyond user interface patterns, and further explore interaction design patterns.

The usage of software design patterns [6] has already gained widespread acceptance from both academia and industry. The success of software design patterns may in part be due to the fact that the pattern solution is represented as pieces of software specification "ready to be used". Moreover, the languages used to represent the solution in a software design pattern are the same languages used to specify the software independent of patterns: the UML family of notations.

Unfortunately, in HCI there is no *de facto standard* language for representing the user-system interaction. This somewhat hinders the widespread and efficient use of HCI design patterns. Moreover, analogously to software engineering, a single representation language may not be enough to address distinct issues and abstraction levels in HCI design, from abstract interaction to the concrete user interface. In this paper, we do not claim to have a definitive answer for this challenge. Instead, we follow on the footsteps of Paula and Barbosa, who briefly proposed to use the interaction modeling language MoLIC [2] as an interaction language for representing the recommended solution in interaction patterns [10]. In this paper, we present an example that illustrates how different user interface design patterns may be connected using MoLIC to compose the interaction sequences that users may perform to achieve a certain goal. The example gives preliminary evidence of the feasibility and usefulness of MoLIC for representing the solution part of HCI design patterns at the interaction level.

Our approach is somewhat akin to the work about task patterns [7,9,12]. We shifted the focus, however, from task to interaction sequences. Although our proposal is more dependent on the technological platform, we chose to do so in order to keep the solution at a level of abstraction that can be directly used or adapted in the construction of the interactive solutions. This is not to say that we substitute task patterns; only that we chose to address an intermediary level of abstraction. By specifying the user-system interaction, we may include in the design patterns some breakdown repair mechanisms, that are usually absent in task patterns.

In the next section, we briefly present some definitions of design patterns and discuss some of its usages in both design and engineering of software artifacts. The third section presents the MoLIC interaction modeling language. We then describe a small-scale study and the investigated user interface design patterns, drawing some preliminary questions that were left unaddressed by these patterns, and describing how MoLIC can be used to complement those patterns. The final section discusses some of the issues addressed in the paper and draws some concluding remarks.

2 On Design Patterns

By observing and documenting successful architectural designs, Christopher Alexander managed to establish a new paradigm for representing knowledge about complex, situated design decisions. He was interested in knowledge that emerges from practice, rather than defining standards and formulas. Alexander's patterns were defined in a narrative style, enriched by relevant contextual information. The motivation for the pattern and its underlying rationale helped the "pattern users" make decisions on how their problem at hand fitted the described pattern, whether some adaptation was necessary, or even when a novel solution should be designed. An important aspect of Alexander's patterns was that the pattern was described from the point of view of the persons who would use the "architectural solution". His focus was notably on the "user experience" of the persons who would inhabit or circulate in the design spaces [1].

It is important to observe the situated nature of design patterns. According to Tidwell, "they are not abstract principles that require you to rediscover how to apply them successfully, nor are they overly specific to one particular situation or culture. Instead, they are somewhere in between: a pattern describes possible good solutions to a common design problem within a certain context, by describing the invariant qualities of all those solutions" [12].

When considering the larger picture, however, we note that patterns may not always be easily combined to create a whole coherent solution. As stated by van Welie and van der Veer, "A pattern by itself is just a small piece of the entire design knowledge "puzzle". Each pattern describes a proven solution to a problem in a certain design context. When all the pieces of the puzzle are "put together", we can see how an entire body of design knowledge is unfolded. Understanding this puzzle is the long-term goal in pattern-research. It will show the paved roads of design, but it will also say when the road should be abandoned in search of new and innovative solutions" [15].

We believe that patterns will not always provide all the pieces of the puzzle. Most HCI patterns include user interfaces sketches or storyboards, representing the relevant aspects of the concrete user interface. In addition to these static solutions, we also need to represent interaction sequences that span individual presentation units. Upon inspection of pattern collections, we observe that there isn't a widely accepted representation language for describing or specifying the possible interactions users may have with the system.

Our hypotheses are: (1) we need a glue language to bind pattern solutions together, to help us evaluate the solution as a coherent whole; (2) this glue language should represent interaction sequences, from the user's point of view. The expression *glue language* here means a language that can be used to connect ("glue") patterns together and cover all the "holes" in the model (interaction sequences for which there are no defined patterns). Our hypotheses are in line with Paula and Barbosa, who stated that "some application-specific interactions cannot be captured in patterns. An interaction representation language should be able to organize and compose both specific and pattern-derived interaction specifications into an application "blueprint". This will help designers not only to build applications faster, but also to develop a more coherent whole" [10]. This usage is analogous to software design patterns, where the solution recommended in most patterns is represented in UML diagrams (typically class and sequence diagrams) [6].

In order to evaluate our hypotheses, we have developed a case study that uses the MoLIC language defined in [2] as such a glue language. The goal of using MoLIC in this work is twofold: (1) to complement the specification of the solution described in design patterns with respect to interaction as a process; and (2) to do so using a language than can serve as a glue language. The expression *glue language* here means a language that can be used to connect ("glue") patterns together and cover all the "holes" in the model (interaction sequences for which there are no defined patterns).

An additional consideration of our study is the use of a single language in both design and engineering activities. Here, *design* corresponds to the creative activity of *conceiving* a novel solution to a unique problem, whereas engineering is the *usage* of a predefined solution (represented in a design pattern, for instance)

This approach has worked well in software engineering, where UML was elected the glue language that binds patterns together, providing a blueprint of the complete application. This is possible because UML was used in representing the design solution itself that was described in each pattern [7]. The drawback of software design patterns, from an HCI standpoint, is that the patterns are described from the point of view of system components.

3 Modeling Interaction

MoLIC stands for Modeling Language for Interaction as Conversation [2]. It has been defined within the theoretical grounding of the semiotic engineering of human-computer interaction [5].

Semiotic engineering characterizes the user interface as a meta-communication artifact, through which designers communicate with users about how users may or should interact with the system [5]. It views the user interface as a designer-to-users message, representing the designer's solution to what he believes are the users' problems, needs, and preferences [5]. In this message, he is telling users, directly or indirectly, what he had in mind when he conceived the application: "Here is my understanding of who you are, what I've learned you want or need to do, in which preferred ways, and why. This is the system that I have therefore designed for you, and this is they way you can or should use it in order to fulfill a range of purposes that fall within this vision." (p.84). One of the consequences of this theory is the emphasis on the designers' role as communicators, and the need to better support this role. If users are able to grasp the designers' vision of the application, it is presumed that they should be able to make a more efficient and satisfactory use of the designed artifact.

MoLIC has emerged as an epistemic tool to support the designers' reflection on the interactive solution being conceived, while it's being conceived [11]. Here, interaction design is viewed as conversation design This kind of conversation is unique, however, because the designer is no longer present when the conversation takes place (i.e., during interaction). Instead, he embeds into the user interface a collection of user interface elements that play the role of the designers' spokesperson. It is thus the designer's responsibility to build into this spokesperson (called the designer's deputy) the spectrum of conversations that it will be able to carry out with users. MoLIC helps designers acquire a global view of the application they are conceiving, from a user's standpoint.

MoLIC focuses on conversational content and structure, allowing to represent interactive solutions in a technology-independent notation. It is important to note that different technological environments will often encourage designers to produce different interactive solutions. However, having a common notation promotes documentation and reuse of interactive solutions across environments, making it easier to think about how differences between environments cause different design choices. MoLIC does not represent concrete user interface elements such as widgets and screen layout, nor the full *expression* of the user interface. Instead, it represents the *content* of the user-system interaction that will surface at the user interface, defining which communicative exchanges may/should take place (see [6] for a brief account of Hjelmslev's content-expression dichotomy).

3.1 MoLIC Notation

The basic MoLIC representation is an interaction-as-conversation diagram [2], whose main elements will be briefly described here. The two basic kinds of node in the diagram are the scene and system processing, which represent the user's and system's turn to "say something", respectively. The turn-taking in conversation is marked by transition utterances. When the designer believes that a conversational breakdown has occurred (i.e., the user misunderstood the application, made a mistake or the system behaved unexpectedly), the interaction sequence that corresponds to a recovery path is in fact marked as one or more breakdown repair utterances.

Fig. 1 illustrates a partial MoLIC diagram for achieving a search goal. The first scene, "Search document", is the place where the user should define the search criteria (document title, author's name or publication date) and the format for presenting the results (list or table). Notice that at least one criterion must be provided, otherwise the system will help the user through recovering from her

Table 1. Basic MoLIC elements

Name	Visual representation
Scene	<Scene topic> <Dialogues>
System processing	■
Transition utterance	⟶ pre: <pre-condition> u: <user's utterance> or d: <designer's utterance> post: <post-condition>
Breakdown repair utterance	- - - - - - ▶ pre: <pre-condition> u: <user's utterance> or d: <designer's utterance> post: <post-condition>

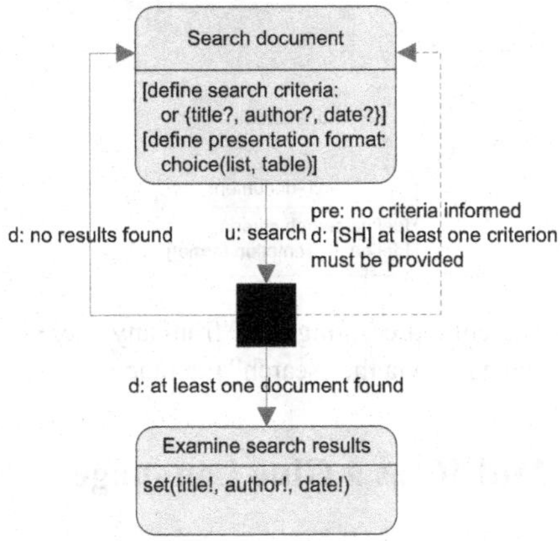

Fig. 1. Sample MoLIC diagram for a search goal

mistake. In the breakdown repair utterance, [SH] means "supported handling". This is the kind of breakdown repair where the designer assists the user in finding out what the problems in the interaction were and gives them a second chance to recover from his mistake.

It is important to note that the system's "turn to talk" is represented in MoLIC as a black rectangle. The goal of this element is to emphasize that the users are not aware of the internal system processing. Instead, the only way that they will get to know what is happening inside the system is by means of the designer's utterances that come out of the system processing. In doing this, we want to, in the early stages of design, encourage a careful representation of the designer-to-user-via-user-interface communication and raise the awareness of the kinds of interaction problems that may occur.

Transition utterances stemming from scenes represent changes in focus or a conclusion of the conversation topic, caused by a user's choice, as indicated by the transition label (e.g. "u:search" in Fig. 1). Those ``stemming from system processes represent the result of that processing, indicating whether the user's request was completed successfully (e.g. "d: no results found" and "d: at least one document found" in Fig. 1) or whether a breakdown or system error has occurred (e.g. "d: at least one criterion must be provided" in Fig. 1).

One may notice that the designer of this diagram chose not to represent the "d: no results found" as a breakdown repair utterance. This is the result of a design choice. In this case, the designer assumed that the user's intent may be to make sure that a certain document doesn't exist (before inserting it into the system, for instance). In other words, the choice between representing a transition as a breakdown repair transition or not depends on what is considered a legitimate user's goal.

Some conversations may occur anytime during user-system interaction. In this case, MoLIC provides a gray scene-like element called ubiquitous access, which represents "any scene" (Fig. 2):

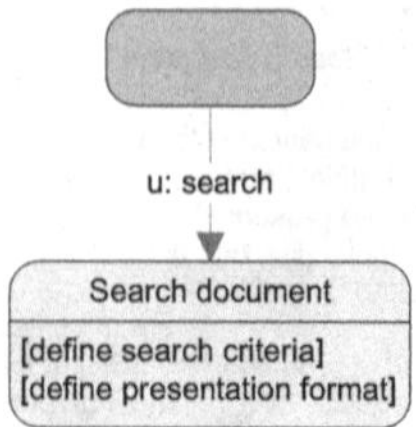

Fig. 2. Ubiquitous access element representing that "from anywhere in the application, the user may access the 'Search document' " via the "search" utterance

4 An Example of MoLIC as a Glue Language

We have developed a small-scale study to investigate the pattern-based specification of an e-commerce application. Three successful (as measured by sales volume) e-commerce websites were investigated, from two different countries. The study was conducted by two HCI researchers. They inspected the websites looking for evidence of the use of user interface design patterns in the check-out process. To help specify how the whole process takes place, a MoLIC interaction-as-conversation diagram was created (via reverse engineering), to bind together the user interface design patterns detected. The resulting interaction-as-conversation diagram constitutes the representation of an interaction design pattern solution, which can be used in the design of future e-commerce applications.

4.1 Identifying User Interface Design Patterns

The first step in the inspection was to identify a collection of HCI design patterns for the web that were used in the websites. Upon inspecting existing patterns collections, the designer chose to use van Welie's web design patterns, a freely available collection derived from research and empirical studies [15]. As in typical design patterns, van Welie's descriptions of each pattern follows the following structure:

- Name: brief (yet significant) description used to refer to the pattern.
- Problem: a description of the problem to be solved, from the user's point-of-view (or from any other stakeholder's point-of-view). The problem should not focus on implementational details; instead, it should be related to users' goals and tasks.
- When to use: the characteristics of the context of use that determine when the pattern can be applied.
- Solution: a concrete and illustrated description of the core solution to the problem. It may be further divided into more specialized solutions for specific contexts, or even provide links to other design patterns.
- Why: the underlying rationale, describing the value of the pattern and why it works.
- Examples: instances of the pattern in use, i.e., where the pattern has been successfully applied. It typically includes a screenshot, and may be annotated.

In this document, we focus on the representation of interaction solutions, as opposed to more static or fragmented presentation units such as web pages or UI components.

We have chosen the following patterns from van Welie's collection to be relevant for the case study [14,16]:

- Login: Van Welie recognizes that a user's login may be done anytime before the user data is actually needed to finish a transaction. The user identifies himself usually using an e-mail address and a password. In addition, help should be provided for users that forget their passwords.
- Main navigation: There should always be a main menu, visible and at a fixed location on the web page. In our case study, we have used the *horizontal* menu: a bar with various clickable items, and should be placed at the top of the page. The currently selected item should be highlighted or have its appearance color altered somehow, to indicate what has been selected and where the user is.
- View:Van Welie suggests a *View pattern* (Fig. 3), which should be used when views are the main elements of the application, and when users need to manage a collection of objects. He also proposes that the list of objects present an abbreviated form of content, and when the user clicks on such expression, the detailed item description should be presented. In addition, he suggests that views be placed in the central portion of the web page, so that users will be able to locate them quickly. If the views become very large, you can use some kind of Paging (being able to directly locate a page by accessing a page index) or Stepping (being able to browse each item using next and previous buttons). The main navigation will be used to switch from one view to another.

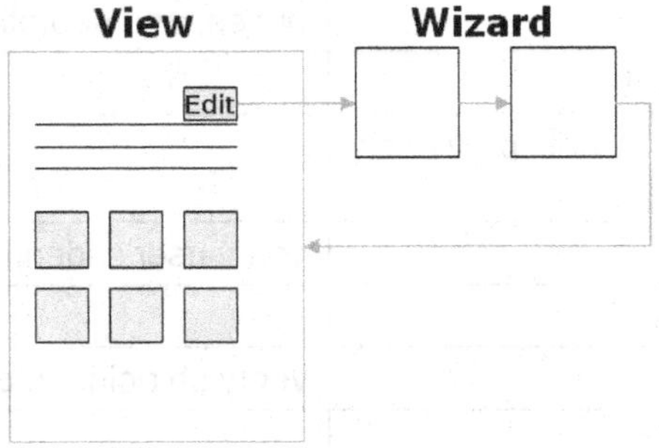

Fig. 3. Van Welie's *view pattern*

From van Welie's collection, some patterns were identified that are specifically related to e-commerce: shopping cart, testimonials, and virtual product display.

- Shopping cart: Users should be able to add many items to the shopping cart without immediately commiting the transaction. They may see the contents of the shopping cart with just one click (and from any web page), and proceed to the checkout at any time.
- Testimonials: E-commerce websites should provide a means for users to give feedback about the quality of the product and or services.

- Virtual product display: It is also desirable for e-commerce websites to virtually interact with the product.

In our example, we will investigate only the final steps of the purchase process, from the moment where there are items in the shopping cart and the user is ready to finalize his shopping at that website. Therefore, only the *login* and *shopping cart* patterns apply.

4.2 MoLIC Interaction-as-Conversation Diagram for e-Commerce Websites

Fig. 4 presents a sample MoLIC diagram of the purchase process defined in two of the inspected websites. Although MoLIC diagrams are supposed to contain the interaction paths that correspond to more than one interrelated goals, for simplicity the figure represents only a fragment for the finalization of the purchase process.

Also for simplicity, the diagram assumes that the user is already registered in the database and knows his password. Thus, the figure omits the interaction exchanges corresponding to the registration of new users and to password requests.

The information contained in the dialog may be defined in the following essential use case [4]:

Finalize shopping transaction

User intention	**System responsibility**
view shopping cart contents	
	present shopping cart contents: products' names, quantities, unit prices, and subtotal
proceed to checkout	
(identify himself, if not previously identified)	
	verify user's identity
define shipping info	
	verify shipping info
define payment info	
	verify payment info
confirm order	
	provide receipt

The diagram in Fig. 4 indicates where each identified user interface design pattern may occur, the user-system dialogues that occur within different patterns and how the various dialogues are connected with one another. It may be seen that, in addition to the user interface patterns, many additional elements are necessary to specify the complete solution, abstracting away user interface details, but defining the user-system dialogues and navigation paths.

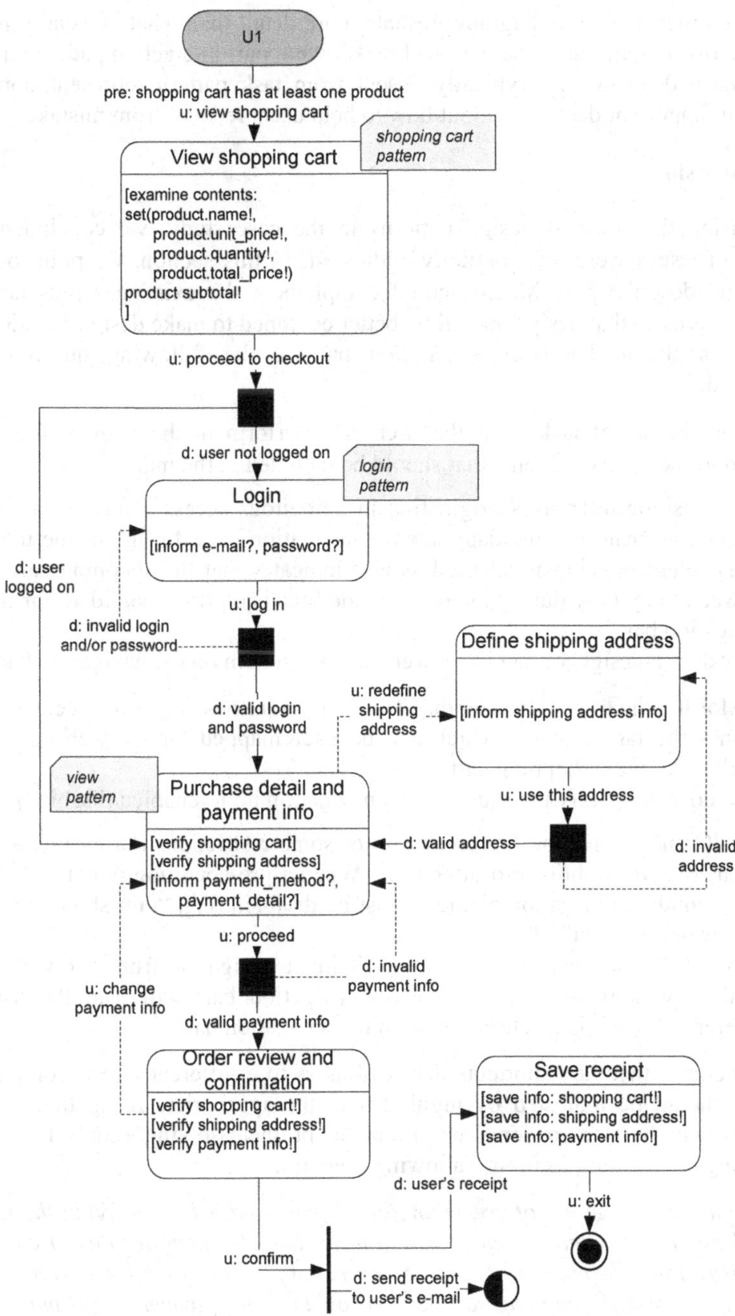

Fig. 4. Interaction-as-conversation diagram for the purchase process found in two e-commerce websites

On the other hand, the diagram presents more detail than what is usually found in task patterns. In particular, the various breakdown repair interaction paths represented by the dashed arrows are typically absent from task pattern representations. This leaves out important decisions about how to help users recover from mistakes.

4.3 Discussion

When using the selected design patterns in the case study, we concluded that a number of issues were only partially addressed. In this section, we point out these issues and describe how MoLIC could complement the existing representation in design patterns so that designers will be better equipped to make design decisions.

When applying the *Main navigation* pattern, the following questions were considered:

- Given the set of tasks that the user may perform in the system, how do we support the choice of items that should be included in the main navigation bar?

  The transition utterances originating in ubiquitous access elements in a MoLIC diagram are natural candidates for the navigation bars. In Fig. 4, the ubiquitous access element (ellipsis labelled as U1) indicates that the shopping cart may be viewed at any time during interaction, and thus is a prime candidate for the main navigation bar.
- How does a designer associate a web page to an item on the navigation bar?

  In MoLIC, the transition utterance from an ubiquitous acess to a scene explicitly defines the target scene, which can be later mapped onto a web page (arrow labelled "u: view shopping cart", in Fig. 4).
- How does he specify the state of each navigation item (enabled/disabled)?

  MoLIC encourages the representation of some restrictions during interaction by means of pre-conditions to utterances. When a pre-condition is not satisfied, the corresponding navigation element must be disabled (e.g. "pre: shopping cart has at least one product").
- How can the designer detect when an indirect navigation from one web page to another (without accessing the main navigation bar) will lead the user to a different "place" (i.e., selected item in the navigation bar)?

  Sometimes there are shortcuts that lead users to a different interaction path, and that should be indicated by highlights in the appropriate navigation elements. This may be due to some opportunistic problem-solving (goals that emerge during interaction), as in the following scenario:

  Aaron is checking out of everythingforsale.com and, when verifying the shipping address, realizes that his address is out of date. He then decides to correct his registration information. After the correction, he comes back to verifying the newly informed shipping address, provides the payment information, and confirms the shopping of the products.

In this example we clearly see that Aaron had one initial goal (to check out of the website), but while carrying out the corresponding tasks he formed a secondary goal (to correct his registration information). When dealing separately with each user goal, this opportunity might go undetected, and the result may be as disastrous as having Aaron lose the previously provided information (i.e. selected products in the shopping cart) when leaving the current task to correct his registration information.

MoLIC easily allows for the representation of intersecting or inter-related goals. In fact, MoLIC encourages the analysis of such shortcuts by representing multiple inter-related goals in the same diagram.

When applying the *View* pattern, the following questions were considered:

- When should the management of collections be performed in a single page, and when should a sequence of pages be used? How do we specify whether, after adding a new shipping address, the user should return to the collection index or whether he should be immediately led to a blank form for adding another item?

  In van Welie's definition of the *View* pattern, it is stated that "typical behavior with forms consists of 'view-edit-return'", as illustrated in **Fig. 5**. However, when the user needs to edit a whole sequence of the collection, this alternative may be inefficient. For instance, imagine a situation in which a manager has a number of requests he needs to deal with. It might be more efficient to deal with them sequentially (**Fig. 6**). In this case, if the system forces him to go back to the web page with the index of requests every time, it would not only be inefficient, but also cause insatisfaction. This kind of rationale may be included in the "When to use" and "Why" parts of the pattern design definition.

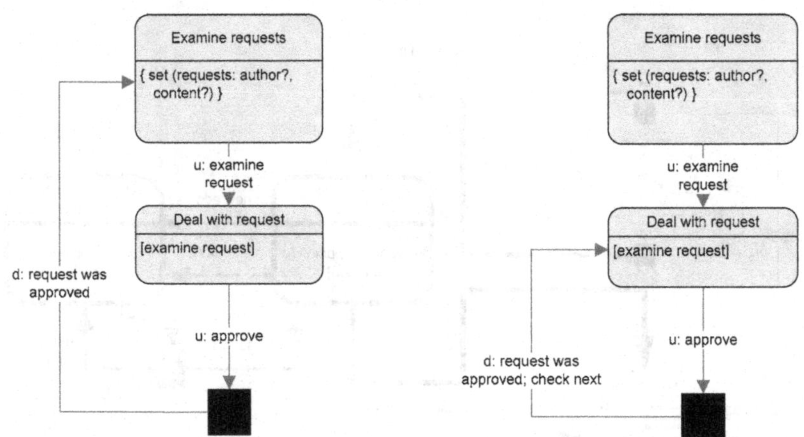

Fig. 5. MoLIC diagram for representing view + edit + return

Fig. 6. MoLIC diagram for representing editing + sequential navigation

- How do we define the common operations of create, update, delete item in a collection? Where (in which page) should they be made available?

  The View pattern is very abstract, in the sense that it doesn't help designers in choosing where in the web pages that compose the pattern they should insert certain elements. It seems that a single task will be supported at each step. However, even in a simple content management system, there a number of possible tasks that are simultaneously available. Using a MoLIC diagram, users are able to specify where the user may say what, and then compare alternative solutions.

Most of the shopping cart pattern is self-contained in an interaction scene, except for the ubiquitous access for allowing the shopping cart to be viewed from any other point in the user interface.

4.4 Applying an Interaction Design Pattern Represented in MoLIC

The third website that was inspected also corresponds to the previously defined essential use case. However, there is a slight difference in the interaction-as-conversation diagram: instead of having a single address associated to the user, there may be multiple addresses, and therefore the user must always choose the address to which the order should be shipped. This distinction makes it necessary for the designers to adapt the solution represented in the diagram previously in **Fig. 4,** resulting in the revised interaction-as-conversation diagram shown in Fig. 7. In order

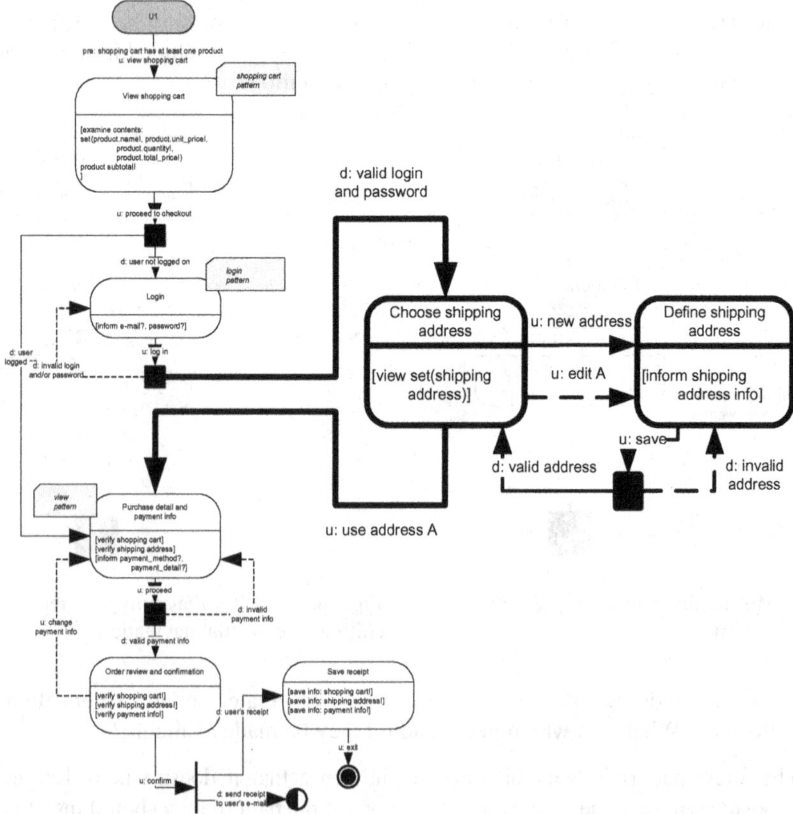

Fig. 7. Interaction-as-conversation diagram excerpt showing the selection and definition of multiple shipping addresses

to transform and adapt a solution, it is necessary that the designer know how to construct MoLIC diagrams.

This example shows that MoLIC can be effectively used to represent different solutions derived from HCI design patterns.

Since MoLIC diagrams are accompanied by a table of domain and user interface signs 2, this information would also be available to interaction designers in representing pattern solutions.

5 Concluding Remarks

In this paper, we have briefly described an example to analyze the feasibility of using MoLIC as a representation language to document design pattern solutions.

The main challenges that we faced when analyzing the literature on HCI design patterns was the lack of a standardized interaction representation language. Taking on the proposal of Paula and Barbosa, we created two interaction-as-conversation diagrams that represent the interaction paths reverse engineered from three successful e-commerce websites, in different countries. These diagrams may be used to represent distinct solutions, according to the context and forces that make up a pattern definition.

Since MoLIC has been used in non-pattern-based interaction design as well, it is a good candidate for a *glue language*, to bind design patterns together into a whole application that may be inspected for consistency and coherence.

Whatever language is chosen, we believe that, for representing HCI patterns, we need to address at least two different levels of representation: a process level, which defines the interaction and navigation; and a user interface level, which defines the relevant concrete user interface elements.

Acknowledgments

The authors thank CNPq for the financial support to this work in the form of individual research grants. They also thank their colleagues at the Semiotic Engineering Research Group for their support and for the fruitful discussions that contributed to this publication.

References

1. Alexander, C. *The Timeless Way of Building*. Oxford University Press. New York, NY. 1979.
2. Barbosa, S.D.J.; Paula, M.G. "Designing and Evaluating Interaction as Conversation: a Modeling Language based on Semiotic Engineering" In Jorge; Nunes; Falcão e Cunha (eds.) Interactive Systems Design, Specification, and Verification – 10th International Workshop, DSV-IS 2003, Funchal, Madeira Island, Portugal, June 2003, Revised Papers Series: *Lecture Notes in Computer Science, vol. 2844*, 2003. pp. 16–33.
3. Borchers, J. *A pattern approach to interaction design*. John Wiley & Sons. 2001.
4. Constantine, L. & Lockwood, L. *Software for use*. The ACM Pres. 1999.

5. de Souza, C.S. *The Semiotic Engineering of Human-Computer Interaction*. The MIT Press. 2005.
6. Eco, U. *A Theory of Semiotics*. Bloomington. Indiana University Press. 1979.
7. Gaffar, A.; Sinnig, D.; Seffah, A.; Forbrig, P. "Modeling Patterns for Task Models". *Proceedings of TAMODIA 2004*.
8. Gamma, E., Helm, R., Johnson, R., Vlissides, J. *Design Patterns*. Addison-Wesley. 1995.
9. Granlund, A., Lafrenière, D., Carr, D.A. "A Pattern-Supported Approach to the User Interface Design Process". *Proceedings of HCI International 2001*. New Orleans, USA. 2001.
10. Paula, M.G., Barbosa, S.D.J. "Bringing Interaction Specifications to HCI Design Patterns". *CHI 2003 Workshop Perspectives on HCI Patterns: Concepts and Tools*. Fort Lauderdale, FL, USA. 2003.
11. Schön, D. *The Reflective Practitioner: How Professionals Think in Action*. New York: Basic Books. 1983.
12. Teuber, C.; Forbrig, P. "Different Types of Patterns for Online-Booking Systems". *Proceedings of TAMODIA 2004*.
13. Tidwell, J. A Pattern Language for Human-Computer Interface Design. Available online at http://www.mit.edu/~jtidwell/common_ground.html (last visited in November 2005)
14. Van Welie, M. Patterns for Designers? Position Paper in CHI 2002 *Workshop on Patterns in Practice*. Available online at http://www.welie.com/patterns/chi2002-workshop/index.html (last visited in November 2005)
15. Van Welie, M.; van der Veer, G. C. "Pattern Languages in Interaction Design: Structure and Organization". *Proceedings of Interact 2003*.
16. Van Welie, *Web Design Patterns*. Available online at http://www.welie.com/patterns/index.html (last visited in November 2005).

An MDA Approach for Generating Web Interfaces with UML ConcurTaskTrees and Canonical Abstract Prototypes

Duarte Costa, Leonel Nóbrega, and Nuno Jardim Nunes

Universidade da Madeira, DME/SCI, Campus da Penteada, Funchal, Portugal
{duarte, lnobrega, njn}@uma.pt

Abstract. UML has become the standard language for modelling in different areas and domains, but it is widely recognized that it lacks support for User Interface Design (UID). On the other hand, ConcurTaskTree (CTT) is one of the most widely used notations for task and dialogue modelling. An important achievement is the proposed notation and semantics for CTT by extending the UML metamodel, proving that task modelling in user interface design can be accomplished by a UML compliant notation. For the interface structure design was proposed that UML's CTT could be complemented with Canonical Abstract Prototypes (CAP) leading to a model-based user interface design method co-specified by the presentation (CAP) and behaviour (UML's CTT) perspectives. In this paper we propose another step in this UID method by defining a specific model compliant with the OMG recommended Model Driven Architecture (MDA), which will be the intermediary between the design model and an implementation of the user interface. This proposal will align the UID method with the MDA recommendation making it possible to automatically generate interface prototypes from conceptual models.

Keywords: Model-Based User Interface Design, ConcurTaskTrees, Canonical Abstract Prototypes, Model Driven Architecture.

1 Introduction

The Unified Modelling Language (UML) has become the standard language for modelling in different areas and domains, but it is widely recognized that the UML lacks support for user interaction and interface design [9]. One of the main reasons is related to the fact that UML-based development is system-centric, meaning that it focuses on the internal system architecture and not on the interactive architecture, thus leading to unusable systems. Although UML provides models and representations for a software development process, none of those diagrams is specifically oriented for User Interface Design (UID).

For the software engineering (SE) community the UML provides a common language for specifying, visualizing and documenting software systems, enabling tool interoperability at the semantic level. The adoption of UML by the human-computer interaction (HCI) community is an important goal since all of these issues are also very important for interactive system development. In [7] the authors propose a

K. Coninx, K. Luyten, and K.A. Schneider (Eds.): TAMODIA 2006, LNCS 4385, pp. 137–152, 2007.

formal UML-compliant model-based User Interface Design approach, which combines a presentation notation (Canonical Abstract Prototypes) with a task modelling notation (ConcurTaskTrees). The Canonical Abstract Prototype notation provides a collection of components in order to build abstract user interfaces. The ConcurTaskTrees notation supports a hierarchical description of the tasks to be performed in an interactive system, providing temporal and semantic relationships.

In this paper we propose another step in the above mentioned UML-based UID approach by integrating it into the Model Driven Architecture (MDA) initiative. The MDA is an Object Management Group (OMG) specification that recommends an approach to system development based on model definition and transformation using standards like the UML. This initiative focuses on model manipulation, leaving the implementation details to a secondary level that ultimately leads to automatic code generation.

The goal of the approach described here is to transform the UID model to a UML-compliant specific model, as recommended in the MDA. The intermediary specific model will provide implementation details that enable automatic generation of code for a specific implementation platform. Although our approach could be applied to different target platforms, here we discuss the challenges of supporting the MDA specification to web-based server-side scripting platforms.

This paper is structured as follows: Section 1 describes the task modelling and abstract presentation concepts in a UML-based approach. Section 2 describes the main concepts for the MDA specification. In Section 3 we describe the specific model that we propose for extending the task modelling and abstract presentation concepts in order to detail the user interface structure and behaviour. Section 4 describes the execution algorithm used for the ConcurTaskTree semantics. In Section 5 we describe the main concepts for the proposed code generation process. In Section 6 we demonstrate the new concepts proposed for the UID method with a modelling and code generation example. Finally we present some conclusions.

2 Task and Abstract Presentation Modelling in UML

In [7] the authors propose a new UID method that combines UML-compliant presentation and task modelling notation. This approach provides a step further in model-based User Interface Design (UID) since it enables UML compliant models, for interaction design, that rely on the new UML 2.0 standard and the enhanced extensibility mechanisms. In essence, the approach defines a Presentation Model, which contains abstract presentation elements for the user interface structure, and a Dialog Model that describes the behaviour of the interaction with a task modelling notation. The proposal defends the co-specification of Presentation and Dialog models as two complementary models for UID.

The need for task modelling support in standard Object Oriented modelling languages has been extensively discussed as a key requirement to bridge the software engineering and Human-Computer Interaction (HCI) arenas. In [9] a UML 1.x extension to support the widely popular CTT notation was proposed. However this approach had weak semantic support since the UML 1.x extensibility mechanisms did not provide the flexibility required to support a notation that included both the hierarchical structure of tasks and the temporal relationships between tasks. In [6] an improved extension to the recent UML 2.x standard was proposed.

This integration between the CTT and the UML 2.x was achieved by extending the UML metamodel and defining new elements and concepts represented in a TaskTree like UML diagram. It was demonstrated that ConcurTaskTrees semantics can be expressed in terms of UML 2.0 activity semantics, allowing an integration of task modelling concepts within the UML. The Canonical Abstract Prototype (CAP) [3] notation proposes a collection of abstract components, for the interface presentation, each specifying an interactive function, such as inputting data or displaying a notification. These components are placed together in order to build abstract interface prototypes. The concepts for the CAP notation are naturally structural so they were defined as an extension to the UML 2.0 Classes package in [7].

Using the CTT and CAP notations extended in UML, a UML-compliant model-based User Interface Design approach was proposed. The UID method described in [7] uses the extended UML 2.0 metamodel with the concepts and semantics of CAP and CTT taking a step further towards integrating the standard specification of UML with concepts for modelling the user interaction. The notation for Canonical Abstract Prototype (CAP) [3] used for the Presentation Model and the notation for ConcurTaskTree (CTT) [5] [11], used for the Dialog Model, were combined and re-defined, providing UML-compliant semantics and notation for User Interface Design.

3 Model Driven Architecture

Model Driven Architecture (MDA) is a specification proposed by the Object Management Group (OMG), defining an information architecture system that is resilient to changes and evolution of the underlying business rules and the associated technological changes. The MDA separates the business logic from the underlying technology platform that implements it. Platform-independent models are created with UML and other standards provided by the OMG.

Those models depict the domain and business rules, separating them from the software code that implements the system. This separation of concerns enables independent co-evolution of the business and technology aspects of the information architecture. This is one of the main benefits in MDA based architectures: being prepared for system evolution at business and technology level.

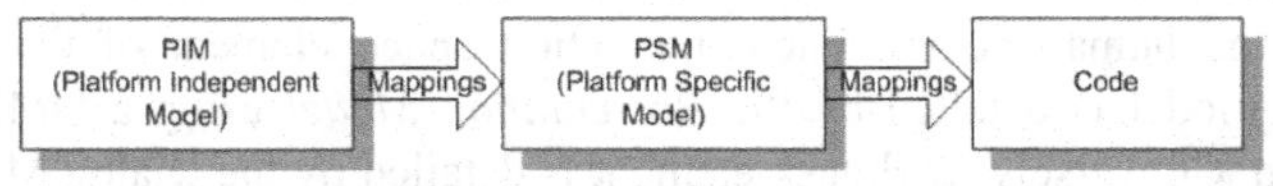

Fig. 1. The main concepts in MDA: PIM, PSM and Mappings

The MDA defines a model-based system structure, put simply, with Platform-Independent Model (PIM) and Platform-Specific Model (PSM). The PSM describe the functionality defined in the PIM for a specific implementation technology, by means of pre-defined transformation mapping rules. Figure 1 represents the main specification concepts of MDA: PIM, PSM and mappings between them.

The PIM is defined with a standard language like UML, supplying a formal specification of the system structure and functionality, abstracting from the technical implementation details. The PSM should also be defined using a standard like UML but are specific to a middleware platform (J2EE, .Net, etc) despite the fact that UML is a technology-independent modelling language.

A key concept in the MDA is the mapping notion. The mappings are a group of rules and techniques used to transform a model in order to obtain another model. To implement these transformations it is fundamental to know the metamodels of the input and output models as well as their mapping rules.

4 Platform Specific Model

In this section we detail the PIM concept from the User Interface Design perspective and then we propose a specific model (PSM) in order to integrate the chosen UID method in the MDA recommendation.

4.1 The PIM in User Interface Design

A PIM should describe the system functionality without considering details about how it will be implemented, providing a higher level of independence between the description of the functionality and the implementation details for the target platform. In a User Interface Design (UID) approach the PIM should reflect the user interface structure and behaviour to a higher degree of abstraction and should not contain any reference to its concrete components. In this way the PIM follows the separation of concerns suggested for UID between the interaction and the interface presentation [12].

The UML-based approach described in [7] defines three model perspectives for the user interface and the related interaction behaviour: *The Conceptual Architecture*, *The Presentation Model* and *The Dialog Model*. The conceptual architecture, which is *UseCase*-driven, defines a high level view of the system architecture, in terms of conceptual class *stereotypes*: *entity*, *control*, *boundary*, *task* and *interaction space* (see [9] for details). The *UseCase* concept element is also present in the *Conceptual Architecture*. The elements that describe the structure and behaviour of the user interface are the <<interaction space>> and the <<task>> class *stereotypes*. The <<task>> classes are used to model the structure of the dialogue between the user and the system, the <<interaction space>> class is used to model interaction between the system and the human actors. Each interaction space element of the *Conceptual Architecture* model is detailed by the *Presentation Model* using a UML-compliant CAP notation. Conversely, each task element is detailed by the Dialog Model using a UML-compliant adaptation of the CTT notation.

In terms of UML metamodel extensions the CAP elements required by the Presentation Model are: *InteractionElement*, *Material*, *Tool* and *Hybrid*. Equally, the following Dialog Model extensions are required by the CTT notation: *TaskTree*, *TaskNode*, and *TaskEdge*. The *Material*, *Tool*, *Hybrid* and *TaskEdge* elements encompass specific relationships with other elements that are discussed later in this paper. We argue that the above-mentioned description of the three models in the UID approach proposed in [7], due to its technological independence nature, fits the PIM concept promoted in the OMG's MDA initiative.

4.2 The Proposed PSM

We describe in this sub-section the PIM elements that should be passed to the specific model. We propose an intermediary Platform-Specific Model (PSM) because, as defined in the MDA recommendation, the PIM should be a technology-free representation of the solution. The technology solution will be reflected in the PSM. The proposed PSM contains the same perspectives defined for the PIM: *Conceptual Architecture, Presentation Model* and *Dialog Model*.

4.2.1 The PIM Elements Passed to the PSM

For the *Conceptual Architecture* part of the PIM, the elements that will be transformed to the PSM are the *UseCase*, the *InteractionSpace* and the *Task* class *stereotypes*. For the structural part defined in the *Presentation Model* view of the PIM, the following elements that represent the CAP semantics and notation should be reflected in the PSM: *InteractionElement* and the corresponding specializations *Material, Tool and Hybrid*. The *Material* element involves the specializations *Container*, *Element*, *Collection* and *Notification*. Conversely, the *Tool* element encompasses specializations: *ToolAction, Create, Delete, Modify, Select and Toggle*. The *Hybrid* element includes the specializations: *ActiveMaterial, EditableCollection, EditableElement, Input and SelectableCollection*.

The original notation for the CAP was defined in [3] and involves 23 elements. In this paper we will only use the most significant in order to illustrate models within a Web context, the full UML metamodel extensions were provided elsewhere in [7]. A metamodel diagram with the CAP elements in UML is represented in Figure 2.

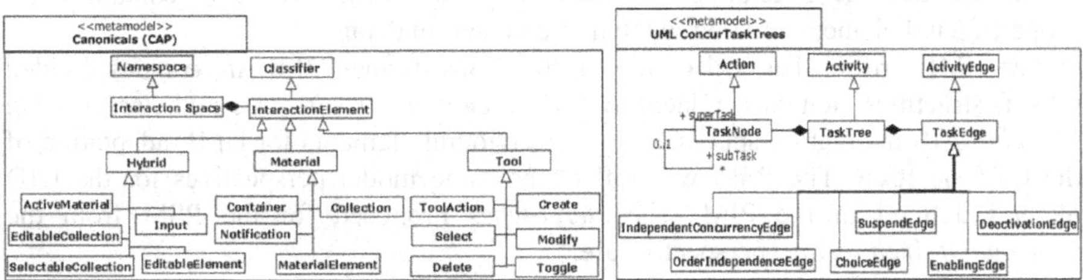

Fig. 2. Extended UML 2.0 metamodel [7] including the CAP and CTT elements used for the PSM proposal

The behavioural component associated with the target user interface, represented in the *Dialog Model* view of the PIM, involves UML's CTT elements reflected in the PSM. Those PIM elements, which are extended from the *Action, Activity* and *ActivityEdge* metaelements in UML 2.0, are *Task, TaskTree and TaskEdge*. The *TaskEdge* element involves the following specialization elements related to CTT temporal operators: *ChoiceEdge, IndependentConcurrencyEdge, DeactivationEdge,*

EnablingEdge, OrderIndependenceEdge, and SuspendEdge. The original semantics and notation for CTT were proposed in [5] [11] whilst the UML metamodel was extended with those elements in [6]. Figure 2 has a metamodel diagram with the CTT elements that extends UML 2.0.

The above-described elements from the three PIM perspectives will be reflected directly into specific elements for the proposed PSM. Those specific elements will be detailed in a later section.

4.2.2 UML Profile: Stereotypes and Tagged Values

UML enables domain-specific models through a set of extension mechanisms (*stereotypes*, *tagged values* and *constraints*) to specialize its elements for a particular application domain. That set of UML extensions is grouped into UML Profiles (a collection of extension elements).

The UML Profiles have an important role in MDA and in code generation techniques [4]. In the MDA specification UML Profiles are particularly important for describing the platform specific model, guaranteeing that the derived models will be consistent with the UML standard, which is one of the recommendations of the MDA.

Thus a UML profile is the recommended technique for the PSM definition. Apart from *stereotypes* that will specialize and extend concepts from the PIM, the UML extensibility mechanisms also include *tagged values*, which enable the possibility of adding characteristics to an element which could not be defined using other UML concepts. As *stereotypes* and *tagged values* are important for the specific model, we will define these extension elements in a UML Profile associated with our PSM proposal.

4.2.3 The PSM Elements

After describing the PIM elements, a proposal for the PSM is required to reflect those elements in a specific target platform. Here we describe a model for the web platform, which, besides the specialized elements from the PIM, will also contain other properties and elements related to the implementation details.

The UML Profile that will be used in the PSM defines UML *stereotypes* divided into: i) structural elements, related to the *Conceptual Architecture* and *Presentation Model* (CAP) interaction spaces, and ii) behavioural elements for UML adaptation of the CTT notation. The PSM will reflect the same model perspectives for the UID method defined in the PIM. The *stereotypes* proposed for the PSM from the *Conceptual Architecture* perspective are:

<<**WebModule**>>; <<**WebAggregationSpace**>>: Mapped from the *UseCase* PIM element.

<<**WebInteractionSpace**>>: Mapped from the *Interaction Space* PIM element. Represents the space within the user interface where the user interacts with the system. This element also defines the link between the *Conceptual Architecture* and *the Presentation Model.*

<<**WebTask**>>: Mapped from the *Task* PIM element. Defines the structure of the dialogue between the user and the system, establishing the behaviour of the user interface. This element also establishes the link between the *Conceptual Architecture* and the *Dialog Model* view.

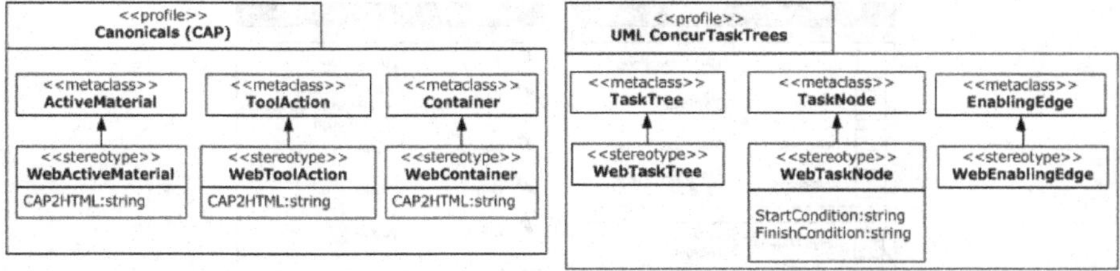

Fig. 3. UML Profiles with stereotypes elements for the Presentation (CAP) and for the Dialog (UML's CTT) Model. For diagram simplification, in CAP Profile, only a metaclass for each subset of Material, Tool and Hybrid is represented. Also for simplification only a metaclass for the TaskEdge subset is represented.

The *stereotypes,* proposed for the *Presentation Model* view in the PSM that will convey the CAP notation are:

<<**WebContainer**>>;<<**WebMaterialElement**>>;<<**WebCollection**>>; <<**WebNotification**>>: Mapped from the subset specialization elements of the *Material* PIM element. A *Material* component represents content, information, data or other user interface (UI) objects manipulated or presented to the user during the course of a task.

<<**WebToolAction**>>;<<**WebCreate**>>;<<**WebDelete**>>;<<**WebModify**>>; <<**WebSelect**>>; <<**WebToggle**>>: Mapped from the subset specialization elements of the *Tool* PIM element. A *Tool* component represents operators, mechanisms or controls that can be used to manipulate or transform materials.

<<**WebActiveMaterial**>>;<<**WebEditableCollection**>>; <<**WebEditableElement**>>;<<**WebInput**>>;<<**WebSelectableCollection**>>: Mapped from the subset specialization elements of the *hybrid* PIM element. A *Hybrid* or *Active Material* is the result of combining the *Material* and *Tool* components classes and represents any component with characteristics of both composing elements, such as a text entry box.

A UML profile package diagram for CAP *stereotypes* and *tagged values* is represented in Figure 3. For the above mentioned *stereotypes* the *tagged values* should be defined in order to describe the relative position of the element in the concrete user interface. Other *tagged values* suggest the concrete user interface element, in this particular case it will be an HTML element. The most significant *tagged value* to be defined for the presentation *stereotypes* is:

"**CAP2HTML**": Sets a value to identify the concrete interface component associated with the *stereotype* that will be implemented in the generated interface prototype. This value albeit initially suggested can be modified later.

In [1] [2] specific mapping was proposed between the CAP concepts and concrete Web UI elements. This enables an initial transformation from the PIM to the PSM, which already corresponds to a concrete Web element stored in the *tagged value* "CAP2HTML". A table with possible mappings from CAP elements to HTML concrete components is shown in Figure 4.

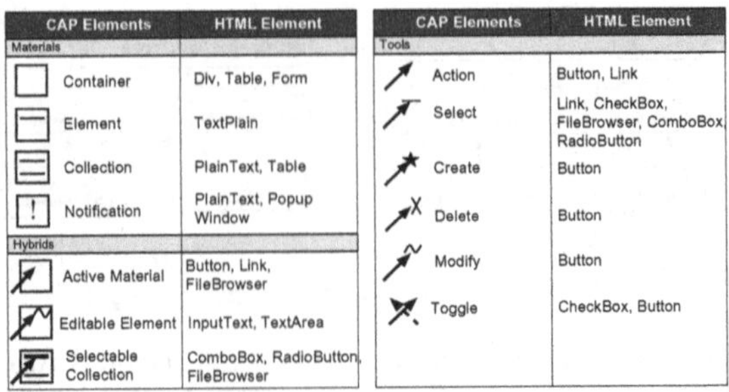

CAP Elements	HTML Element
Materials	
Container	Div, Table, Form
Element	TextPlain
Collection	PlainText, Table
Notification	PlainText, Popup Window
Hybrids	
Active Material	Button, Link, FileBrowser
Editable Element	InputText, TextArea
Selectable Collection	ComboBox, RadioButton, FileBrowser

CAP Elements	HTML Element
Tools	
Action	Button, Link
Select	Link, CheckBox, FileBrowser, ComboBox, RadioButton
Create	Button
Delete	Button
Modify	Button
Toggle	CheckBox, Button

Fig. 4. Suggested CAP to HTML mappings

For PSM elements related to the behaviour (*Dialog Model* view) of the user interface, we propose the following *stereotypes* that are extensions to UML's CTT elements for the PIM:

<<**WebTaskTree**>>: Mapped from the *TaskTree* PIM element. This element will define the root of the UML's CTT that will detail the interaction behaviour. This element will be linked to the *Task* element from the Conceptual Architecture view.

<<**WebTaskNode**>>: Mapped from the *TaskNode* PIM element. This element defines a task or action that will be performed in the interface. This *stereotype* will include *tagged values* to define the start and finish conditions of task execution. The start and finish conditions are related to UML's CTT semantics and are only applied to basic tasks (leaf nodes) because only these types of tasks will reflect a direct user interaction in the user interface. This also means that only the basic tasks (leaves) will be linked to a CAP element in the Presentation Model.

<<**WebIndependentConcurrencyEdge**>>;<<**WebChoiceEdge**>>;<<**WebEnablingEdge**>>;<<**WebOrderIndependenceEdge**>>;<<**WebDeactivationEdge**>>; <<**WebSuspendEdge**>>: Mapped from several PIM temporal operator elements, these elements represent the *stereotypes* for each type of temporal operator described in UML's CTT notation.

For the UML's CTT *stereotypes*, *tagged values* should also be defined, enabling automatic code generation. The most significant *tagged values* related to the behavioural *stereotypes* are:

"**StartCondition**": Sets the value that will identify the condition to check if the *isStarted* state for a task node should be set to *True* or *False*.

"**FinishCondition**": Sets the value that will identify the condition to check if the *isFinished* state for a task node should be set to *true* or *False*.

In Figure 3 is represented a UML profile package diagram with *stereotypes* and *tagged values* for UML's CTT. The graphical representation of the elements in the PSM will be the same as defined for each supported notation. The only difference is that the string "<<stereotype>>" will be attached to PSM's elements.

4.2.4 PIM to PSM Mappings

The transformation process between the PIM and the PSM is executed automatically and will result in the creation of PSM's elements with *stereotypes* and *tagged values*. There is a direct correlation between the PIM and the PSM elements, as suggested by the profile, e.g. a *Container* will be mapped to a <<WebContainer>>, and so on. In the transformation process additional information is also added to *tagged values*, such as the suggested HTML element for the specific CAP and the *Start* and *Finish* conditions for the *TaskNode*.

For simplification of the work, transformation rules (mappings) are defined in a simplified and direct way. The standard *Query View Transformation* (QVT) [13] is still at an initial specification stage, but could be a promising approach to a formalised standard method of defining the mapping rules between the PIM and PSM. The PIM and PSM are serialized in an XMI format, following the OMG recommendation, in order to promote better integration and transformation between the models and from the PSM to the target platform code. The transformation rules are discussed in detail in section 5.2.

5 Task Tree Algorithm

An important consequence of the UID method, described in [7], for UML CTT adaptation is the possibility of simulating the model using a specific execution algorithm. The task tree algorithm allows enabling and disabling of task nodes defined in the tree structure, and related through temporal operators.

The goal of the algorithm is the identification of the tree's tasks necessary to set the state to *Enable* or *Disable*, taking into account the associated temporal operator and user executed tasks. The task nodes that can be executed, which represents a direct interaction with the user, are leaf nodes of the tree. Combining the presentation and UML task notations we can simulate abstract prototypes in a way that enables early usability evaluation of UIs and also leverage the automatic generation of code.

The first step in the algorithm is the creation of a binary tree to be parsed by a recursive method. The binary tree is named an "Execution Task Tree" (ETT) [7] in which all the nodes represent a task or an operator structure. The second step verifies which task nodes are *Enabled* or *Disabled*. The second part of the algorithm that verifies which task nodes were executed (started and finished) is similar to the algorithm defined for the original CTT [5] [11].

Comparing the main aspects of the algorithms defined for the original CTT [5] [11] with that proposed in UML's CTT [7], in both methods the CTT structure must be transformed in a binary tree before parsing the task nodes and processing their state (*Enabled* or *Disabled*). In the method proposed for UML's CTT the operators' precedence is also fundamental as defined in the original CTT [5] [11].

One of the main differences between the two algorithms is related to the initial transformation from CTT structure into a binary tree. While in the CTT binary tree task nodes are created connected by operators, in the proposal for ETT, the tasks and operators are defined as nodes, so all nodes in an ETT represent a task or a temporal operator.

The above algorithm is implemented in the target Web platform resulting in a support structure to execute the interface behaviour as defined in the PSM using UML's CTT semantics and notation.

6 Code Generation Process

In this section we present the main aspects of the code generation process. We start by describing the modeling editor used and the main aspects of the open-source Web platform that will support the implementation. Afterwards we detail some aspects of the model-to-model and model-to-code transformations.

6.1 The Modelling Editor and Target Platform

The *MetaSketch Editor* [8] is a reflexive meta-modelling tool capable of editing models and metamodels. The tool supports the most recent OMG technologies, including XMI 2.1 and Meta-Object Facility (MOF) 2.0, enabling the creation of models in any well-defined notation capable of being expressed as MOF instances. Using the *MetaSketch Editor* we define the PIM elements that extend the UML 2.0 metamodel. Since the PSM is a UML-based model, this tool is also used in order to define and manipulate its elements. We define the metamodel elements proposed in the UID method [7], extending the UML meta-model with CAP and CTT elements. The proposed PSM is defined with regard to the new elements in order to extend the PIM. The CAP and UML's CTT elements are extended by a UML Profile used in the PSM diagrams.

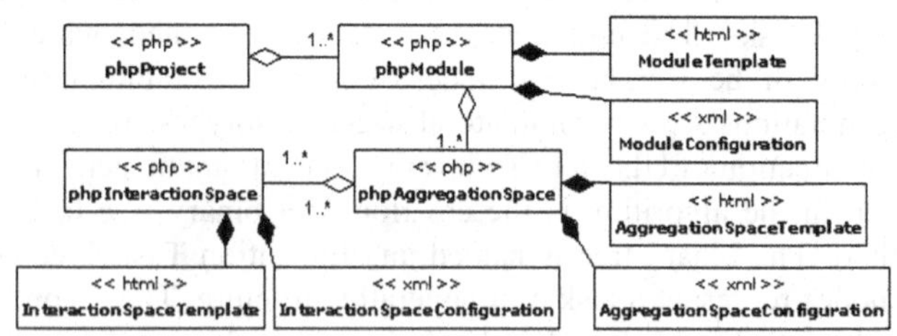

Fig. 5. Class diagram with framework's code elements

The Web implementation platform, used to generate the interface prototypes, is developed in PHP 4.x, an open-source server-side language. With the PHP scripting language was built the *Hydra framework* for implementing web user interfaces being the base of the platform. The *Hydra framework* uses the same concepts defined in the UID method providing traceability between the models and the code, which is an important item in a model-driven process. The code structure that fits the framework requirements has the following main code classes: *phpProject*, *phpModule*, *phpAggregationSpace* and *phpInteractionSpace*.

The *phpModule* is used to organize the implementation code, while the *phpAggregationSpace* will originate a web page, composed by *phpInteractionSpace* elements. The *phpInteractionSpace* is the framework base unit and provides the user interaction and presentation. The *phpModule*, *phpAggregationSpace* and *phpInteractionSpace* are coded as PHP classes and each one has two other associated code artefacts: (i) A configuration artefact and a (ii) presentation template artefact.

The configuration artefact is defined using XML and contains the behaviour rules and other configuration parameters like data source options, validation rules, data fields etc. The template artefact is created using HTML and is responsible for the presentation of the associated PHP class (*phpModule*, *phpAggregationSpace* or *phpInteractionSpace*).

In Figure 5 are described the main code elements for the implementation platform. For simplicity reasons, we are not using any existing UML Profile for Web or XML, instead we defined only the following stereotypes: <<php>> for a PHP Class; <<html>> for a HTML template; <<xml>> for a XML artefact. More information about UML profiles for Web Modelling and XML is provided elsewhere in [14] [15].

6.2 PIM-to-PSM and PSM-to-Code

The transformation from the PIM to the PSM is executed using the PHP's application *Model2Code* where the transformation rules are configured. The PIM's file is parsed, the transformation rules are applied and the process finishes creating the PSM's XMI file. The transformation rules at this stage of the work are defined as a set of direct mappings. In future work could be necessary to use a standard like QVT [13] to formalise the mapping rules between the PIM and PSM. The most significant model-to-model transformation rules are described in Table 1.

Table 1. PIM-to-PSM (1) and PSM-to-Code (2) most significant transformation rules

(1) PIM element >>>	is mapped to >>> PSM element
UseCase	WebModule and
InteractionSpace	WebInteractionSpace
Task	WebTask
TaskTree	WebTaskTree
TaskNode	WebTaskNode. The tagged values *StartCondition* and *FinishCondition* are set with default values;
TaskEdge	WebTaskEdge;
Canonicals (CAP) [*InteractionElementName*]	Web[*InteractionElementName*]. The tagged value *CAP2HTML* is set following the mappings in Figure 5;

(2) PSM element >>>	is mapped to >>> Code Artefact
WebModule	PHP Class, a XML file and a HTML
WebAggregationSpace	PHP Class, a XML file and a HTML template file
WebInteractionSpace	PHP Class, a XML file and a HTML template file
UML's CTT Profile: WebTask, WebTaskTree, WebTaskNode and WebTaskEdge	UML's CTT Profile semantics are placed in a XML File (the same associated with the
CAP's Profile: Web[*InteractionElementName*]	Parameters in the HTML Templates and in XML file (the same associated with the *WebInteractionSpace*)

The resulting PSM and its elements can be edited and modified, using the *MetaSketch Editor*, promoting an independency level between the PIM and the generated PSM. When the PSM is finished, the correspondent XMI file is loaded to PHP's application *Model2Code* and parsed into an internal structure. In the next step, the application cycles through the internal structure, applying for each element a pre-configured code template, which is parsed with information obtained earlier from the model.

The code templates, pre-configured in *Model2Code* application, are associated with a model element or property. The parsing results from the code templates compose the project code structure. The main transformation rules to obtain the code artefacts from PSM's elements are describe in Table 1.

The resulting code structure, as described in Table 2, starts by a project main directory that contains base classes for the *Hydra framework* and main configuration which defines parameters like used data sources (Database or WebServices connections), etc. An important item is the "/modulos" directory which contains the generated code artefacts from the PSM's elements. In this directory are created sub-directories for each *WebModule* element defined in the model. Each *WebModule* directory contains the *WebAggregationSpaces* and *WebInteractionSpaces* code structure, composed by PHP Classes, XML and HTML Template files. The *WebTask* and *WebTaskTree* semantics, containing the user interface behaviour rules, are placed in the same XML file associated with the *WebInteractionSpace*.

Table 2. Tables with the (1) main code structure and with (2) detailed structure for each WebModule element

(1) Main Directories	Contains:
/classes	Hydra framework classes
/conf	Main configuration files
/css	Framework definitions
/html	Framework definitions
/imagens	Framework definitions
/javascript	Framework definitions
/modulos	WebModule's Sub-Directories
/templates	Global presentation structure

(2) WebModule's Sub-Directories	Contains:
/classes	PHP Classes for WebInteractionSpaces
/classes/eagr	PHP Classes for WebAggregationSpaces
/classes/modulo	PHP Class for WebModule
/conf	XMI Files for WebInteractionSpaces
/conf/eagr	XMI Files for WebAggregationSpaces
/conf/modulo	XMI File for WebModule
/templates	HTML Templates for WebInteractionSpaces
/templates/eagr	HTML Templates for WebAggregationSpaces
/templates/modulo	HTML Template for WebModule

The *Hydra framework* code structure is flexible, providing that the generated classes, templates and configuration code can be modified after the automatic code generation, to refine any aspect of the web user interface.

7 PSM Modelling Example

In this section we present a full practical example of the proposed UID method by defining a PIM, the related PSM and the generated code. The example is a simple web interface meant for sending e-mail.

The PIM includes elements for the structure, with CAP notation, and also elements for describing the interaction with UML's CTT notation.

The *Conceptual Architecture* elements for the user interface are as follows:

- "**SendMail UseCase**": *UseCase* element;
- "**SendMail InteractionSpace**": *Interaction Space* element that represents the interface presentation perspective;
- "**SendMail Task**": *Task* that represents the interface dialogue or behavioural perspective;

The *Presentation Model* elements, which are associated with and detail the "**SendMail InteractionSpace**" element, are as follows:

- "**SendMail Dialog**": *Material Container* for all the structural elements;
- "**EnterToAddress**", "**EnterSubject**" and "**EnterBodyMessage**": are *EditableElement* components;
- "**SelectFile**: is a *SelectableCollection* component;

- "**AttachFile**", "**Cancel**" and "**SendMessage**": are *ToolAction* components;
- "**ReturnReceipt**": is a *Toggle* component;

Figure 6 represents the PSM *Presentation Model* diagram with the used *stereotypes* in the example.

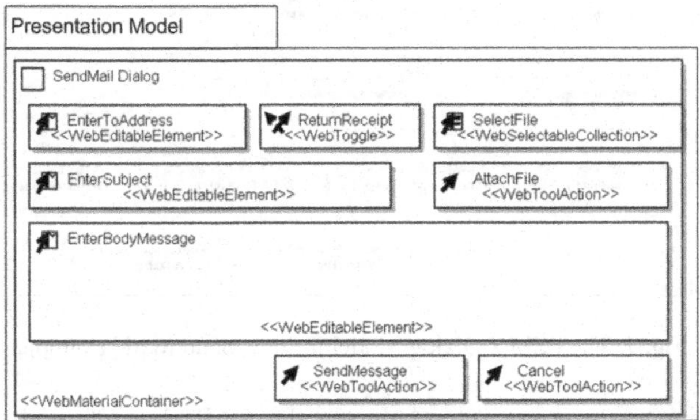

Fig. 6. The PSM's Presentation Model for the "Send Mail" example

The *Dialog Model* elements represented in UML's CTT, which are associated with and detail the "**SendMail Task**" element, are as follows:

- "**SendMail RootNode**": *TaskTree* element that represents the root node ;
- "**EnterSubject**", "**ReturnReceipt**", "**AddAttach**" and "**EnterBodyMessage**": Optional *Task* nodes, meaning that property *Optional* is set to *True*.
- "**Z**": Temporal operator *Deactivation*;
- "|": Temporal operator *Independent Concurrency*;
- ">": Temporal operator *Enabling*;

All the others elements ("**ComposeMail**", "**Cancel**", etc) are task nodes and they are represented in Figure 7. The tree leaf nodes that represent basic tasks are direct associated with presentation CAP elements and have the same name, e.g. the "**Cancel**" task node is associated with the "**Cancel**" *ToolAction* component.

Analysing the *Dialog Model* (see Figure 7) we can see that in the initial state all the basic tasks are disabled except for the "EnterToAddress" and "Cancel" nodes. If "Cancel" is chosen all the others elements will be disabled, thus finishing the interaction. When the "EnterToAddress" is inserted, the basic tasks (and the correspondent CAP) "EnterSubject", "EnterBodyMessage", "ReturnReceipt", "SelectFile" and "SendMessage" are enabled. After this step it is possible to send the e-mail message or edit the other options before sending it. If we choose "SelectFile" the element is disabled and the "AttachFile" is enabled.

With the above elements, that defines the PIM, and with the mapping rules defined in section 5.2, we create the PSM, adding *stereotypes* and certain information about the concrete implementation elements in *tagged values*. In the PSM some information

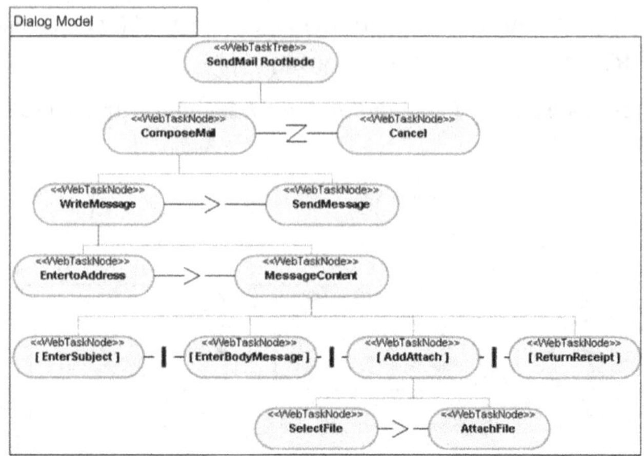

Fig. 7. The PSM's Dialog Model for the "Send Mail" example

is added relating to mapping rules between the CAP elements and concrete Web components which are stored in the *tagged value* "CAP2HTML".

In our example, following the suggested mappings in Figure 4, we map the CAP *SelectableCollection* component to an HTML *FileBrowser* concrete component and the *ToolAction* component is defined as an HTML *SubmitButton*. The *Material Container* is mapped, in this case, to an HTML *Form* structure because of the *ToolAction* component contained. As described previously the UID method used, defines an association relationship between the CAP elements and UML's CTT basic task (tree leaf node) elements. Each basic task node in the Dialog Model could have a one-to-one relation to a CAP element from the Presentation Model. This relationship is relevant to the PSM in detailing the start and finish conditions for the task node, being also fundamental in order to obtain the task *Enabled* or *Disabled* state.

At the current stage of our proposal and due to the interaction web context the start and finish conditions were simplified and will occur simultaneously. For example, the task "EnterToAddress" is related with a CAP *EditableElement* and is mapped to a HTML *InputText* component. The *tagged values* for start and finish conditions will be set as "Value Not Null" and only when the Web server receives the *InputText* field with a value will mark the task as finished, then processing the *Enable/Disable* state. From the PSM XMI representation, the implementation code is generated for the Web platform, as described in section 5. Regarding the main aspects of the generated code, the implementation platform supports the separation between the presentation components and behavioural components, leading to a close relationship with the PSM elements. As detailed in section 5.1 and 5.2, the presentation code artefacts are organized in a group of templates and classes. The behavioural code artefacts are composed of a group of XML files that contain UML's CTT semantics.

Figure 8 has the concrete HTML interface generated automatically from the PSM (*Dialog* and *Presentation*) in the example. With this example we confirmed that the PSM elements are transformed into code components, generated automatically, obtaining an executable prototype of the user interface, completing in this way all the

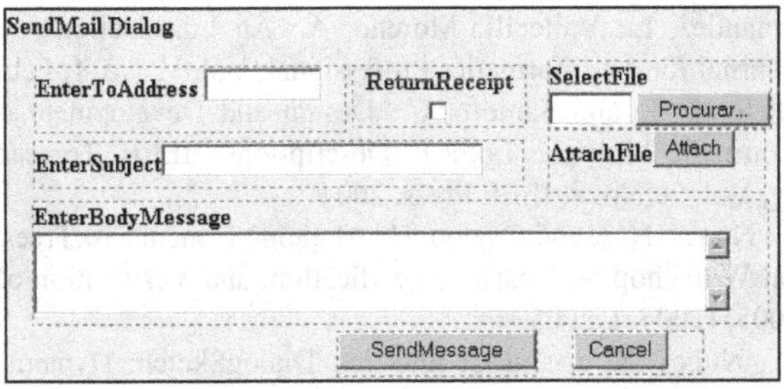

Fig. 8. The interface prototype generated with the PSM for the "Send Mail" example

steps required in a development process of a user interface from the analysis and design through to the implementation code.

8 Conclusions

The approach in [7] extends UML 2.0 metamodel with task modelling and abstract presentation concepts for model-based User Interface Design (UID). The proposal stands for the co-specification of Presentation and Dialog models as two complementary models using Canonical Abstract Prototypes and UML's ConcurTaskTree notation, respectively providing a formal way to express the main aspects for UID.

The approach described in this paper takes a step further by extending the UID approach for the MDA specification. Starting from the Dialog and Presentation models we proposed a Platform-Specific Model (PSM) and an UML Profile in order to detail the requirements for automatically generating Web interfaces. With this MDA and UML compliant solution, we can obtain from the design models a fully functional Web interface prototype in order to simulate it in an earlier stage or to deploy a final interface. This solution is one of the firsts that integrates abstract modelling for UID with MDA, providing automatic code generation from user interface models.

Our proposal provides satisfactory results concerning generated Web interfaces. It is fully compliant with the modern OMG technologies and supports the longstanding HCI best practice of separation of concerns. We believe the approach described here proves the feasibility of bridging SE and HCI under common ground of the UML and MDA.

References

[1] Campos, P. and Nunes, N.: Canonsketch: A user-centered tool for canonical abstract prototyping. In Proceedings of DSV-IS'2004, 11th International Workshop on Design, Specification and Verification of Interactive Systems, Springer-Verlag, 2004.

[2] Campos, P. and Nunes, N.: Tools of the Trade: The Practitioners' Tools and Workstyles. IEEE Software accepted for publication, 2006.

[3] Constantine, L. and Lockwood, L. A. D.: Software for use : a practical guide to the models and methods of usage-centered design. Addison Wesley, Reading, Mass, 1999.

[4] Fuentes-Fernández, L., Vallecillo-Moreno, A.: An Introduction to UML Profiles. The European Journal for the Informatics Professional, Vol. V, No. 1, February 2004
[5] Mori, G., Paternò, F. and Santoro, C.: Design and Development of Multidevice User Interfaces through Multiple Logical Descriptions. IEEE Transactions on Software Engineering, Vol. 30,No. 8, IEEE Press, 2004
[6] Nóbrega, L., Nunes, N. J. and Coelho, H.: Mapping ConcurTaskTrees into UML 2.0. 12th International Workshop on Design, Specification, and Verification of Interactive System (DSV-IS'2005) (2005a). 2005.
[7] Nóbrega, L., Nunes, N. J. and Coelho, H.: DialogSketch: Dynamics of the Canonical Prototypes. 4th International Workshop on TAsk MOdels and DIAgrams for user interface design: For Work and Beyond (TAMODIA'2005) (2005b), Gdansk, Poland, September 26-27, 2005, (to appear) ACM Press.
[8] Nóbrega, L., Nunes, N. J. and Coelho, H.: The Meta Sketch Editor, A reflexive modeling editor. In Proceedings of CADUI'2006. 2006.
[9] Nunes, N. J. and Falcão e Cunha, J.: Towards a UML profile for interaction design: the Wisdom approach. In Proc. of UML´2000 Conference, Kent – UK, A. Evans (Ed.), Springer Verlag LNCS, New York (2000) 50-58.
[10] Nunes, N. J.: Object Modeling for User-Centered Development and User Interface Design: the Wisdom Approach. PhD Thesis, University of Madeira, Funchal, Portugal, April 2001.
[11] Paternò, F: Model-Based Design and Evaluation of Interactive Applications, Springer Verlag, 1999
[12] Puerta, A. R., and Eisenstein, J.: Towards a General Computational Framework for Model-Based InterfaceDevelopment Systems. In Proc. of the 4th International Conference on Intelligent User Interfaces1999. ACM Press, New York, NY, 1999, 171-178
[13] Tata Consultancy Services Revised submission for MOF 2.0 Query / Views / Transformations RFP, QVT-Partners, 2003
[14] David Carlson: Modeling XML Applications with UML: Practical e-Business Applications. Addison-Wesley Professional, 2001
[15] Jim Conallen: Building Web Applications with UML. Addison-Wesley Professional, 2002
[16] Vanderdonckt, J.: A MDA-Compliant Environment for Developing User Interfaces of Information Systems. Proc. of Conference on Advanced Information Systems Engineering (CAiSE'2005), Porto (2005)

High-Level Modeling of Multi-user Interactive Applications

Jan Van den Bergh, Kris Luyten, and Karin Coninx

Hasselt University – transnationale Universiteit Limburg
Expertise Centre for Digital Media – Institute for BroadBand Technology
Wetenschapspark 2
3590 Diepenbeek
Belgium
{jan.vandenbergh,kris.luyten,karin.coninx}@uhasselt.be

Abstract. With the shift of networked software applications away from the desktop computers and into home appliances comes the challenge of finding new ways to model this type of software. The most important home appliance that has new found computing capabilities is the television set. Through television people can now be participants instead of viewers, and use interactive software to enter the participative stage. Staged participatory multimedia events are a subset of this kind of interactive software that have a predefined temporal structure that lets television viewers and mobile users become participants in a distributed multimedia event. In this paper, we introduce an interaction model that is part of modelling language for staged participatory multimedia events. We show how the language can be mapped on UML constructs and shortly discuss related work using a common example.

1 Introduction

The current era is sometimes referred to as the communication age; many innovations over the last few years relate to enhanced communication facilities and systems that support the creation of communities that have members who would otherwise not be able to even meet eachother. This trend is also visible in most "passive" media as television shows. Television shows become increasingly interactive and engage the viewer to participate instead. Television games are not longer created by production studios and distributed by a broadcasting agency but are also recorded and broadcasted by people at home. The whole community can create and participate. A next step in this evolution could be that interactive television shows will involve even more user interaction and awareness of other participants. These *staged participatory multimedia events* (SPME) will be organized for (and by) individual communities.

The design of such shows poses some engineering challenges which should not be presented to the final creators of the shows. In this paper we present part of a language we created to support the design of such shows. A short overview of this language, SpIeLan (short for SPme InterfacE LANguage) is presented in

K. Coninx, K. Luyten, and K.A. Schneider (Eds.): TAMODIA 2006, LNCS 4385, pp. 153–168, 2007.

section 2. After which we will discuss into more detail the part of the language that allows specification of interaction between users and the system components. This language was created to overcome some specific problems with current solutions for specifying behaviour of multi-user interactive applications and to be relatively easy to translate into software by the asynchronous component framework that will be used to implement SPMEs. The interaction language was designed specifically to allow the user to directly see the link between the user interface of the users with different roles and the functionality that is executed on server-side components. Section 3 provides more detailes about the structure and the elements of the diagram. A discussion of the notation, including a broad-brush comparison with some related work is provided in section 4. Finally, a conclusion and future work are presented.

2 SpIeLan

The SpIeLan consists of three different model types: the scenario model, the presentation model and the template model. Each of these three models was made with a specific usage in mind.

The scenario model describes the overall structure of a staged participatory multimedia event. It defines a sequence of scenes and how different roles are actively involved in these scenes. Each scene is an instance of a certain template. Each template is associated with a certain screen-layout, described in the presentation model, and a set of interactions that can occur within the template, defined in the template model. Figure 1 illustrates the relation between the models.

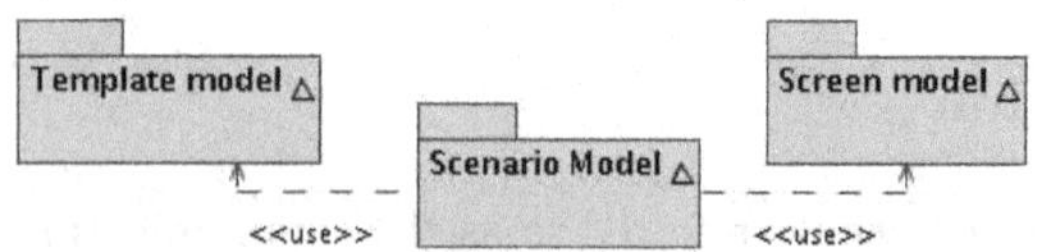

Fig. 1. Overview of the models supported by the SpIeLan

Due to the characteristics of the models, the scenario model and the presentation model will be mostly used by the creators of a show, while the template model will be used by the more technical people. The creators are envisioned to drag and drop scenes onto the scenario diagram and to tune the usage of these scenes through the use of parameters that are provided. The way in which the user interface components are linked with software components and when which function of the framework is activated are considered to be less important to them and are hidden in the template diagram. They can make changes to the presentation model however. For more details about the scenario model and the presentation model we refer to [10], which provides a discussion of both models and how high-level prototypes can be generated from only those two models.

3 Template Model – Interaction Language

3.1 Overview

The template model specifies the interaction between users of a staged participatory multimedia event and the system as well as the temporal relations between these interactions. The requirements we set for the language are as follows:

- The language should support interaction of multiple users with a single system. Each of the users has one role, but this role can change at runtime. A role change is however established by the system. A users role determines the user interface that is displayed to the user and the interactions that are possible.
- The presence of multimedia and awareness of other users are very important for the establishment of staged participatory multimedia events and thus they should be represented in the language.
- A template and the interactions specified in it should be useable in a number of contexts, so a certain degree of abstraction was desired. E.g. it should not specify which concrete hardware features (such as for example color keys on a remote control) should be used to trigger some interaction, however the fact that interaction should take place had to be shown clearly
- It should be possible to map the specification onto a framework of server-side interaction components which uses an asynchronous messaging system for establishing interaction.
- The integration with the other models should not be too confusing.
- the system should be usable by end-users, i.e. people whose main job is not to get some programming job done, but who might program in order to get their job done.

The proposed specification is the result of some iterations with informal evaluations between them. It consists of two main areas, a header and the main content. The header specifies the name of the template, parameters and results of the template [1] and all roles that are involved in the template. For each role, all parts of the user interface that are visible to that user are specified as well as the media-sources they provide. A special role, *All*, exists to avoid unnecessary dubble specification of user interface elements that are visible to all users. An example of such header is shown in figure 2.

The second area gives the functionality of interaction components that is used in the templates, their temporal relationships and the parts of the user interface that provide information to this functionality or display results to the users. The discussion of this part of the language is discussed in the following two sections. Section 3.2 discusses how server-side functionality is described, while section 3.3 describes the symbols used to express the parts of the user interface.

An example of a template model can be seen in figure 5, which is elaborately discussed in section 3.4.

[1] A template instance can take information generated in another template and give information back at the end of its execution.

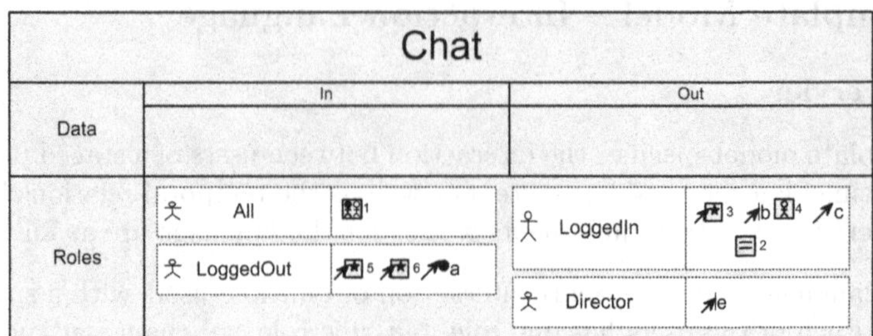

Fig. 2. Example header

3.2 Server-Side Behavior

The interaction diagram describes how and when server-side functionality is activated. The server-side functions that are to be executed are modeled using two symbols: *Interaction* and *MultiUserInteraction* of which the structure is shown in figure 3(a) and figure 3(b), respectively. Both contain four sections from top to bottom:

- The name of the function of an interaction component that is triggered
- The name of the interaction component offering the function
- The parameters of the function and its results.
- Events that can start (`In:Start`) or stop (`In:End`) the execution of the function, or that are sent during the execution of the function (`Out`).

The generalized semantics of an *Interaction* and an *MultiUserInteraction* is partly [2] shown in figure 3(c) and figure 3(d) respectively using UML [8] activity diagrams as specified. The former describes an interaction that is started when an event, specified in the section `In:Start`, is received by an interaction component. This interaction component then starts executing the specified functionality *Function* [3]. This might cause sending an event, specified in the section `Event1` to another interaction component. The execution of *Function* is stopped when an event, specified in the section `Event2` is received. A cleanup action can still be executed, which can for example be used to send the results to the participant's television set. Note that no events need to be specified. In this case, the Interaction is started when the previous one is ended and it stops when f has finished execution.

The semantics of a MultiUserInteraction is similar to that of an Interaction, but differs in the fact that it can be started and execute multiple times before completion. This means that at least one event needs to be specified in the section `In:Start`. When this event is received by an interaction component, it starts executing the specified functionality. In the mean time, however, it can

[2] Only the server part is shown, the parts for the clients is not shown.

[3] In the UML diagrams, the actual execution of the server is represented by the unlabeled actions.

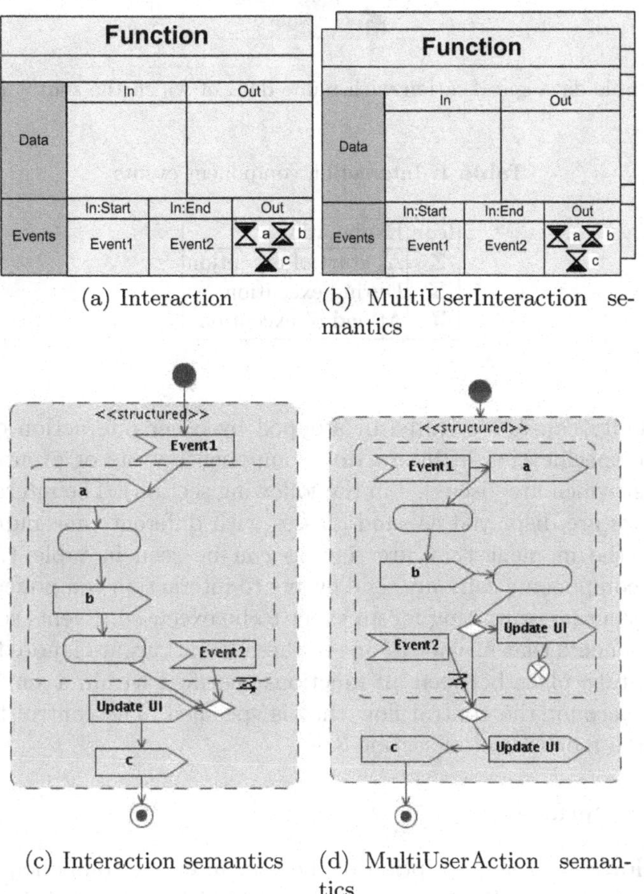

(a) Interaction (b) MultiUserInteraction semantics

(c) Interaction semantics (d) MultiUserAction semantics

Fig. 3. Semantics of the SpIeLan Interaction and MultiUserInteraction using UML 2.0 syntax. Corresponding events in figure (a) and (c), and (b) and (b) have corresponding labels.

keep on receiving the specified event. The execution of a MultiUserInteraction ends, when no more events can be received because an event, specified in the section `In:End` is received or no more events can be received because all possible event sources are exhausted. This can happen when all participants of the roles that can cause the events can only send the event a limited number of times and they have all reached that limit.

The parameters and results are shown as dotted rectangles that have a left and right part (an example can be seen in figure 4). The left part is used to give information about type of parameters and results, the right part displays shows the name of the variable. The left part of the symbol for parameters and results is also used to express the relationship with user interface components. More details about the relation with the user interface is given in the following section, while an example will clarify the overall structure and semantics of the language.

Fig. 4. Example data specification with name data of which the source is a recorded media type

Table 1. Interaction component events

Icon	Explanation
⧗	At start of execution
⧗	During execution
⧗	At end of execution

Functionality can be activated or stopped by other interaction components through the specification of interaction component events or events generated by the users (which are discussed in the following section). The interaction component events are displayed as sand glasses with different time indications depending on the moment they are sent as can be seen in table 1. Note that interaction components can only send events to interaction components that are currently executing or waiting for an event to be executed. Events sent to interaction components that are not in one of these situations are ignored. Exchange of data can take place between all functions specified within a single diagram, taking into account the control flow that is specified. The control flow will be explained into more detail in section 3.4.

3.3 User Interface

Specification. For the description of the user interface components, we chose the Canonical Abstract Prototype notation [2], which provides abstract icons for the functionality offered by a certain part of the user interface. Three major types of abstract components exist with different subtypes: *generic abstract tools* ↗ (actions, operators, mechanisms or components that can be used to operate on materials), *generic abstract material* □ (containers, content, information, data that is operated upon) and *generic abstract active material* ↗□(a combination of both other types). A set of in total twenty one generic components is defined in the original abstract prototypes notation. For a detailed discussion of these generic components and other features of the Canonical Abstract Prototypes, we refer to [2].

In earlier work[10] we defined two additional generic components to enhance the description of the user interfaces of staged participatory multimedia events. Both generic components are types of generic material and provide show some kind of presence information (such as a live video stream of a participant, an emoticon, an avatar or her/his name and status). The first, the participant element ▣ , provides presence information about one participant, while the second, the active participant collection ▣, provides this information about a group of participants. This latter component also has the option to mark some participants as active. In a chat application, such component could be used to show the contact list and highlight the last x contacts from which messages were received.

In contrast to the original Canonical Abstract Prototypes notation [2], each icon that identifies an abstract component has an associated label to relate it with the roles that can see it. For example, the activeParticipantCollection in figure 6, abstract component 1, is only visible to users that have the role `LoggedIn`.

Bindings with interaction specification. The values parameters of *Interactions* and *MultiUserInteractions* can have different sources. The values can be specified explicitly in the specification, they can come from results of other *Interactions* and *MultiUserInteractions* or they can originate from users. In the latter case, different sources can be identified: user interface components, recorded audio or video, or, live audio or video. Similarly, the results of *Interactions* and *MultiUserInteractions* can be displayed in the user interface. When a generic user interface component is used to display results or is used as a source for parameter values, the corresponding icons and a character identifying the user interface component are shown in the left part of the data-specification.

A user can trigger or end the execution of some functionality provided by an *Interaction* or a *MultiUserInteraction*. In this case, the generic tool or interactive material triggering or ending the execution of an event is placed in the area `In:Begin` or `In:End` respectively.

3.4 Example

Figure 5 shows an example of an interaction specification of a simple chat application. The heading shows the name of the template, `Chatting` in addition to the roles that are relevant: `LoggedIn`, `LoggedOut` and `Director`. No parameters or results are specified. Below the heading, one can see the control flow of the template, which is inspired on the control flow in UML activity diagrams.

The control flow can also be modeled as a token that starts at the start node, a black dot. One token than flows through the edge to the following node in the diagram. In figure 5 this is a fork node (a black rectangle). In a fork node, the token splits in one token per outgoing edge. When all local preconditions are met (all specified events are received by the interaction component), the interaction component starts executing the specified behavior. In the example, this means that once a user has requested to log in with a valid login and password, that user is logged into the system and the contact-lists of all users get updated. In parallel, the `MessageServer` waits until it receives an event `e` from the `Director` that will start the shut down process. When this process starts, the event `d` is sent which stops all processing of messages, logs out all logged in users and stops the ability of users that are not logged in to use the chat service.

Once one user is logged into the system, a token leaves the Interaction `Login`, splits at the fork node and three tokens flow to the specified MultiUserInteractions that enable sending and receiving of messages, the login of other users and the logged in users to log out. Once all users have logged out, the execution

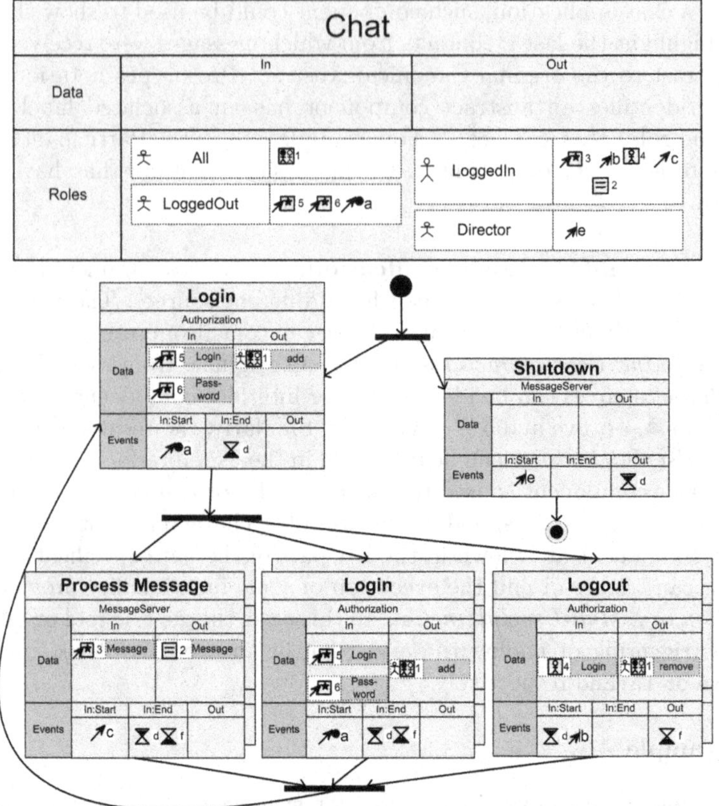

Fig. 5. Chat specification - template model

of the MultiUserInteraction `Logout` stops. This triggers the event `f` which also stops the other MultiUserInteractions. Once these have all successfully stopped execution, tokens have flown over all incoming edges of the join node, starting the flow of a token over the outgoing edge, which again starts the Interaction Login when a valid login and password are specified by a user (in user interface components `5` and `6`).

The interaction stops when the final node is reached (a circle with a black dot in it). In the example in figure 5 the execution ends when the `Director` has shut down the `MessageServer`. Note that the example specification does not guarantee a completely clean end of the system. This would have required an additional join node and additional edges.

When multiple paths are possible from an Interaction or MultiUserInteraction to another one in the diagram, but only one of them can be executed at runtime, the one whose preconditions are first met, gets executed. In terms of token flow this means that the token does not flow on the edges before the preconditions at the end of the edge are met.

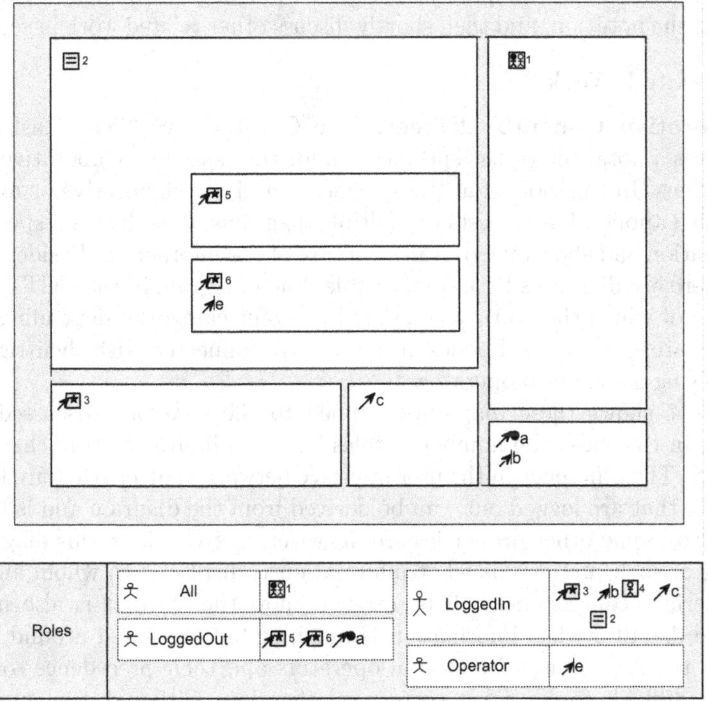

Fig. 6. Chat specification - screen model

Figure 6 shows the screen model that corresponds to the template model, specified in figure 5. All user interface components that are used in the template diagram to specify which data they contain, are allocated to a certain region on the screen. Notice that a single region can contain more than one symbol for a user interface component. This enables us to show the user interface specification for multiple roles at different moments in time in a single diagram.

The user interface components are shown on the screen whenever an interaction could retrieve data from it or push data to it. In the chat example, this would result in the appearance of the user interface components which allow entering login and password from the start of the template for users with the role `LoggedIn` and the contactlist (abstract component `1` would be visible from the moment at least one user is logged in. The designer can however override this behavior if desired.

4 Discussion

In this section, we will first focuss our discussion of related work on specification languages that also focuss on user interaction in detail and are supported by publicly available tools, the Collaborative ConcurTaskTrees and UML Activity

Diagrams and shortly compare our proposed language with them regarding usability of the notation, and then shortly discuss other related work in section 4.2.

4.1 Related Work

Collaborative ConcurTaskTrees. The Collaborative ConcurTaskTrees [5] (CCTT) is a notation for the specification for the tasks in collaborative interactive systems. In this notation, the specification of a collaborative or multi-user interactive application consists of multiple diagrams. One diagram specifies the collaboration and shows the overall structure of the interaction. Besides this diagram there are diagrams for each user role. Each diagram in the CCTT is a tree structure of which the nodes are tasks of different categories depending on how the tasks are executed. All nodes in the tree are connected with their right-hand sibling using a temporal operator.

Figure 7 shows these diagrams, applied to the example, discussed in section 3.4. In this case, the number of roles has been limited to two: chatters and operators. The difference in the user interface between chatters that are logged in and those that are logged out, can be derived from the diagram and is therefore eliminated. Some other properties are, however, less visible in this diagram. An example of such property is what information is displayed to whom and which user interface components will be used to show the data. It is also not clear from the diagram what information is manipulated or passed around between different tasks. The use of temporal operators and their precedence sometimes makes it difficult to construct correct specifications, although tool support for the notation helps to find and identify problems.

The use of three diagrams instead one, makes the creation of the specification more complex, especially since the current tool support does not have the possibility to put different diagrams side by side. The specification however allows to specify behavior for each role that is not present in the overview diagram, which enables the creation of richer clients. This feature is however of no use in this situation because all information processing is done at server-side. Roles in CCTT are allocated to different diagrams which makes getting an overview in an application in which roles are dynamic more difficult.

The notation offers no obvious way to specify which interaction component is responsible for executing which behavior. This is natural because specification of such implementation related things is out of the scope of the Collaborative ConcurTaskTrees, which is a cognitive model.

UML Activity Diagrams. Activity diagrams, as defined in UML 2.0 [8], are another way to specify multi-user interactive applications. Activity diagram semantics in UML 2.0 is based on the semantics of petrinets and uses tokens to denote both the object and the control flow.

Figure 8 shows a possible specification of the example in section 3.4 using the UML 2.0 syntax, extended with CUP 2.0 [9] to show the categories of the actions and show the actors that execute the actions or trigger the events. Figure 8 shows two diagrams; one for specifying the behavior of the chat-client and one for the specification of the chat-server.

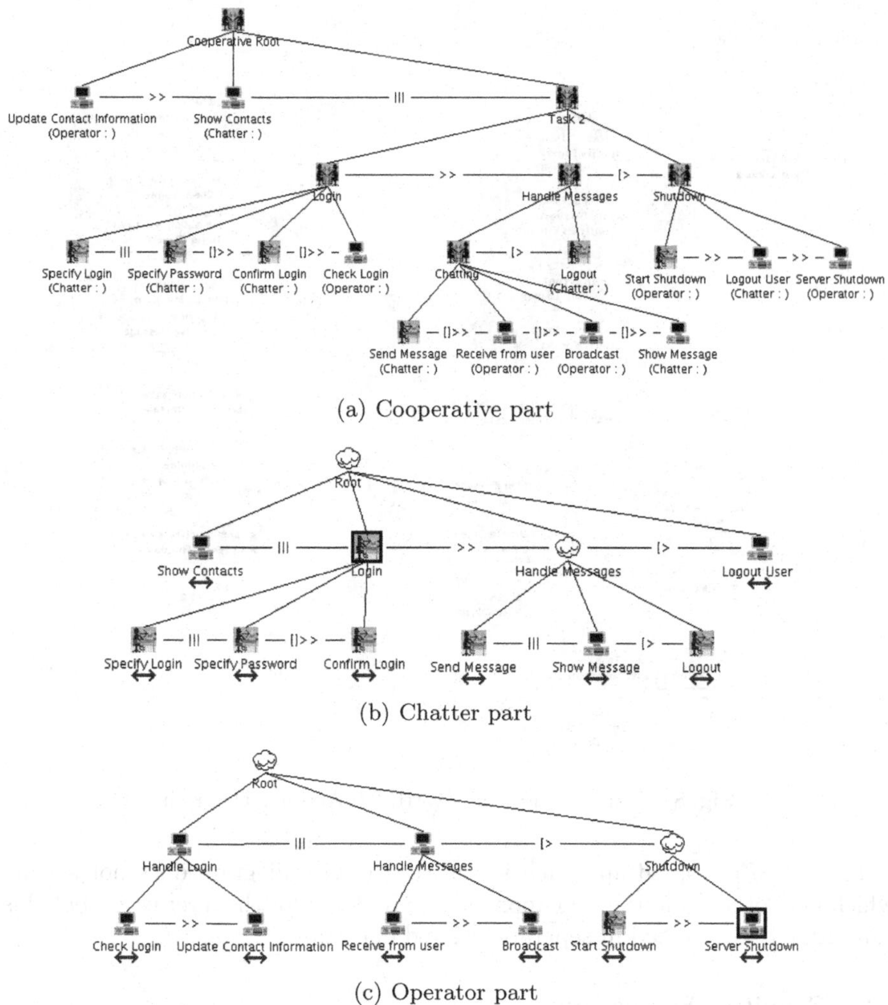

(a) Cooperative part

(b) Chatter part

(c) Operator part

Fig. 7. Chat specification - Cooperative ConcurTaskTrees

We chose to use two diagrams for this specification because we found no way to clearly specify both the client behavior and the server behavior in a single diagram. These two diagrams were created from scratch and not by transforming the specification discussed in section 3.4 using the mapping shown in figure 3. The specification in UML however relies heavily on the usage of some new syntax for UML 2.0, such as the interruptable regions (the dashed rounded rectangles in the diagram), which stops all execution within that region when an event has been received (such as for example the `server shutdown` element in figure 8. A drawback of the specification in the figure is that the interaction between the client and the server is not directly clear from looking at the diagrams.

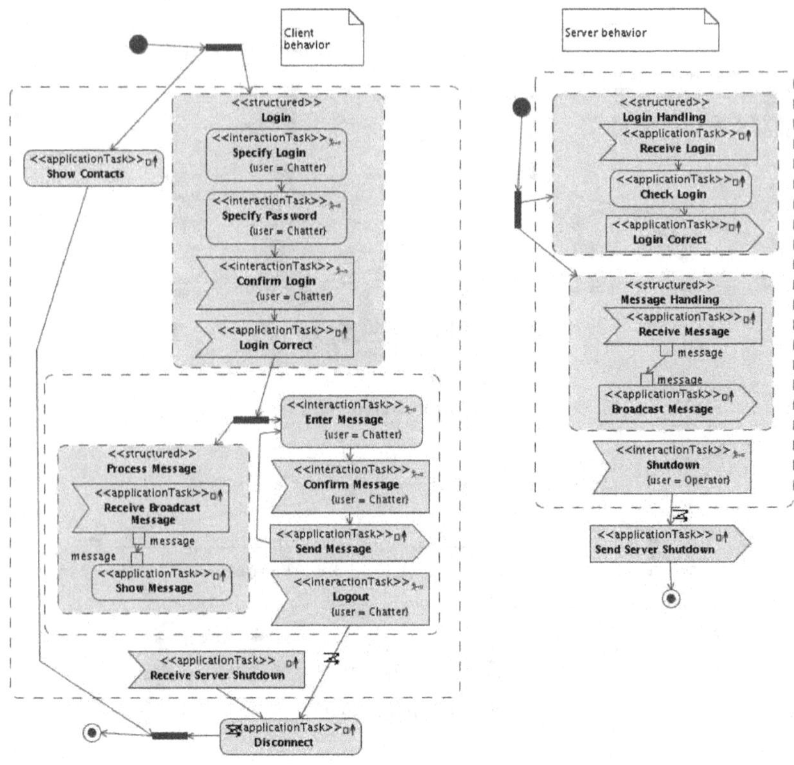

Fig. 8. Chat specification - UML 2.0 Activity Diagram

In most UML-based approaches [7,9] the activity diagram does not specify which kind of user interface components are required for the interaction but this can instead be specified in separate, related diagrams.

4.2 Cognitive Evaluation

When designing a new language it is important to get a good idea of the usability of the notation from early in the design process. Since it is difficult to do usability testing of a programming or design language without complete and appropriate tool support, we already did an initial evalution of the interaction language we designed using the Cognitive Dimensions Framework [4]. This framework gives a common terminology to discuss usability issues and shows which factors should be minimized or maximized for a specific task.

Table 2 gives an overview of a subset of the cognitive dimensions that are part of the earlier mentioned framework together with a rating of the desirability of these dimensions as they can be found in [3]. The remainder of this section contains a discussion of those dimensions proposed notation.

All notations suffer from some sort of *viscosity*, resistance to change. The proposed language suffers from viscosity when an additional interactions are to

Table 2. Cognitive dimensions of modification tasks

Property	Profile
viscosity	harmful
hidden dependencies	harmful
premature commitment	harmful
abstraction barrier	harmful
abstraction hunger	useful
secondary notation	very useful
visibility, juxtaposability	important

be added to the diagram, possibly requiring other interactions to be moved. Also addition of adding user interface components as a source for or target of data can imply multiple actions; the data symbols might have to be resized. The UML activity diagram suffers from a similar viscosity artifacts due to nesting of artifacts and lack of appropriate space. The viscosity of the Collaborative ConcurTaskTrees is of a different nature although lack of space might be a problem as well [4]. Changes to a task in one diagram might have to be repeated in other diagrams. Addition or removal of a task can also imply changing the category of another task as well as adding or removing temporal relations or even abstraction levels.

The problem of *hidden dependencies* is larger in both Collaborative ConcurTaskTrees and activity diagrams, since one will have to use multiple diagrams to specify the necessary activities and additional dialog boxes or diagrams to specify the user interface components. The proposed notation has limited hidden dependencies; most relevant information is explicitly shown in the diagram and only a single diagram is used where other notations require more diagrams. The usage of only a single diagram has the consequence that the resulting notation is less flexible, in that it is not possible to model interaction that has no relation with server-side behavior. This is, however, not perceived to be a problem for the targeted domain.

Premature commitment can be an issue in the proposed notation, e.g. using a MultiUserInteraction instead of an Interaction might involve recreating all associated information (events and associated user interface components) and possibly connected control flows. Although appropriate tool support can easily eliminate this problem. Other problems with the proposed notation as well as the Collaborative ConcurTaskTrees as the UML activity diagram notations were also hinted at in the discussion of viscosity, namely space allocation problems.

The number of *abstractions* needed to get to a functional diagram is probably lower in the Collaborative ConcurTaskTrees than in UML activity diagrams and the proposed notation. Although the closer mapping to the implementation in the latter two notations might make these abstractions not as difficult to deal with.

[4] Repetitive viscosity can occur if space has to be allocated for an additional child for a task to the left of several other tasks since each task to the right has to be moved.

The proposed notation does not allow to make abstractions within the context of one template. This contrasts with the UML activity diagrams which are allow the definition of custom abstractions and thus are abstraction tolerant, and the Collaborative ConcurTaskTrees notation which is abstraction hungry; it requires the creation of user-defined abstractions.

Secondary notations are best supported in UML activity diagrams, which allow the specification of comments inside diagrams as well as organization of the diagram in a way that is logical to the user. This freedom is partially reached through the usage of *connectors* which allow object and control flows to be visually interrupted and continued in another place of the diagram. Furthermore size and position can be used to convey information if desired. This latter freedom also exists to a limited degree in the proposed notation, while the Collaborative ConcurTaskTrees notation has no support for secondary notations.

The last properties are *visibility and juxtaposability* of which the latter is totally dependent on the offered tool support and will be left out of this discussion. Visibility within the notation was a major concern in the design of the proposed notation, which is reflected in the explicit representation of the information that is considered to be important int he modeled applications. This is one of the reasons that things like user interface components as well as their relation to the involved roles are represented explicitly in the proposed notation in contrast to the other discussed notations. It is our firm believe that the increase in visibility gained through the explicit representation of such information outweighs the increase in viscosity and abstraction barrier which are the consequence of the extra abstractions that are involved.

We can conclude that our proposed notation has better results regarding visibility for our purposes and has less hidden dependencies compared to the other discussed notations. These advantages however come at the price of a slight increase in viscosity and abstraction barrier. In the other areas, the proposed language does not score significantly better or worse than the other discussed notations disregarding the increase in expressiveness of a single diagram.

Other related work. Multi-user interactive applications are heavily researched when these applications offer support for collaborative work. Which also involve many technical issues like synchronization, locking, floor control, etc. Boyle and Greenbergh [1] support the design of multimedia groupware by providing a toolkit that allows to quickly prototype multimedia groupware applications. By not taking into account scalability issues and providing high-level access to often used features of multimedia groupware, they can create functional prototypes of such applications with a few lines of code.

Our work is more related to the design of the interactivity of the distributed multimedia application. van der Veer and van Welie [11] provide an overview of more task-based notations and whether they support some features necessary for their goal; the analysis, design and evaluation of groupware. They concluded that no single notation was satisfactory and proposed a process, DUTCH, that uses multiple notations integrated through a shared ontology.

DialogSketch [6] uses extensions of the UML metamodel to define a task model and a presentation model. The task models are expressed using a combination of the ConcurTaskTrees notation [5] and the UML activity diagram resulting in a tree-based notation. The presentation model is expressed using a UML version of the Canonical Abstract Prototypes [2]. They focus on the definition of single user applications.

5 Conclusion

We introduced a new interaction model for the specification of multi-user interactive multimedia applications with a focuss on user interaction and server-side behavior. The discussed model builds on the foundations provided by UML and Canonical Abstract Prototypes and extends and combines these in order to provide a compact description of a multi-user interaction system, which we evaluated using the Cognitive Dimensions framework [4]. The discussed notation is part of SpIeLan, a language to describe staged participatory multimedia events (SPME). Such events a special kind of interactive television shows with a high degree of participation of the television "viewers". The language has been used to describe a limited set of SPME and is supported by a tool.

Automated generation of both mid-fidelity and high-fidelity prototypes from these models is planned for the near future. Better tool support that helps to reduce some weaknesses identified in the cognitive evaluation is another path for future development which will be accompagnied with user testing.

Acknowledgements. This research was performed within the IWT project Participate of Alcatel Bell. Part of the research at the Expertise Centre for Digital Media is funded by the ERDF (European Regional Development Fund), the Flemish Government and the Flemish Interdisciplinary institute for Broadband Technology (IBBT). Special thanks goes to Steven Huypens for the feedback and discussion of the ideas presented in this paper.

References

1. Michael Boyle and Saul Greenberg. Rapidly prototyping multimedia groupware. In *Proceedings of the 11th International Conference on Distributed Multimedia Systems (DMS'05)*, IL, USA, September 2005.
2. Larry L. Constantine. Canonical abstract prototypes for abstract visual and interaction design. In *Proceedings of DSV-IS 2003*, number 2844 in LNCS, pages 1–15, Funchal, Madeira Island, Portugal, June 11-13 2003. Springer.
3. Thomas Green and Alan Blackwell. *Cognitive Dimensions of Information Artifacts: a Tutorial*, 1.2 edition, October 1998.
4. Thomas R. G. Green and Marian Petre. Usability analysis of visual programming environments: A 'cognitive dimensions' framework. *Journal of Visual Languages and Computing*, 7(2), 131–174 1996.

5. Giulio Mori, Fabio Paternò, and Carmen Santoro. CTTE: support for developing and analyzing task models for interactive system design. *IEEE Transactions on Software Engineering*, 28(8):797–813, 2002.
6. Leonel Nóbrega, Nuno Jardim Nunes, and Helder Coelho. Dialogsketch: dynamics of the canonical prototypes. In Marcin Sikorski, editor, *TAMODIA*, pages 19–25. ACM, 2005.
7. Nuno Jardim Nunes. *Object Modeling for User-Centered Development and User Interface Design: The Wisdom Approach.* PhD thesis, Univ. da Madeira, 2001.
8. Object Management Group. *UML 2.0 Superstructure Specification*, October 8 2004.
9. Jan Van den Bergh and Karin Coninx. Cup 2.0: High-level modeling of context-sensitive interactive applications. In *Proceedings of MoDELS 2006*, number 4199 in LNCS, pages 140–154, Genova, Italy, October 2006. Springer.
10. Jan Van den Bergh, Steven Huypens, and Karin Coninx. Towards Model-Driven Development of Staged Participatory Multimedia Events. In *Proceedings of DSV-IS 2006*, LNCS, Dublin, Ireland, July 2006. Springer. To be published.
11. Gerrit van der Veer and Martijn van Welie. Task based groupware design: Putting theory into practice. In *Proceedings of the conference on Designing interactive systems: processes, practices, methods, and techniques*, pages 326 – 337, New York City, New York, USA, 2000. ACM Press.

Goals: Interactive Multimedia Documents Modeling

Pedro Valente and Paulo N.M. Sampaio

University of Madeira (UMa), Distributed Systems and Networks Lab. (Lab-SDR),
Campus da Penteada 9000-390
+351 291 705 {024, 291}
{pvalente, psampaio}@uma.pt

Abstract. Multimedia has been largely applied to develop attractive and functional applications that allow achieving useful user-tasks. These sophisticated applications are usually developed using bottom-up approaches regardless of the complexity of the implementation. Furthermore, the design of complex Interactive Multimedia Documents (IMDs) introduces an additional complexity; the authoring of these applications can be an error-prone task considering the increasing number of media objects participating in these documents and the synchronization among them. For this reason, the authoring of IMDs should be supported by a structured methodology based on an intuitive abstraction that facilitates the design of complex IMDs. This paper presents *Goals* a top-down use-case driven, architectural-centric, UML based methodology that allows for the intuitive authoring of complex IMDs through the structured modeling of the presentations aspects, content and the complete behavior of these documents.

Keywords: Interactive Multimedia Documents, Software Engineering, UML, Modeling, Multimedia Authoring, Goals.

1 Introduction

The area of document engineering describes in general all the aspects of the conception and presentation of Interactive Multimedia Documents (IMDs). The IMDs have been widely used in several domains, such as: medicine, education, entertainment, government, etc. The IMDs describe the simultaneous presentation of different types of media objects (audio, video, text, etc.) which can be integrated in some form supporting different types of user-interactions (navigation, selection, etc.) as well.

Therefore, during the design of these documents some aspects must be considered such as the types of media objects to be used, the logical and temporal synchronization among these objects, the application domain, and even the network infrastructure that will be used to support the multimedia communication.

This paper presents *Goals* (Goal-Oriented Approach led Software), a methodology to guide the authoring of complex IMDs from the user requirements definition to the design of these documents. For this purpose, *Goals* provides the complete modeling of the different levels of a multimedia document (e.g. content, presentation, behavior and user interactions) assuring the traceability from use cases to code generation.

K. Coninx, K. Luyten, and K.A. Schneider (Eds.): TAMODIA 2006, LNCS 4385, pp. 169–185, 2007.

There are some UML-based methodologies for IMD modeling in the literature [11], [1], [5]. In most cases, the UML (as well as non UML-based methodologies) is applied to solve some specific multimedia problems, such as user interaction and synchronization. However, these efforts fail to guide the user (modeler) to model simple and usable software, inducing him to develop complex models that combine different relevant multimedia information which are difficult to use and maintain. Furthermore, traceability is not an explicit concern in most of the works. *Goals* overcomes most of the limitations of existing methodologies, as presented along this paper, for the design of complex educational IMDs.

This paper is organized as follows: Section 2 introduces the main levels for the modeling of complex IMDs. Section 3 presents a simple IMD which is used throughout the paper to illustrate *Goals*. Section 4 identifies the modeling techniques that are the basis of *Goals*. Section 5 enumerates and exemplifies the steps of *Goals* and section 6 presents some conclusions of this work.

2 Modeling Interactive Multimedia Documents

In order to propose an approach for the modeling of IMDs, it is indeed important to understand how these documents can be structured. Thus, an IMD can be described according to a multi-level structure [10]: (i) *Content level*, which describes the information itself associated with each component of the document; (ii) *Presentation level*, which describes how and where each component of the document will be presented, and; (iii) *Conceptual level*, which describes the behavior of the IMD associated with the temporal and logical relations among the components of the document.

Besides, an authoring model should also consider the possible user interaction methods. Thus, the model should also describe anchors and links for hypermedia navigation and other methods such as selection and data input. These structures are briefly discussed in the following sections.

2.1 Content Level

The *Content level* defines the information associated with each component of the IMD. Basically, the *Content level* describes the primitive data (media data) related to each media object of the IMD. In this level, the information about access (URL), manipulation of primitive data and metadata shall be declared.

2.2 Presentation Level

The *Presentation level* defines the spatial, temporal and sound characteristics for each component of the IMD. Thus, this level is composed by:

- The *spatial characteristics* of each visible component, such as the size, spatial position (absolute or relative to a virtual coordinates system) and presentation style;
- The *temporal characteristics* for the presentation of each dynamic component, such as the presentation speed, the initial and final position of presentation, and the number of possible repetitions;

- The characteristics related to *sound* are useful to define, for instance, the initial volume for the presentation of an audio sequence.

2.3 Conceptual Level

The *Conceptual level* is responsible for describing the components of a document and their logical and temporal relations:

- The *components* of a document are related to the description of the content of this document through a structure of modules with different semantics and granularity, for example: chapters, sections, sub-areas, etc.
- The *logical* structure of an IMD is related to the different possibilities a user has to navigate inside the document's structure. According to Ginige [6], three basic types of structures can be defined: linear, hierarchical and network. The choice of the most appropriate structure to an IMD depends upon the purpose of this document.
- The *temporal relations* are described based on events that can be produced during the presentation of an IMD. These events can be *synchronous* (when their occurrence can be predicted previously, such the start or end of presentation of an image), or *asynchronous* (when their occurrence can not be predicted, such as the occurrence of a user interaction). The temporal relations describe not only the parallel and/or sequential presentation among media objects, but also the causal relations among them. In particular, the *causal relations* describe the conditional dependencies among the events associated with the components of an IMD. For instance, if a user interaction occurs over media object *B*, it interrupts the presentation of object *C*.
- *User interaction* and subsequent system response is also defined at conceptual level. Thus, interactivity can be divided into the following categories: *navigation*, *presentation control*, *environment control* and *information input*.

3 An Interactive Multimedia Document

The methodology based on UML presented in this paper can be applied to support the design of complex IMDs, although, in order to illustrate the application of this methodology, a simple interactive multimedia scenario is applied and presented in Figure 1. This IMD describes the parallel presentation of an interactive image (*interactiveButton*) with the sequential composition of an exclusive presentation of two audio objects (*audio1* and *audio2*) followed by a video object (*video*). In this case, all the components of and exclusive presentation will be presented, although never simultaneously, following the semantics of this operator as described in [14].

The presentation duration of objects *audio1*, *audio2*, *video*, and *interactiveButton* are respectively [0,5][1] seconds, [0,5] seconds, indefinite[2] and [0,20] seconds and the following synchronization constraints are considered: (i) the presentation of the

[1] [x,y] – x represents the minimal duration and y represents the maximal duration (of the presentation).

[2] An indefinite duration characterizes the presentation of an object inside the interval $[0,+\infty]$.

exclusive composition of *audio1* and *audio2*, and *interactiveButton* must start simultaneously, (ii) the presentation of *video* and *interactiveButton* must end simultaneously, (iii) clicking *interactiveButton* or double-clicking *video* interrupts both *interactiveButton* and *video*, and (iv) the presentation of *video* can only be interrupted by the occurrence of a user interaction. The main issues related to the design of IMDs using *Goals* are addressed in the sequel, illustrated using the previous scenario.

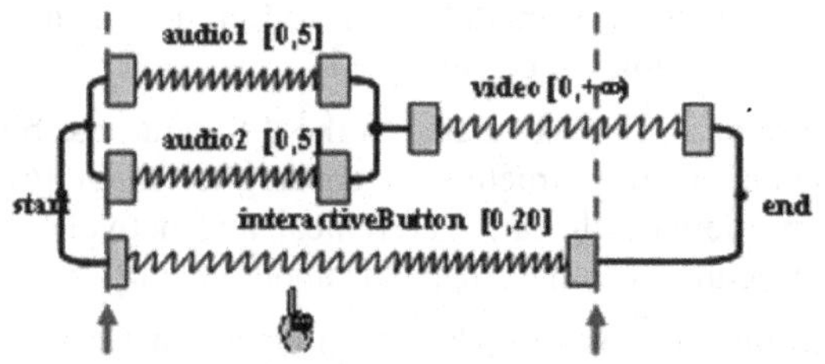

Fig. 1. Illustration of an interactive multimedia scenario

4 Goals Basis

The methodology proposed within *Goals* for the modeling of IMDs is based on different techniques. Indeed, as presented in section 2, different abstractions are needed to represent the main structures (levels) of these documents.

The main techniques applied by *Goals* are UML [9], *Wisdom* [8], *Usage-Centered Design* [2] (*Essential Use Cases* [3] and CAPs [4]) and *Concur Task Trees* [13]. UML provides the basic notation of the methodology, *Wisdom* provides the main software engineering process, *Usage-Centered Design* provides specific techniques for requirements definition and user interface design, while *Concur Task Trees* provide the technique for user-task modeling.

4.1 Goals Modeling Techniques

Before presenting the modeling of IMDs using *Goals*, it is important to consider the different techniques applied for this purpose.

4.1.1 UML

Unified Modeling Language (UML) [9] is an object-oriented (OO) modeling language for specifying, visualizing, constructing, and documenting the artifacts of software systems. UML, version 0.9, appeared in 1996, published by Grady Booch, Jim Rumbaugh, and Ivar Jacobson, and was an attempt to normalize the semantics and notation of other existing OO languages.

UML has become the standard modeling language in software industry and has been, from the late 90's, the reference to a number of other methodologies, notations and techniques that restrict UML's models and/or extend the existing notation. In particular, RUP [7], the *Rational Unified Process*, developed initially by the Rational

Corporation, is the software development process that explains how to apply UML. RUP is considered a heavyweight; today, the use of lightweight methodologies (UML based or not) is generalized in the software engineering industry, contributing with precise techniques to solve specific problems related to e.g. requirements definition, human-computer interaction or user interface design. Some examples are *Wisdom* [8], *Usage-Centered Design* [2], and *ConcurTaskTrees* (CTT) [13].

4.1.2 Wisdom

Wisdom was proposed as a solution to bridge usability engineering and software engineering, and, as a way to apply software engineering in Small Software Development Companies [8]. *Wisdom* is an evolutionary, prototyping, UML-based method. The *Wisdom* method provides a tool to rapidly achieve a stage of implementation based on a few and easy to understand sequence of diagrams, effectively reducing the great quantity of models provided by UML and RUP, focusing on the essentials of the system being developed. The main diagrams proposed within *Wisdom* are illustrated in the Figure 2.

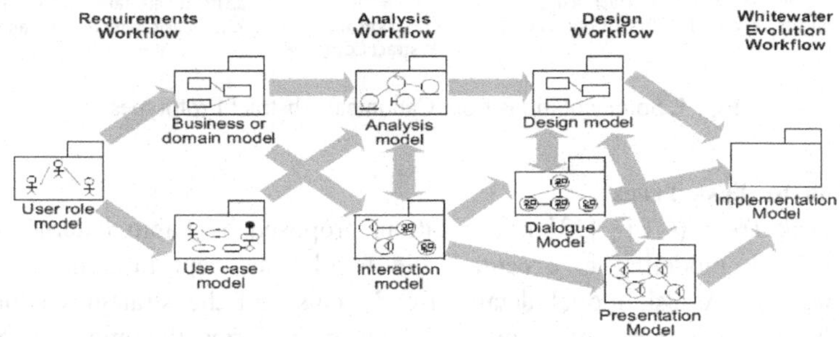

Fig. 2. Wisdom Architecture

4.1.3 Essential Use Cases

Usage-Centered Design (UCD) [2] is an object-oriented based approach for interactive system design that firstly applied the already existing *essential use cases* [3]. *Essential use cases* are an evolution of concrete use cases, which (concrete use cases) are usually used in a large variety of scope, detail, focus, format, structure, style, and content by both software engineers and Interface Designers, that results in imprecision in the definition of the requirement.

By definition, an *essential use-case* is a simplified, abstract, generalized use-case defined in terms of *user intentions* and *system responsibilities* [3], its independent from technology and focuses in what the user really needs to accomplish. Constantine's *essential use-cases* provide a way to connect the design of the user interface back to the essential purpose of the system and the work it supports, contributing to close a gap between software engineering and interface design [8]. An illustration of the application of essential use-cases is depicted in Figure 3.

user intentions	**system responsibilities**
identify self as customer	
select help option	present help options
describe problem	request description
	offer possible solutions

Fig. 3. Example of the application of an Essential Use Case

4.1.4 Canonical Abstract Prototypes

Canonical Abstract Prototypes (CAPs) [4] are part of the Usage-Centered Design [2]. CAPs allow for the modeling of a complete set of user interactions that can occur in the components of the user interface. The use of CAPs can largely contribute for the better and faster understanding of the functionality of the user interface, especially if a software development team exists. Some of the most commonly used CAPs notations are depicted in Figure 4.

(a) (b) (c)
(a) generic abstract tool,
(b) generic abstract material,
(c) generic abstract active material.
Basic symbols for Canonical Abstract Components

(a) (b) (c)
(a) abstract collection container
(b) abstract selection
(c) abstract selectable collection material
Extension and elaboration of basic symbols for Canonical Abstract Components

Fig. 4. Some notations from Canonical Abstract Prototypes

4.1.5 Concur Task Trees

Concur Task Trees (CTT) [13] is a notation, proposed by Fabio Paternò for task modeling. Task modeling is a central and familiar concept in human-computer interaction [12]. A task model details users' goals and the strategies adopted to achieve those goals in terms of actions that the users performs, the objects involved in those actions and the underlying sequencing of activities.

The CTTs are based in a graphical notation that supports the hierarchical structure of tasks, which can be interrelated through a powerful set of operators that describes the temporal relationships between subtasks. CTTs were adapted to fit *Goals* modeling, combining the tasks identified (using the Task and Audio Task stereotypes, see Figure 6) with the system behavior (the system response, Controls, see Figure 6) in the same diagram.

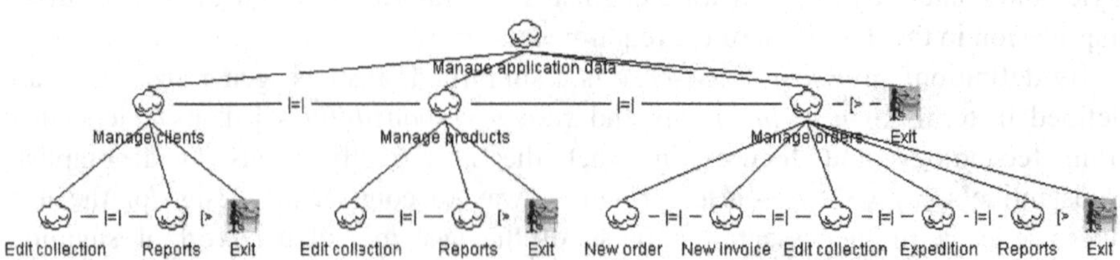

Fig. 5. Example of the application of the Concur Task Trees

5 Illustrating the Methodology

This section introduces the steps for the modeling of IMDs based on *Goals*. For this reason, it is important to identify the modeling technique adopted for each step, and the associated IMD design level, according to the IMDs design architecture presented in section 2 for the description of the *content*, *presentation* and *conceptual* (including user interactions) levels, and the suggested modeler which can all be the same person as usually occurs. Thus, consider Table 1 which points out each step of *Goals*.

Table 1. Steps of Goals methodology

Step	Modeling Technique	IMD Level	Modeler
1*	Use Case	Requirements	Analyst Architect
2*	Activity Diagram + Interaction Spaces	Requirements	Analyst
3	Interaction Model	User Interaction	Analyst
4	Navigational Model	Presentation	Analyst IMD Author
5*	Presentation + Interaction	Presentation + User Interaction	IMD Author
6	MM[3] Domain Model	Presentation + Content	Analyst
7	MM Object Model	Presentation + Content	IMD Author
8	Presentation + MM Object Model	Presentation + Content	IMD Author
9	Conceptual Model	Conceptual	IMD Author
10	Temporal Model	Conceptual	IMD Author
11	MM Architecture	Conceptual	Architect

* is considered an essential Step.

In the table, steps 1, 2 and 5 are highlighted as essential steps (*), once, with these 3 steps it's possible to achieve acceptable IMD definition for simple cases, once, the tools used in these models are accurate enough for this purpose.

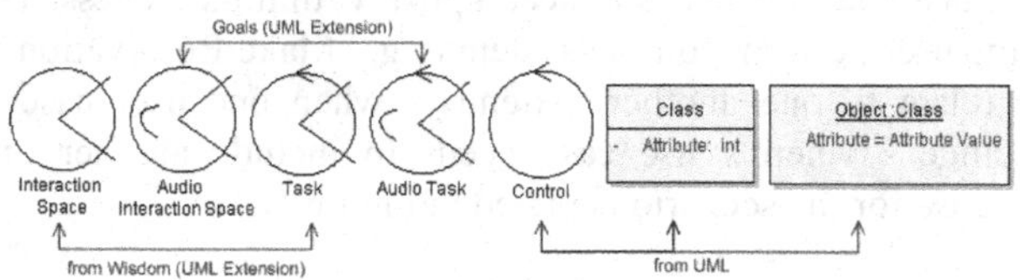

Fig. 6. Main notations of Goals

[3] MM – Multimedia.

Figure 6 depicts the main notations used throughout the steps of *Goals*. An *interaction space* (audio or not) represents a *user interface* in which is possible to exist or not a user interaction, a *task* is an action that the user makes over the *user interface*, a *control* is a component (code) of the system that implements some functionality, and, *class* and *object* represent data (of the system), being an object an instantiation of a class (see [9] for more information on instantiation).

5.1 Step 1 – Use Cases

A *use case* identifies a part of the application that will solve some specific problem, and which will result in a part of the software that represents a useful and complete user *task*. This should be enough to understand the scope of the implementation within the application being built, but in order to complete the understanding of the usage, the *use case* should be complemented with other (optional) information relevant to the IMD author(s): (i) the *High Level Concept* defines in one sentence what the complete IMD (or application) should do (not only this use case); (ii) *Process Identification* defines in which situation this *use case* will take place; (iii) *User Characterization*, that identifies user characteristics that may influence the application being built; (iv) the *Environment Description* (optional) may also influence the overall result; lightning conditions or noise influence may be relevant.

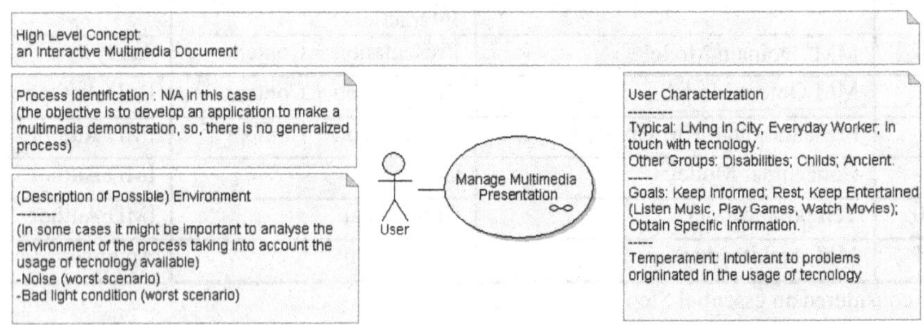

Fig. 7. Step 1 – Use Case and complementary information

In order to specify the *use case*, it's necessary to identify the *user*(s). The *user* represents a single person or a group of *users* that want to achieve the same goal, and more than one group of *users* can use the same *use case*. The *use case* is named according to the task the *user* needs to accomplish within its process. The *use case* is an action that the user performs on the system (e.g. "Make Reservation"). Notice that *use cases* can relate to one another (extends - when one user case complements another, or include - when a use case needs to include another one). Figure 7 illustrates a *use case* for the scenario depicted in Figure 1.

5.2 Step 2 – Activity Diagram + Interaction Spaces Identification

The *activity diagram* details the *tasks* that both *user* and *system* need to accomplish in order to complete successfully the (*essential*) *use case* [2]. This diagram is separated into *user intentions* and *system responsibilities*. *User Intentions* are *tasks* that the *user* wants to accomplish on the system, which at this stage can be or not by means of interactions, being most times a high level *task* representing what the user is doing at this step in order to complete his *task* (e.g. "Reserve Room"). Contrarily, *System responsibilities* are the response of the system to the *task* accomplished by the *user* (e.g. "Confirm Room Reservation").

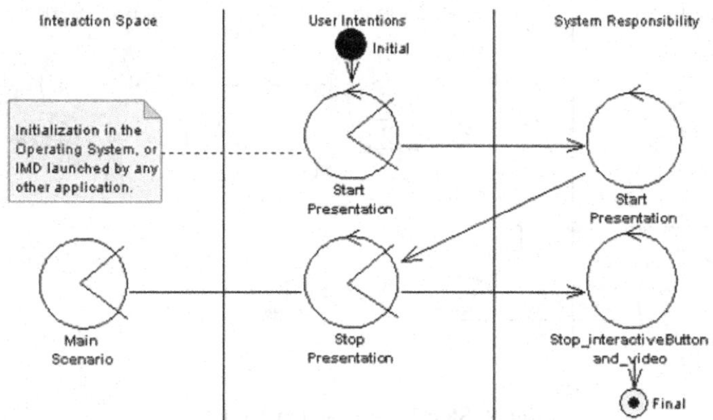

Fig. 8. Step 2 – Activity Diagram

The *activity diagram* can begin in either side, system or user. Usually, in common cases, 3 to 6 *tasks* are enough so that *user* is able to accomplish what he needs. Of course, the number of *tasks* depends on the complexity of the overall *use case* purpose. In general, more than one *user task* and more than one *system responsibility* can be executed in sequence.

For instance, consider the *activity diagram* associated with the previous IMD which is depicted in Figure 8. In this diagram, the *user intentions* initially describe the start of the IMD presentation, which is immediately accomplished by the system (*System Responsibility*). During the presentation, the user can interact any time to stop the presentation (by clicking *InteractiveButton* or double-clicking *video*, as presented in Step 3).After the *activity diagram* is completed, the user interfaces (*interaction spaces*) in which the *tasks* will be performed must be described.

5.3 Step 3 – Interaction Model

The *interaction model* details (decomposes) *tasks* into *sub-tasks*, and, the corresponding *system responsibilities* into *sub-system responsibilities*. The higher level description of an interaction model diagram is a combination *task-system responsibility* from the activity diagram presented in step 2. Thus, a *task* from the activity diagram is decomposed by means of *concur task trees* (CTT [13]) up to the description of an interaction within the *user* interface. Similarly, corresponding *system responsibilities* (which are controls or system functions) are decomposed (if needed) into lower level controls, which are executed whenever that *user task* takes place.

An operator must be specified among the sub-*tasks* in order to determine their order. These operators can be: *Choice* (T1 [] T2); *Independent concurrency* (T1 ||| T2); *Disabling* (T1 [> T2); *Enabling* (T1 > T2); *Suspend/Resume* (T1 |> T2); *Order independent* (T1 |=| T2). For further information on the operators see [13].

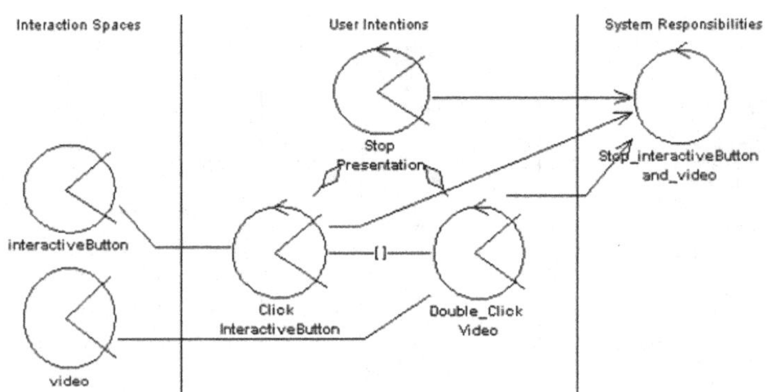

Fig. 9. Step 3 – Interaction Model

This decomposition should be made until reaching specific interaction with the system (e.g. "confirm reservation", which means clicking a button) or, until it is clear to the modeler that the author of the IMD will fully understand the rest of the process that will achieve the *user's* objective. Then, such as in the *activity diagram*, it is necessary to identify in which *user* interfaces (*sub-interaction spaces* in this diagram) the *tasks* will be performed.

For instance, Figure 9 illustrates the *Interaction Model* for the previous IMD. According to this figure, the combination "Stop Presentation"- "Stop Interactive Button and video" are placed at top of the diagram. In particular, the *user intention* "Stop Presentation" is decomposed until reaching interface interaction ("Click Interactive Button" or "Double Click Video"), and, when any of this interactions exist, the function "Stop Interactive Button and video" (*system responsibility*) will be executed. In this case, this function does not need to be decomposed.

5.4 Step 4 – Navigational Model

Briefly, the navigational model provides the modeling of the different possibilities of navigation among the scenarios of an IMD. The IMD presented in this paper is very simple, for this reason the navigation model is the same as the one presented in Step 5 – Canonical Abstract Prototypes + Interaction (only the *interaction space* classes). The association "navigation" (not used in this toy example) can be applied between two *interaction spaces* meaning that the target *interaction space* will replace the initial *interaction space*.

5.5 Step 5 – Presentation (Canonical Abstract Prototypes) + Interaction

The *presentation* is the visual construction (design) of the user interface. It is based on the *interaction spaces* identified in the *navigational model* (step 4), and the visual aspect of each area is modeled using *Canonical Abstract Prototypes* (CAPs [4]). CAPs allow the modeling of a complete set of user interactions that can occur in the components of the user interface. For instance, for the selection of a room, a list must be displayed; the appropriate CAP must be used to specify this situation. CAPs are applied to detail all the *interaction spaces* of an IMD.

The *interaction spaces* identified in the previous steps can be associated with *regions* (which describe spatial coordinates for the presentation of interactive and non-interactive media). Furthermore, the description of all the user interaction identified in the *interaction diagram* (step 3) can be associated with the respective *interaction space* where it occurs.

For instance, consider Figure 12 (left side only) which describes the *CAP + Interaction model* for the previous IMD. In the description of this picture "Main Scenario" represents the complete user interface, and is decomposed into *sub-interaction spaces*: "main window" (that has no interaction associated); "video" (inside which will be presented a video stream); "interactiveButton"; and "Audio Exclusive" (through which will be presented two audio streams). Note that since "Audio Exclusive" describes an audio channel, it is also considered as an *interaction space*, and it is represented using a different stereotype: the *audio interaction space.* Furthermore, the "Click Interactive Button" and "Double Click Video" tasks re associated with their corresponding *interaction spaces*. Complementarily, CAPs are used to specify that "interactiveButton" and "video" generate a *stop/end/complete* action and that "video" is a *container* (see [4] for the description of CAPs tools and materials).

5.6 Step 6 – Multimedia Domain Model

The *multimedia domain model* describes the information concerning the content of each media composing the IMD and each visual region for the presentation of these media.

The description of the regions and media content is described, as follows:

- The *regions domain model* specifies the attributes of each *region* for the presentation of a media. Thus, the *interaction spaces* identified in the *presentation* (step 5) are transformed into generic UML classes. The representation can also be made using the *interaction space* stereotypes. For this purpose, the necessary attributes for each *region/interaction space* were defined, and a pattern was proposed for each kind of *region* (audio, video, image, etc.) with their appropriate attributes.

- The *Media Domain Model* defines which media will be presented on the IMD. For this purpose, a pattern was proposed as well for each kind of media (audio, video, text, etc.).

It is important to emphasize that in order to cover all the features for the design of IMDs, the attributes for the definition of the *regions domain model* and *media domain model* were based on the description of these components from the language SMIL

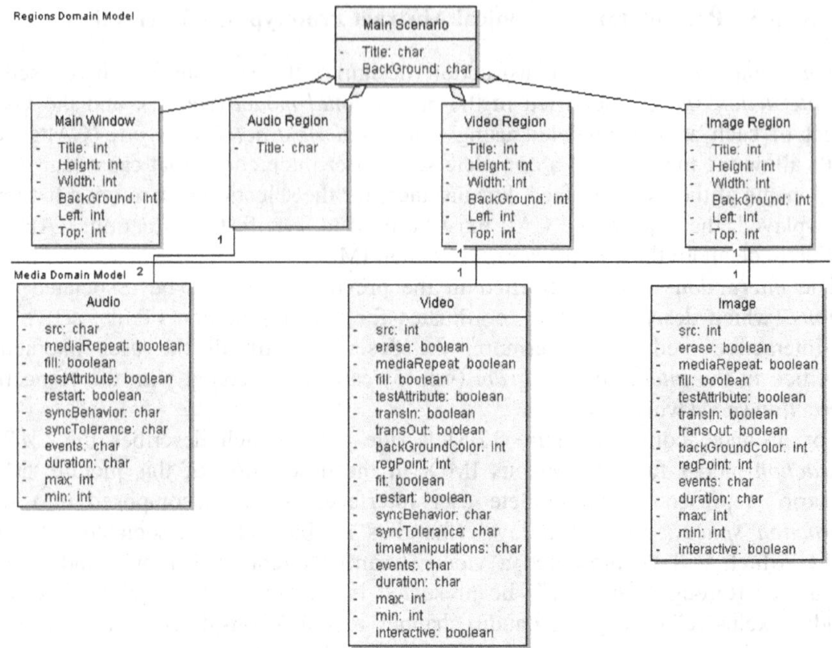

Fig. 10. Step 6 – Multimedia Domain Model

[14]. Notice that in this model "Audio Region" has two audio sequences associated, and that, contrarily, "Video Region" and "Image Region" will only present a video and an image respectively.

5.7 Step 7 – Multimedia Object Model

The *object model* describes the instantiation of the class diagrams (*multimedia domain model*) associated with each region and media of the IMD as illustrated in Figure 11.

During the definition of the *object model*, if there are more than 1 media to be presented in a unique region, this media has to be instantiated several times

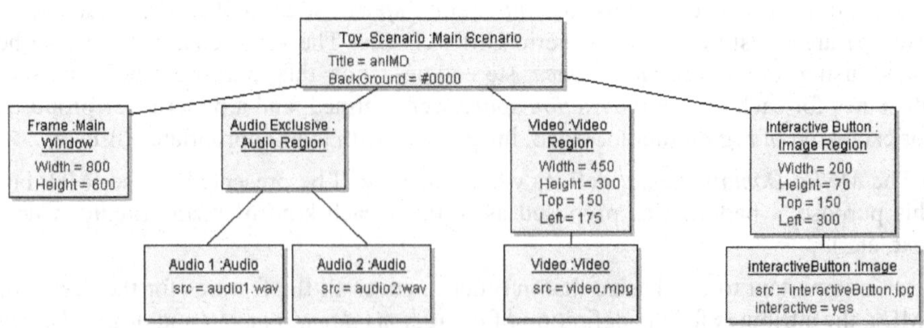

Fig. 11. Step 7 – Object Model

(according to the number of media). The definition of each instantiation considers the description of each appropriate attribute for each media and/or region.

5.8 Step 8 – Presentation + Object Model

This step of the methodology aims at associating the visual design of the interface (step 5) with the *multimedia object model* (step 7). For this purpose, each region of the interface is associated with a respective region class described by the *object model* (step 7). Similarly, for each identified region, the instantiation of one or more media (from the *object model*) is associated with this region.

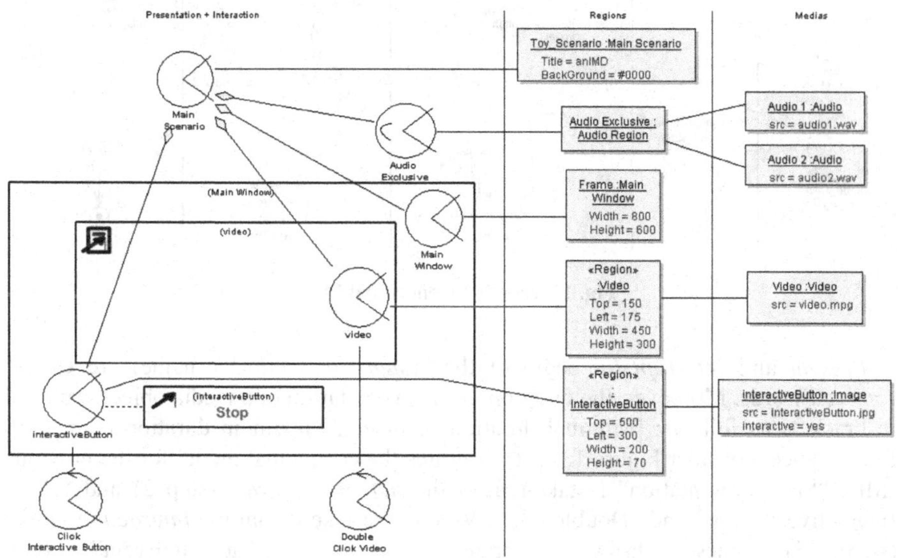

Fig. 12. Step 8 – Presentation + Object Model

5.9 Step 9 – Conceptual Model

Conceptual model details each *system responsibility* identified in the *interaction model* (step 3) with an activity diagram. For this purpose, all the *tasks* that are *user interactions* are placed on the left of the diagram (see Figure 13), and each *system responsibility* is detailed in a sequence of new *sub-systems responsibilities* using an activity diagram.These diagrams can be described as: (i) *sequence* (one *system responsibility* after another), (ii) *parallel* (two or more *system responsibilities* are executed at the same time) or (iii) *exclusive* (all the system responsibilities are executed but never simultaneously [14]).

Furthermore, *causal relations* among media objects can also be described. These *relations* assume that a media object presentation can be initiated or interrupted whenever an appropriate event takes place (e.g., start of a media object or a user interaction). Thus, the start or interruption of a media presentation can be associated with a *system responsibility*, and the causal relation between two system responsibilities can be described by the definition of an *event* at the beginning of the *relation*, and by the action (*Present* or *Interrupt*) that must be executed at the end of the relation.

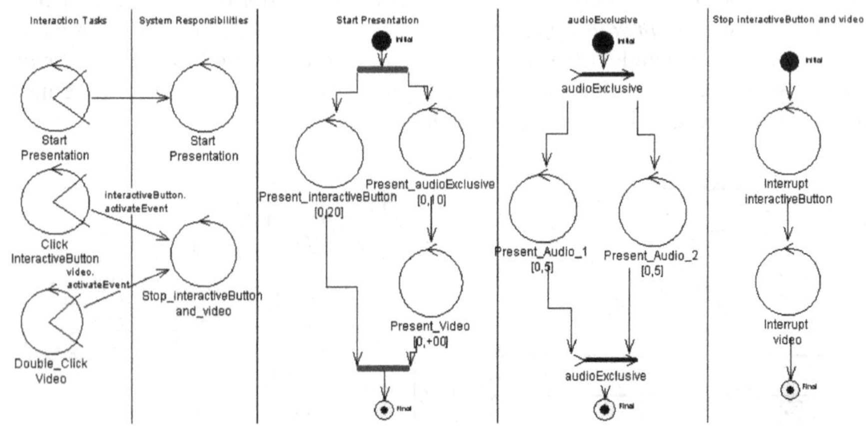

Fig. 13. Step 9 – Conceptual Model

Present and *Interrupt* (at begin of the *system responsibility* name) are *Goals*' reserved words. Moreover, the duration of the presentation of a media object is placed in brackets as follows: [Minimal duration of media, Maximum duration of media]. For instance, consider Figure 13 that illustrates the conceptual model for the previous IMD. "Start Presentation" is taken from the *activity diagram* (step 2) and "Click Interactive Button" and "Double Click Video" are taken from the *interaction model* (step 3), these tasks generate the *event* "activateEvent" (e.g. interactiveButoon.endEvent) (considering SMIL [14]), which leads to the *Interruption* of "interactiveButton" and "video" characterizing a *causal relation*.

Both "Start Presentation" and "Stop InteractiveButton and Video" are detailed until reaching all *Present* and *Interrupt* functions for each media object of the IMD. Notice that in the "audioExclusive" activity diagram a different stereotype is used instead of the regular UML fork (like in "Start Presentation").This is the fork used in *Goals* to specify an *exclusive presentation*.

Moreover, notice that using a CASE tool it's possible to represent a composite element which can be further detailed within other (sub-)activity diagrams. This is an important potentiality of *Goals*, since it eliminates scalability problems. An alternative view of the (logical/temporal) behavior of the system is the *temporal model* (step 10).

5.10 Step 10 – Temporal Model

The *temporal model* is a graphic (timeline) description of the *media* presentation in time which also describes the *causal relations*, based on *user interaction* or not. This timeline is described into three different parts: (i) the first one (on the left upper side of the graphic) describes the *presentation* of all the media objects identified in the conceptual model (step 9); (ii) the second one (on the right upper side of the graphic) describes the *presentation behavior* of the media objects of the IMD in time. For this purpose, this presentation must describe the parallel, sequence and exclusive presentation of all the media objects of the IMD with their respective presentation duration. Furthermore, the *causal relations* among the media objects can also be described in this part of the graphic; (iii) the third part of the graphic (on the down side of the graphic) describes the possible occurrence of *user interactions* associated with a media object described in the second part of the timeline.

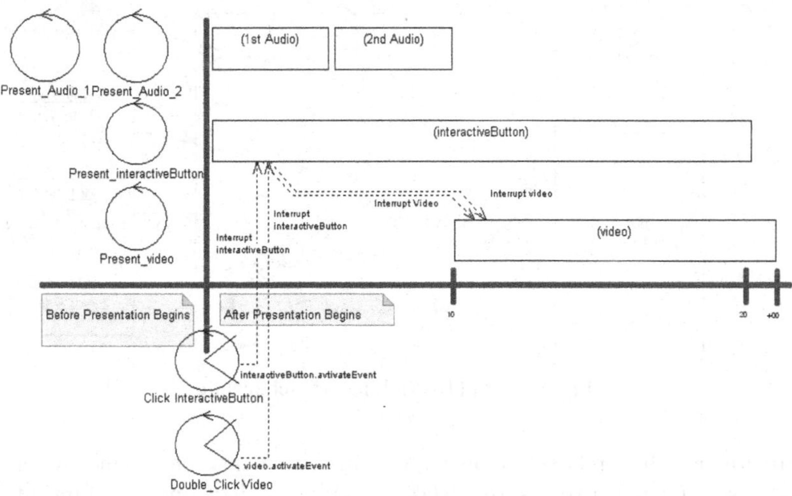

Fig. 14. Step 10 – Temporal Model

Moreover, it might be important to also describe on this graphic the *system responsibilities* (not originated from user interaction) and their impact on the *presentation* of the *media objects. Tasks* and *system responsibilities* that influence the medias presentation are placed along the time line from the first moment that they can occur. Consider Figure 14 which depicts the *temporal model.* It's possible to identify each *Present* and *Interrupt* functions that influence the presentation of elements.

The *causal relation* generated from the "Click Interactive Button" can be described from: "Click Interactive Button" -> "Stop Interactive Button and Video" -> "Interrupt interactiveButton"-> "Interrupt Video" identified in the *conceptual model* (step 9), from where the causal relations "Interrupt InteractiveButton" and "Interrupt video" were derived. A similar situation happens for "Double Click Video" and is also represented in the diagram.

5.11 Step 11 – Multimedia Architecture

The *Multimedia architecture* is the representation of all relevant *components* of the *system* and their *relations*. The structure of these *components* (which are relevant for the implementation) is organized from left to right (see Figure 15). These components are: *interaction spaces, tasks, system responsibilities* and *medias*.

An *architecture* of the system is essential to evaluate the system size (and complexity) and to control the system implementation, once, it is possible to identify the precedence of implementation between *components*, e.g. in order to be able to implement the *control* "Start Presentation" the controls for the presentation of "video", "interactiveButton" and "audioExclusive" must already be available.

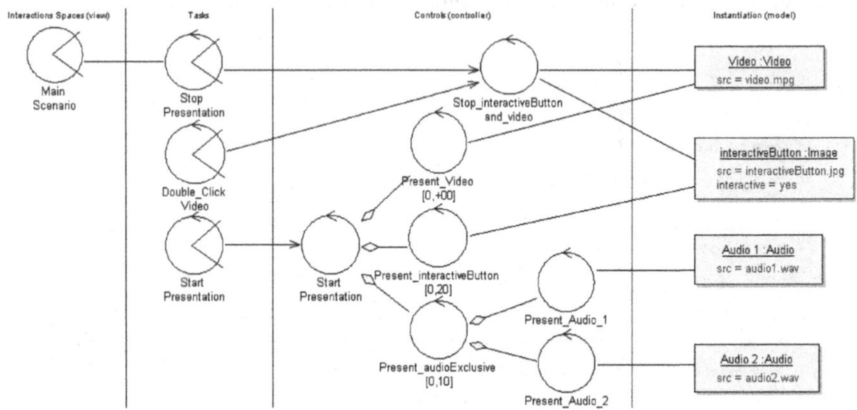

Fig. 15. Step 11 – Multimedia architecture

Furthermore, the architecture is an overall documentation of the system that encourages dialogue between system stakeholders (e.g. client and development team) in order to reach negotiation over, for instance, the implementation project or system maintenance for the introduction of new requirements.

Despite the proposal of 11 steps for the design of Interactive Multimedia Documents, these steps support completely the design of complex IMD, and, once each step focus on an isolated part of the construction some steps can be omitted to make the process more agile.

6 Conclusions

This work presents *Goals*, a methodology that aims to bridge software engineering and multimedia authoring. *Goals* is a lightweight, use case-driven, architectural centric methodology that guides the software conceptualization by means of the simplification of the system design concerning usability and maintainability.

The use of *Goals* induces the author of an IMD into a straight lined (few iterations are suggested) and fast software definition process towards implementation. The models of the methodology are intended to be simple, intuitive and scalable.

A simple example is used to illustrate how the methodology can be applied, however, *Goals* can be used to develop complex IMDs and can be easily complemented with Wisdom [8] to model complex software engineering applications that also support multimedia.

As for future works, the methodology shall consider the modeling of user aspects such as Quality of Experience (QoE) and Quality of Service (QoS) requirements which will be included in a tool to support multimedia authoring with Goals with automated IMD generation using SMIL [14]. In the meanwhile, Goals can be applied using any UML 2.0 [9] compliant CASE tool. In this work, special attention will be taken to usability, regarding the integration of both system and media information in order to achieve self-explained applications.

References

1. Bari, M., Martin, C.: Modeling interactive multimedia presentations. In proceedings of m-ICTE 2005 June 7-10th (2005).
2. Constantine., L.: Usage-Centered Engineering for Web Applications. IEEE Software, vol. 19, no. 2, Mar/Apr (2002) p. 4.
3. Constantine, L., Lockwood, L.: Structure and Style in Use Cases for User Interface Design. In Object Modeling and User Interface Design, (Addison-Wesley, 2001; ISBN: 0201657899). M. van Harmelen (ed.) (2001).
4. Constantine, L.: Canonical Abstract Prototypes for Abstract Visual and Interaction Design. In Proceedings of DSV - IS'2003 – 10th International Workshop on Design, Specification and Verification of Inter-active Systems, LNCS - Lecture Notes in Computer Science. Berlin: Springer-Verlag. Joaquim Jorge, Nuno Nunes, and João Falcão e Cunha (eds.) (2003)
5. Fuentes, L., Troya, J. M., Vallecillo, A.: Using UML profiles for documenting web-based application frameworks. Annals of Software Engineering (2002) 13:249-264
6. Ginige, A., Lowe, D.B., Robertson, J.: Hypermedia Authoring. IEEE Multimedia, Vol. 2, No. 4 (1995).
7. Kruchten, P.B.: The Rational Unified Process (An Introduction). Addison Wesley (1999)
8. Nunes, N.: Object Modeling for User-Centered Development and User Interface Design: The Wisdom Approach. PhD. Thesis, Universidade da Madeira (UMa), Funchal, Madeira (2000).
9. Object Management Group OMG: Unified modeling language superstructure, version 2.0. final adopted specification, OMG document ptc/2003-08-02, August (2003).
10. Sampaio, P.N.M.: A Methodology for MHEG-5 Implementation from E-LOTOS Specification. M.Sc. Thesis (in portuguese), Federal University of São Carlos (UFSCar), São Paulo, Brazil (1998).
11. Sauer, S., Engels, G.: UML-based Behavior Specification of Interactive Multimedia Applications. Proceedings of IEEE Int'l Symposium on Human-Centric Computing Languages and Environments (HCC); IEEE Computer Society, Stresa, Italy, 5--7 September (2001) 248--55.
12. Nóbrega, L., Nunes, N. D., Coelho, H.: Mapping ConcurTaskTrees into UML 2.0. Paper accepted in DSV-IS (2005).
13. Paternò, F., Mancini, C., Meniconi, S.: ConcurTaskTrees: A Diagrammatic Notation for Specifying Task Models. In Proceedings of INTERACT 1997, Sydney, Chapman & Hall (1997) 362-369.
14. W3C: Synchronized Multimedia Integrated Language (SMIL), URL: http://www.w3.org/AudioVideo/

Using Task Models for Cascading Selective Undo

Aaron G. Cass and Chris S.T. Fernandes

Union College, Schenectady, NY 12308 USA
{cassa, fernandc}@union.edu

Abstract. Many studies have shown that selective undo, a variant of the widely-implemented linear undo, has many advantages over the prevailing model. In this paper, we define a task model for implementing selective undo in the face of dependencies that may exist between the undone action and other subsequent user actions. Our model accounts for these dependencies by identifying other actions besides the undone one that should also be undone to keep the application in a stable state. Our approach, which we call *cascading selective undo*, is built upon a process-programming language originally designed in the software engineering community. The result is a formal analytical framework by which the semantics of selective undo can be represented separately from the application itself. We present our task model, the selective undo algorithm, and discuss extensions that account for differing kinds of inter-action dependencies.

1 Introduction

Most applications that support an undo command use a *linear undo* model. Under this model, only the most recent user action is retracted, and multiple consecutive executions of the undo command iterate backwards through the history list. In general, given user actions $A_1, ..., A_n$, issuing an undo command will only undo action A_n, and one cannot undo any action A_i without also undoing actions $A_{i+1}, ..., A_n$.

However, the *selective undo* model, introduced by Berlage [3] and studied more formally by Myers and Kosbie [7], has long been studied as an alternative to the linear model. In selective undo, a user can undo an arbitrary action A_i without undoing other actions. This has significant advantages over the linear model. First, collaborative environments necessitate the implementation of a non-linear model. If multiple users are editing the same shared document over a network simultaneously, then any particular user's most recent *local* action may not be the most recent *global* action in the system. Therefore, any undo implementation must be selective by nature.

Second, selective undo encourages a user's exploration of an application, especially when the application allows for tasks to be done in an arbitrary order. Consider a word processor user who wants to change a document from a current state $\mathcal{A}$ to another state $\mathcal{B}$, but is unsure of the exact steps she should take to accomplish this. It would be preferable for the user to be able to perform a series of tentative steps from $\mathcal{A}$ towards $\mathcal{B}$ all the while knowing that she could return to state $\mathcal{A}$ at any time via undo – even if other unrelated tasks, such as the changing of a word at the behest of the spell checker, were performed during the exploration process. Selectively undoing the tentative steps

K. Coninx, K. Luyten, and K.A. Schneider (Eds.): TAMODIA 2006, LNCS 4385, pp. 186–201, 2007.

without changing the results of the spell checking allows for greater flexibility than the linear model.

One of the biggest challenges in the implementation of selective undo, however, is in defining what should happen to subsequent user actions in the history list that are semantically dependent on the selectively undone item. Consider the following word processor commands:

1. Type "hello".
2. Italicize "hello".
3. Copy "hello".
4. Paste in position x.

Selectively undoing the second action could result in the removal of italics from either the original and the pasted text or just the original text, depending on how we define the pasted text's relationship to the original. Indeed, the repercussions of not dealing with dependencies can be more severe than just an unexpected change in formatting. In general, the selective undoing of a user action that creates an object A will result in ambiguity over how to interpret a subsequent user action in the history list that affects the value of some property of A. Dependencies such as these must be considered for a selective undo mechanism to handle complex tasks. In previous work, these dependencies are accounted for in limited ways, such as treating some tightly dependent user actions as null operations during undo [5] or disallowing the undo action if the result will not be meaningful [3]. We propose a different alternative – allowing an undone action to cause the undoing of other user actions until a meaningful state is reached (with appropriate user feedback and override controls). We believe this *cascading selective undo* offers more flexibility than previous approaches.

In this paper, we introduce a paradigm for cascading selective undo that explicitly models and tracks dependencies that exist between user actions. We model these dependencies using a process language originally designed for the software development community. We believe this to be a good match since software engineering is a domain in which dependencies between user tasks frequently occur, and thus provides fertile ground for determining appropriate undo semantics. In addition, tools already exist in the software engineering community for capturing dependencies in complex process or workflow models. Conversely, the tools which are used for software development can greatly benefit from a feature allowing selective undo.

Section 2 discusses related work in the area of selective undo. Section 3 explains our approach, detailing why we believe structure should be placed on user tasks, outlining motivating examples, and presenting our algorithm for cascading selective undo. Section 4 highlights future extensions to this approach, and Section 5 gives concluding remarks.

2 Related Work

The semantics as to how selective undo should work have not converged in the literature. Many implementations use the *script* paradigm [2], in which the result of undoing action A_i alone is equivalent to the result reached by executing user actions:

$$A_1, ..., A_{i-1}, A_{i+1}, ..., A_n$$

in that order. That is, if the list of user actions is viewed as a script, undoing one action is equivalent to removing that action from the script, with no other changes. This can result in side effects the user may or may not have intended, such as the changing of the pasted text's formatting in the example above. On the other hand, selective undo as discussed in the GINA system [3] simply restores the values of an undone item's properties to what they were immediately before the original execution of the user action. For our example above, this results in the removal of italics from just the original text. This ambiguity in the definition of selective undo points to the disparity between the way undo is perceived by interface programmers compared to users [1, 6]. Relationships between actions are often known to users of an application because they know how they are trying to use the system, but the system does not know the relationships and therefore cannot act on them.

Myers and Kosbie [7] later adopted the selective undo semantics used in GINA when they implemented their Amulet user interface. By implementing *command objects*, they organized user actions into a hierarchy which allowed higher-level commands to be invoked by lower-level commands. Their system not only supported selective undo, but selective reusability of arbitrary commands on new objects. However, since Amulet supported GINA semantics, their support for dependencies associated with selective undo is limited to undoing the values of command objects' properties. If a user used two command objects A and B where the output of using A was piped as input into B, the selective undoing of A may leave B in a semantically unstable state.

Regarding undo in collaborative frameworks, Abowd and Dix [1] point out that even *defining* undo from a user's perspective can be a daunting task. Chen and Sun [4] use the script model to implement their Any Undo feature (described in [11]) in the GRACE collaborative graphical editing system. Prakash and Knister [9] augment their DistEdit package–a group text editor building kit–with a form of selective undo where a *Conflict* function is used to check to see if two operations are dependent on each other in such a way that one cannot be undone with the other also being undone. And Ressel and Gunzenhäuser [10] use dynamic transformation rules to effect undo in a collaborative system by allowing transformations to affect future transformations in a pre-determined way. However, in all of these systems, any accounting of dependencies is done through the implicit encoding of them into the undo algorithms themselves. A major novel aspect of the model we propose is that dependencies and undo semantics are abstracted to an external representation. This allows the semantics of undo to be separately represented apart from the application code itself.

3 Our Approach

Before detailing a couple of examples that will be used to explain our approach, let us first explain that the approach assumes that an application imposes structure on how a particular user interacts with it. We argue (a) that imposing some structure on the use of technology can have distinct benefits for supporting users and (b) that many applications already do this. Consider, for example, automated teller machines (ATMs). Most ATMs ask the user to enter a personal identification number (PIN) before any other action. The underlying reason to request a PIN is that the user must be authenticated before the system withdraws money from their bank account. However, the system need not authenticate the user as the first action – it can wait to get authentication when it is directly needed. However, there are good (usability and security) reasons to request the PIN first. Therefore, imposing structure has benefits and is currently done in applications of many sorts.

Of course, not all structures are good for all uses or all users. A task structure designed to help one use *PowerPoint* to create an organization chart will clearly not help one create a slide presentation. So, instead of forcing one structure, we propose that multiple structures be made available, thus creating different *applications* that use the underlying application as a basic technology – in essence, the user interacts with the composition of the underlying application and a structure that specifies a *way of using the application*. We also propose that these models be relatively high-level, thus allowing the user to flexibly use the low-level application for low-level tasks but guiding them to string the low-level tasks together to solve the higher-level objectives.

Note that users of current applications have (at least a rough) understanding of the way they wish to use their applications. Unfortunately, the user does not have a way to indicate to an application how the application will be used and therefore cannot get specific guidance from the application itself. We propose that users can choose the way they want to use a system by choosing a particular task model, thus informing the system of their choice. The system can therefore use the chosen task model to constrain use of the system, thus guiding the user in their task.

Note also that the task models are not created by the end users of the system. While end users can certainly be involved in the specification of ways of using applications, we imagine that these models will be generated by domain experts. These experts will create specific task models that they expect with be of value, either because they describe very common tasks, popular uses of the underlying application, or uses needed within a particular organization.

The task models can be arbitrarily flexible, effectively removing all constraint on use. So, the approach we describe does not require imposing arbitrary structure – but we expect that when structure is imposed, we can give the user benefits. In particular, knowing the structure of the task the user is trying to accomplish can help us provide what we believe is a more natural mechanism for the *undo* command that takes this structure into account. It is the meaning of undo in these structured situations that we discuss in this paper. We start with an explanation of two examples that illustrate the desired behavior of undo in different scenarios.

3.1 Motivating Examples

Consider, as a running example, a scenario in which two authors are using a presentation application, such as *PowerPoint*, to create a single presentation, and they wish to impose a structure upon their presentation in the form of sections, subsections, etc. with the slide being the most basic unit of a section. They wish to have a Table of Contents slide at the beginning of the presentation that shows a list of the section names. This slide is then repeated at the beginning of each section with the next immediate section name highlighted.

We consider two examples to demonstrate the mechanics of cascading selective undo.

Example 1. Consider the following user actions:

1. User 1 begins the process of adding a section by creating a section header.
2. User 2 updates the Table of Contents slide to include the new section.

Suppose User 1 then decides against the creation of the new section and undoes step 1. Since the Table of Contents slide content is dependent on the existence of sections, the update in step 2 should also be undone. In other words, the undo should cascade to step 2. It is this dependency that must be represented. At first glance, this action is equivalent to what would happen under the linear undo model, but the second example shows how selective undo reacts in a more complex situation.

Example 2. Consider the following set of user actions. To save space, we have grouped multiple user actions into single steps in places where the point of the example is not affected:

1. User 1 creates slides A_1 through A_n.
2. User 1 creates section title slides S_1 through S_m.
3. User 1 creates the Table of Contents slide.
4. For each slide A_i, User 1 places it into its appropriate section, S_j.
5. User 2 creates slides A_{n+1} through A_{n+k}.

Suppose that after User 2 creates the last k slides, User 1 realizes that the section structure is not appropriate and wishes to delete it, perhaps because the new content does not fit in the existing structure. Selectively undoing step 2 would accomplish this. Intuitively, we want our undo mechanism to be aware that the presentation structure is independent of the slides, so that undoing step 2 would cascade to steps 3 and 4 but not to step 5. While this accomplishes the same goal as deleting the structure manually, undo is more efficient because the structure, with all of its nested subsections, may be spread throughout the presentation, making it difficult for the user to find and delete all occurrences by hand.

Both of these examples show how cascading could be used to bring the user document back to a stable state. We now describe the language and algorithms that we have developed to accomplish this.

3.2 Modeling Dependencies

Any number of formalisms could adequately model control dependencies between tasks. However, some software engineering researchers have developed *process-programming* languages [8], which not only model task dependencies, but also enable automated execution of these task models to track user progress on the tasks. We chose to use

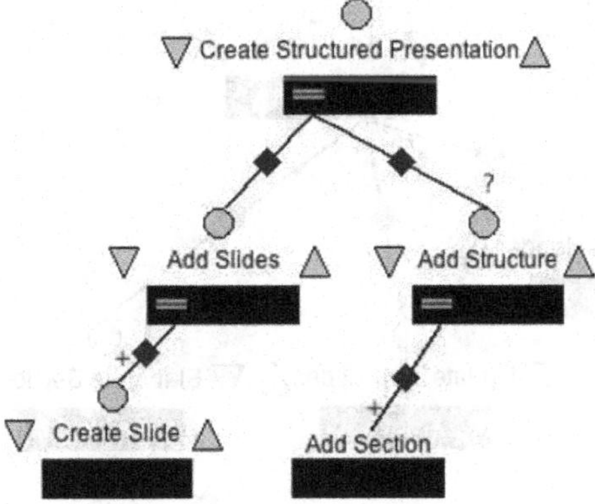

Fig. 1. A Little-JIL program that shows the overall process, elaborated further in other figures, for creating a structured presentation

Little-JIL [13], a recently-developed, feature-rich, graphical process-programming language. One of the authors (Cass) has been involved with the development of this language and the infrastructure that supports it, and has used it to develop a software design tool. We now show how this language can be used in the context of the previously-described examples.

Figures 1, 2, and 3 show a task model[1] for the application presented in the previous section. The task model represents the overall task as an elaborated hierarchy of tasks, while the *kind* of a parent task determines the order of execution of its child tasks. The Create Structured Presentation task in Figure 1 is of the *parallel* kind, as indicated by the two horizontal bars. Because it is a parallel task, its children, Add Slides and Add Structure, can be performed in any order, to be chosen by the users of the system. In essence, we are saying here that these tasks do not depend on one another for the reasons outlined in the previous section.

Figure 1 also shows the cardinality mechanism of the language. The question mark on the edge above Add Structure indicates that this task is optional in this context. The users of the system need not add any structure to the presentation. However, if they decide to add structure, they must add one or more sections, as indicated by the plus sign on the edge above Add Section. Note that Add Structure is parallel, indicating that the sub-tasks involved in adding sections do not depend on each other – sections are independent.

Note also the two tasks Create Slide and Add Section. Create Slide is a leaf task, a primitive task actually performed by a user, as indicated by the lack of a task kind. Add Section on the other hand, is a *reference*, as indicated by lack of the triangles on either side of the task name[2], and is therefore further elaborated somewhere else.

[1] We use the word *task model* to emphasize that we do not specifically require a process-programming language. In the software engineering literature, task models are called *process programs* and tasks are called *steps*.

[2] These triangles represent pre- and post-requisites, which are not used in this example.

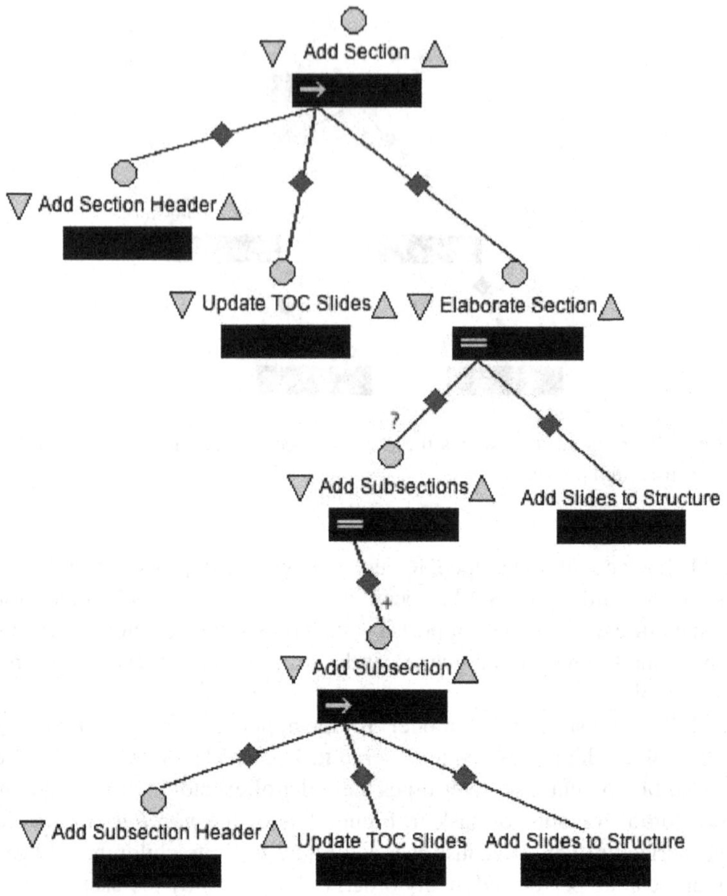

Fig. 2. An elaboration of the Add Section step from Figure 1

In this case Add Section is elaborated in Figure 2. As indicated by the arrow, Add Section is a *sequential* task and thus its child tasks must be performed in left-to-right order. The user must add a section header first, update the corresponding table of contents slides, and then elaborate the section. What is not shown in the diagram is that not all of these tasks need be performed by the same user. In fact, it is relatively easy to arrange for some of the tasks to be automated – for example, the system could automatically update the table of contents pages because such pages are fully determined by the section and subsection headers added by users.

Note that this particular way of creating presentations is not novel, and in fact there are applications that directly support this method (for example, the Beamer [12] LaTeX package). However, we aim for a more flexible, general approach that would support multiple ways of using the same underlying tools to perform different tasks – by encoding the different ways of using the tools in task models, the system can support and guide the users to use the tools in different, useful ways.

Table 1. The different task kinds supported by Little-JIL

Kind	Symbol	Description
Sequential	→	Child tasks must be performed in left-to-right order.
Parallel	=	Child tasks can be performed in any order, possibly overlapping.
Choice	-O-	One child task, chosen by the users, must be performed.
Try	⤃	Child tasks are tried in a specified order; task is done when one child succeeds.

Note that there are other task kinds not used in our example (see Table 1). By changing the task kinds, we can easily create different user experiences. For example, changing the kind of the Create Structured Presentation task to *sequential* indicates that one should create slides first and then add structure. For novice users, one might want to give more precise guidance, while for experts, one might want more choice and parallel tasks.

Continuing with the example, Elaborate Section involves (optionally) adding subsections and adding slides to the section (if we did not want to add slides to the section, we would not have added the section). Add Subsections is defined similarly to Add Structure. Both reference Add Slides to Structure, which is elaborated in Figure 3.

Though not shown, the language also supports a *parameter-passing* mechanism. For example, to enable Add Slides to Structure to be used in the two previously-described contexts, we can define it to take as a parameter the name of the section or subsection to which to add slides. Update TOC Slides would also take the section or subsection header as a parameter.

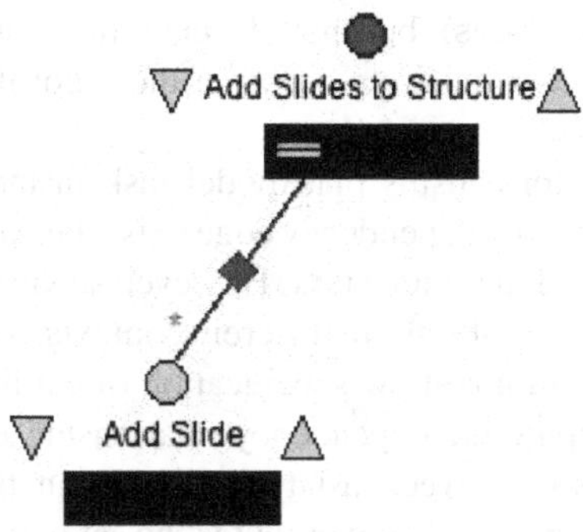

Fig. 3. An elaboration of the Add Slides to Structure step from Figure 2. The star (*) cardinality indicates that zero or more slides may be added by the user.

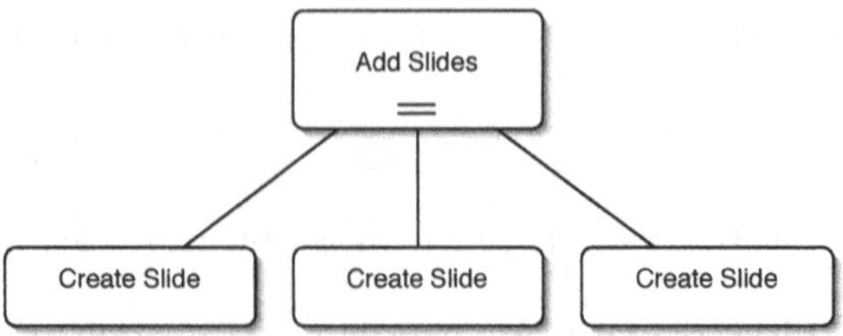

Fig. 4. A possible instance tree for the Add Slides task

3.3 The Main Cascade Algorithm

Given the dependencies modeled in a task model of the kind outlined above, and given a user request to undo one of the tasks, a cascading selective undo algorithm must calculate the *cascade*, i.e. the set of tasks that must also be undone if the requested task is to be undone. The algorithm must ensure that if only the selected task and the tasks in its cascade are undone, the system will arrive at a meaningful state. In other words, the algorithm must ensure that the system after the undo command is completed is one that could have been reached by following the task model on a path from the starting state.

To clarify the context in which such algorithms must work, let us note here that the task model is *instantiated* as the users interact with the system. The tasks in the task model represent *types* of tasks that are instantiated in different contexts. For example, Elaborate Section is instantiated with different parameters. As another example, consider the *instance tree* shown in Figure 4, which is one possible instantiation of the Add Slides sub-tree from the task model. In this example, there are three instances of Create Slide, indicating that users have created three slides using the system. Note that the instances are different. In particular, the first instance of Create Slide is different from the second instance – the second instance is optional because the first one will have satisfied the cardinality of the task. Both instances share the same parent instance (an instance of Add Slides), but they differ in this important context. The task model is therefore a model of task types, while the algorithm must work with task instances.

Simpler task-modeling formalisms that model task instances directly afford relatively simple cascade logic – if a dependency edge exists between the task instances, the target task is in the cascade of the source task. However, such simpler task-modeling formalisms would not allow reuse of tasks in different contexts, would not model naturally-hierarchical tasks, and would not allow specification of cardinality. Our algorithm, on the other hand, must compute the dependency relationship between pairs of task instances based on relationships between task types. The input, therefore, to our algorithm is a task instance to be undone, while the output is the set of all task instances that must also be undone to cause the system to arrive at a state consistent with the task model. The main algorithm, which deals only with control dependencies specified by the task kinds, follows:

```
COMPUTECASCADE(t)
Input: Task instance t to be undone.
Output: Cascade for t.
1: C ← {t}
2: if t is root task then
3:     return C
4: p ← t.parent
5: k ← p.kind
6: C ← C ∪ COMPUTECASCADE(p)
7: if k = SEQUENTIAL ∨ k = TRY then
8:     C ← C ∪ subtrees(p.childrenAfter(t))
9: return C
```

The algorithm, as outlined above, assumes that task instances have the following attributes:

– *parent*: The parent of task instance.
– *kind*: The task kind of the associated task.

In addition to these attributes, task instances need a *childrenAfter* function, which returns the children of the task that are to the right of the given child – that must come after the given child in the sequential ordering of the sub-tasks. We also use a *subtrees* function to find all tasks in the subtrees rooted at those children.

Theorem 1. COMPUTECASCADE(t) *correctly computes the set C of all existing tasks dependent on t by a control dependency specified in the task model.*

Proof. Consider a task s dependent on t by a control dependency in the task model. Because the only dependencies we consider are those specified by the task kinds, s depends on t because they share a common ancestor, $\mathcal{A}$, that makes that dependency explicit. Parallel and choice kinds do not control the order of execution of their subtrees, so $\mathcal{A}$ is neither parallel nor choice – it must be of sequential or try kind. We know that s is not in a sub-tree to the left of t's sub-tree at $\mathcal{A}$ – this would imply that s *necessarily* had to be performed before t, not the other way around. Therefore, s is in a sub-tree to the right of t's sub-tree at $\mathcal{A}$. Because the recursion starts at t and moves up the tree, the algorithm eventually reaches a child of $\mathcal{A}$ and then line 8 of the algorithm adds s to the set C.

Similar logic can be used to show that no task is added to C if it is *not* dependent on t. Therefore, we have shown that the set C is equivalent to the set of tasks dependent on t.

Let us now return to the motivating examples to see how the above algorithms would produce the desired results. Figure 2 shows the tasks relevant to Example 1: namely Add Section Header and Update TOC Slides. When the Add Section Header task is undone, the sequential control dependency of its parent causes line 8 of the main cascade algorithm to execute. This causes all children of the sequential node Add Section which are to the right of Add Section Header to also be undone, including the update of the table of contents. Note that if the Elaborate Section task had also been completed by the user (to include subsections, for example) then that task would have been undone as well.

Example 2 involves a larger part of the task model. Steps 1 and 5 of the example, dealing with the creation of slides, is handled by the subtree rooted at the Add Slides node in Figure 1. Steps 2-4, dealing with structure, is handled by the subtree rooted at the Add Structure node in the same figure, whose child node Add Section is fully modeled in Figure 2. In this example, undoing the creation of all of the section title slides is equivalent to undoing *all* of the Add Section tasks. In other words, it is equivalent to undoing the parent node, Add Structure. When the algorithm is applied, all nodes on the path from the Add Structure node to the root of the task model, which in this case is just the Create Structured Presentation node, will also be undone. However, note that because the Add Slides task has an explicit parallel dependency relationship with Add Structure, none of the slide creation steps will be undone, which is exactly the desired result for steps 1 and 5 of Example 2. The final step is to observe that, unlike the previous example, the user wishes to undo a non-leaf node. For that case, we also wish to undo all leaf node tasks that are descendants of Add Structure. This will cause the individual user steps 2, 3, and 4 of Example 2 also to be undone, as desired. Note that this requires additional work beyond computing the cascade – we consider descendant tasks separately from the cascade.

3.4 Extensions to the Approach

The algorithm presented above details proper semantics for cascading selective undo for cases in which nominal control flow defines all the dependencies between tasks. However, the approach can be extended to take advantage of cardinality specifications and data dependencies.

Cardinality. Open-ended cardinalities open up an interesting possibility for selective undo. Consider, for example, undoing a task instance that is attached to an edge with + cardinality, such as one of the Create Slide instances shown in Figure 4. If the user wants to undo all tasks instances attached to the edge, it is clear that the parent must also be undone because the cardinality specification requires at least one sub-task. However, if we are undoing only some of the tasks, leaving at least one completed task attached to the edge, the cardinality can be satisfied by the remaining tasks. In the case where the parent is a parallel task, we can safely avoid further cascading (aside from the recursive searching for sequential and try ancestors) because the siblings do not depend on one another. The algorithm for this approach is similar to the one above, except for the special case noted here.

Note, however, that this extension would not always produce the result the user wanted – if the user wants to undo a task so that they can redo it in a different way or with different information, then we require that the parent task be undone, because in order for tasks to be performed, their parent tasks must not have been completed. We therefore plan to investigate ways of giving the user the choice of these two interpretations – perhaps presenting both cascades.

Data Dependencies. In some situations, data dependencies between tasks can be known *a priori*. For example, a task that modifies a slide clearly depends on the task that created the slide. In the current system, we model some of these data dependencies using the parameter-passing mechanism, which specifies parameter passing between parent and child tasks. If a task $\mathcal{B}$ depends on data from a sibling task $\mathcal{A}$, we indicate this by passing a parameter from $\mathcal{A}$ to its parent and subsequent passing of the same parameter from this parent to $\mathcal{B}$. Note that this is not limited to direct siblings – we can specify data flow between any two tasks that share a common ancestor. However, this mechanism only allows specification of data dependencies between $\mathcal{A}$ and $\mathcal{B}$ if $\mathcal{A}$ and $\mathcal{B}$ are already related by a control dependency. In particular, if the common ancestor is a parallel task, the system cannot guarantee that the parameter received by $\mathcal{B}$ is the one produced by $\mathcal{A}$ – $\mathcal{A}$ might not yet have executed at the time that $\mathcal{B}$ starts. Therefore, the set of data dependencies specified in our task models is a subset of the control dependencies already specified.

In some situations, this is not enough to model all known data dependencies. For example, we might wish to have an Add Section Cross-Reference task as an optional child of Create Slide in our running example. This task might need the section header as a parameter from the Add Section Header task that created the section, which therefore means that Add Section Cross-Reference must happen *after* the corresponding Add Section Header task. In the current language, we cannot specify this data dependency without forcing sequential control dependency between the two tasks. Our plan is to add independent data dependencies to the language. Of course, when we have added these new dependencies, our undo algorithms will have to consider them in computing the proper cascade for a user's undo request. This should be possible by taking the union of the data dependency cascade with the one computed by the main algorithm.

Note that not all data dependencies can be known *a priori*. Consider a development environment for creating Java programs. At runtime, the user might create a method in a previously-created class, even though the task model did not require that the method be created in exactly this class. If the user requests that we undo the creation of the class, clearly the creation of the method must be part of the cascade. Because this data dependency is created by the user's actions and not required by *a priori* dependencies, the previously-outlined approach cannot capture it. Berlage [3] suggests that these kinds of dependencies should be modeled in the tool and that they can be used to disallow undo commands that result in "meaningless" states. We suggest taking this a step further by using these dependencies in calculating the proper cascade. Our new algorithms will have to support this.

4 Future Work

In addition to the extensions outlined above, the development of which we already have underway, we plan further improvements to the approach as well as development of visualizations to support users in using it. We further plan to run experiments to assess the usability of the approach.

4.1 Dealing with Exceptions

Little-JIL [13] also has an exception handling mechanism, which allows the specification of scoped handlers that respond to exceptions thrown from tasks up the hierarchy.

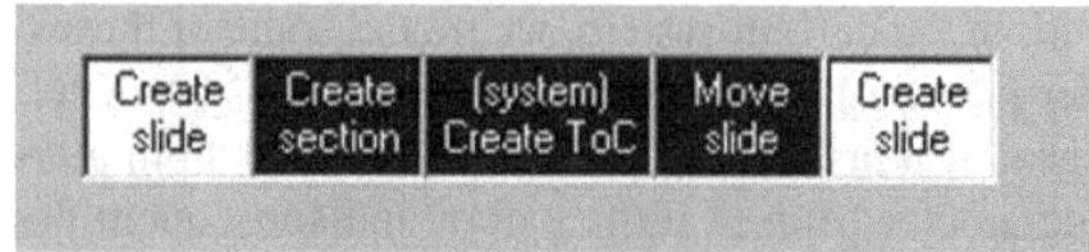

Fig. 5. One possible visualization of a cascade. The user has selected "Create Section" to undo.

This presents some additional issues for selective undo. If a user action causes an exception to be thrown, then undoing that action should cause a cascade to the exception handler, which should also be undone. Because exception handlers are themselves represented as task hierarchies, consisting of an arbitrary number of subtasks with control dependencies between them, undoing an exception handler involves undoing those subtasks.

Cascading of undo operations to exception handlers is not currently handled by our system, but will be in future implementations. One interesting open question is if users should be allowed to *directly* undo exception handlers themselves, perhaps with the intent of redoing the handling in a different manner. This is under investigation.

4.2 Limiting Scope of Undo

There are scenarios in which an operation cannot be undone. For example, an application might have a finite history list or it might model a real-world permanency. (One cannot undo a transaction if the seller has already spent the money or the buyer has already consumed the good.) In these situations where a full cascade is not possible, the application should disallow undo. However, the undo logic may not realize that it is in this situation until a cascade is already in progress. In this case, we must be able to reverse the effects of the cascade. Alternatively, the cascade could throw an exception, to be handled as we discussed above. There are plans to address these issues in future versions.

4.3 Visualization for the Approach

An important aspect we have not yet discussed is how a cascading undo will be represented to the user, both before and during the cascade. When the user selects an action to be undone, it should be clear what the cascade will affect. In Example 1, one wouldn't want the user to be surprised when the Table of Contents slide is altered. One possible visualization would be to simply show the user all affected actions, including system actions. An example appears in Figure 5. Alternatively, we could couple a user's selection with an explanation of why other actions were being affected. Explicit control dependencies would allow such explanations to be created dynamically.

4.4 Task Model Inference

The approach described here assumes that the task model is known ahead of time. Several task models might exist for a particular application, but the user chooses one of those models when they begin using the system. Of course, this can be limiting. In the longer term, we plan to explore approaches that would infer the task model the user intends to use by monitoring low-level user actions. Then, instead of first choosing a task model, the user can explore with relatively more freedom early on in a session before giving enough context to the system that the system can then start to help the user make continued progress.

Of course, if the user can choose a task model at the beginning of use, they can also change task models mid-way through a session. Again, under the current approach, the user must make an explicit choice. However, we envision an approach that would monitor user actions and reinterpret the user's choice at those points when the user attempts tasks that are not in the currently "chosen" task model.

4.5 Evaluation of the Approach

There are several important questions to answer with respect to the usefulness of selective undo to end users. Some of these questions are:

1. Does our interpretation of selective undo semantics match user expectations?
2. Would a user choose to use selective undo over linear undo?
3. Would a user choose to use selective undo instead of performing an alternate set of tasks? (a more general case of the above question)

We have begun experiments to help answer these questions. Here we describe one completed experiment and two yet to be carried out.

In the first experiment, we have tried to determine whether a user would choose to apply selective undo instead of the traditional linear model. We provided subjects with a series of drawing tasks, and asked them to show the state the drawing should be in after one of the tasks is undone. We then coded their responses to infer which undo model each subject performed. In this experiment, we found that cascading undo is chosen more than the other two and linear undo is chosen extremely infrequently.

However, we cannot conclude from this experiment that undo is more desirable than performing an alternate set of tasks. To explore this question, we plan an experiment where we guide subjects to create and edit elements in a document to reach a certain state before asking each subject to transform the document to a different state. If this different state is well-chosen, the subjects can choose a selective undo to reach the state, but they can also use a different set of tasks (creation, editing, or deleting tasks) to reach the same visible state. We predict that subjects will choose selective undo over using a different sequence of tasks, except perhaps if the alternate sequence is very short.

In another experiment, we wish to determine if users can predict what will happen (i.e. the end state) if either linear or selective undo is used in a given context. We will give the user a series of tasks on a familiar application and then tell the user that either linear undo or selective undo will be used at a particular point. We will then ask the user to predict what the document will look like after that particular type of undo has been executed. We expect to use a broad, computer-literate population for this experiment in order to determine if a particular paradigm for selective undo is the "natural" one.

5 Conclusions

We have presented cascading selective undo, which maintains the advantages over linear undo that have long been touted while also capturing dependencies between user tasks that are necessary in many contexts to ensure that undo results in a meaningful state. Our approach exploits task models designed by application developers and chosen by users – task models that we argue provide much needed guidance in complex domains and provide additional context information to the system when the user requests an undo action.

Our novel approach uses Little-JIL, a process modeling language from the software engineering community, to explicitly represent task models with control dependencies. Little-JIL provides precise representation of control dependencies that have allowed us to develop algorithms that determine appropriate cascading of undo at any point in the user experience. It is also robust enough to allow for complex task models where the semantics of selective undo are not straightforward. Extensions to our main algorithm account for the complexities in the model, including cardinality, exception handling, and data dependencies.

We are currently planning experiments to test the viability of selective undo to end users. Results will allow us to refine our model, the language upon which it is based, and implementations of selective undo. We already have a Little-JIL-based implementation of a software design tool that shows that the language is capable of representing complex executable task models. It does not yet support undo (selective or otherwise), but based on the knowledge gained from the current work, and the experiments outlined in the section on future work, we plan to add a selective undo mechanism to the tool in the near future, and thus learn whether the approach described here is feasible for developers as well as for users.

References

1. G. D. Abowd and A. J. Dix. Giving undo attention. *Interacting with Computers*, 4(3):317–342, 1992.
2. J. E. Archer, Jr., R. Conway, and F. B. Schneider. User recovery and reversal in interactive systems. *ACM Transactions on Programming Languages and Systems*, 6(1):1–19, 1984.
3. T. Berlage. A selective undo mechanism for graphical user interfaces based on command objects. *ACM Transactions on Computer-Human Interaction*, 1(3):269–294, 1994.
4. D. Chen and C. Sun. Undoing any operation in collaborative graphics editing systems. In *GROUP*, pages 197–206, 2001.
5. A. Dix. Moving between contexts. In P. Palanque and R. Bastide, editors, *Design, Specification and Verification of Interactive Systems '95*, pages 149–173. Springer, 1995. Toulouse, France.
6. R. Mancini, A. J. Dix, and S. Levialdi. Dealing with undo. In *Proc. of INTERACT'97*, Sydney, Australia, 1997. Chapman and Hall.
7. B. A. Myers and D. S. Kosbie. Reusable hierarchical command objects. In *Proc. of the ACM Conf. on Human Factors in Computing (CHI 96)*, pages 260–267. ACM Press, 1996.
8. L. J. Osterweil. Software processes are software, too. In *Proc. of the Ninth International Conf. on Software Engineering*, Mar. 1987. Monterey, CA.

9. A. Prakash and M. J. Knister. A framework for undoing actions in collaborative systems. *ACM Transactions on Computer-Human Interaction*, 1(4):295–330, Dec. 1994.
10. M. Ressel and R. Gunzenhäuser. Reducing the problems of group undo. In *GROUP*, pages 131–139, Phoenix AZ, USA, 1999.
11. C. Sun. Undo any operation at any time in group editors. In *Computer-Supported Cooperative Work (CSCW)*, pages 191–200, 2000.
12. T. Tantau. *User's Guide to the Beamer Class, Version 3.06.* http://latex-beamer.sourceforge.net, Oct 2005.
13. A. Wise, A. G. Cass, B. S. Lerner, E. K. McCall, L. J. Osterweil, and S. M. Sutton, Jr. Using Little-JIL to coordinate agents in software engineering. In *Proc. of the Automated Software Engineering Conf.*, Grenoble, France., Sept. 2000.

Exploring Interaction Space as Abstraction Mechanism for Task-Based User Interface Design

Christian M. Nielsen[1], Michael Overgaard[2], Michael B. Pedersen[3], Jan Stage[4], and Sigge Stenild[5]

[1] NNIT A/S, Lottenborgvej 24, DK-2800 Lyngby, Denmark
cmne@nnit.com
[2] KMD A/S, Selma Lagerlöfs Vej 300, DK-9220 Aalborg East, Denmark
michael@netmo.dk
[3] ETI A/S, Bouet Moellevej 3-5, DK-9400 Nørresundby, Denmark
mbpedersen@gmail.com
[4] Aalborg University, Department of Computer Science, DK-9220 Aalborg East, Denmark
jans@cs.aau.dk
[5] Guppyworks, Odensegade 7, DK-2100 København Ø, Denmark
zilentninja@gmail.com

Abstract. Designing a user interface is often a complex undertaking. Model-based user interface design is an approach where models and mappings between them form the basis for creating and specifying the design of a user interface. Such models usually include descriptions of the tasks of the prospective user, but there is considerable variation in the other models that are employed. This paper explores the extent to which the notion of interaction space is useful as an abstraction mechanism to reduce the complexity of creating and specifying a user interface design. We present how we designed a specific user interface through use of design techniques and models that employ the notion of interaction space. This design effort departed from the task models in an object-oriented model of the users' problem and application domains. The lessons learned emphasize that the notion of interactions spaces is a useful abstraction mechanism that can help user interface designers exploit object-oriented analysis results and reduce the complexity of designing a user interface.

Keywords: User interface design, task models, model-based user interface design, abstraction, object-oriented, domain models.

1 Introduction

Models and specifications are key elements in many software development projects. It has been documented that software development based on specifications produce systems with a high level of functionality and robustness [1]. Accordingly, it has been suggested that specifications are crucial in projects where high technical complexity makes software reliability and verification paramount, e.g. batch systems, process control systems, complex systems and safety-critical systems [18]. In many interactive systems, the user interface accounts for a large part of the code and is a major source of complexity [1].

K. Coninx, K. Luyten, and K.A. Schneider (Eds.): TAMODIA 2006, LNCS 4385, pp. 202–216, 2007.

In software engineering, it is generally agreed that developers use abstraction and decomposition to cope with complexity in software design [6], [9], [22], [24]. This use of abstraction and decomposition as vehicles for human reflection has also been denoted as the analytical mode of operation [13]. The analytical mode of operation relies on abstraction mechanisms, which are concepts or language constructs that support abstraction and decomposition. The notion of objects and classes is an example of abstraction mechanisms that support abstraction and decomposition of phenomena in a problem domain [5][21]. Designers employ these concepts for taming the complexity of a software design effort. In user interface design, the notion of task is an example of an abstraction mechanism that is used in several model notations.

More recently, the importance of abstraction in user interface design has been emphasized for other reasons. The broad variety of mobile devices that are being developed are proving to be a challenge for user interface designers because they offer only limited and different means of interaction and small screens [6][8]. Moreover, the diversity of the mobile platform makes it imperative to design on an abstract level [3]. This latter argument can be generalized to any type of multi-platform system.

Model-based user interface design aims to support an analytical mode of operation in user interface design with a range of models and mappings between them [10]. It has been emphasized that within this approach, there is no consensus about the models to use and the notations employed in the models [3].

The purpose of this paper is to move beyond specific model notations by exploring an abstraction mechanism for user interface design. The aim is to identify an abstraction mechanism and establish to what extent it supports abstraction and decomposition in user interface design. In the following section 2, we present related work in model-based user interface design and discuss potential abstraction mechanisms. The results presented in this paper are based on a case study of the process of designing the user interface of an interactive location-aware mobile system to support communication in a specific safety-critical application domain. The domain was the fuel department of a coal-based power plant. This case study is presented in section 3. Section 4 provides an overview of the results from an object-oriented analysis that was conducted prior to the case study. Section 5 presents the process and result of designing the user interface of the mobile application. Section 6 elaborates on the lessons learned from the case study. Finally, section 7 provides the conclusion.

2 Related Work

Model-based user interface design includes two major streams of work. The first stream focuses on model features and mappings between models. The aim is to develop computerized tools to support the models and transformations between them, e.g. [4], [20]. A key topic in this stream is denoted as the mapping problem, which refers to the need for handling transformations from one model to another [3], [10]. The main problem in this stream is to derive models of concrete user interfaces from more abstract models. This has been described as the abstract-to-concrete gap [15]. Some tools handle this gap by requiring human intervention in certain activities of the design process [23].

The second stream of work in model-based user interface design focuses on the creative process that is conducted by human designers. The aim is to provide tools and techniques that support humans in handling the complexities involved in the design task. This has also been denoted as design heuristics [19].

Our work is within the second stream. With this approach it is crucial to develop strong abstraction mechanisms that can help designers tame the complexities of the user interface design task.

The literature reflects three different types of abstraction mechanisms that have been suggested for user interface design. The first type originates from user interface technology. In the Cameleon reference framework [2], the most abstract description of a user interface is a logical model that is based on elements that are abstractions of existing widgets [10]. Thus this approach employs an abstraction mechanism that is derived from existing user interface technology.

The second type of abstraction mechanisms originates from the domain of the prospective users of the system. Some focus on the tasks of the users. Tasks are a key element of the application domain of a system [12]. Most task-driven design techniques exploit hierarchically organized task structures with temporal dependencies between sub-tasks to derive models of user interfaces [20]. Others focus on the objects of the users' work. This is a key element in the problem domain of a system [12]. Finally, there are attempts to include both tasks and objects [11].

The notion of interaction space is an interesting abstraction mechanism for model-based design of user interfaces. It is used in the Wisdom (Whitewater Interactive System Development with Object Models) method [16], [17]. An interaction space is a part of the user interface that facilitates some specific interaction between the user and the system. It is a class that will be used to generate elements for the user interface. Examples of interaction spaces are higher-level widgets such as windows, menus and panels. It has a graphical representation that can be used in combination with models based on the UML notation.

The concept of views has been suggested as a vehicle for design of the user interface. For a given task, the designer defines how many views are needed to support that task. Then the sub-tasks of that task are distributed on the views [23]. This idea is similar to interaction spaces in the sense that an abstract concept forms the basis for design. However, a view represents a screen or part of a screen and thereby, it is less abstract than an interaction space that can represent any mean for interaction.

In the rest of this paper, we explore to what extent the notion of interaction space is useful as an abstraction mechanism for user interface design. The discussion is based on a case study that is presented in the following section.

3 Case Study

The case study was conducted at Nordjyllandsværket, a coal-based power plant situated in Northern Jutland in Denmark, see Figure 1. The plant produces central heating, electricity, and by-products that are used in the production of cement. We limited the case study to the fuel department of the power plant, see the diagram in Figure 1.

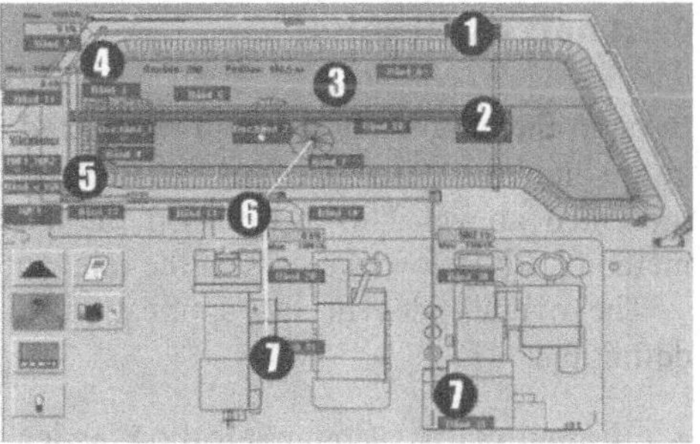

Fig. 1. Nordjyllandsværket and the fuel department

The plant is divided into two independent production plants (the two locations #7). The coal for the two plants is supplied from a central storage area (locations #2 and #3). The fuel-department is responsible for delivering the coal used in the two production plants, amounting daily to 5000 tons of coal for each.

The employees in the fuel department continuously monitor and control the transportation of coal. They must ensure that the correct amount of coal arrives to the correct location and that the coal has certain properties and quality. To ensure this, the coal is processed (locations #4 and #5) before transporting it to the final location (location #7). Another important task is to prevent the coal in the storage area from self-combusting.

The employees perform a variety of different tasks to ensure that the needed amount of coal is delivered to the two production plants. To coordinate the tasks described above, quick and easy communication is important, and in some cases even essential in order to carry out the job in a safe and efficient manner. At the present, the devices used for communicating are VHF-radios (walkie-talkies), DECT wireless phones, and some times mobile phones. The control tower (location #6) is the only location where all the necessary information is accessible and it is also the place where employees can operate and control most of the machinery.

Every element of the transportation of coal can be controlled through the existing system, but only through a complex coordination process. When a problem arises, which cannot be solved from the control room, for example in the Grinder building (location #5), the person situated here trying to solve a problem does not have access to the relevant information. Furthermore specific parts of the machinery can only be controlled from inside the Grinder building. The only way to gain access to the information systems in the control room is by communicating with a person in the control room either by phone or walkie-talkie.

Often the phones are not usable because of the weak signal; hence the only tool for communicating is the walkie-talkie. Several problems are related to the use of this device. Many conveyor-belts run underground, which disrupts the signal, and the machines and conveyor belts are often placed inside concrete buildings, which also disrupts the signal. Finally, there is a deafening noise inside these buildings, which makes talking to each other difficult, and using any kind of mobile device for verbal communication is virtually impossible.

4 Analysis Results

Prior to the case study, we had conducted an object-oriented analysis of a location-aware mobile communicator to support employees in the application domain presented above. This was based on OOA&D, a typical object-oriented analysis method [12]. Below, we present the relevant results from this analysis.

The overall idea of the application was summarized in the following system definition:

- **Functionality:** Communication device with machine state indication and support for communication
- **Application Domain:** Transport of coal around the power plant, preparation and mixing of coal, monitoring of conveyer belts and problem solving/prevention in production line
- **Conditions:** Safety critical, noisy environment, dusty conditions, above- and underground, employees have basic IT training/knowledge
- **Technology:** Pocket PC with Microsoft visual studio 2003 .Net and WLAN
- **Objects:** Employee, mobile unit, conveyer belt, magnet, screener, grinder, control room computer
- **Responsibility:** Context-aware mobile communication support system that monitors production line state and facilitates cooperation and communication in a noisy environment

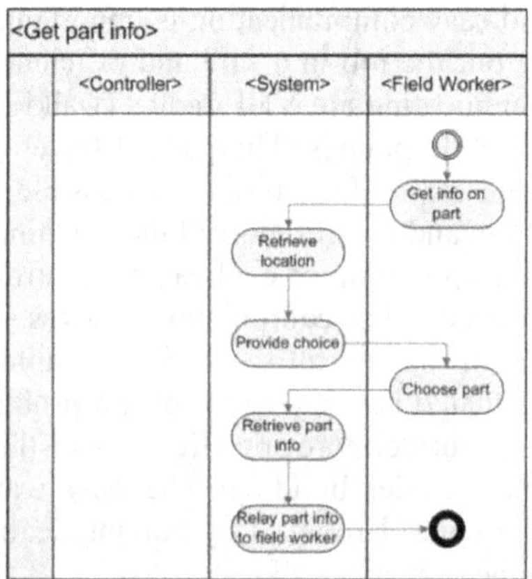

Fig. 2. Essential task flow diagram for getting information about a part of a machine

Two main models were produced during analysis. The users' work tasks in the application domain were described in terms of use cases. We identified nine use cases that should be supported by the system. We modelled each of these. There are two roles in the problem domain: controller and field worker. In order to model their different responsibilities and to emphasize the purpose of the system, we expressed the work in terms of activity models with responsibilities. Wisdom [17] denotes this as an essential task flow diagram. For an example, see Figure 2.

The problem domain was described by a class diagram and a set of statechart diagrams. The class diagram depicts the physical locations, the communication, and the users relevant to our system, see. Figure 3 For each class, there was also a state chart diagram that describes the detailed behaviour for objects from this class.

Finally, the analysis produced a list of 22 functions that the system should include. The list describes each function and specifies its complexity and type.

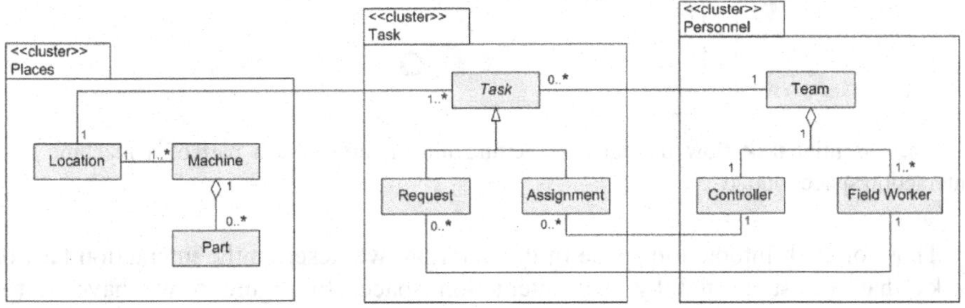

Fig. 3. Class diagram for the whole problem domain

5 User Interface Design

The user interface design departed directly from the results of the object-oriented analysis.

5.1 Individual Interaction Models

We started making individual interaction models. For each essential task flow diagram, we made an individual interaction model. This model provides a set of interaction spaces that are needed to support a user that is carrying out the task.

An individual interaction model is defined by taking the corresponding task flow diagram and on the right hand side of this diagram drawing up the interaction spaces that is needed to support each activity in the diagram.

This is illustrated in Figure 4, where we have added two interaction spaces on the right hand side. These two are examples of two interaction spaces that can be applied in many cases: browser and view [17]. The browser is an interaction space that shows and enables selection of a number of objects of a class. In this case it shows the parts that are visible at a specific location, and the user is able to select one of these objects. The view provides information about a single object. In this case it is information about the part the user has chosen.

The next step is to add what Wisdom refers to as task classes that are related to individual interaction spaces. However, here we discovered a source of confusion. The whole diagram describes how a task is carried out, and as part of that, we describe something that is also referred to as tasks. In order to differentiate, we denoted the activity related to an interaction space as an interaction task.

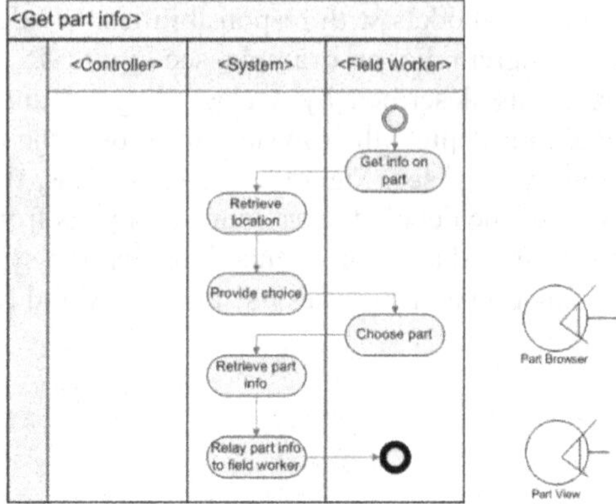

Fig. 4. Essential task flow diagram for getting informationabout a part of a machine with interaction spaces added

Thus for each interaction space in the diagram, we describe the interaction task or tasks that are supported by that interaction space. In Figure 5 we have added interaction tasks for the two interaction spaces.

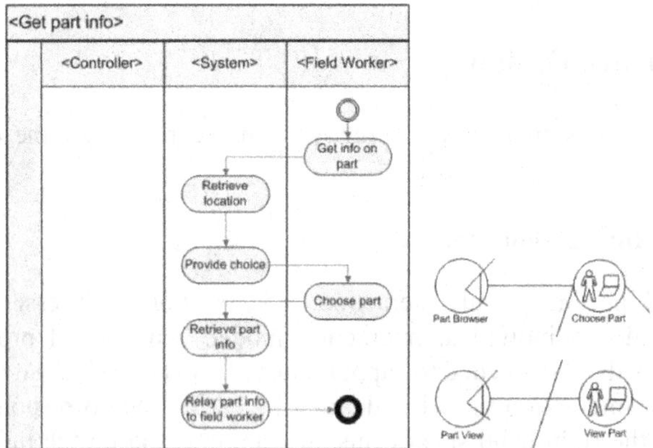

Fig. 5. Essential task flow diagram for getting information about a part of a machine with interaction spaces and interaction tasks added

This is done for each essential task flow diagram. In our case, we had nine diagrams, so we ended up with 9 individual models like the one shown in Figure 5.

5.2 General Interaction Model

When all of the individual interaction models are complete, they are combined into a general interaction model. The general interaction model describes all the interaction spaces and interaction tasks that the system must support.

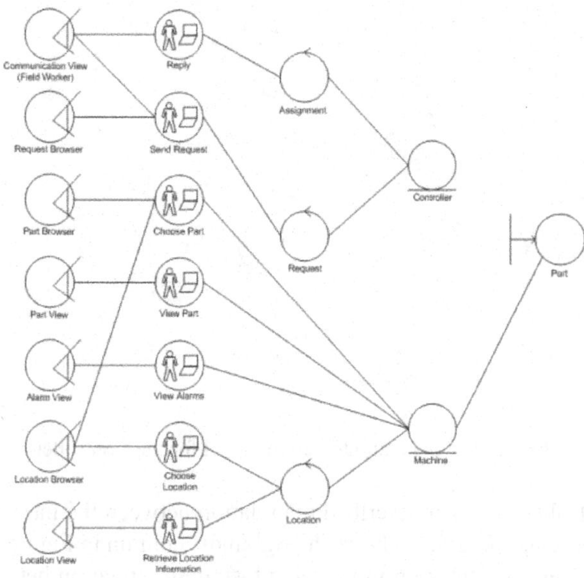

Fig. 6. The general interaction model for the Field worker

In our case, we had two roles, controller and field worker, and in the task models, we had divided the description between them. Thus we were able to relate the interaction spaces to each role. Therefore, we decided to make a separate general interaction model for each of the roles. Figure 6 shows the general interaction model for the Field worker. A general interaction model was also made for the Controller This is illustrated in Figure 7. For both models, the first version of the general interaction model only included the two leftmost columns.

In the process of mapping the individual interaction models into the general interaction model, repeated task classes and interaction spaces were eliminated.

5.3 Relation to Problem Domain Classes

Up to this point, the user interface design involved only the task models from the results of the object-oriented analysis. However, we also used the class diagram, see Figure 3. This was done by relating each interaction task to the objects it involved. This is illustrated in the rightmost columns of Figure 6. For example, the choose part interaction task involves an object from the Machine class which in turn involves an object from the Part class.

The different symbols used for the problem domain classes are not important for this example. Thus this part of the general interaction diagram describes the relation between the interaction model and the problem domain model that is described on the overall level by the class diagram.

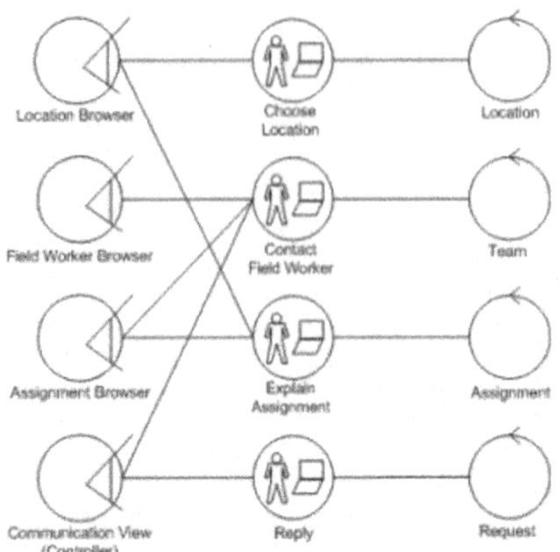

Fig. 7. The general interaction model for the Controller

For the Controller, we also described the relation between the interaction tasks and the classes in the class diagram. This is the rightmost column in Figure 7.

Both of these general interaction models illustrate the relation between interaction spaces and problem domain classes. Each interaction task is related to one problem domain class. This is a useful criterion for assessing the interaction tasks you have defined; if an interaction involves more than one class, it might be considered to break it down further.

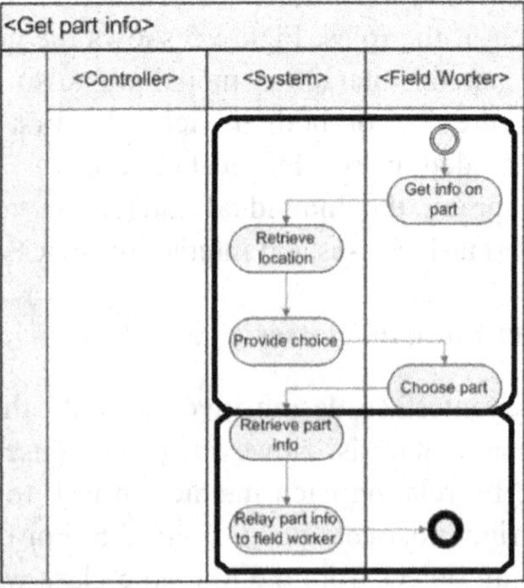

Fig. 8. Essential task flow diagram for getting information about a part of a machine with two overall states for interaction tasks added

5.4 Updating Task Flow Diagrams

The work process described in a task flow diagram involves a number of interaction tasks. For the diagram in Figure 5, there are two interaction tasks: choose part and view part. We have used this relationship to describe more structure in the task flow diagrams. We did this by creating an overall state for each interaction task. This is illustrated in Figure 8.

This provides a clear relation between the use of the interaction spaces of the system and the description of the users' work in the task flow diagrams. It describes the sequence in the use of the system. In Wisdom, this is modelled in a so-called dialogue model [17].

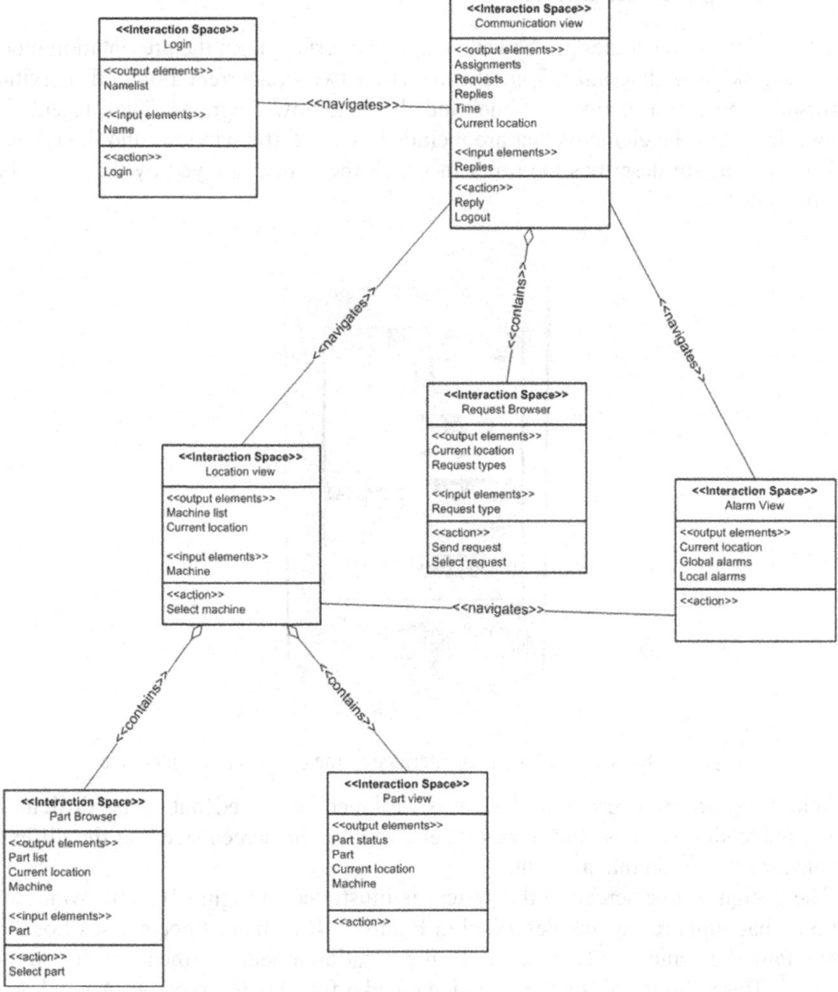

Fig. 9. The presentation model for the whole system

5.5 Creating the Presentation Model

The general interaction diagrams were used for creating a presentation model for the system. The presentation model describes the classes that will be used to generate object in the user interface. It is a single model for the whole system that is based on the interaction spaces. The interaction spaces are transformed to classes one by one, and they are related to each other with object-oriented structures.

The presentation model for the whole system is shown in Figure 9. The attributes of the classes in the diagram are defined from the detailed class diagram for the problem domain, and the operations are defined by distributing the function list from analysis on the individual presentation model classes.

5.6 Designing the User Interface

The last activity was to design the concrete user interface from the presentation model and the task flow diagrams. This encompassed two concurrent flows of activities, corresponding to the dialogue model and the task flow diagrams. The presentation model describes the elements that are included in a specific window, and the relevant task flow diagram describes the order in which they are employed by the user when solving a task.

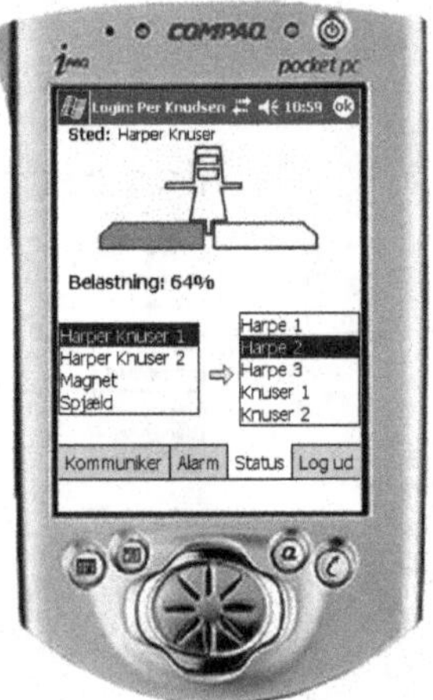

Fig. 10. One screen of the user interface of the communication device

When the concrete user interface was designed, it turned out to be difficult to group objects on screens, and it was crucial to take the screen size and the different means for interaction into account.

The design of one screen in the system is illustrated in Figure 10. This window is the one that support the task described in Figure 2. It includes three classes Location View, Part View and Part Browser in the presentation model, see the lower left part of Figure 9. Based on this design, we implemented a functional prototype. A window of this prototype is shown in Figure 10.

The prototype was implemented in the .Net Compact Framework. This forced some alterations to the design of the individual screens of the prototype. One major change was that the tab panes had to be moved to the bottom of the screen, as it was impossible to place them at the top. Also using the navigation button of the PDA for navigation between the tab panes had to be excluded due to an error in the .Net Compact Framework. Instead, navigation was accomplished by finger touch. Furthermore, it was impossible to determine the size of each tab pane, which made it questionable whether they where large enough to be used for finger touch navigation. Finally, the bottom of the screen could not be used as it was reserved for other PDA functionality.

The usability of the implemented prototype was evaluated in two ways: (1) a heuristic inspection performed by five usability experts [14], and (2) a field evaluation in cooperation with five employees at the power plant, who are the prospective users of the mobile system. In the field test, the workers used the system while members of the development team controlled the communication with the PDA in order to simulate a realistic work process. After the work tasks were completed, the user was interviewed about the usability of the system.

The overall results of these evaluations showed us that the system was indeed usable. The employees were positive towards actually using the system instead of the walkie-talkie. One of them even said that he actually found this way of communicating better because he was sometimes disturbed by all the non-work related talk taking place over the VHF-radio. The employees all agreed that, especially in the locations, where the noise level is high, the system would be very useful, and they would want to use the system, if it was fully implemented. Despite disagreeing on how detailed information that the system should provide in the status and alarm sections, they all found the presented information useful in both solving problems and monitoring the production line.

6 Lessons Learned

Through the case study of designing the user interface for the mobile communication device for the power plant, we learned the following lessons:

- The results from the object-oriented analysis was a productive basis for user interface design
- The models that we used were well related to each other
- The notion of interaction spaces was a useful abstraction mechanism (we got hold of the task)
- The abstraction allowed us to focus on the essential elements and defer detailed design issues
- The design process enabled us to produce a novel user interface design
- Methodological support for the detailed user interface design was needed

The design process departed from the results of an object-oriented analysis. Selected results from the analysis were directly applicable, and we had no need to make additional analysis activities. Thus the case study demonstrates that it is possible to tie object-orientation and user interface design together. The results from the application domain analysis provided the overall framework, as the task models were used to derive and specify interaction spaces. The problem domain model was used to qualify the description of interaction spaces and to provide details for the design of interface elements.

We used a combination of models from an object-oriented analysis method [12] and Wisdom [17]. This combination worked well in the sense that it covered the necessary activities of user interface design.

The notion of interaction spaces was used to define elements in the user interface that would support the users' individual tasks. This enabled us to handle the complexity of the user interface without getting burdened with details about widgets and other concrete elements. Thereby, the notion provided a useful abstraction mechanism.

The abstraction was linked to the models of the users' tasks. In our case study, we used essential task models, but other task models might be used instead. This relation meant that we could describe the essential elements of the user interface first. Later, we could deal with the detailed design issues, and the decisions on these details did not affect the decisions on the essential elements.

The user interface we designed grew out of the case we worked with. The idea of illustrating the machine and providing two connected menus with machines and part was new for this type of application. We have designed other communication devices for other application domains. However, this design was substantially different. The abstraction in terms of interaction spaces facilitated the creative process.

When we created the detailed design of the user interface, we had no methodological support. In this process it would have been useful to have guidelines for defining the specific details of the individual user interface elements.

We also discovered a fundamental problem in the design process. If our task flow were too detailed, it became very complicated to describe interaction spaces and interaction tasks. We solved this problem by relating interaction tasks to the problem domain model's class diagram. An interaction task should involve one class, and handle everything related to that class. Thus the class diagram defines the level of granularity for the interaction model.

7 Conclusion

This paper describes experience from a case study where we conducted a model-based design of the user interface of a mobile communicator for a safety-critical domain. In this process, we exploited results from an object-oriented analysis. The design process was supported by selected model notations from the Wisdom method. The case study indicated that the notion of interaction spaces is useful as an abstraction mechanism in the design process. It can help user interface designers exploit object-oriented analysis results and reduce the complexity of designing a user interface. The user interface design process was successful to the extent that the different activities produced results that were relevant for the following activities, we created a novel design and the usability evaluation of a functional prototype gave positive results.

These conclusions are based on a single case study. In addition, the case was to design a mobile communication system for a safety-critical domain. It would be interesting to try out the presented approach on other cases.

Acknowledgments

We are grateful to the employees of the fuel department at Nordjyllandsværket for giving us the opportunity to use the fuel department as the case in our design process. The project in which the research behind this paper was carried out is partly financed by the Danish Research Councils (grant number 2106-04-0022).

References

[1] Boehm, B., Gray, T., and Seewaldt, T. Prototyping versus Specifying: A Multiproject Experiment. *IEEE Trans. Software Eng. SE-10*, 3 (May 1984), 290-303.
[2] Calvary, G., Coutaz, J., Thevenin, D., Limbourg, Q., Bouillon, L. and Vanderdonckt, J. A Unifying Reference Framework for Multi-Target User Interfaces. *Interacting with Computer, 15*, 3 (2003), 289-308.
[3] Clerckx, T., Luyten, K., and Coninx, K. The Mapping Problem Back and Forth: Customizing Dynamic Models while Perserving Consistency. In *Proceedings of TAMODIA 2004*, ACM, 33-42.
[4] Clerckx, T., Winters, F. and Coninx, K. Tool Support for Designing Context-Sensitive User Interfaces using a Model-Based Approach. In *Proceedings of TAMODIA 2005*, ACM, 11-18.
[5] Coad, P. and Yourdon, E. *Object-Oriented Analysis*, second edition. Prentice-Hall, Englewood Cliffs, New Jersey, 1991.
[6] Dey, A. K. and Abowd, G. D. Towards a Better Understanding of Context and Context-Awareness. In *Proceedings of CHI 2000*, ACM.
[7] Dijkstra, E. Notes on structured programming. In *Structured Programming*. Academic Press, London, 1972, 1-82.
[8] Dunlop, M. D. and Brewster, S. A. The challenges of mobile devices for human computer interaction. *Personal and Ubiquitous Computing, 6*, 4 (2002).
[9] Langefors, B. *Theoretical Analysis of Information Systems*. Studentlitteratur, 1966.
[10] Limbourg, Q. and Vanderdonckt, J. Adressing the Mapping Problem in User Interface Design with UsiXML. In *Proceedings of TAMODIA 2004*, ACM, 155-163.
[11] Mahfoudi, A., Abed, M. and Abid, M. Towards a User Interface Generation Approach Based on Object Oriented Design and Task Model. In *Proceedings of TAMODIA 2005*, ACM, 135-142.
[12] Mathiassen, L., Munk-Madsen, A., Nielsen, P. A. and Stage, J. *Object-Oriented Analysis & Design*. Marko Publishing, Aalborg, 2000.
[13] Mathiassen, L. and Stage, J. The Principle of Limited Reduction in Software Design. *Information Technology & People, 6*, 2-3 (1992), 171-185.
[14] Nielsen, J. and Molich, R. Heuristic Evaluation of User Interfaces. In Proceedings of CHI 1990, ACM, 249-256.
[15] Nobrega, L. Nunes, N. J. and Coelho, H. DialogSketch: Dynamics of the Canonical Prototypes. In *Proceedings of TAMODIA 2005*, ACM, 19-25.
[16] Nunes, N. J. and Cunha, J. F. Wisdom: A Software Engineering Method for Small Software Development Companies. *IEEE Software*, 2001.
[17] Nunes, N. J. and Cunha, J. F. Wisdom - Whitewater Interactive System Development with Object Models. In M. van Harmelen (Ed.), *Object Modeling and User Interface Design*. Addison-Wesley, 2001.

[18] Parnas, D. Software Aspects of Strategic Defense Systems. *Communications of the ACM, 28*, 12 (Dec. 1985), 1326-1335.
[19] Prinebeau, C. and Vanderdonckt, J. Exploring Design Heuristics for User Interface Derivation from Task and Domain Models. In *Proceedings of CADUI 2002*, 103-110.
[20] Reichart, D. Forbrig, P. and Dittmar, A. Task Models as a Basis for Requirements Engineering and Software Execution. In *Proceedings of TAMODIA 2004*, ACM, 51-58.
[21] Rumbaugh, J., Blaha, M., Premerlani, W., Eddy, S., and Lorensen W. *Object-Oriented Modelling and Design*. Prentice-Hall, Engelwood Cliffs, New Jersey, 1991.
[22] Wirth, N. *Systematic Programming. An Introduction*. Prentice-Hall, Englewood Cliffs, New Jersey, 1973.
[23] Wolff, A., Forbrig, P., Dittmar, A. and Reichart, D. Linking GUI Elements to Tasks – Supporting an Evolutionary Design Process. In *Proceedings of TAMODIA 2005*, ACM, 27-34.
[24] Wulf, W. Languages and structured programs. In R.T. Yeh (Ed.), *Current Trends in Programming Methodology*. Prentice-Hall, New Jersey, 1977.

Comparing NiMMiT and Data-Driven Notations for Describing Multimodal Interaction

Joan De Boeck, Chris Raymaekers, and Karin Coninx

Hasselt University, Expertise Centre for Digital Media (EDM)
and transnationale Universiteit Limburg
Wetenschapspark 2, B-3590 Diepenbeek, Belgium
{joan.deboeck,chris.raymaekers,karin.coninx}@uhasselt.be

Abstract. In the past few years, multimodal interaction is gaining importance in virtual environments. Although multimodality makes interaction with the environment more intuitive and natural for the user, the development cycle of such an environment is often a long and expensive process. In our overall field of research, we investigate how model-based design can help shorten this process by designing the application with the use of high-level diagrams. In this scope, we developed 'NiMMiT', a graphical notation especially suitable for expressing multimodal user interaction. We have already experienced the benefits of NiMMiT in several in-house applications, and are currently assessing the value of NiMMiT with respect to existing notations. In this paper we report on our comparison of NiMMiT against some well known data-driven modeling notations.

1 Introduction

Interactive Virtual Environments (IVEs) are computer generated worlds that allow the user to intuitively interact with the data or objects in this world. To improve the intuitiveness of the interaction, the communication between the human and the system often is multimodal: information is not only exchanged visually and kinesthetic, but also via haptics, sounds or spoken messages. Due to the complexity of the virtual worlds, and the complexity of the human senses, designing such IVEs is more often than not a very time consuming and expensive process.

For several years, our lab has been conducting research on optimising interaction in IVEs using multimodal techniques. Several solutions using force feedback [1], speech or two handed input [2] already have been described in our former work. Even though we have gradually developed a code framework, each solution ended up in hundreds of lines of code to be written before being able to use the proposed interface. To shorten the design and development cycle, we developed NiMMiT (Notation For Multimodal Interaction Techniques), a visual notation optimised to describe human interaction in such IVEs.

NiMMiT has already shown its usefulness in several in-house applications, and will soon be integrated in other domains and other frameworks. At the same time,

K. Coninx, K. Luyten, and K.A. Schneider (Eds.): TAMODIA 2006, LNCS 4385, pp. 217–229, 2007.

there is a growing need for tool support. NiMMiT has been developed, driven by the specific needs to model multimodal interaction techniques at a high level, minimising the amount and the complexity of the code to be written. For the development of NiMMiT we conducted a thorough research and studied several other existing graphical notations. As our current experience, and the future applications allow us to conclude that the NiMMiT approach looks promising, we decided to perform a more formal evaluation of the current version of NiMMiT against other existing solutions. In this paper, we will specifically focus on the data-driven notations, other state-driven notations will be evaluated similarly in our next work.

In the next section, we first briefly explain how we developed NiMMiT. Thereafter, we show the basic building blocks of our notation. In section 4, as an example, we explain the Voodoo-Dolls interaction technique [3] using NiMMiT. Subsequently, we try to express the same technique using some other diagrams. Finally we discuss the comparison of the different notations and state our conclusions.

2 Describing User Interaction

A possible solution to shorten the development cycle of an interaction technique (IT) is to *describe* the interaction, rather than *implementing* it. The description can be performed using a high-level graphical notation. The proposed notation should be suitable for

- allowing designers to communicate about the functionality of an IT, using an easy-to read diagram
- allowing an application framework to interpret (an XML-based equivalent of) the diagram, so it can be used for automatic execution.

The notation must provide enough low-level information for a framework to execute the diagrams, but it also needs to be high-level and easily readable for a designer to reason about the IT. Several general notations exist, such as State Charts [4], Petri-nets, Coloured Petri-nets [5] and UML [6]. Other notations, are extended or optimised to support user interaction in particular. Examples are InTml [7], ICon [8] and ICO [9][10].

To our opinion, to describe interaction, a notation should also satisfy the following criteria:

Event Driven: Interaction techniques are inherently driven by user-initiated actions, which we define as events. Human interaction is multimodal by nature. Multimodality can be seen as a combination of unimodal events (e.g. pointer movement, click, speech command, gesture, etc.). Hence, events are 'the initiators' of the interaction.

State Driven: While interacting with it, the system not always has to respond to all available events. Mostly, certain events must have been occurred before other events are enabled. Therefore, we define an IT as a finite state machine,

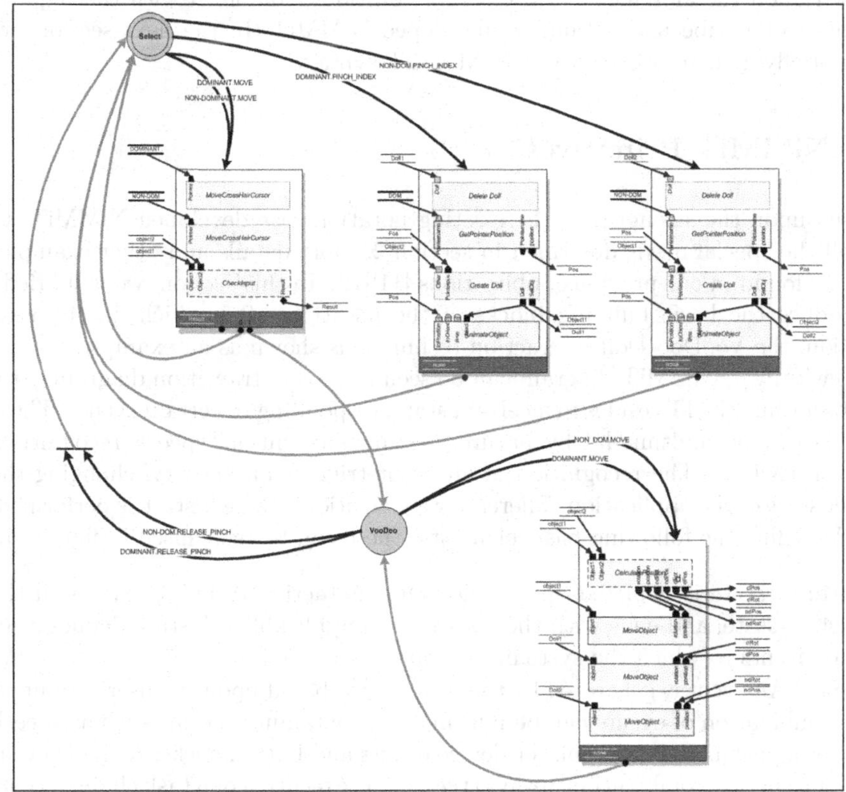

Fig. 1. NiMMiT Diagram of the VooDoo-doll interaction Technique

in which each state defines to which events the system will respond. The occurrence of an event invokes some action to the system, followed by a state transition.

Data Driven: Limiting our vision on interaction techniques solely to a finite state machine would be too restrictive, and it would violate the requirement of automatic execution. It is clear that user interaction implies some important data flow, internally (e.g. the collision between the virtual hand and an object in order to move that object). Obviously, certain data must be exchanged between the different actions within the interaction technique.

Hierarchical Reuse: Some subtasks of interaction techniques recur rather frequently. Selecting objects is an example of a very common component. When modelling a new interaction technique, the designer should be able to reuse descriptions that were created earlier. Therefore, the notation should support a hierarchical build-up, so an existing diagram of an interaction technique can be reused as a subtask of a new description.

Based upon the aforementioned existing notations, combined with the requirements to describe interaction, we developed NiMMiT. In the next section, we will briefly give an overview of the NiMMiT syntax.

3 NiMMiT Primitives

Based upon the strengths of the existing notations, we developed NiMMiT, to fulfill the special needs described in section 2. More details and other examples can be found in our previous publications [11][12]. In this section, we will briefly introduce the basic building blocks of the notation, after which, in the next section, the VooDoo-Doll interaction technique is shown as an example.

Basically, a NiMMiT diagram can be seen as a state transition diagram. At a certain time, the IT resides in a certain state, responding to certain events. These events can be multimodal by nature: gesture recognition, speech recognition, button clicks,... The recognition of an event triggers an activity, changing the inner state of the application. Thereafter a transition to a next state is performed.

We define the following basic elements (these can be recognised in figure 1):

State: A state is depicted as a circle. The interaction technique starts in the start-state, and ends with the end-state (if applicable). A state defines a set of events to which the system responds.

Event: An event is generated by the framework, based upon the user's input. A combination of events can be multimodal, containing actions such as speech recognition, gestures, pointer device events and button clicks. A single event or a specific combination always triggers the execution of a task chain. Events are depicted as an arrow pointing away from the state.

Task Chain: A task chain is initiated by an event and is depicted as a shaded rectangle in the diagram. A task chain is a linear succession of tasks, which will be executed one after the other.

Task: A task is a basic building block of the actual execution of the interaction technique. Typically, tasks access or alter the internal state of the application. E.g., when running in a typical 3D environment, a task can be 'collision detection', 'moving objects', 'playing audio feedback',... Tasks can be predefined by the system, but designers can also define their own custom tasks using C++ or a scripting language. Tasks can have input and output ports, on which they receive or send parameters or result values. Input ports are required or optional, indicated by a black or a grey input port respectively.

Labels: As data can be shared throughout a diagram, NiMMiT needs a system to (temporarily) store values. This is done in 'labels', which can be seen as high-level variables. Labels are depicted in the diagram beside the task chains and are always connected to the input or output ports of a task.

State Transitions: Finally, when a task chain has been executed completely, a state transition moves the diagram into the next state. A choice between multiple state transitions is also possible, based upon the value of a certain label.

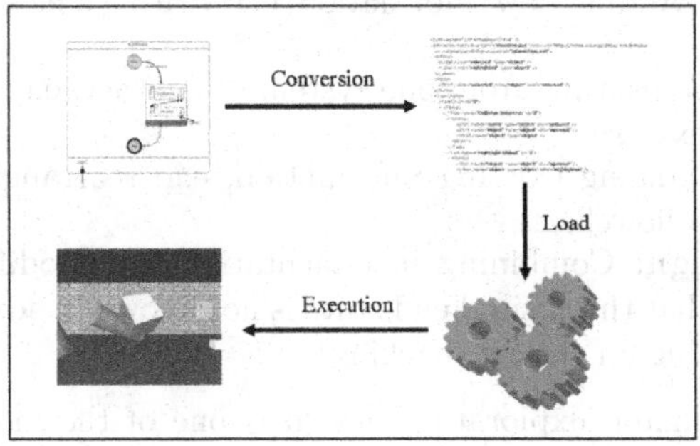

Fig. 2. Execution of a NiMMiT Diagram

A NiMMiT diagram does not support concurrency in principle, but several diagrams can run simultaneously and can be synchronised at any time. More advanced multimodality such as complementary and redundancy as described in [13] are possible. This is described more in detail in [12].

To meet our requirement of execution, a diagram is saved to an XML equivalent. That XML is read and interpreted by an application framework, as shown in figure 2.

4 Evaluation Approach

In this section, we will first define the evaluation criteria, which we will adopt for the assessment. Then, we will explain the VooDoo-Dolls interaction technique [3] as a case study. In the next section, we first elaborate on VooDoo-dolls, using NiMMiT. Subsequently, we try to describe the same IT using other data-driven notations. We opted to elaborate on InTML and UML: InTML, because it is a purely data-driven notation, and UML as it is the most fundamental standard. Finally, we discuss the different diagrams and their suitability to describe ITs against the defined criteria.

4.1 Evaluation Criteria

The evaluation of graphical notations is not an exact process which often results in variegated and/or subjective conclusions. To minimise the impact of subjective impressions, we will first define on which criteria the notations will be evaluated, however one can criticise that selection of criteria is subjective in some respect, as well. The criteria are based on Green's 'Cognitive Dimensions of Information Artefacts' [14][15]. Cognitive Dimensions are, as the author says, 'discussion tools that give names to concepts that their users may only have half-formulated'. The CD framework comes with 14 dimensions which focus on different aspects of the notation. Each dimension can either be positive or negative, dependent on the application in which the notation is applied. Green distinguishes four possible applications:

Incrementation: Adding new information; e.g. writing a new piece of programming code.

Transcription: Translating from one system to another; e.g. copying book details to an index card.

Modification: Changing existing information; e.g. rearranging and changing some parts of a flowchart.

Exploratory design: Combining incrementation and modification, with the characteristic that the desired end state is not known in advance; e.g. sketching, programming on the fly (hacking).

In our research domain, exploratory design is one of the most important applications of a high-level notation. As the notation is mainly intended to easily design, try and modify interaction techniques, a diagram is often designed step by step in a trial-and-error manner. Since the evaluation of a dimension is highly dependent on the application, we evaluate the selected notations in the scope of 'Exploratory design'.

The CD framework defines the folowing cognitive dimensions: abstraction, hidden dependencies, premature commitment, secondary notation, viscosity, visibility, closeness of mapping, consistency, diffuseness, error-proneness, hard mental operations, progressive evaluation, provisionality, role-expressiveness.

In the scope of this paper, and the evaluation of the particular notations, the following dimensions are relevant:

Abstraction is a grouping of elements to be treated as one entity. The **abstraction barrier** is the minimum number of abstractions that must be known before the notation can be used. **Abstraction tolerant** systems allow users to make their own abstractions, but don't require to do so. In our solution we strive to a low abstraction barrier, but an abstraction tolerant notation.

Diffuseness expresses the verboseness of a notation. A notation for interaction techniques must be not to diffuse.

Role-Expressiveness describes how easy it is to distinguish the different components or logical blocks in a notation. It is clear that the notation in our application must be as role-expressive as possible.

Viscosity is the resistance of a notation to change, or in other words the implications of a small change on the entire diagram. As we take the exploratory design as the main application for the notation, a high viscosity is adverse.

Progressive Evaluation means that the work in progress can be easily checked for as far as it is finished. This means that only a part of the entire solution can be evaluated. It is clear that in exploratory design, this is important.

Premature Commitment expresses in what amount a designer must make some decisions in advance before the proper information is available.

4.2 VooDoo-Doll Interaction Technique

In order to assess the selected notations, we have chosen to elaborate on the VooDoo-Dolls interaction technique [3], because it is a well known two-handed metaphor, which results in fairly easy diagrams in all notations, while still demanding most of the requirements of multimodal interaction. We will assume that if this IT can be easily modelled using the evaluated notations, there is a good chance that other techniques will fit, as well.

Voodoo-Dolls is a two-handed IT used to manipulate (distant) objects in 3D. By moving one of the hands, a crosshair cursor (attached to that hand) is moved accordingly. If the cursor moves over an object and the index and thumb of that hand are closed ('pinch'-event) a 'doll' is created and attached to the corresponding hand. A doll is a representation of the original virtual object, but scaled and attached to the movements of that hand. As soon as two dolls are defined, the manipulation phase of the IT starts. By moving the doll of the dominant hand, with respect to the doll of the non-dominant hand, the original object is moved with respect to the other object. When the thumb and the index are released, the doll is removed and the original object keeps its new location. The aim of this IT is to manipulate objects at any scale (close-by and far) with respect to each other. E.g. if the user creates a doll of a tea-pot in the dominant hand, and a table on the other side of the room in the non-dominant hand, he can easily put the pot on the table by moving both dolls with respect to each other.

5 Evaluation Results

5.1 NiMMiT

NiMMiT Diagram

Referring to figure 1, the IT starts in the 'Select'-state. Here the system responds to four events: either a move of the dominant or the non-dominant hand, or a 'pinch' (closing thumb and index) of one of the hands. If a 'pinch' occurs, dependent on the hand, one of the task chains at the right side of the diagram is executed, creating a doll for that hand. Each time one of the hands moves, the crosshair cursors of both hands are updated and the system checks if there are already two dolls present. If not, a state-transition to the original state is performed. Otherwise, we arrive at the 'VooDoo'-state. If the hands are moved now, the activated task chain calculates the object's new position with respect to the reference object (attached non-dominant hand's doll), and the object and the dolls are moved accordingly. When the user releases the pinch of one of the hands, a transition to the 'Select'-state is performed and a new doll can be made.

Evaluation

If we compare the NiMMiT diagram against the aforementioned criteria, we see that NiMMiT has a reasonable **abstraction** barrier, since it consists of about 10 constructs. It is allowed for a designer to define custom abstraction at the level of hierarchical diagrams. Concerning the **diffuseness**, there are no unnecessary structures, although one can have objections against the explicit internal labels

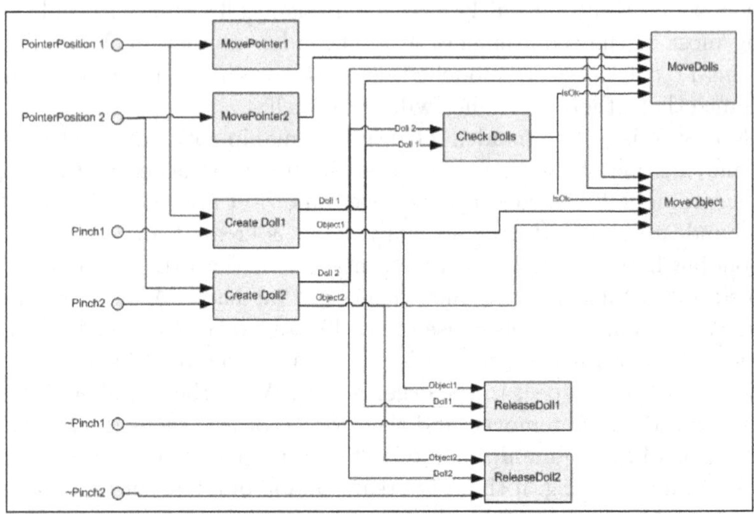

Fig. 3. InTML Diagram of the VooDoo-doll Interaction Technique

within a task chain (see bottom-most task chain in figure 1). As there is a clear syntactic difference between states, task chains, events and transitions, the notation is enough **role-expressive**. The **viscosity** is reasonable, although changes in a task-chain can have an influence on the data flow of the entire diagram. As the diagram must not be fully functional before it can be run, **progressive evaluation** is supported. Finally, as a drawback of any graphical notation, some **premature commitments** are required for positioning the primitives within the diagram.

5.2 InTML

InTML Diagram

InTML [7] is a purely data-driven notation to describe the execution of an application at a high level. It does not support states, but uses 'filters' instead. A filter can be seen as a 'black box', performing some activity based upon its inputs, while returning the output at its output ports. Important to know is that the control flow of the diagram is implicitly driven by the data, as a filter is only executed as soon as it contains a valid input on all of its input ports.

Figure 3 shows a possible diagram in InTML of the VooDoo-Dolls interaction technique.

At the left hand side, the user's input is shown. The positions of the user's dominant and non-dominant hand always are valid inputs. Hence, the filters moving the cursors (crosshairs) are constantly executed. As soon as the user closes the thumb and the index of a hand, the 'Pinch'-variable becomes valid, and a doll is created. The 'Create Doll' filters create a doll from the object which is indicated by the crosshair cursor. It returns the object and its doll. As soon as both dolls are created, the 'checkdolls' filter returns 'true', as it has a valid input on all ports. The returned value activates the 'MoveDolls' and 'MoveObject' filters, which moves the dolls and the object according to the movements of the user's hands. As soon as a pinch is released and a valid doll exists, the doll is released in the 'ReleaseDoll' filter.

Evaluation

InTML has a minimal **abstraction barrier**, as it only consists of three constructs. However, to our knowledge, the notation does not allow users to define their own abstractions. The low barrier, however, means that the **diffuseness** will increase, as for more complex structures more primitives are needed. This will have its implications to the **viscosity**, as well. E.g. if the 'Object In Hand' metaphor [2], with more mutual exclusive phases should be described, more additional filters will be necessary to enable or disable certain parts of the diagram. Moreover, if one of the first filters must be changed, it has implications on all subsequent filters. Next, in our opinion, the **role-expressiveness** of the notation is not optimal, since recognising functional blocks in the diagram is only based upon their location. Although difficult to check in practice, we can imagine that **progressive evaluation** is supported so that it is not required to finish the entire diagram before it can be tested. Finally, here again **premature commitments** are required for the positioning of the notation's primitives.

5.3 UML Activity Diagrams

UML Diagram

Figure 4 shows the same interaction technique, modelled using UML activity diagrams. We start at the topmost node, where we wait for the occurrence of one of the events. When a pinch is recognised, the doll belonging to that hand is created, and it is saved in a datastore. When the hands are moving, the crosshair cursors are constantly updated, and the 'CheckInput' activity checks if two dolls are currently present. When the check fails, the current node is repeated.

As soon as two dolls become available, the bottommost node is executed. Each time one of the hands is moved, the new position of the dolls and the objects is calculated. The objects are moved accordingly, restarting the same activity node again. When a pinch of one of the hands is released, an interruptible edge brings the token back to the first activity node.

Evaluation

The UML **abstraction barrier** is somewhat higher. In this diagram only 11 constructs are used, but inherently, as the standard is more extensive, it is not inconceivable that more structures must be known. UML allows for user defined abstraction but does not requires this, which is the approach we prefer. The **diffuseness** of the notation is good, however when we do not define specialised

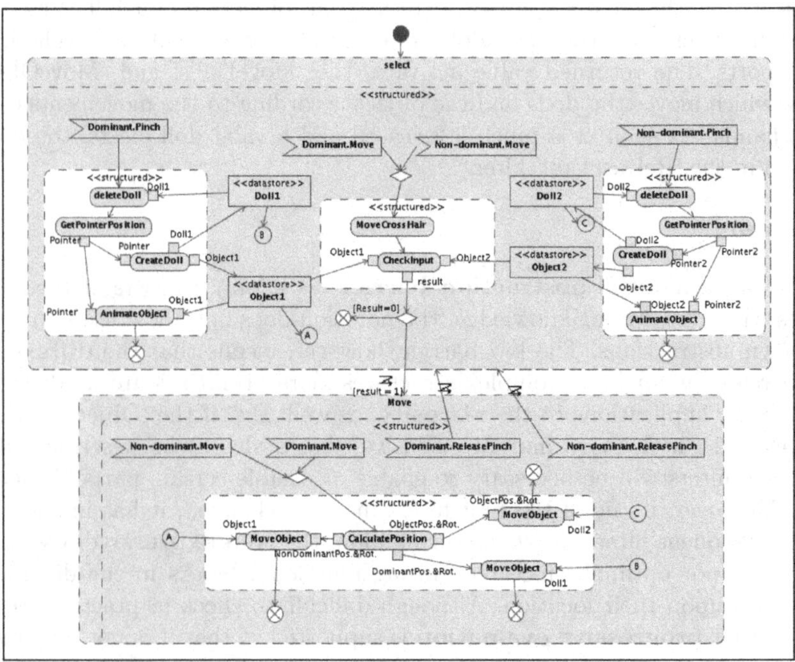

Fig. 4. UML Activity Diagram of the VooDoo-doll interaction Technique

stereotypes, there is some overhead of specific structures (such as datastores, structured activity nodes and interruptable regions) which are needed for syntactic and semantic correctness. The **role-expressiveness** and the **viscosity** are acceptable, although there is no syntactic difference between control flow and data flow, which can be seen as a minus. Finally, it appears that **progressive evaluation** can be supported. Finally, within UML, once again, **premature commitments** are required for the positioning of the primitives, resulting in a higher viscosity.

5.4 Discussion

We can summarise the results for the cognitive dimensions in the main application of an exploratory design as shown in table 1.

Comparing the three notations to each other, we can notice that InTML has a minimal **abstraction** barrier with only three constructs. However this will lead to a higher **diffuseness**. Moreover, InTML has no support for other user-defined abstraction. In contrast, UML and NiMMiT use a higher but comparable number of constructs. This makes the abstraction barrier higher, but still acceptable. Both notations have some syntactical overhead, but they do not form a real problem concerning the readability of the diagrams.

The **roll-expressiveness** of InTML is low. As a result of the low number of constructs, the only way to distinguish functional blocks is by their location.

Table 1. Cognitive Dimensions for the notations

	InTML	UML	NiMMiT
Abstraction	Minimal barrier No additional abstr	Acceptable barrier Abstr Tollerant	Acceptable barrier Abstr Tollerant
Diffuseness	Quite Verbose	Some overhead of extra structures	Some overhead of internal labels
Role-Expressiveness	Functional blocks only recognisable by location	Acceptable	States and Tasks are well distinguishable
Viscosity	Strong implications in subsequent filter	Some data flow issues	Some data flow issues
Progressive Evaluation	Supported	Supported	Supported
Premature Commitment	Only for location of primitives	Only for location of primitives	Only for location of primitives

The role-expressiveness of UML is significantly better, but we regret that there is no syntactic difference to indicate data flow and control-flow, as we prefer to see both as separate entities within an interaction technique. Because NiMMiT makes a clear syntactic distinction between states, events, tasks and transitions, we prefer the role-expressiveness of NiMMiT.

Diagrams in InTML can quickly grow as the interaction technique consists of more mutual exclusive phases, resulting in a higher **viscosity**. Moreover, InTML is based on the principle of executing filters as soon as it receives a legal value on all of its input ports. This means that a change to a filter, will inherently propagate to the next filters, resulting in a higher viscosity, again. UML and NiMMiT appear to have a similar viscosity. Changes to the diagram will inherently have implications to the data flow of the remainder of the diagram; however, as data flow is not the main aspect of the diagram, the impact will be lower as with InTML.

Finally, it appears that all notations support **progressive evaluation**, which is desirable in the context of an exploratory design. Since InTML, NiMMiT and UML are all graphical notations, they all require some **premature commitments** with respect to the location of the primitives. As far as we can see, this is the only occurrence of premature commitments, which is acceptable.

In summary, we can conclude that, according to the proposed criteria, InTML is less suitable to describe user interaction, in the experimental environment in which we want to apply it. NiMMiT and UML are very similar and are both suitable. The overhead of the UML notation in the example can be easily reduced by defining suitable stereotypes. However, we are somewhat concerned about the underlying complexity of the entire UML standard, which must be known for the integration of frameworks for automatic execution and the development of tool support. Using stereotypes will facilitate the use of the notations, but will even increase this underlying complexity. UML is indeed a very general and powerful standard, but only a very small part of it is applicable for describing user interaction. On the other hand, NiMMiT is especially designed for describing user interaction, and is therefore more dedicated to this domain.

Keeping the findings above in mind, it is difficult to make an exclusive choice between both notations. However, the research in this paper has led to some concrete recommendations for the NiMMiT syntax to be improved, such as the removal of internal labels within a task chain, or an improved abstraction tolerance so that complex diagrams can be simplified by user defined abstractions.

6 Conclusions and Future Work

We evaluated NiMMiT, a graphical notation dedicated to describe interaction techniques against other existing data-driven notations. Compared against criteria, based on Green's 'Cognitive Dimensions', we can conclude that purely data-driven notations (such as InTML) are less suitable to describe interaction techniques. The general standard UML appears to be comparable to NiMMiT. However, we still have our concerns to adopt the UML standard, as this will complicate the development of tool support and the integration of interpreters in our model-based approach.

As a result of this research, we will concretely update the NiMMiT notation, and at the same time keep an eye on the usage of UML in the domain of VE-development.

As stated in the introduction, this paper focussed on the comparison of NiMMiT against data-driven alternatives, in particular. In a next step, we plan to evaluate NiMMiT in a similar way against the family of the state-driven notations, such as Petri-Nets and ICO.

Acknowledgements

Part of the research at EDM is funded by ERDF (European Regional Development Fund), the Flemish Government and the Flemish Interdisciplinary Institute for Broadband Technology (IBBT).

NiMMiT has been developed within the VR-DeMo project (IWT 030248), which is directly funded by the IWT, a Flemish subsidy organization.

The authors also want to thank Jan Van den Bergh for his valuable contributions applying the UML notation.

References

1. De Boeck, J., Raymaekers, C., Coninx, K.: Aspects of haptic feedback in a multi-modal interface for object modelling. Virtual Reality Journal **6** (2003) 257–270
2. De Boeck, J., Cuppens, E., De Weyer, T., Raymaekers, C., Coninx, K.: Multi-sensory interaction metaphors with haptics and proprioception in virtual environments. In: Proceedings of the third ACM Nordic Conference on Human-Computer Interaction (NordiCHI 2004), Tampere, FI (2004)

3. Pierce, J., Stearns, B., Pausch, R.: Voodoo dolls: seamless interaction at multiple scales in virtual environments. In: Proceedings of symposium on interactive 3D graphics, Atlanta, GA, USA (1999)
4. Harel, D.: Statecharts: A visual formalism for complex systems. In: Science of Computer Programming. Volume 8. (1987) 231–274
5. Jensen, K.: An introduction to the theoretical aspects of coloured petri nets. In: W.-P. de Roever, G. Rozenberg (eds.): A Decade of Concurrency, Lecture Notes in Computer Science. Volume 803., Springer-Verlag (1994) 230–272
6. Ambler, S.: Object Primer, The Agile Model-Driven Development with UML 2.0. Cambridge University Press (2004)
7. Figueroa, P., Green, M., Hoover, H.: InTml: A description language for VR applications. In: Proceedings of Web3D'02, Arizona, USA (2002)
8. Dragicevic, P., Fekete, J.D.: Support for input adaptability in the ICON toolkit. In: Proceedings of the 6th international conference on multimodal interfaces (ICMI04), State College, PA, USA (2004) 212–219
9. Navarre, D., Palanque, P., Bastide, R., Schyn, A., Winckler, M., Nedel, L., Freitas, C.: A formal description of multimodal interaction techniques for immersive virtual reality applications. In: Proceedings of Tenth IFIP TC13 International Conference on Human-Computer Interaction, Rome, IT (2005)
10. Palanque, P., Bastide, R.: Petri net based design of user-driven interfaces using the interactive cooperative objects formalism. In: Interactive Systems: Design, Specification, and Verification, Springer-Verlag (1994) 383–400
11. Coninx, K., Cuppens, E., De Boeck, J., Raymaekers, C.: Integrating support for usability evaluation into high level interaction descriptions with NiMMiT. In: Proceedings of 13th International Workshop on Design, Specification and Verification of Interactive Systems (DSVIS'06), Dublin, Ireland (2006)
12. Vanacken, D., De Boeck, J., Raymaekers, C., Coninx, K.: NiMMiT: A notation for modeling multimodal interaction techniques. In: Proceedings of the International Conference on Computer Graphics Theory and Applications (GRAPP06), Setbal, Portugal (2006)
13. Coutaz, J., Nigay, L., Salber, D., Blandford, A., May, J., Young, R.M.: Four easy pieces for assessing the usability of multimodal interaction: The CARE properties. In: Proceedings of INTERACT95, Lillehammer (1995) 115–120
14. Green, T.: Cognitive dimensions of notations. In: People and Computers, Cambridge University Press, Cambridge, UK (1989) 443–460
15. Green, T., Blackwell, A.: Cognitive dimensions of information artefacts: a tutorial. http://www.ndirect.co.uk/ thomas.green/workstuff/papers/ (2005)

Incorporating Tilt-Based Interaction in Multimodal User Interfaces for Mobile Devices

Jani Mäntyjärvi[1], Fabio Paternò[2], and Carmen Santoro[2]

[1] VTT Technical Research Centre, Kaitoväylä 1,
90571 Oulu, Finland
[2] ISTI-CNR, Via G. Moruzzi 1,
56124 Pisa, Italy
{Jani.Mantyjarvi, Fabio.Paterno, Carmen.Santoro}@Isti.Cnr.It

Abstract. Emerging ubiquitous environments raise the need to support multiple interaction modalities in diverse types of devices. Designing multimodal interfaces for ubiquitous environments using development tools creates challenges since target platforms support different resources and interfaces. Model-based approaches have been recognized as useful for managing the increasing complexity consequent to the many available interaction platforms. However, they have usually focused on graphical and/or vocal modalities. This paper presents a solution for enabling the development of tilt-based hand gesture and graphical modalities for mobile devices in a multimodal user interface development tool. The challenges related to developing gesture-based applications for various types of devices involving mobile devices are discussed in detail. The possible solution presented is based on a logical description language for hand-gesture user interfaces. Such language allows us to obtain a user interface implementation on the target mobile platform. The solution is illustrated with an example application that can be accessed from both the desktop and mobile device supporting tilt-based gesture interaction.

Keywords: Model-based design of user interfaces, gestural interfaces for mobile devices, tilt interfaces.

1 Introduction

Pervasive environments are characterized by seamless connectivity and various types of devices, through which a user can interact with applications. This creates challenges in implementing the means for interaction, and several interaction modalities e.g. graphical, vocal, gesture, touch, and tactile can potentially be used. Also, different devices have different operating platforms, and user interfaces must be described in different ways: for example some devices support browsers and the user interface can be implemented with XML-based mark-up languages e.g. X/HTML, VoiceXML, X+V etc., while in other devices access to system level software is required to enable the functionality for supporting specific modalities. Model-based approaches [16] [20] can be useful to address such increasing complexity by providing meaningful abstractions that allow designers to focus on the main

K. Coninx, K. Luyten, and K.A. Schneider (Eds.): TAMODIA 2006, LNCS 4385, pp. 230–244, 2007.

conceptual aspects without being distracted by a plethora of low-level implementation details.

While support for model-based development of multimodal interfaces, limited to graphical and vocal modalities, has already been investigated [1][17][19], so far no proposal to address gesture interaction with mobile devices through model-based design has been put forward. This paper presents an in-depth discussion of problems and challenges related to gesture interfaces for mobile devices and a solution for interface development able to target mobile devices supporting gestures.

The structure of the paper is as follows: after discussing related and background work, we highlight the challenges related to designing gesture interfaces for mobile devices from abstract interface definitions. We then present a solution for enabling hand gesture UI development for target mobile platforms with the Multimodal TERESA environment. The approach is illustrated with an example application. Lastly, discussions and conclusions are provided along with indications for future work.

2 Related Work

Obrenovic et al. [15] have investigated the use of conceptual models expressed in UML in order to derive graphical, form-based interfaces for desktop or mobile devices or vocal devices. UML is a software engineering standard mainly developed for designing the internal software of application functionalities. Thus, it seems unsuitable to capture the specific characteristics of user interfaces and their software. The ICO formalism for user interfaces has shown to be suitable to model and specify multimodal interfaces mainly for analysis in safety-critical application [2], and it has limited automatic support for generation of multi-modal interfaces from such specifications.

One interesting effort to ease multimodal interface development is ICARE [4]: it provides a graphical environment for a component-based user interface exploiting various modalities and modules that allow various compositions of such modalities. In this paper we present a different approach: we show how we can derive multimodal interfaces starting with logical descriptions of tasks and user interfaces obtained through general, platform-independent notations. We still provide the possibility of combining the modalities in various ways, but at different granularity levels (inside a single interaction object and among several interaction objects). While some other work has been carried out to apply transformations to logical descriptions to derive multimodal interfaces [19], our work has been able to provide an authoring environment that is able to suggest solutions for identifying how to combine various modalities and allows designers to easily modify them in order to tailor the interface generation to specific needs. This result has been obtained by extending a previously existing authoring tool [14][17] that was limited to creating graphical and/or vocal interfaces.

In the research area of gesture-based interfaces, Rekimoto [18] carried out pioneering work on tilt-based interaction. Later on, Hinckley presented a study on how tilt actions and other sensors could be used in mobile devices [8]. More recently, other studies have been conducted from various viewpoints e.g., Murray et al. have applied control theory to tilt interaction [7]. The project XWand has studied a concept of multi-modal interaction for pervasive environments [21]. In this approach a handheld device equipped with inertial sensors is utilized to control various functionalities embedded in a room. Camera-based technologies are also used in mapping hand gestures to interaction commands. In [13], a handheld device with inertial sensing is utilized to control devices and applications in public spaces. The same paper also presents an in-depth examination of approaches for user dependent and independent gesture recognition. Also, the mobile-device, entertainment and consumer electronics industries have presented product concepts utilizing hand gesture interaction [10, 11]. However, all these contributions on gesture interaction have not addressed model-based generation.

3 Background

To provide some background on our approach the specific aspects of gestural interaction in mobile devices are identified and discussed. In addition, we introduce the framework for enabling model-based design of multi-modal user interfaces and situate the support for hand gesture interaction within such a framework.

3.1 Hand Gesture Interaction Through Inertial Sensing

In this subsection we discuss hand gesture interaction and interface design, as well as the challenges they pose for model-based UI design.

Some primary uses of hand gestures in interaction tasks include triggering, selection, and navigation. The design of gesture interfaces in general is a challenging task. The results obtained from pen-gesture and hand-gesture interface design studies are quite similar [9, 10]: gestures must be easily remembered by a user and captured reliably by a recognition system to ensure positive user experience. There are many challenges arising from the nature of gestures: the number of gestures is infinite; gestures can be simple or more complex; lastly, gestures are personal, e.g. the same gesture can be performed with different speed, scale and orientation of the hand.

There are various types of gestures. From the viewpoint of recognition systems they can be divided into three categories [9, 13]:

- Measure and control – measured signals tilt, rotation or amplitude are directly mapped onto interaction events.
- Discrete gestures – more complex gestures e.g. symbols, are captured with machine learning methods, and the beginning and end of a gesture are indicated by pressing and releasing a button.
- Continuous gestures – more complex gestures are captured with machine learning methods, and recognition runs continuously.

There are also various types of sensors available for various devices that may limit the amount and types of gestures supported by a target platform, e.g. a mobile device.

These challenges affect the design of recognition methods and set requirements on how to utilize gestures in end-user devices.

The gestures recognised on a device can be specified or a user can personalize them [9, 11]. In the case of fixed gestures, there usually is a set of trained models with a pre-defined gesture vocabulary in a gesture manager - a gesture recognition service located in a device - producing a set of pre-established consequences. On the other hand, in the case of personalized gestures, the manager may contain a predefined fixed set of trained models. However, the user also has the possibility to edit (add, remove, re-name, etc.) the existing set and, moreover, may train new gestures and link them to specific device actions.

The important role of gestures must be borne in mind in the design of multimodal interfaces. Gestures can potentially be used in navigation and in providing control commands. So a user interface supporting gesture interaction must combine at least the graphical and gesture modalities. In addition, vocal or tactile modalities can potentially be included in mobile devices. For example, let us consider the basic interaction elements: prompt, input and feedback. In interaction with a mobile device supporting gestures, several modalities should be used in a complete interaction: graphical for the prompt, gestures for providing input, and vocal, tactile and/or graphical for feedback.

In summary, the main challenges related to designing gesture-enabled interfaces for mobile devices using model-based approach are that gesture descriptions must tolerate uncertainty from gesture recognition. However, this applies mainly for more complex gestures while simple gestures, e.g. tilt gestures are provided usually with 100% accuracy. In addition to fixed naming of gestures, there must be support for defining customized gestures. Since inputting (control, activate, select and navigate) is the primary purpose of gesture interaction and it is impossible to prompt and give feedback through gestures, various types of interaction elements must be carefully combined with other modalities in the user interface to ensure a functional final UI for a target device. Moreover, in the model-based approach the description language defining the gesture UI (gesture vocabulary) must be general and flexible for allowing both stationary and customisable gesture sets.

In this paper, we present a solution able to support multi-device applications involving mobile devices with gesture control. Our development environment supports fixed simple and complex gesture sets. Gesture sets supported by development environment are presented in Figure 1.

Particular in gesture interfaces, tilt gesture means that a user may tilt a device, for example to left/right/backward/forward, to initiate some UI action. Tilt events are recognized by a gesture recognition software using signals from accelerometers. Arrow-, symbol- or other free form gestures mean that a device is waved to various directions and shapes of gestures imitate given shapes, arrows or symbols, etc. These types of gestures are more complex from gesture recognition viewpoint and they require machine learning-based recognition algorithms. Due to gesture sensing hardware availability only tilt gestures are supported in our target platform.

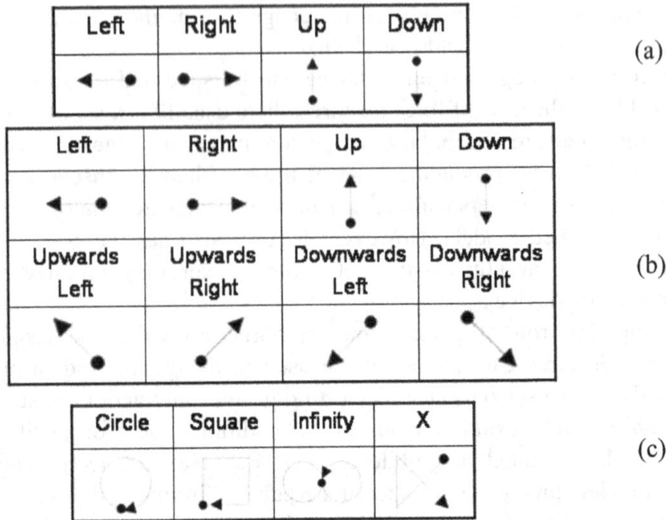

Fig. 1. Illustration of the gestures sets supported. *a)* Tilt set, *b)* Arrow set, c) Symbol set. Dot means the start of the gesture while black triangle (end of arrow) refers to end of gesture.

3.2 Model-Based Approaches

In the research community in model-based design of user interfaces there is a consensus on what the useful logical descriptions are [5, 16, 20]:

- The task and object level, which reflects the user view of the interactive system in terms of logical activities and objects that should be manipulated to accomplish them;
- The abstract user interface, which provides a platform independent description of the user interface;
- The concrete interface, which provides a platform dependent but implementation language independent description of the user interface;
- The final implementation, in an implementation language for user interfaces.

Thus, for example we can consider the task "select a work of art", this implies the need for a selection object at the abstract level, which indicates nothing regarding the modality in which the selection will be performed (it could be through a gesture or a vocal command or a graphical interaction). When we move to the concrete description then we have to assume a specific platform, for example the graphical desktop, and indicate a specific platform-dependent interaction technique to support the interaction in question (for example, selection could be through a radio-button or a list or a drop-down menu), but nothing is indicated in terms of a specific implementation language. By platform we mean a set of interaction resources that share similar capabilities (for example the graphical desktop, the vocal one, the cellphone, the graphical and vocal desktop). When we choose an implementation language we are ready to make the last transformation from the concrete description into the syntax of a specific user interface implementation language. We prefer to use the term platform independent for the abstract level rather than the term modality independent because a multimodal system is a system that processes two or more combined user input modes (such as speech, pen, touch, gestures, …) but we can have platforms that use the same input modes but with rather different available interaction resources (for example in terms of screen size) that heavily affect the possible task support and thus requiring different strategies for adapting the user interfaces to their features in order to obtain usable results.

The advantage of this type of approach is that it allows designers to focus on logical aspects and takes into account the user view right from the earliest stages of the design process. In the case of interfaces that can be accessed through different types of devices the approach has additional advantages. First of all, the task and the abstract level can be described through the same language for whatever platform we aim to address. Then, in our approach we have a concrete interface language for each target platform. Thus, a given platform identifies the type of interaction environment available for the user, and this clearly depends on the modalities supported by the platform itself. Actually, in our approach the concrete level is a refinement of the abstract interface depending on the associated platform. This means that all the concrete interface languages share the same structure and add concrete platform-dependent details on the possible attributes for implementing the logical interaction objects and the ways to compose them. All languages in our approach, for any abstraction level, are defined in terms of XML in order to make them more easily manageable and allow their export/import in different tools.

Another advantage of this approach is that maintaining links among the elements in the various abstraction levels allows the possibility of linking semantic information (such as the activity that users intend to do) and implementation, which can be exploited in many ways. A further advantage is that designers of multi-device interfaces do not have to learn the many details of the many possible implementation languages because the environment allows them to have full control over the design through the logical descriptions and leave the implementation to an automatic transformation from the concrete level to the target implementation language. In addition, if a new implementation language needs to be addressed, the entire structure of the environment does not change, but only the transformation from the associated concrete level to the new language has to be added. This is not difficult because the concrete level is already a detailed description of how the interface should be structured.

This means that the main challenge we had to address for supporting gestural interactions with mobile device through a model-based approach was the design of a concrete interface language for this platform. This language on the one hand should be the refinement of the general abstract language and on the other hand should contain all the relevant information necessary to generate then an implementation for this target platform in any language able to support it. In particular, as first implementation environment we have used the Microsoft Visual Studio 2005 with C# language enriched with the libraries for controlling the 2D accelerometer from Ecertech (http://ecertech.com).

4 A Logical Language for Gesture Interface

The XML concrete gesture interface language is a refinement of the abstract TERESA language [3]. It provides support for various types of gestures, which can be associated with the interaction types supported. It covers some gesture sets, e.g. basic tilt-set, free form arrow and symbol sets. Defining more complex custom sets also enables support for user-defined gestures. The concrete gesture interface language defines an interface using default settings and a number of presentations, each of which consists of definitions of the relevant interactors (interaction or only output) as well as the composition operators.

In the following the CUI declarations are presented. For all presentations, the gesture settings define which gesture sets are used:

```
<!ELEMENT default_settings (graphic_settings, gesture_settings, operators_
      settings, interactors_settings)>
<!ELEMENT gesture_settings (change_focus*, gesture_sets*)>
<!ELEMENT gesture_sets (tilt, arrow, symbol, custom*)>
```

The important issue in interacting with a multi-device application using gestures is simply to navigate between elements on a UI. For gesture UI it is crucially important to highlight the current focus of interaction. Changing the focus is defined as default settings within the gesture modality. In our example changing the focus is done by using basic tilt commands:

```
<!ATTLIST change_focus
      next (%tilt_act;) #REQUIRED
      previous (%tilt_act;) #REQUIRED>
```

Showing the focus graphically on a target platform can be done by highlighting graphical elements, such as, font-change, box, colour, etc.

In the tool, the gesture actions can be associated with interactors. The gesture actions are defined by default with the following sets:

```
<!ENTITY % tilt_act "null | tilt_left | tilt_right | tilt_forward | tilt_backward">
<!ENTITY % arrow_act "null | arrow_left | arrow_right | arrow_up | arrow_down |
    arrow_downwd_left | arrow_downwd_right | arrow_upwd_left |
    arrow_upwd_right ">
<!ENTITY % symbol_act "null | circle | square | infinity | x">
```

In multimodal UI, gestures can be potentially used only for input. In particular, they are suitable for control and selection. The relevant input-interactors to be used with gestures are indicated in Figure 2. The control interactor includes navigator and activator elements, while the selection interactor includes single and multiple selection elements. Such types of interactions also need to operate in parallel with graphical elements such as buttons or various types of lists. Graphically, interactors can be implemented using many objects, such as links, various types of buttons and menus and boxes.

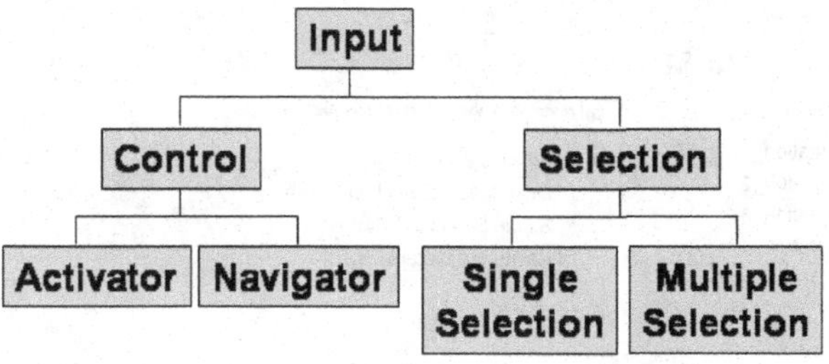

Fig. 2. Gesture-supported interaction interactors

Input interactors for gestures are defined as extensions to existing graphical ones; while defining graphical description definitions state gestures for interactors from the given sets.

```
<!ELEMENT activator  (button, gesture*)>,
<!ELEMENT navigator (button, gesture*)>,
<!ELEMENT single ((radio_button | list_box | drop_down_list), gesture*)>,
<!ELEMENT multiple ((check_box | list_box), gesture*)>,
```

where gesture element is defined with given gesture set(s) with possible gesture entities.

5 Gesture Interface Development

The Multimodal TERESA tool [14] already supports development of graphical and vocal modalities and enables interfaces implemented in XHTML, XHTML Mobile Profile, VoiceXML and X+V. In order to extend the interoperability of the tool for various types of platforms we have chosen the Pocket PC OS for our target platform and the C# implementation language for the target platform. The Microsoft environment provides robust support for PDAs. Our authoring tool has been extended in order to define gesture actions for interacting with a mobile device supporting gesture interaction. A screenshot of the user interface editor of the tool when defining the application user interface supporting graphical+gesture modalities is shown in Figure 3.

The structure of the control panel of the tool is described in [14]. For supporting gesture modality there is a new Gesture Attributes- area in the Concrete Properties subpanel. Moreover, the Multimodal Properties panel supports the specification of the relevant CARE (Complementary, Assignment, Equivalence and Redundancy) properties [6], which can be used to set how the supported modalities are utilized by a user to reach a goal. In addition, how to compose the modalities can be better analyzed by considering the different phases of an interaction (prompt, input, feedback). In the case of gesture-based interactions it is reasonable to output information only graphically. In this case outputting information refers to providing prompt and feedback, so the property for outputting data is graphical assignment by default.

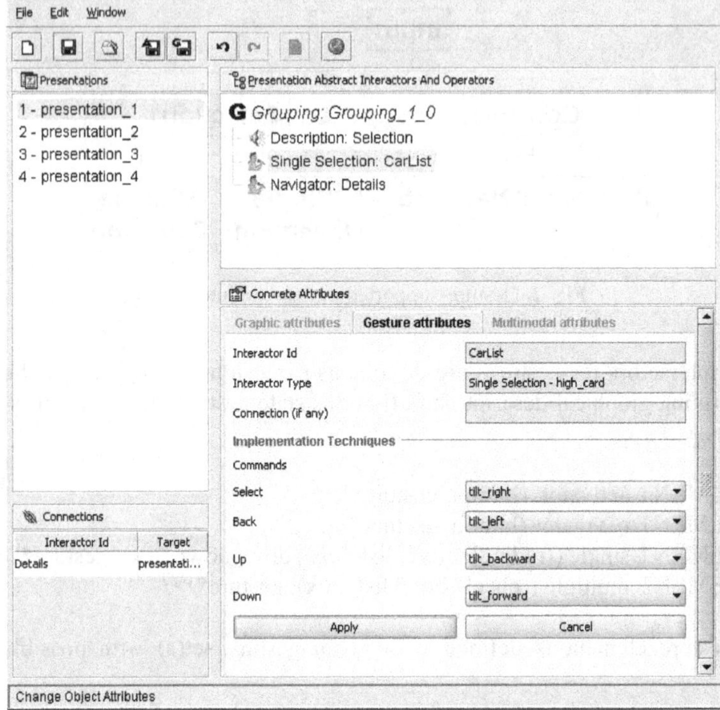

Fig. 3. Screen view of a UI development tool when designing graphical+gesture interface for a mobile device for our example

A user should be able to interact using either the graphical or gestural modalities. Thus, the property for inputting information is equivalence, while graphical assignment can be another option. In the case of composition operators (grouping, hierarchy, ordering and relation), the only relevant property is graphical assignment for the same reason as in the output-only interactor (the gestural modality cannot be used to output information).

Graphic attributes related to fonts, background, and graphical objects such as text and image descriptions are set on the tool for CUI. In the final UI generation phase, they are converted to corresponding definitions on target language by using corresponding classes, methods and properties.

On a target implementation, the user interface is defined in the following way. Firstly, interaction objects are associated to presentations and graphics and gesture attributes are set in the tool. Then, during the final UI generation the selected interactors are used to define corresponding controls by using the corresponding classes on the target language. Activators and navigators are implemented as buttons while single and multiple selectors are implemented using radio-button, check-box, list-box or drop-down-list. Regarding composition operators, grouping of UI object on a final UI is supported by using boxes including the relevant elements.

The gesture events supported are defined in a tool. In the code of the final UI, the commands defined are set as alternative choices for activating defined controllers either graphically or gesturally (when modalities are equivalent). For a target platform, equivalent gesture controls are implemented in the following manner. Elements of the generated graphical UI layout with event handlers are defined. The gesture events are associated with state transitions between interactor elements. When generating this part of code the input is taken from connections between presentations from the CUI. In order to incorporate interoperability a designer should make sure that naming of gesture actions in the tool matches to gesture events produced by GestureManager on a target platform. On a target platform, showing and moving focus graphically according to tilt-gestures is carried out by adding focus-related methods and properties to the state transitions of the user interface. The focus of the active state is shown through graphical highlighting.

The type of application that we have considered is form-based, meaning that the interactive part of the UI on various platforms (desktop and mobile device) consists mainly of interactive forms.

In our approach for producing UI for the selected target platform in Microsoft C# (supported by Visual Studio 2005), we assume that there is a project for containing libraries or an interface to a software producing gesture events (GestureManager - recognition software). In Microsoft Visual Studio 2005 a user interface is (mainly) defined through the Windows Forms, which, in C#, are defined as <name>*.cs* and <name>*.designer.cs* –files. The first file type contains the source for defining functionality of the form - together with other sources files while the latter file type defines the graphical layout of a window (Form). The <name>*.designer.cs* –files can be created traditionally by typing or automatically when designing layout by drag and drop in the Designer tool of the Interface Development Environment. The goal in our transformation is to generate content to the <name>*.designer.cs* –files and to the <name>*.cs* –files for defining graphical and gesture actions.

As discussed above, due to gesture sensing hardware availability only tilt gestures are supported in our target platform. In our tilt interaction model, vertical tilt actions (tilt_forward - next, tilt_backward - previous) cause a change of focus among interactors, i.e. vertical tilt allows navigation between interactors. Horizontal tilts, right or left, respectively define the actions selection and step back. After an interactor (e.g. a drop-down menu) is activated with tilt_right, vertical tilt can be used to navigate amongst elements on the menu. Once again, tilt_right defines activation of the selected item and tilt_left exits the current selection mode (e.g. returning to the upper level). The complete specification of the user interface through the tool defines the interaction with the application on a target language. After the final UI generation, the parts of code generated along with image and text resources are included into a project in the IDE, which must be then compiled and installed to a device. On mobile devices this can be done through over-the-air (OTA) transfer.

6 Example

This section illustrates the development of gesture enhanced mobile application with a scenario and an example application.

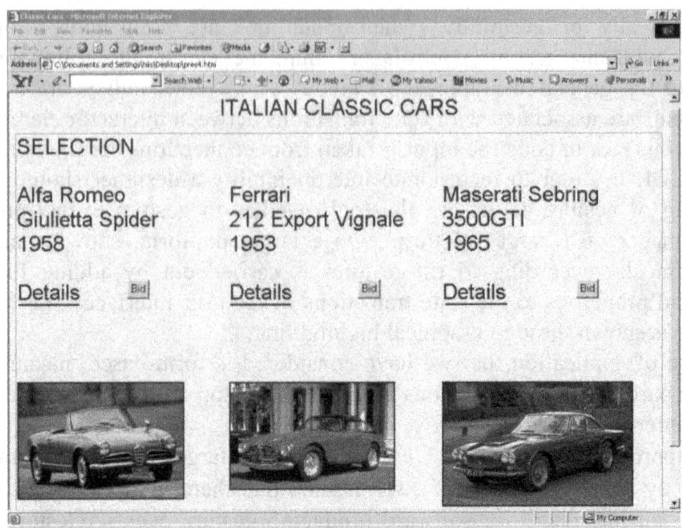

Fig. 4. The user interface for the desktop application

Our usage scenario considers Giovanni, who searches information on classic Italian cars. He accesses a desktop application, which provides him with information on such cars. The application allows him also to place offers on cars. Later, Giovanni decides to go and have a look at the car selection. The car sales point also supports mobile access for describing cars and for making offers. When Giovanni enters the sales point place, his mobile receives notification on the possibility of installing an Italian Classic Cars application.

He accepts the installation and starts to use the application. Our scenario is one possible usage scenario regarding mobile and pervasive services and applications. Services have various implementations available to support constantly widening selection of mobile and pervasive target platforms. For this reason, it is necessary to be able to provide development environment from which various versions of interfaces and applications can be fluently generated. The desktop UI generated by using the tool supports only graphical modality while the mobile device version also generated by the tool supports graphical and gesture modalities, and appearance and functionality of the application are adapted according to properties of a mobile terminal, as set in the tool.

User interfaces for desktop and for mobile device developed using our authoring tool are shown in Figures 4 and 5, correspondingly. The accelerometer able to sense gestures is the small box at the bottom of the PDA (Figure 5. Upper image).

The desktop application is implemented through a Web site showing overview of the selection with links to details and trading. The application on a mobile device is implemented as executable application. It utilizes tab-type-UI, since it provides users with an idea on several views, which can be changed by tilting horizontally. The main selection view on mobile device shows names of cars implemented as a list box, which can be browsed up and down with vertical tilting. Details link and Bid-button

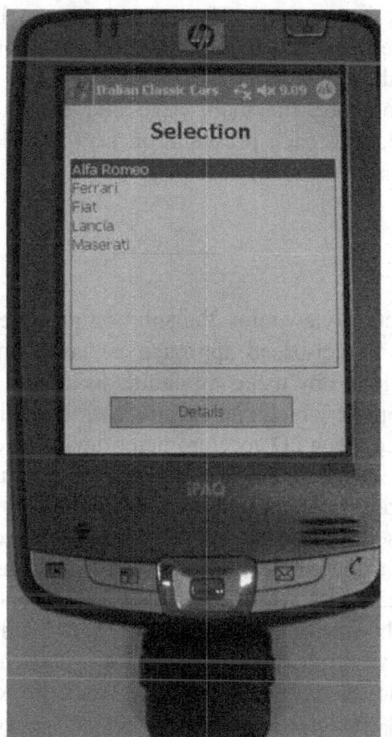

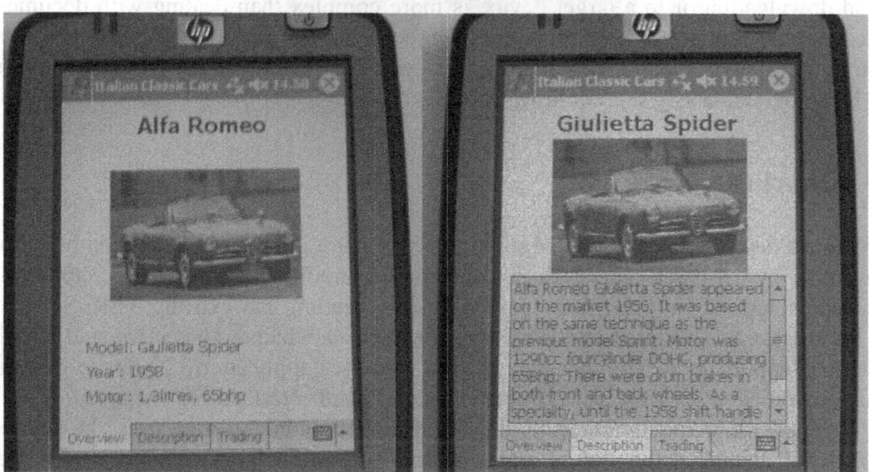

Fig. 5. Application on a mobile device. *Upper image*: Main selection view; *Bottom-left image*: Overview of selected car; *Bottom-right image*: Description of the selected car.

are changed into tabs on a mobile device. By tilting right the overview presentation of the selected car (Figure 5. Bottom-left image) can be accessed as illustrated in our tilt interaction model. By tilting again right another presentation, description, can be accessed (Figure 5. Bottom-right image), etc. By tilting left previous presentations are shown until main view is accessed. The interactors can be used in parallel with graphical modality. Overview-tab on a mobile device shows the basic description while the description-tab shows extended description. On the desktop version, the overview is shortly shown on the main page and details behind details-link. On mobile application objects in each presentation are grouped together to a compact presentation suitable for small display.

7 Discussion

From the gesture interaction viewpoint, the solution proposed for developing gesture user interfaces using a model-based approach is based on experiences with hand gestures interfaces developed by using miniaturized inertial sensors (accelerometers, magnetometers, gyroscopes), which can be attached to small hand-held devices. We have a device using an Ecertech 2D accelerometer device (it can be seen in the bottom part of the upper photo in Figure 5). The solution is demonstrated with a simple tilt gesture set and the target application can be extended to support to more complex shape-based or customised gestures enabled by 3D inertial sensing HW. The solution can also be generalized to be applicable to other types of hand gesture interfaces, in which gesture events are sensed by other means, e.g. cameras etc.

In order to increase the interoperability of the TERESA development environment for supporting pervasive embedded devices the chosen target implementation language in our concrete example is C# running on a Pocket PC operating system, instead of a Web-based application. Although generating the executable application and downloading it to a target device is more complex than dealing with document descriptions supported by browsers, we see that in the near future pervasive computing environments will involve various types of embedded wireless devices, which not necessarily support browsers.

8 Conclusions

We have discussed issues related to design of gesture interfaces. A solution based on using a model-based approach for developing multimodal interfaces supporting gesture interfaces is presented. It is obtained extending the existing TERESA tool. The solution is illustrated with a concrete example in which both desktop and mobile device applications are generated. The mobile application supports gestural interaction. The desktop platform provides graphical interface for prompt, feedback and input while the interface in the multi-modal mobile device uses the limited graphical resources for prompt and feedback and allows gesture interface for user input. Actually, the mobile device uses both modalities in equivalent manner by providing a user with additional options for performing commands through gestures. The approach is illustrated with real application example using a quite simple set of gestures. We would like to point out that the approach may support any set of gestures supported by the target platform.

The approach also shows the interoperability of the framework, since the target platform is a PDA with Pocket PC operating system. The form-based application is compiled after applying code generated from the tool and then the application must be downloaded to the mobile terminal.

Future work will be dedicated to integrating this functionality to migratory interface environments and to extend it to support multi-modal gesture interaction with mobile devices. Also, we plan to develop applications with a more complex and free form sets of gestures supported by the target platform.

Acknowledgments. Our thanks to ERCIM for support.

References

1. Abrams, M., Phanouriou, C., Batongbacal, A., Williams, S., Shuster, J., 1994. UIML: An Appliance-Independent XML User Interface Language, Proceedings of the 8th WWW conference.M., Chang, C.-C.K., Gravano, L., Paepcke, A.: The Stanford Digital Library Metadata Architecture. Int. J. Digit. Libr. 1 (1997) 108–121.
2. Bastide, R., Navarre, D., Palanque, P., Schyn A. & Dragicevic, P., A Model-Based Approach for Real-Time Embedded Multimodal Systems in Military Aircrafts, Proceedings ICMI 2004, pages 243-250, ACM Press.
3. Berti, S., Correani. F., Paternò, F., Santoro, C., The TERESA XML Language for the Description of Interactive Systems at Multiple Abstraction Levels, In Workshop Organized at Advanced Visual Interfaces 2004, pp. 103-110.
4. Bouchet, J., Nigay, L. Ganille T., ICARE software components for rapidly developing multimodal interfaces. Proceedings ICMI 2004, pages 251-258, ACM Press.
5. Calvary, G., Coutaz, J., Thevenin, D., Limbourg, Q., Bouillon, L., Vanderdonckt, J. A Unifying Reference Framework for Multi-Target User Interfaces. Interacting with Computers. Vol. 15, No. 3, June 2003, pp. 289-308.
6. Coutaz J., Nigay L., Salber D.,.Blandford A, May J., Young R., 1995. Four Easy Pieces for Assessing the Usability of Multmodal Interaction: the CARE properties. Proceedings INTERACT 1995, pp.115-120.
7. Eslambolchilar, P., Murray-Smith, R., Tilt-based Automatic Zooming and Scaling in Mobile Devices - a state-space implementation, Mobile Human-Computer Interaction MobileHCI 2004: 6th International Symposium, Glasgow, UK, September 13-16, 2004. Proceedings. Stephen Brewster, Mark Dunlop (Eds), LNCS 3160, Springer-Verlag, p120-131, 2004.
8. Hinckley, K., Pierce, J., Sinclair, M., Horvitz, E., Sensing Techniques for Mobile Interaction, ACM UIST 2000 Symposium on User Interface Software & Technology, CHI Letters 2 (2), pp. 91-100.
9. Kela, J., Korpipää, P., Mäntyjärvi, J., Kallio, S., Savino, G.,Jozzo, L., Di Marca, S., Accelerometer-based gesture control for a design environment, In Personal and Ubiquitous Computing, Springer, DOI 10.1007/s00779-005-0033-8,(online), 2005.
10. Kim, S-H, Ok, J., Kang, H.J., Kim, M-C., Kim, M., An interaction and product design of gesture based TV remote control, In CHI '04 extended abstracts, Vienna, Austria, 2004, pp. 1548 – 1548.
11. Linjama J., Kaaresoja T., Novel, minimalist haptic gesture interaction for mobile devices, In Proc.Nordic-CHI, 2004, Tampere, Finland, pp. 457 – 458.
12. Long AC, Landay JA, Rowe LA. Implications for a gesture design tool. In: Human Factors in Computing Systems (SIGCHI Proc.). ACM Press, 1999. 40-47.

13. Mäntyjärvi, J., Kallio, S., Korpipää, P., Kela, J., Plomp, J., Gesture interaction for small handheld devices to support multimedia applications, In Journal of Mobile Multimedia, Rinton Press, Vol.1(2), pp. 92 – 112, 2005.
14. Mori, G. Paternò, F. Santoro C., Design and Development of Multi-Device User Interfaces through Multiple Logical Descriptions, IEEE Transactions on Software Engineering, August 2004, Vol.30, N.8, pp.507-520, IEEE Press.
15. Obrenovic, Z., Starcevic D., Selic B., A Model-Driven Approach to Content Repurposing, IEEE Mutimedia, Januray March 2004, pp.62-71.
16. Paternò, F., "Model-Based Design and Evaluation of Interactive Application". Springer Verlag, ISBN 1-85233-155-0, 1999.
17. Paternò, F., Giammarino, F., Authoring Interfaces with Combined Use of Graphics and Voice for both Stationary and Mobile Devices, Proceedings AVI'06, ACM Press, May 2006.
18. Rekimoto J., Tilting operations for small screen interfaces, ACM UIST 1996, 1996., pp. 167-168.
19. Stanciulescu A., Limbourg Q., Vanderdonckt J., Michotte B., Montero F., A Transformational Approach for Multimodal Web User Interfaces based on USIXML. Proceedings ICMI 2005, pages 259-266, ACM Press.
20. Szekely, P., 1996. Retrospective and Challenges for Model-Based Interface Development. 2nd International Workshop on Computer-Aided Design of User Interfaces, Namur, Namur University Press.
21. Wilson A, Shafer S. Between u and i: XWand: UI for intelligent spaces. Proceedings of the conference on Human factors in computing systems, CHI 2003, April 2003. pp 545-552.

An HCI Model for Usability of Sonification Applications

Ag. Asri Ag. Ibrahim[1,2] and Andy Hunt[1]

[1] The University of York, Heslington, YO10 5DD, York, United Kingdom
[2] University Malaysia Sabah, Lock Bag No.2073, 88999 Kota, Kinabalu, Sabah, Malaysia
{aaai500, adh2}@york.ac.uk

Abstract. Sonification is a representation of data using sounds with the intention of communication and interpretation. The process and technique of converting the data into sound is called the sonification *technique*. One or more techniques might be required by a sonification *application*. However, sonification techniques are not always suitable for all kinds of data, and often custom techniques are used - where the design is tailored to the domain and nature of the data as well as the users' required tasks within the application. Therefore, it is important to assure the usability of the technique for the specific domain application being developed. This paper describes a new HCI Model for usability of sonification applications. It consists of two other models, namely the Sonification Application (SA) Model and User Interpretation Construction (UIC) Model. The SA model will be used to explain the application from the designer's point of view. The UIC Model will be used to explain what the user might perceive and understand.

Keywords: Usability, Sonification, Usability Inspection, Human Computer Interaction (HCI), Usability Inspection Material, Perception.

1 Introduction

Sonification is the representation of data using non-speech sound for the purpose of communication and interpretation. The specific conversion process and technique involved in transforming the data into sound representation is called the *sonification technique*. There are many techniques currently available in data sonification such as parameter-mapping [5], model-based sonification [6], audification [25] and so forth. These techniques are normally guided by the type of data to be presented and the required user tasks that the sonification can support such as program debugging [10], multi channel data display [5], stock market prediction [22], computer network auralisation [27] etc. Sometimes the type of 'tasks' is not clear especially for sonification applications that involve data exploration. This makes the usability aspects quite difficult to implement and evaluate in such applications.

However, the issue of usability is no longer an option, but rather a requirement for sonification applications. We believe that, the usability of applications is very much influenced by the specific sonification technique employed. One or more techniques might be required by a sonification application. However, a technique is not always

K. Coninx, K. Luyten, and K.A. Schneider (Eds.): TAMODIA 2006, LNCS 4385, pp. 245–258, 2007.

suitable for all kinds of data or domain; and often we use custom techniques, where the design is tailored to the nature of the data and the user's required tasks within the application. Therefore, it is important to assure the usability of the techniques for the specific domain application being developed. To produce a usable sonification application, it is important to understand the technique as well as how the users will interact with the application. Since the output will be in the form of sound, it is also important to understand how the sound will manipulate the capability of human auditory system.

In this paper, we propose a new HCI model for usability in sonification applications. It is used to explain and understand sonification applications (at the design stage) and how they might be interpreted by the users. This is done through two different models namely the Sonification Application Model (SA Model) and the User Interpretation Construction Model (UIC Model).

Our starting point is *Norman's Model of HCI* (as shown in Fig. 1) which is expanded using *three elements of sonification* (as shown in Fig. 2.a)). This gives rise to our *HCI model for usability of sonification applications* (which is shown in Figure 2.b)). Norman's model consists of two gulfs - namely execution and evaluation. The *execution* gulf is the gap between the effects that the user intends to achieve and the actions provided by the system. The *evaluation* gulf is the gap between what the users want to do and what they actually manage to achieve; thus it provides a way for users to determine whether or not they achieve their goal.

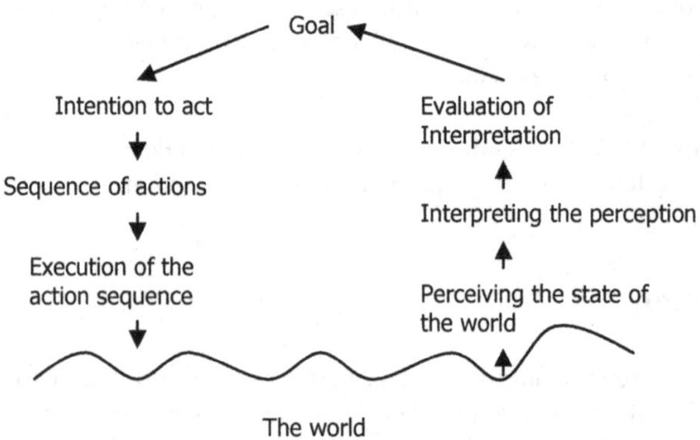

Fig. 1. Norman's Seven Stage Model of Human Computer Interaction [28]

In our model, the effects that the user intends to achieve (user requirements) and the actions provided by the system are dealt with separately. The user requirements are described as *goals* and *abstract tasks*. An example of an existing analysis of user requirements for sonification applications is *TaDa* (Barrass, 1997). '*The world*' in Norman's model relates to our system (in this case is a sonification application) which provides interactivity with the users and produces sounds as the output. This sonification application is described using our SA Model. The output of sonification applications is normally sound, representing the data that the user perceives. Norman's model mentions this in the evaluation gulf that involves perception, interpretation and evaluation. We explain this through our UIC Model.

Both models are created based on (a) the definition of sonification, (b) our assumptions about the usability of sonification applications, (c) a data state model, (d) issues in designing sonification applications; and (e) seven stages of Norman's Human Computer Interaction. All of these will be explained in this paper.

In summary, both the SA Model and the UIC Model can be used to explain what the application offers and what will be interpreted by the users. The application is considered usable if what it offers (SA) is interpreted (UIC) correctly as what was intended by the users as stated as their goal and abstract tasks.

2 Definitions

2.1 Sonification

Sonification is defined as the representation and transformation of data/information using non-speech sound for the purposes of facilitating, communication, comprehension or interpretation by listening [1] [2] [3].

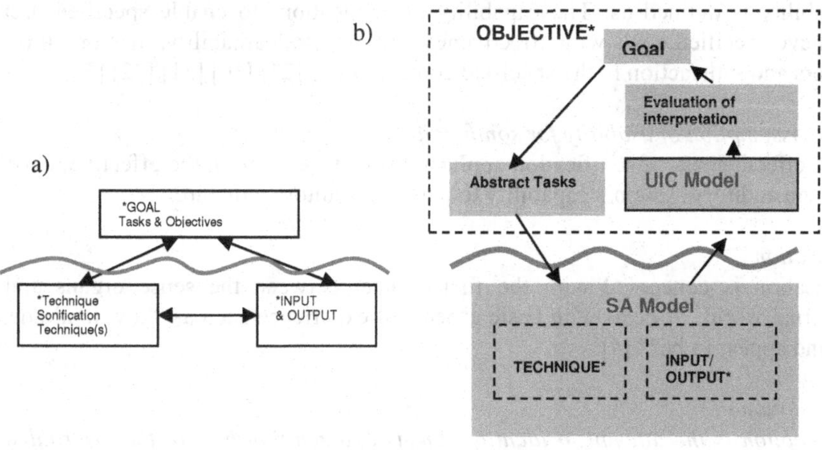

Fig. 2. a) Three important elements from the definition of Sonification. b) General framework of our HCI model for the Usability of Sonification Applications, based on Norman's Model and three important elements of sonification.

From the definition, we clarify the term sonification from three distinctive elements specifically (a) *Technique,* (b) *Input/output* and (c) *Goals* as presented in Fig. 2 a). The 'technique' refers to how the data is transformed into sounds. The 'input/output refers to the data/information as the input and the sounds as the output of the transformation (technique). And the 'goals' concern what the application (including the 'technique' and 'input/output') wants *to achieve.*

These three elements of sonification (Technique, Input/Output and Goals) as illustrated in Figure 2 a) are important to our HCI model. By comparing Norman's model (Figure 1) and the three elements of sonification; and imagining that the curly line is the interface and interaction between the users and the application, the 'Technique and Input/output' (used in the SA Model) can be considered as part of the application (the 'world' in Norman's model). The 'Goals' element in sonification is divided into the 'user requirements' and 'sound interpretation' of the application. The interpretation will be explained through our UIC Model, which involves the perceiving, interpreting and evaluating stages in Norman's model. This is illustrated in 2 b).

The definition of usability for sonification will be based on the existing definitions of *usability*, *sensation*, *perception* as well as *our usability assumption* as explained below:

2.2 Usability

Below are several definitions of usability for sonification applications as well as an assumption which we will find useful.

Usability

Usability is defined as: The capability of applications to enable specified users to achieve specified goals with effectiveness, efficiency, learnability, memorability, low errors and satisfaction in the specified context of use [24] [30] [31] [32] [33].

Our Assumption of usability for sonification applications

The effectiveness of sonification applications is dependent on the effective use of the human auditory system's capability to perceive auditory structure.

Sensation

Sensation is concerned with the first contact between the sense organs and the external world. It deals with basic aspects of experience such as "how loud does the sound appear to be?" [4].

Perception

Perception is the attempt to identify objects and relationships in the external world [4]. The focus is on how we form a conscious representation of the objects and object relationships. The processes involve *selecting, organizing* and *interpreting* the sensory data into a useful mental representation of the world. The perception question is related to the question "Can you identify the sound?"

Based on the definitions and our assumption above, we can summarize that the purpose of usability study for sonification applications is as follows:

*To understand and investigate how the main usability factors (efficiency, learnability, memorability, satisfaction and error handling) will support the effectiveness of sonification applications in manipulating the human auditory system's capability in the process of selecting, organizing and interpreting the sound (*sonified data*) and its structure into useful mental representations or information.*

Therefore, the application is said to be effective if the user's intended tasks can be accomplished with high accuracy and completeness. This will have happened if the user gets a useful mental representation from the sound as what it "*should and could be*". This can be achieved if the intended structure of the data and the perceptual structure of the sound coincide.

In summary, it is important to give detailed attention to each element of sonification (*Technique, I/O and Objective*) and explain them as the interaction between the user and the application. Therefore, our models give more attention to the questions below:

1. How is the data or information [*as the Signified or Input*] transformed [*by the Technique*] into sound representation [*as the Signifier or Output*]? – **Sonification Application Model (SA Model)**
2. How can the application help the user to perceive the sound as a useful mental representation of the original data [*as the goal*]? – **User's Interpretation Construction Model (UIC Model)**

3 Sonification Application Model

This section explains the **Sonification Application (SA) Model**. This model is used to explain a sonification application from the designer's point of view, including what would the user would like to do and to know. Besides describing the data transformation processes, it is also important to consider any interactivity of the system with the user.

To relate our model to 'usability', we need to look at existing issues in sonification application design. These issues are based on previous research and user testing of various sonification applications. Due to space limitations, we list here a few of the most important issues as examples. We have split them into two categories; (1) *Signified issues* [*data, data attributes, information etc.*] and (2) *Signifier issues* [*physical sound parameters, sound perception parameters, sound etc.*]. Examples of issues in the signified category are data scaling [5] such as increasing or decreasing the data values; data set reduction [6] such as reducing the data dimension; and mental image of the data [7] which involves an investigation of the user's imagination about the data. Examples of issues in the signifier category are musical knowledge requirements [8] [9] [10] [11] such as whether or not the user must have knowledge of musical theory for a better understanding; sound type (musical and non-musical) [12] [13] to avoid fatigue; number and type of acoustic parameters [12] [14]; Perceptual Issues [10] [12] [15] [16] [17]; sound aesthetics [18]; the number of signals that can be played at the same time [19] [20]; sound density [18]; sound structure[12] and so forth.

We use a data state model to describe the conversions processes as well as the input and output of sonification applications. The data state model is inspired by [21] as it involves data transformation processes. The transformation processes explain how the data is transformed from its original form into the final sounds. These transformation processes are used to explain the *technique* in Sonification applications. The data and sound parameters involved in all the transformation processes are considered as the *I/O* (input/output).

To ensure that detailed attention is given to the transformation processes, Input/Output and users' interactivity, the sonification application model should consist of the elements below (which appear as the rows in the table in Figure 3):

1. Technique – *[transformation processes]*
2. *I/O – [data/information and sounds]*
3. Interaction – *[interaction between the users and the application in all the transformation processes]*
4. Users – *[Users involvement in all the transformation processes]*

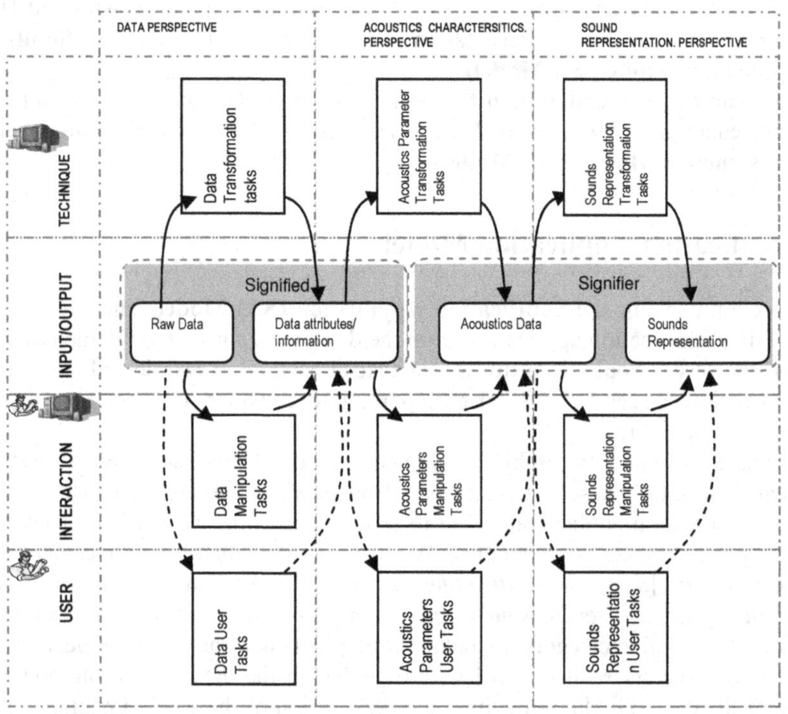

Fig. 3. Sonification Application (SA) Model

Interaction is important in the model because some of the applications allow the users to manipulate and interact with the final sound representation [23], acoustics parameters [5] or even the data [5][6][22]. This is illustrated as the '*interaction*' row in Figure 3. The user aspect is also important as most sonification applications are domain dependent. Therefore, explanation of user's knowledge and what they should know are important as these influence how they use and interpret the system and its sound outputs.

In the SA model, both *interaction* and *user* layers focus on the designer's point of view, including what the user needs to do and to know. What the user might perceive and understand will be explained later in the UIC Model. These two different points of view towards the users are important to know whether or not what was designed will be well interpreted by the users.

Wittgenstein ((1953) cited from Barrass, 1997[26]) said that the meaning of a sign is not the object it signifies but rather the way it is used. Therefore, the signifier does not necessary carry a direct representation or meaning of signified but rather the tasks or the function of the signified. This is where the *interaction* and *user* parts (*in the diagram*) will play important roles to elaborate a more meaningful of signifier towards the signified that it represents. Both parts can be used to explain how to use the sound.

Basically, the 'technique', 'interaction' and 'users' layers are used to explained the data transformation processes starting from its original form via an intermediate "ready to play" form and then into the final sound. We call the transformation processes *data transformation, acoustics parameters transformation and sounds transformation.* These produce three different perspectives – namely data, acoustic characteristics and sound representation perspectives as shown in Figure 3 above. In terms of tasks analysis (excluding the Input/Output level), there are at least nine different tasks categories which can be used to explain the processes involved in creating sounds from data (*as shown in Figure 3*).

In general, the tasks at the '*technique*' level are those performed by a system to process, manipulate and transform data into sound representations without user interruption. Tasks at the '*interaction*' level are those performed by the user through interactions with a system. And the tasks at the *'user'* level are those entirely performed by the user independent of the system.

These three types of tasks can be further divided into three different perspectives. For instance, *'acoustics user tasks'* are those performed by users without interacting with a system which relate to acoustics parameters such as judging the loudness level of sound from two different instruments. *'Data manipulation tasks'* are those performed by users through interactions with a system which relate to data changes, such as selecting either to sort the data in ascending or descending order; or choosing which data dimension of multidimensional data is to be sonified.

In summary, in this section, we have described briefly the Sonification Application Model, existing design issues categories and the first questions of how the data or information (*Signified or input*) is transformed (*Technique*) into sound (*Signifier or output*), which is illustrated in Figure 3 above.

4 User Interpretation Construction Model

This section describes the second question about how sonification applications can help users to perceive the output sound as useful mental representations. To answer this question, we model the possible user activities and interactions with sonification applications and relate them with what the users might interpret. The model is also based on the definitions of *sensation* and *perception* as defined earlier.

Since the users will be listening to sound representations, this will directly involve '*sensation*', which is concerned with the first contact with the sound. It is then followed by '*perception*', which is our attempt at identification and interpretation. It involves processing '*perceived sound* into '*useful mental representations*' of the world.

In our previous assumption of usability, effectiveness depends on the capability of users to '*perceive'* auditory structure as what it should be. Therefore, our model is based on the definition of '*perception'*, which involves *selecting, organizing* and *interpreting* activities.

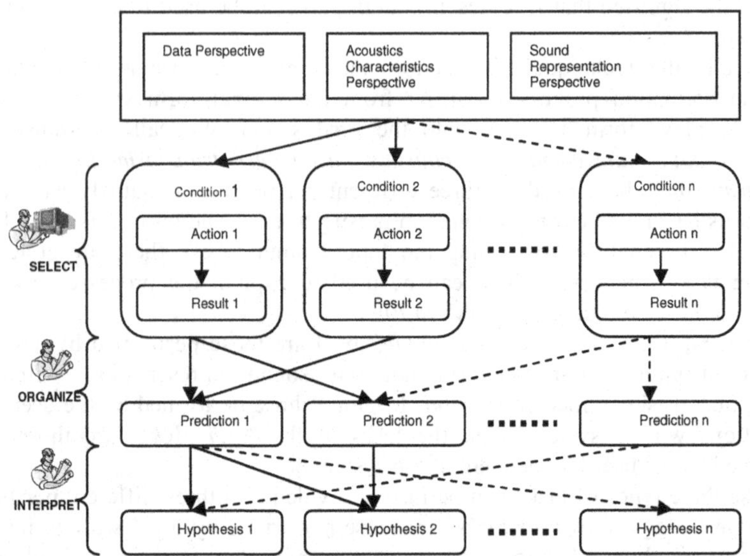

Fig. 4. User's Interpretation Construction (UIC) Model for Sonification Applications

In sonification applications, variations in sounds are heard due to changes or differences which occur in the data set. Such variations might also occur due to different approaches on how users interact and manipulate the same data.

The differences in sounds might attract the user's attention, which will produce different *conditions* during the first contact with the sound (*sensation*). This will produce questions from the users that are at a relatively low level, such as '*Can I hear the high pitch?*', or '*Can I identify the object?*' [4]. Conditions are the possible *answers* or *results* of these questions; or the possible useful sounds. This is illustrated as selection level in our model as shown in Figure 4 above. Selection is a discriminating process where the user selects potential useful sound representations. Among all the outputs, probably only a few of them are significant and will attract the user's attention, which eventually become the final conditions. Therefore, this level it is more concerned with filtering and attending only to significant conditions that might contain the required information.

The 'filtered conditions' are organized in the following level called 'Organizing'. This is the activity where the user constructs, arranges or puts together several conditions into a statement or structure. These 'organized conditions' or statements are called 'prediction'. Prediction is a statement about future conditions. In this level, the user will try to predict from all the available filtered conditions. The prediction is based on one or more conditions and focuses on predicting 'what will happen' or 'what does that mean?'

In the 'interpret' level, the user tries to make sense, conceptualize or conceive the significance of the prediction. This is performed based on at least one or more predictions from the previous level. The combinations of several predictions form a statement called a *hypothesis*. A hypothesis is a proposed explanation of a phenomenon based on several predictions (*which are also based on the sound with or without interaction*) of the application.

We will explain briefly the model through a simple physical analogy – '*exploring the number and type of different materials used on a surface*'. Let us assume that there are two types of interactions involved; *knocking* and *scratching*. Every action will produce different sounds, which will create several different *conditions*. Among all the conditions, probably only a few of them are important and will attract to the user, which will eventually become the '*final conditions*' for the users. That is why it is called the '*selection*' level. This level involves filtering and attending only to important conditions that might contain the important and required information.

Let us assume that the possible conditions are represented by the sets below:

1. *'knocking' conditions = {knock1-soundA, knock2-soundB, knock3-soundC}*
2. *'scratching' conditions = {scratch1-soundA, scratch2-soundB, scratch3-soundC, scratch4-soundD}.*

The 'knocking' action (interaction) has three conditions (*possible information*) while '*scratching*' action has four conditions that might attract the user. In the '*organize*' level, the user tries to organize the available conditions and make predictions about the surface. Such prediction is based on one or more conditions and focuses on drawing up a set of rules in the user's head which helps them to understand the role of their interaction with the surface'. From the conditions above, some examples of prediction are;

1. *'if the 'knock' action produces sound A, the scratch action should also produce a more or less equivalent sound for the same area',*
2. *'if the knocking produces sound C and the scratching also producing sound C, it could be made from the same materials'*
3. *'knocking has produced three different sounds, therefore, three different materials might exist'*
4. *'scratching has produced four different sounds, therefore, four different materials might exist'; and*
5. *'Sound D does not appear in knocking actions, it might not be a new material"*
6. *Sounds from knocking and scratching might not be related, therefore, sound D might be a new material.*

In the '*interpretation*' level, users try to make sense of and interpret the outputs through several predictions. The combination of several predictions is used to form a *hypothesis*. A hypothesis is a proposed explanation of a phenomenon based on several predictions (*which are also based on the sounds either with or without interaction*). Some examples of possible hypotheses from the predictions above are:

1. *Based on the prediction number 1, 2 and 5, it is hypothesized that: 'different materials exist if the knocking sounds are more or less the same with the scratching sounds'*
2. *Based on the prediction number 3, 4 and 6, it is hypothesized that: 'differences of sounds in knocking and scratching are because they are not related'*
3. *Based on the prediction number 1, 2, 3, 4 and 5, it is hypothesized that: 'if the sound does not appear in both type of interactions, it cannot be considered as different material, and therefore, the number of materials exist in the surface can be referred to the lowest number of sounds between the two types of interactions'*

By doing this, we are actually producing the possible user perceptions of the sound representation.

As explained earlier in the definition of usability for sonification applications - where *'the intended structure of the data'* and *'perceptual structure of the sound'* coincide, the user can get a useful mental representation. By comparing what we have explained in this section with the previous section – *'what the application or designer would like the users to do and to know'* with *'what the user might perceive and understand'*, the sonification application is said to be effective if these two coincide. If this has happened, the task could be accomplished with high accuracy and completeness and therefore, the application is said to be effective. As a result, these two models are important and should be integrated in one *'HCI model of usability for sonification applications'* as illustrated earlier in 2 b).

5 HCI Model of Usability for Sonification Applications

The bigger picture of the HCI model is shown in Figure 5. The Goal is a description of something to be achieved by using the application. Tasks analysis involves determining the *abstract tasks* for the application. The abstract tasks explain the user requirements, regardless of what the application offers. The abstract tasks will then need to be explained from the designer's point of view, which includes what the application will do, and what the application expects the users to do and to know (*SA Model*). For the purpose of evaluation, we will then need to analyze the possible interpretation through the *UIC Model* which includes selecting, organizing and interpreting. Finally comes the *'evaluation of interpretation'* that will determine whether or not the goal has been achieved.

The *evaluation*, *interaction*, *perception, organizing* and *interpretation* can be repeated until the task is accomplished or the goal is achieved. If this happens, it will create an interaction loop between the users and the application itself (also illustrated in Figure 5). Outside the scope of this paper is a thorough analysis of how the existing research focuses could be fit into this model. For instance TADA [26] (Tasks Analysis-Data Analysis) focuses on Tasks and Signified or data; Model-based sonification technique [6] focuses on interaction and the signified; Parameter mapping focuses on signified and signifier [1] [5], semantic approach [29] focuses on signified; and Syntactic [8][12] and Pragmatic focus on signifier (refer to Figure 5 above). This shows that the previous 'design approach' and 'sonification technique' can be

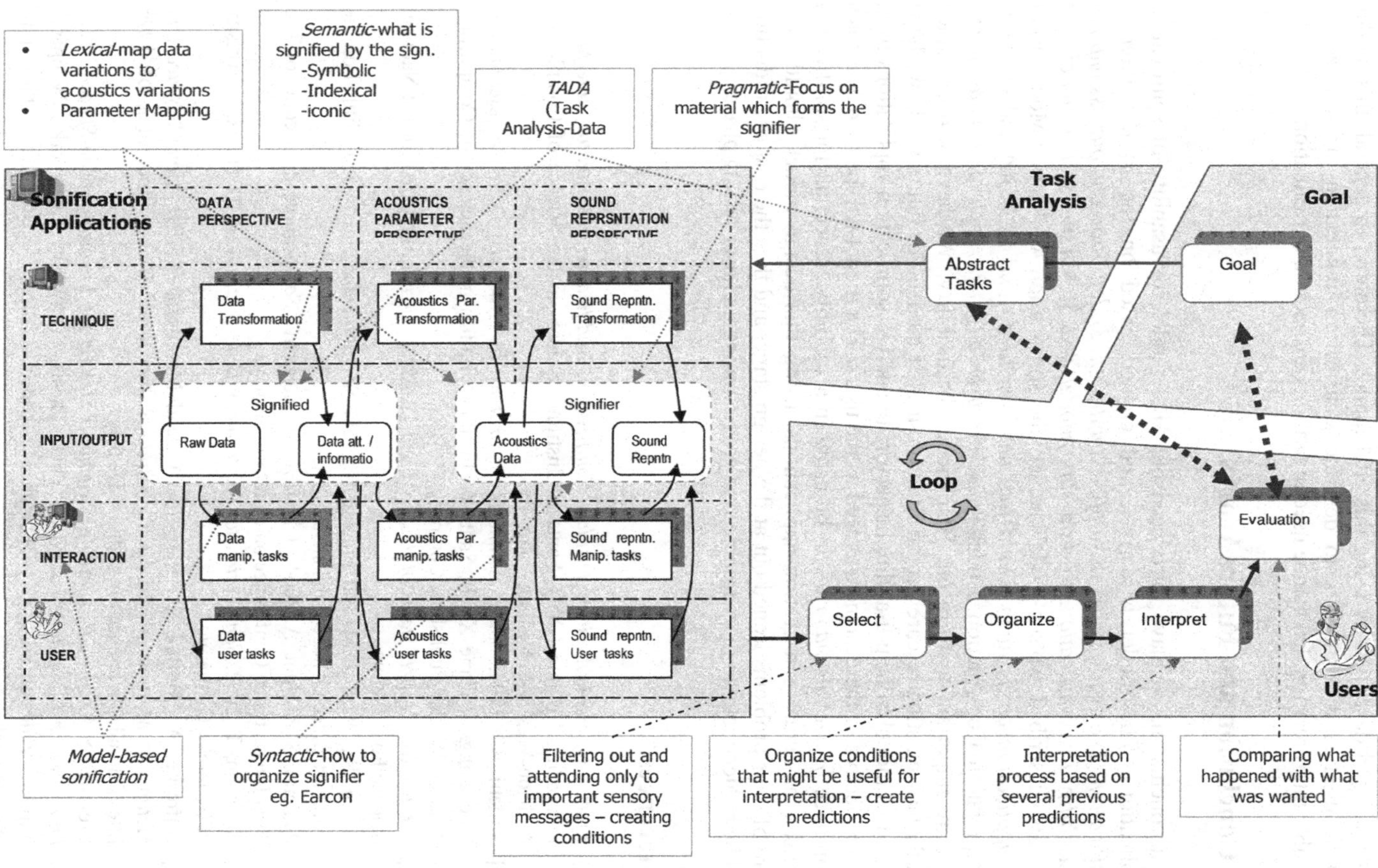

Fig. 5. HCI Model for Usability for Sonification Application

explained and described by using this HCI model. Therefore, in general, this model can be used as a framework to describe sonification applications as well as its possible interpretation that can be used in usability inspection or evaluation.

6 Conclusion and Future Works

As a conclusion, we have introduced our HCI model for usability of sonification applications. The model is derived and created based on the 1) *definition of sonification*, 2) *existing issues in sonification design, 3) definition and our assumption of usability for sonification, 4) data state model and 5) Norman's HCI model.* We have also described two sub-models namely the Sonification Application Model [*what the application or designer would like the user to do and to know*] and the User Interpretation Construction Model [*what the user might perceive and understand*]. Both are important to form our HCI model for usability. We have also explained briefly how existing research could fit into our HCI model. For future work, we hope to use this model to help usability inspectors to analyze sonification applications from the perspective of the designers as well as the users. The model will be used as a basis to produce *inspection materials* to be using in a usability inspection for sonification application. Future sonification applications, using this design model, should have more of their problems ironed out at the design stage, and thus the cost of production will be reduced, due to more trouble-free programming and user-testing phases.

References

[1] Kramer G. 1994. *Auditory Displays Sonification, Audification and Auditory interfaces.* Proceeding Volume XVIII, Santa Fe Institute, Studies in the Science of Complexity, Addison-Wesley Publishing Company.

[2] Scaletti ,C. 1994. *Sound Synthesis Algorithms for Auditory Data Representations.* Proceedings Volume XVIII, Santa Fe Institute, Studies in the Science of Complexity, Addison-Wesley Publishing Company.

[3] *Sonification Report: Status of the Field and Research Agenda.* Prepared for the National Science Foundations.

[4] Coren ,S., Ward ,L.M. and Enns ,J.T. 1999. *Sensation and Perception*, Fifth Edition. Harcourt Brace College Publishers. USA.

[5] Pauletto, S. & Hunt, A. 2004. *A Toolkit for Interactive Sonification.* Proceeding of The 2004 International Conference on Auditory Display.

[6] Hermann, T. 2002. *Sonification for Exploratory Data Analysis.* PHD Thesis, University of Bielefeld, Germany.

[7] Dufresne, A., Martial, O., Ramstein, C. and Mabilleau, P. 1996. *Sound, Space and Metaphor: Multimodal Access to Windows for Blind Users.* Proceeding of 1996 International Conference on Auditory Display.

[8] Brewster ,S.A. 1994. *Providing a Structured Method for Integrating Non-Speech Audio into Human-Computer Interface.* PhD Thesis, University of York. Webpage: http://www.dcs.gla.ac.uk/ %7Estephen/ papers/ theses/ Brewster_ thesis.pdf. Downloaded: Jan 2005

[9] Stevens, R. 1996. *Principles for The Design of Auditory Interfaces to Present Complex Information to Blind Computer Users*. PhD Thesis, University of York. Webpage: http://www.cs.man.ac.uk/~stevensr/papers/thesis-rds.pdf. Downloaded: Jan 2005.

[10] Vickers, P. & Alty, J.L. 2000. *Musical Program Auralisation: Empirical Studies*. Proceeding of the 2000 International Conference on Auditory Display.

[11] Edwards, A.D.N., Challis, B.P., Hankinson, J.C.K. and Pirie, F.L. 2000. *Development of a Standard Test of Musical Ability for Participants in Auditory Interface Testing*. Proceedings of the 2000 International Conference on Auditory Display. Website: http://www-users.cs.york.ac.uk/ ~alistair/ publications/ pdf/ MAT.pdf , Downloaded: January 2001.

[12] Brewster, S.A., Wright, P.C. and Edwards, A.D.N. 1992. *A Detailed Investigation into the Effectiveness of Earcons*. The Proceedings of The 1992 International Conference on Auditory Display.

[13] Lodha, S.K., Beahan, J. Heppe, T., Joseph, A. & Zane-Ulman, B. 1997. *MUSE: A Musical Data Sonification Toolkit.* Proceeding of the 1997 International Conference on Auditory Display.

[14] Stevens, C., Brennan, D. and Parker, S. 2004. Simultaneous Manipulation of Parameters of Auditory Icons to Convey Direction, Size and Distance: Effects on Recognition and Interpretation. Proceedings of the 2004 International Conference on Auditory Display.

[15] Alty, J.L. & Rigas, D.I. 1998. Communicating Graphical Information to Blind Users Using Music: The Role of Context. CHI 98 Los Angeles CA USA.

[16] Stevens, R.D., Brewster, S.A., Wright, P.C. and Edwards, A.D.N. 1994. *Design and Evaluation of an Auditory Glance at Algebra for Blind Readers*. Proceeding of the 1994 International Conference on Auditory Display.

[17] Edworthy, J. & Hellier, E. 2002. *Designing Urgency into Sound*. Proceeding of Design Sonore Conference 2002, Paris.

[18] Leplatre, G. & McGregor, I. 2004. *How to Tackle Auditory Interface Aesthetics? Discussion and Case Study.* Proceeding of the 2004 International Conference on Auditory Display.

[19] Rober, N & Masuch, M., 2004. *Interacting With Sound: An Interaction Paradigm For Virtual Auditory Worlds*. Proceedings of the 2003 International Conference on Auditory Display, Sydney Australia.

[20] Cunningham, B.S. & Ihlefeld, A. 2004. *Selective and Divided Attention: Extracting Information From Simultaneous Sound Sources*. Proceeding of the 2004 International Conference of Auditory Display, Australia.

[21] Daude S. & Nigay ,L. 2003. *Design Process for Auditory Interfaces*. International Conference on Auditory Display, Boston, USA.

[22] Janata, P. & Childs, E. 2004. *Marketbuzz: Sonification of Real-time Financial Data*. Proceeding of the 2004 International Conference on Auditory Display, Sydney, Australia.

[23] Zhao ,H., Plaisant ,C., Shneiderman ,B. and Duraiswami ,R. 2004. *Sonification of Geo-Referenced data for Auditory Information Seeking: Design Principle and Pilot Study.* Proceedings of the 2004 International Conference on Auditory Display.

[24] Neilsen, J. 1993. *Usability Engineering.* Academic Press. Morgan Kaufmann. UK

[25] Florian, D. 2001. *Using Audification in Planetary Seismology*. Proceeding of the 2001 International Conference on Auditory Display.

[26] Barrass, S. 1997. *Auditory Information Design*. Phd Thesis. The Australian National University.

[27] Malandrino, D., Daniela, M., Negro, A., Palmieri, G. and Scarano, V. 2003. *NeMoS: Network Monitoring with Sound.* Proceeding of the 2003 International Conference on Auditory Display, Boston, USA.

[28] Norman, D.A. 1988. *The Design of Everyday things.* Third printing 2000, First MIT Press edition, 1998. USA

[29] Gaver ,W.W. 1994. *Using and Creating Auditory Icons.* Proceeding Volume XVIII, Santa Fe Institute, Studies in the Science of Complexity, Addison-Wesley Publishing Company.

[30] Bevan, N. & Macleod, M. 1994. *Usability Measurement in Context.* Behaviour and Information Technology, 13, 132-145.

[31] Bevan, N. 1995. *Usability is Quality of Use.* Proceedings of the 6th International Conference on Human Interaction, Yokohama.

[32] Bevan, N. 2001. *International Standard for HCI and Usability.* International Journal of Human Computer Studies, 55(4),533-552.

[33] Bevan, N., Kirakowski, J. & Maissel, J. 1991. *What is Usability?* .Proceeding of the 4th International Conference on HCI, Stuttgart.

Non-functional User Interface Requirements Notation (NfRn) for Modeling the Global Execution Context of Tasks

Demosthenes Akoumianakis, Athanasios Katsis, and Nikolas Vidakis

Dep. Applied Information Technology & Multimedia,
Technological Education Institution of Crete,
Estavromenos 715 00 Heraklion – Crete
da@epp.teiher.gr, k.thanasis@gmail.com, vidakis@epp.teiher.gr

Abstract. This paper describes the rationale behind a user interface requirements management notation and a supporting tool suite. The notation is being developed to facilitate the design of interactions based on an account of non-functional requirements (NFRs), thus the acronym NfRn for the technique. NfRn is a graphical notation which is used to specify an interactive system's global execution context (GEC). The resulting depiction is referred to as the Global Execution Context graph (GECg). The GECg is a visual construction, which consists of nodes, representing interaction scenarios, and directed links representing scenario relationships designating alternate execution, concurrency, ordering, and set-oriented relationships between two scenario nodes. The technique is particularly useful for specifying certain NFRs – such as adaptability, adaptivity, scalability and portability – which are especially relevant for anytime, anywhere access. In the paper, we demonstrate the application of the technique in the context of an on-going research project aiming to build an 'electronic village' of local interest in the region of Crete.

Keywords: Context models, HCI Notations, Scenarios, User interfaces.

1 Introduction

In the recent history of HCI researchers have proposed a variety of modeling techniques to facilitate diverse design- and/or specification-oriented targets. For instance, techniques such as GOMS [1], TAKD [2] and UAN [3] are representative of an HCI research line with strong ties to cognitive science and the mental characteristics of computer-based tasks (e.g., interaction as problem solving, hierarchical structure of tasks). On the other hand, declarative modelling of users, tasks, user-computer dialogue and application domains has given rise to a variety of techniques and tools, widely known as model-based user interface design and development (for a review see [4]). In the recent past, the latter community has experienced considerable development, exploiting notations (e.g., UML) and scripting methods (e.g. XML) developed and made popular by neighbouring research communities in software engineering and the WWW respectively. Exemplar results of this research activity include UML extensions such as UMLi [5] and the UML profile

K. Coninx, K. Luyten, and K.A. Schneider (Eds.): TAMODIA 2006, LNCS 4385, pp. 259–274, 2007.

described in [6], a variety of tools for cooperative task modelling such as CTTE [7] and multiple user interface description such as Teresa [8], as well as various XML compliant mark-up languages such as UsiXML [9] that describes the user interface for multiple contexts of use such as Character User Interfaces (CUIs), Graphical User Interfaces (GUIs), Auditory User Interfaces, and Multi-Modal User Interfaces.

One issue of significance to the present work is the sufficiency of the existing proposals to cope with early phases of design where requirements are being explored and concepts are formed. Moreover, we are primarily interested in Non-Functional requirements (NFRs) and the impact they may have on the HCI design of nomadic applications. Specifically, our concern relates to the suitability of existing notations to facilitate the novel requirements prevailing in nomadic and ubiquitous applications - such as scalability, object mobility / migration, security, platform independence, location awareness, personalization / individualization - commonly referred to as NFRs or quality attributes [10]. Clearly, the established UML notations as well as the UML-based extensions mentioned earlier offer no obvious mechanism to allow designers to model explicitly such software quality attributes in the course of analysis and design. Moreover, there is no obvious link to the relevant HCI considerations. The work described in [11] is a partial on-going effort addressing partially the issue, as it deals only with UML class diagrams. This realization has been the driving concern in recent efforts aiming to extend UML so as to facilitate support for modelling global applications [12] and their respective properties and quality attributes (e.g., mobility, performance, object migration, security).

On the other hand, the model-based user interface development paradigm seems to address some of these concerns partially and in an ad hoc manner. Specifically, model-based development has indeed delivered a number of possible solutions to generating user interfaces for multiple platforms (for instance [8]) but these do not result from an explicit account of designated NFRs. In fact, model based development practitioners need not be aware of such constructs as NFRs. Instead, in the majority of cases, platform-aware user interface versions are generated by manipulating, either automatically or semi-automatically, an abstract task model which is incrementally transformed to a concrete instance. The mappings of abstract tasks to concrete object classes are governed by various techniques including selection rules and temporal operators which usually define relationships between tasks in the abstract task model [8], or graph grammars [13]. Such methods, together with platform-specific information may indeed suffice to generate a platform-aware user interface implementation. However, the above takes place without having the designer explicitly address the underlying NfR of platform independence or portability. Instead, the design work focuses on the mechanics of mapping abstract components to concrete instances.

It is worth therefore questioning the generality of this approach with regards to other NFRs such as personalization, adaptability or scalability. It should be noted that our premise is not that model-based and task-oriented development cannot cope with such challenges. On the contrary, we strongly believe that it is perhaps the only engineering paradigm that can be refined to cope with the emerging requirements. However, this would require a substantial shift from task-level to goal-oriented and activity modelling and linking with recent advances in goal-oriented requirements engineering and requirements-driven system development (e.g., [14]).

In cases where NFRs such as the above become prominent engineering goals, the user interface design work involved cannot focus solely on the task or the abstract interaction object levels, but should extend to address the activity level. Phrased differently, we claim that in modern applications, the designer is increasingly required to be able to articulate the global execution context of the systems tasks, rather than being solely concerned with the development of an abstract task model from which incrementally, either through mappings or transformations, a platform-aware user interface is generated. Recently, we described a proposal for a specifications-based technique which may be used to provide a candidate solution to the problem [15]. In this paper we develop further the basic notation, present a supporting tool environment and demonstrate their application in the context of an on-going research and development project aiming to construct an 'electronic village' of local interest covering the tourism sector of the region of Crete (see Acknowledgement).

2 Scenarios, NFRs and the Task GEC

The present work links with neighbouring software engineering requirements management, systems evolution and HCI design. The common theme across these areas is the notion of scenarios and scenario-based techniques. Our intention is therefore to describe a scenario-based method for populating the global execution context of tasks using designated NFRs. This is based on the premise that HCI design lacks a coherent and detailed macro-level method (in the sense defined in [24]) for including change management in the user interface development process. In other words, although there is a plethora of micro-level techniques useful to study change in the context of HCI, there is no integrated frame of reference for identifying and propagating change across stages in the course of the design and development processes. It is also argued that formalizing change management in relation to designated NFRs, which are explicitly accounted in the context of human-centred development, can provide a useful frame of reference. In the remaining of this section we define terms of reference and elaborate on relevant work, thus establishing the technical target of the present work.

2.1 The Scenario-Based Perspective

Depending on their field of application, there has been a wide range of formal and semi-formal methods and notations to facilitate scenario-based analysis. In software engineering, scenario-based methods have been developed to facilitate a variety of targets including scenario elicitation and generation, scenario evolution, scenario quality assurance, etc. Out of the range of these efforts, of particular relevance to the present work are those emphasising scenario-based requirements engineering. Specifically, Sutcliffe et al. (see [17]) developed a method and software assistant tool for scenario-based requirements engineering, which expanded pathways through a use case as well as suggesting alternative scenarios from a limited taxonomy of failure types. Although this tool did take environmental influences into account when generating alternative scenarios, it generated too many possible scenarios. In [18] Sutcliffe and Ryan developed a Scenario Requirements Analysis Method (SCRAM), which recommended a combination of concept demonstrators, scenarios and design rationale. The SCRAM method uses scenarios with a prototype artefact in order to help users relate the design to their work/task context and discover requirements defects by interactive walkthrough. Leite et al., in [19] defined a template for scenarios and developed a semi-automatic scenario construction process which delivers narrative descriptions of scenarios. In [20] the authors addressed the problem of missing scenarios with a method supported by their CREWS-SAVRE tool, which facilitates automatic generation of new scenarios for consideration by an analyst, using a library of standard models and alternative sequences of use case events. More recently Breitman et al., in [21] seek to establish a more active role of scenarios in the course of software construction. They argued that scenarios evolve as software construction proceeds, and proposed a method and a supporting tool to facilitate scenario evolution. Non-narrative scenario notations have also been researched extensively. For example, scenario-based specification notations, such as message sequence charts (MSCs) and UML sequence diagrams, are popular as part of requirements specifications. Also various UML notations are intended to cover all aspects of systems analysis from requirements management to software design and deployment.

The above brief overview indicates that in the past decade scenario-based requirements engineering has experienced substantial growth both in methods proposed and supporting tools. In the vast majority of these methods, scenarios are introduced as static resources for specifying functional requirements or reflecting and/or envisioning use. Once the system is delivered and deployed, scenarios in the majority of the cases die out. Thus, any future development of the system will typically disregard both the initial set of scenarios and the thinking, which gave rise to the system in question. It would be both interesting and challenging to consider scenarios in a more dynamic context, whereby initial scenario formulations and their accompanying rationale remain as persistent design resources which are progressively enriched with new insight derived from improved understanding of the system's contexts of use. This would enable the analyst to consider system evolution in relation to evolution of the initial set of scenarios. In effect, this leads to the need for methods to manage change in requirements engineering. Our interest is to link such changes with the context in which they occur.

2.2 Change Management and the GEC

Change in interactive software is inherently linked with the context in which a task is executed. Typical context parameters include the target user, the platform providing the computational host for the task or the physical or social context in which the task is executed. Traditionally, interactive software was designed to cope with minimal and isolated changes, related primarily to the user, since no other part of the system's execution context (i.e. platform or context of use) was viable to change. As more and more software and information systems adopt Internet technologies and protocols for greater openness and interoperability, the changes that can take place are far more complex and demanding, as the closed computing environment is replaced by the open, dynamic and almost unbounded nature of the Internet. In the new distributed and networked information-processing paradigm, change management entails a thorough understanding of the GEC of tasks.

In our previous work [16] we presented a methodology and a suite of tools for designing user interfaces as a composition of task contexts. A task context was defined as an interactive manifestation (or a style) of an abstract task (i.e. a task comprising abstract interaction object classes). For example, a selection is an abstract task, which can be interactively manifested either as an explicit choice from a list box, or choice from a check box or selection from a panel of options. Each alternative was designated as a distinct task context with explicit rationale and interaction style, describing conditions for style activation/deactivation, object classes, attributes of object classes, preference and indifference expressions, default conditions, etc.

Building on this early conception of a task context, in [15] the global execution context of an abstract task T was defined as a five tuple relation $\langle T, g, S, f, C \rangle$ where g is the task's goal to be achieved by alternative scenarios $s_i \in S$, and a function $f(s_i)$ which defines the maximally preferred option of S, given a designated set of constraints C. Such a definition, allows us to model change in interactive software in terms of certain conditions or constraints which propagate alternative interactive behaviours to achieve task-oriented goals. Each constraint in C is a predicate of type $c(type, parameter, value)$. Three types of constraints are relevant, namely user constraints, platform constraints and context constraints. In light of the above, it is now argued that change δ in the execution context of a software system occurs if and only if there exists at least one constraint in C whose parameter value has been modified. The result of recognizing δ and putting it into effect causes the deactivation of a $s_i \in S$, which was the status prior to recognizing δ, and the activation of a new $s_j \in S$, which becomes the new status. In the context of user interface design, it is therefore of paramount importance to identify the changes which may reasonably take place in a system's execution context, model them in terms of constraints relevant to user interface, and detail the interactive scenarios through which the user interface can cope with the designated changes. To this effect, the study of NFRs early in the design process can help populate and structure the required design space.

2.3 The GEC Through NFRs

In [15] we argued that populating the GEC of a task by considering designated NFRs entails two primary considerations, namely explicit modelling of the designated NFRs and modelling how the NFRs intertwine. We also described how both these targets can be facilitated by using the concepts and notation of the NFR Framework [22] to model specific NFRs such as adaptability, personalization and ubiquity to gain insight to the GEC of a set of tasks. Specifically, we argued that each designated NfR can be elaborated in terms of a softgoal interdependency graph comprising hierarchical decomposition of softgoals. Moreover, we studied explicitly the NfR of adaptability and described how it intertwines with other NFRs such as scalability, individualization and platform independence (see Fig. 1).

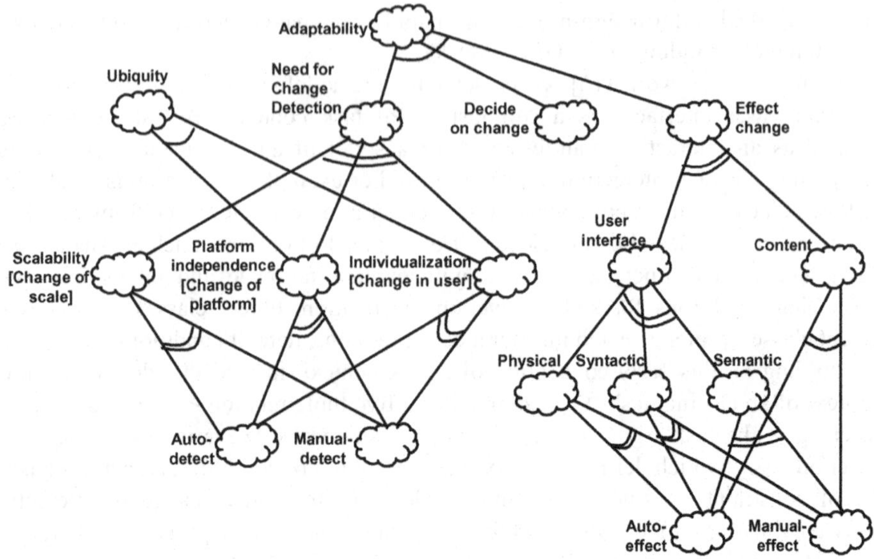

Fig. 1. Softgoal hierarchy of the NfR of adaptability

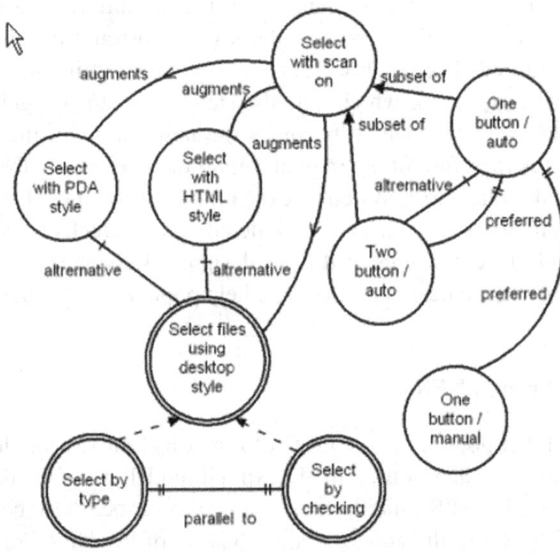

Fig. 2. Example of the GECg

To gain insight to the GEC, the analyst should proceed to examine the implications of each softgoal. This is typically done through scenarios which embody the designated softgoal. The result is documented in the global execution context graph which is a visual construction, depicting three primary elements, namely base (or reference) scenarios, envisioned growth scenarios (embodying softgoals), both designated as nodes in the graph, and scenario evolution mechanisms which are represented as scenario relationships linking scenario nodes. Two scenarios can be related with various relationships, which depict alternate execution, concurrency, ordering, and set-oriented relationships between two scenario nodes. As an example, Fig. 2 depicts a visual layout of the global execution context of a task 'select files' in a classical ftp application. The graph depicts one reference scenario, namely 'select files using desktop style' which can be realized by two parallel scenarios 'select by type' or 'select by checking'. The graph introduces two growth scenarios ('select with PDA style' and 'Select with HTML style') which are alternative to the basic reference scenario. Each growth scenario as well as the reference scenario can be augmented with 'Select with scan on' which in turn may be realized by two alternatives namely the 'One button / auto' or 'Two button / auto'. Moreover, the 'One button / auto' is preferred to 'One button / manual'.

In light of the above, it stands to argue that a system's global execution context graph can provide designers with useful information regarding:

- The range of alternative execution contexts considered appropriate.
- The conditions which characterize activation / deactivation of growth scenarios; this entails an elaboration and justification of each of the relationships appearing in the graph.
- Guidance in the choice of what paths to traverse or walk through under specific conditions.
- Choice of suitable system architecture; for example relationships of the type `alternative_to` and `augments` designate the systems adaptable components, while the relationship type `parallel_to` points out adaptive features of the target implementation

3 Populating the GECg

Populating the GECg is a process involving several analytic steps. These steps introduce on the one hand a micro-method for an evolutionary management of requirements, while on the other hand they establish a list of requirements for the NfRn tool and the supporting environment which is presented in the next section. Consequently, in the following we first describe briefly basic terms and then present details of a scenario evolution mechanism which leads to the GECg.

3.1 Scenario Types

As in the case of other research studies, we consider scenarios to be descriptions of a computer-mediated situation (either existing or envisioned). Such description should have certain characteristics to be complete. Specifically, a scenario should clearly specify a goal, which is to be achieved by certain (user or system) actions. Actions specify the content of the scenario, which is expressed using a suitable representation. The representation may change depending on the stage of the scenario's life cycle, which indicates the phase in the system development (i.e. requirements analysis, requirements validation, software specifications or design), which the scenario is intended to serve. At any time in its life cycle, the system's requirements are expressed through a set of scenarios, which are referred to as 'base' or 'reference' scenarios. A system's evolution is considered as a transformation of a set of base scenarios, which results in the generation of new requirements expressed through growth scenarios. Growth scenarios are typically generated following a critique (or screening) of a base or reference scenario. The critique may be informal, based on intuition, or semi-formal making use of an analytic technique (see below). Irrespective of the screening method, the result of critiquing is a set of growth scenarios, which are linked to the base scenarios through relationships.

3.2 Scenario Evolution Mechanisms

The term evolution describes a phenomenon encountered in many different domains. It generally implies progressive change in the properties or characteristics of domain entities. These changes are typically incremental and small relative to the entity as a whole but exceptions to this may occur. Our interest in this article is to consider changes in the type, nature and scope of scenarios in requirements engineering and to describe a method for persistent change management. To this effect, our aim is similar to the notion of scenario evolution described in [21], although our motivating rationale is different.

3.2.1 Scenario Screening

The essence of screening is in defining appropriate filters or adopting alternative perspectives to critique a base scenario. It is therefore a scenario inspection technique in the sense described in [19], [23], which can be realized through different instruments. Typical screening or filtering instruments include checklists and heuristics as in discount usability evaluation [27], issues as in IBIS [28], questions as in QOC [26] or claims as in Claims Analysis [25]. In this paper, we add to this literature by exploring NFRs (i.e., adaptability, scalability, individualization) as an instrument for screening a base scenario. It may also be advisable to combine instruments to facilitate the screening process. In general, the choice of instrument is dependent on subjective parameters, such as the inspector's familiarity with certain instruments, the commitment to formal, semi-formal or informal techniques, as well as the availability of an implemented version of the requirements described in the base scenario. In any case, the guiding principle in screening a scenario is to conduct the inspection so as to identify design breakdowns of either current or future work practices [29].

Table 1 indicates an example of a screening process realized using a designated set of NFRs, and the corresponding (somewhat generic) design breakdowns. It is worth pointing out that the new requirements derived as a result of screening and identifying design breakdowns may not be distinct. Instead, they may intertwine requiring further analysis; this issue is further elaborated in the next section using a set of scenario relationships. In general, screening delivers three main outcomes, namely a list of designated filters, a set of design breakdowns and a corresponding set of new requirements and their rationales.

Table 1. Screening using NFRs and corresponding design breakdowns

NFR		Example of design breakdown	New requirement
Platform independence		"...the system can be accessed under a specific environment e.g., Windows and it is not available as WWW or WAP application or service ..."	*Allow choice of delivery medium or style (i.e. HTML, WAP, Windows style)*
Scalability		"... the content of the system does not scale up or down to meet platform or access terminal requirements or capabilities ... "	*Detect context of use and allow operation in text-only style through a kiosk*
Adaptation	Adaptability	"...the system cannot be customised either automatically or manually to diverse requirements..."	*The system should be customisable to the user's language*
	Adaptivity	"...when in operation the system does not monitor user's interaction behaviour to adjust aspects of interaction..."	*The system should convey an auditory feedback upon completion of critical tasks*
Context awareness		'...the system takes no account of the context of use to accordingly modify its interactive behaviour..."	*Allow context monitoring and switching between designated interaction styles*
Localisation		"...the system can not be localised..."	*Allow choice of language*
Accessibility		"...the system is not accessible by certain target user groups..."	*Interview user to determine capabilities (i.e. motor, visual, cognitive etc), and accordingly adapt system*

It is important to note that in this type of screening the objective is not merely to identify a particular system or system specification to be selected out of a range of plausible ones. Instead, the aim is to identify how the same system (or its tasks) performs against the screening heuristics and to reveal design breakdowns. The greater the number of design breakdowns identified, the richer the insight gained of the system's global execution context.

3.2.2 Compiling Growth Scenario

Compiling growth scenarios is a two-phase process. In the first phase, growth scenarios are derived to address the new requirements identified during the screening phase. Therefore they are directly related to the screening rationale, while the intention is to envision possible solutions to the corresponding design breakdowns. In terms of syntax, growth scenarios are exactly the same as base scenarios. In other words, a growth scenario should clearly specify the goal it addresses, as well as the (user or system) actions to achieve the goal. Moreover growth scenarios come in similar representations as the base scenarios (i.e. narratives, bulleted sequence of actions, diagrammatic notation, etc). The second phase entails an analysis of the space of growth scenarios with the intention to compile aggregate growth scenario by identifying common elements. This is achieved by relating growth scenarios through relationships designating alternate execution, concurrency, ordering, and set-oriented relationships between the scenarios. These relationships are the primary mechanism for specifying the global execution context of the tasks in the reference scenario in terms of designated NFRs.

Alternative to. Two scenarios are related with the alternative_to relationship when each serves exactly the same user goals but one and only one can be active at any one time. This is formally expressed as follows: $\forall$ g $\in$ Goal, alternative_to $(g(S_i), g(S_j), NFR)$. In general, two scenarios related with an alternative_to relationship are considered as indifferent with regards to all other quality attributes except the ones designated in the alternative_to declaration. It is also worth noting that alternative_to provides the main operator for specifying adaptability of a system or a user interface with regards to the designated NFR (e.g., platform independence).

Augmentation. Augmentation captures the situation where one scenario in an indifference class is used to support or facilitate the mostly preferred (active) scenario within the same indifference class. In general two scenarios related with an augments relationship serve precisely the same goal through different interaction means. An example illustrating the relevance of the augments relationship is the case where scanning is introduced as an additional interaction technique. In such a case, the scanner is explicitly activated upon button press, while there are alternatives such as one button auto scan, one button manual scan, etc.

Preference. This relationship extends the alternative_to relationship for the case where, given a goal g and $g(S_i)$ alternative_to $g(S_j)$ and $i, j > 1$. In such cases, there should be a preference order for S_i and S_j specified by a preference condition or rule. When executed, the preference condition should place candidate scenarios in a preference ranking (indifference classes), while the most preferred scenario (first indifference class) is the one to be activated. The range of scenarios in a preference class may augment one another. For instance, Fig. 2 declares 'one button / auto' scenario as being preferred to 'one button / manual' scenario.

Parallelism. Parallelism in the execution of interaction scenarios (or concurrent activation) is a common feature in a variety of interactive applications and, when properly supported, it can serve a number of desirable features such as adaptivity, multimodality and increased usability. For the purpose of the present work, two scenarios are related with a parallel_to relationship when they serve the same goal and are active concurrently.

4 NfRn Tool Support and Case Study

The concepts presented in the previous section are being further explored in the context of on-going R&D aiming to provide a computer-based environment for building the GECg of computer-mediated tasks. The current version of the system, called NfRn, provides a test-bed for evolutionary scenario management supporting all types of scenarios introduced earlier. The system is currently being validated in the context of the eKoNEΣ project (see acknowledgement). eKoNEΣ is an R&D project which started in 2006 with the distinct objective to establish a local electronic village

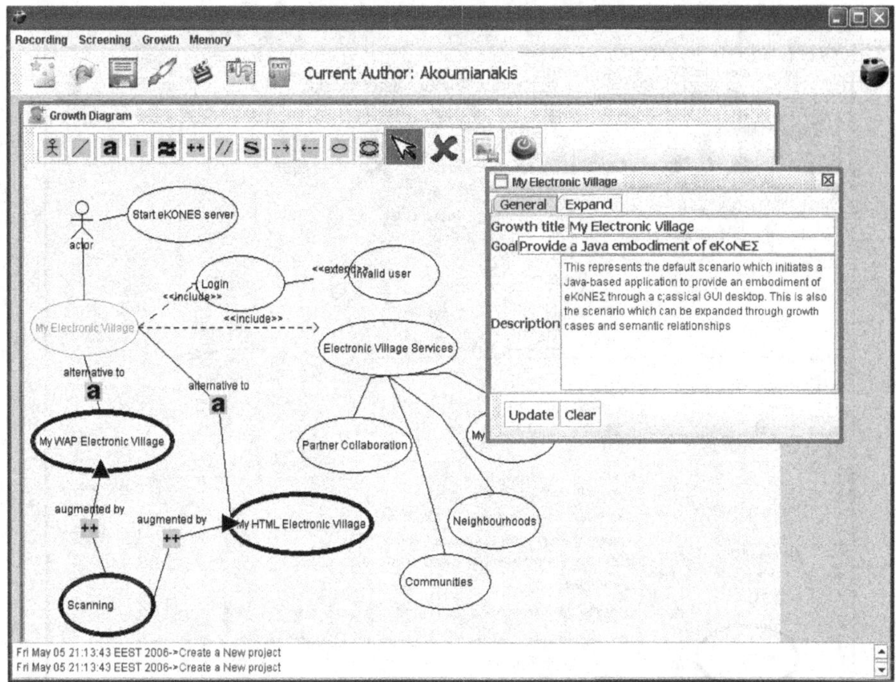

Fig. 3. An example of the GECg using the NfRn suite of tools

on tourism in the region of Crete. The project is currently in its initiation phase where concepts are being formed and articulated through scenarios and user-involved prototyping. A variety of scenarios are being considered ranging from static scenarios such as the visual depiction of the electronic village at a point in time to dynamic scenarios emphasizing behavioural patterns of participants leading to activity aggregation / desegregation, etc. In what follows we will briefly present both the use of the NfRn and the early mock-ups which are being developed in the course of concept formation.

Fig. 3 presents an instance of the NfRn system depicting tentative scenarios of use of the eKoNEΣ system. As shown, a diagrammatic depiction of the GECg is similar to an extended use case diagram. In the example presented in Fig. 3 the emphasis is on the description of alternative interactive embodiments of the electronic village across different platforms (desktop Java, HTML and mobile terminals). Each alternative platform is associated with a distinct growth scenario. The specific growth scenarios depicted are 'My WAP Electronic Village' and 'My HTML Electronic Village'. Each of them is linked with the base scenario (i.e., 'My Electronic Village') via the alternative_to relationship as shown in Fig. 4. The current version of the tool supports generation of the expanded GeCg (i.e. the graph, the issues and the rationale) as an XML file. An extract of this file for our reference example is summarized in Fig. 5.

It is worth pointing out that scenarios related with the `alternative_to` relationship declare the adaptable features of a system. Thus for example Fig. 6 – Fig. 8

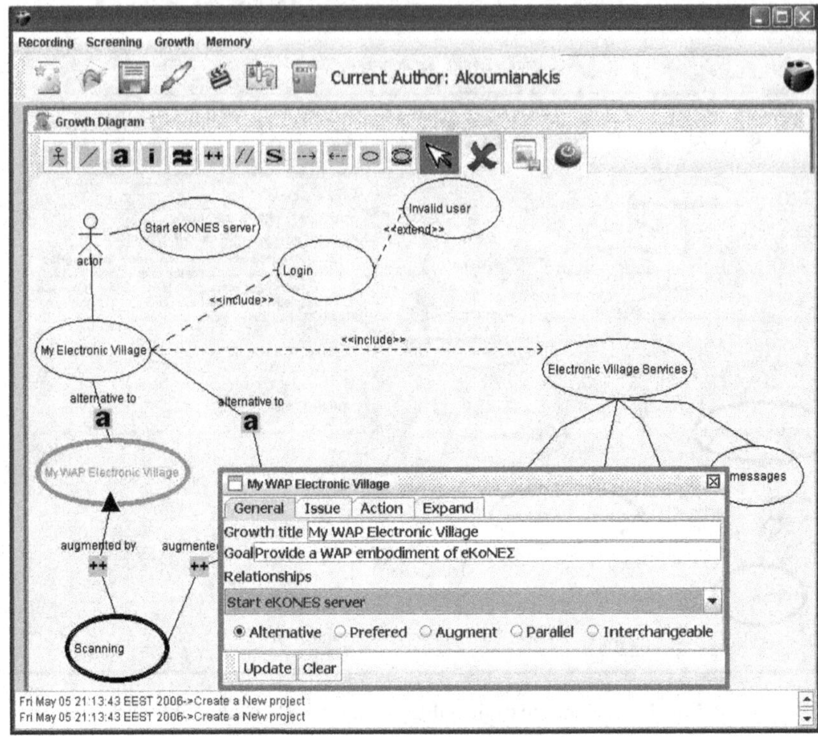

Fig. 4. Declaring scenario relationships

```
<Project-Diagram author="Akoumianakis">
   <actor>
      <UseCase name="Start eKoNES server">
      </UseCase>
      <UseCase name="My Electronic Village">
         <goal>Provide a Java embodiment of eKoNEΣ</goal>
         <description> …esents the default scenario...</description>
         <issue id="1">
            <relationship type="alternative to">
            <GrowthCase name="My HTML Electronic Village">
            <goal>test</goal>
                <issue id="3">
                <relationship type="augmented by">
                    <GrowthCase name="Scanning">
                    <goal>test</goal>
                    </GrowthCase>
                </relationship>
                </issue>
            </GrowthCase>
            </relationship>
         </issue> …
   </actor>
</Project-Diagram>
```

Fig. 5. Example XML created from NfRn tool

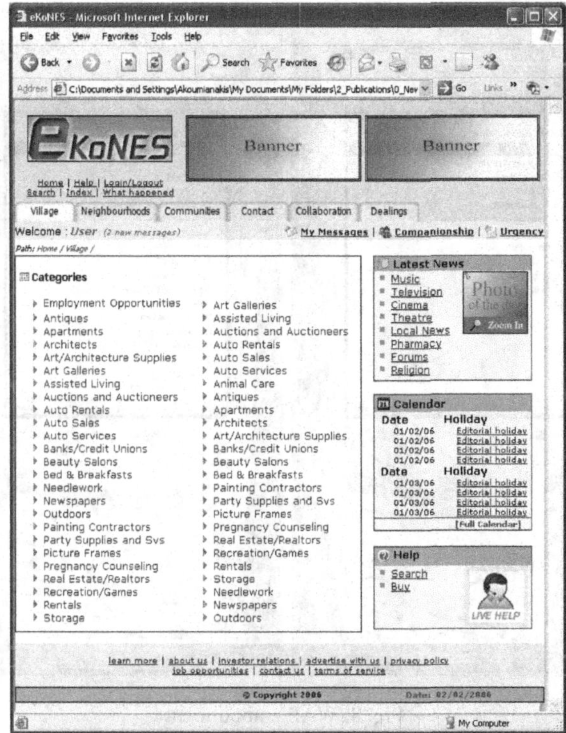

Fig. 6. HTML embodiment

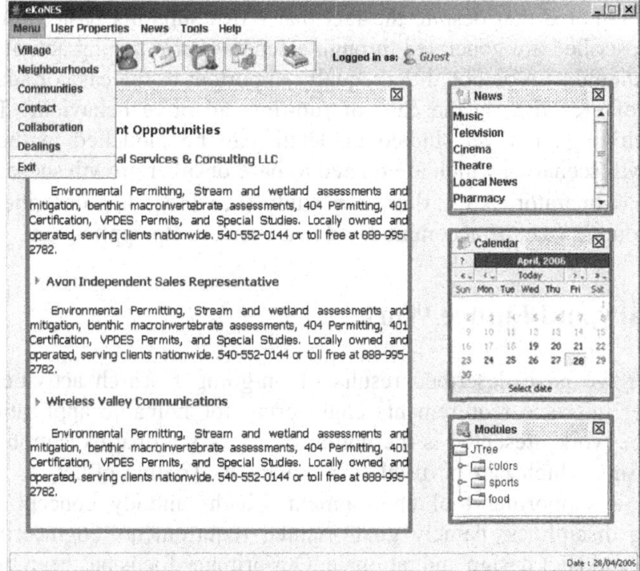

Fig. 7. Java based GUI embodiment

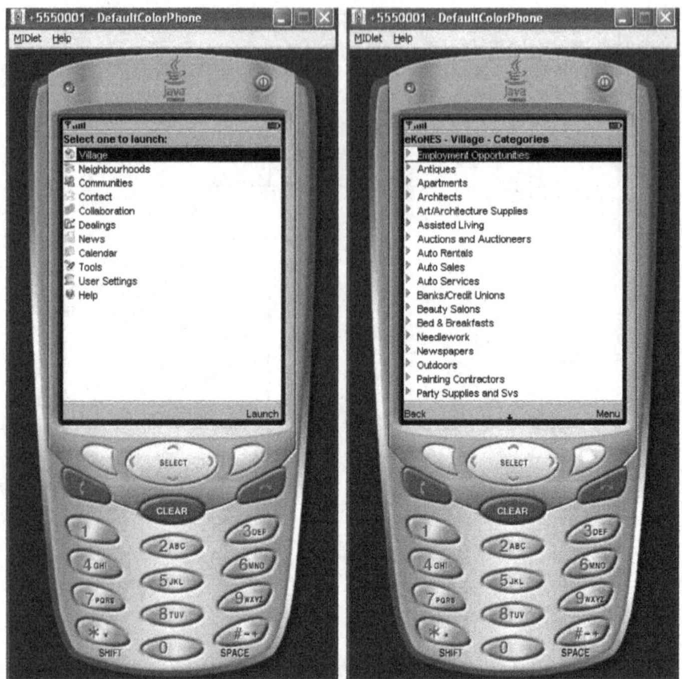

Fig. 8. WAP embodiment

illustrate examples of alternative interactive embodiments of the basic functionality and services of the electronic village.

It should be noted that despite the fact that NfRn supports basic prototyping, the prototypes described are generated through a separate prototyping activity and stored in NfRn. It should also be noted that equally important to the case of adaptability, in the context of eKoNEΣ, is the case of run-time adaptive behaviour. This type of behaviour, although not yet studied in detail, can be modelled in the NfRn tool through growth scenarios which are related to base or other growth scenarios with the `parallel_to` operator. An earlier case study (see [15]) has described how such adaptive encounters can be accommodated in a standard ftp application.

5 Summary and Future Work

In this paper we have described results of on-going research activities aiming to facilitate user interface requirements engineering for nomadic applications. A core concept in the work presented is the notion of a task's global execution context and the mechanisms which can be used to populate it. To this effect, we presented a method and a supporting tool environment which embody concepts from three neighbouring disciplines, namely goal-oriented requirements engineering, scenario management and HCI design and rationale. Our primary focus has been the NfRn tool and the support it provides for analytic construction of the global execution context graph. Future work will seek to address several extensions both in the methodology and the tool. In terms of methodological extensions, we are studying the development of a scenario specification language to formalize the semantic description of scenarios. On the other hand several refinements of the `NfRn` tool are currently under development. Specifically, an on going activity seeks to expand the (currently primitive) user interface prototyping features supported by the tool so as to establish a link between scenarios (either reference or growth), their underlying rationale and interactive embodiments. In this context, we are also exploring the possibility of linking the `NfRn` tool outcomes with existing task-based notations (e.g., CTT [7]) and model-based user interface tools (e.g., Teresa [8]).

Acknowledgments. Part of this work is co-funded by the General Secretariat of Research and Technology of the Greek Ministry of Development in the context of the Project eKoNEΣ (KP-24) of the Operational Programme of the Region of Crete. Partners in eKoNEΣ are: The Department of Applied Information Technology and Multimedia of the Advanced Technological Education Institution of Crete (Prime Contractor), the Department of Electronics and Computer Engineering of the Technical University of Crete, the Department of Music and Acoustic Technology of the Advanced Technological Education Institution of Crete, Forthnet S.A, Anixe S.A, and the Heraklion Chamber of Commerce and Industry.

References

1. Card, S.K., Moran, T.P. and Newell, A., The Psychology of Human-Computer Interaction. Hillsdale, N.J.: Lawrence Erlbaum, (1983).
2. Diaper, D., Johnson., P., Task analysis for knowledge descriptions: theory and applications in training. In J. Long and A. Whitefield, editors, Cognitive ergonomics and human-computer interaction, Cambridge University Press, (1989).
3. Hartson, H. R., et al., The UAN: A User-oriented Representation for Direct Manipulation Interface designs. ACM Transactions on Information Systems, Vol, No 3, (1990) 181-203.
4. Pinheiro da Silva, P., User Interface Declarative Models and Development Environments: A Survey. Lecture Notes in Computer Science, (1946) 207–226.
5. Pinheiro da Silva, P., Paton, W.N., User interface modelling in UMLi, IEEE Software (2003), 62-69.
6. Blankenhorn, K.: A UML Profile for GUI Layout, Master's Thesis, University of Applied Sciences Furtwangen, Department of Digital Media, (2004).
7. Mori, G., Paterno, F., Santoro: CTTE: Support for Developing and Analyzing Task models for interactive system design. IEEE Transactions on S.E., 28(9), (2002) 1-17.
8. Mori, G., Paterno, F., Santoro: Design and Development of Multidevice user interfaces through multiple logical descriptions. IEEE Transactions on Software Engineering, 30(8), (2004) 1-14.
9. UsiXML: http://www.usixml.org/.
10. Mylopoulos, J., Chung, L., Nixon, B. : Representing and using non-functional requirements: a process-oriented approach. IEEE Trans. Software Engineering 18 (6), (1992) 483-497.

11. Cysneiros, L-M., Leite, JCSP.: Using UML to reflect non-functional requirements. Proceedings of the 2001 conference of the Centre for Advanced Studies on Collaborative research (CASCON), IBM Press, Toronto, (2001) 202-216.
12. Baumeister, H., Koch, N., Kosiuczenko, P., Stevens, P., Wirsing, M., UML for global computing. In Corrado Priami, editor, Global Computing. Programming Environments, Languages, Security, and Analysis of Systems. IST/FET International Workshop, GC 2003, Rovereto, Italy, Feb. 914,2003, Revised Papers, volume 2874 of LNCS, (November 2003).
13. Limbourg, Q., Vanderdonckt, J., Addressing the Mapping Problem in User Interface Design with USIXML, Proc TAMODIA Prague, (2004) 155-164.
14. Castro, J., Kolp, M., Mylopoulos, J., Towards requirements-driven information systems engineering: the Tropos project. Information Systems 27, (2002) 365–389.
15. Akoumianakis, D., Pachoulakis, I. Scenario Networks: Specifying User Interfaces with Extended Use Cases. In P. Bozanis and E.N. Houstis (Eds.): PCI 2005, LNCS 3746, (2005) 491–501.
16. Akoumianakis, D., Savidis, A., & Stephanidis, C., Encapsulating intelligent interaction behaviour in unified user interface artefacts, Interacting with Computers (12), (2000) 383-408.
17. Sutcliffe, A., Scenario-based requirements analysis. Requirements Engineering (3), (1998) 48–65
18. Sutcliffe AG, Ryan M., Experience with SCRAM, a Scenario Requirements Analysis Method. In: International Conference on Requirement Engineering, (1998) 164–171.
19. Leite JCSP, Hadad GDS, Doorn JH, Kaplan GN., A scenario construction process. Requirements Engineering 5(1), (2000) 38–61.
20. Maiden, N., Minocha, S., Manning, K., Ryan. M., CREWS SAVRE: Systematic scenario generation and use. In ICRE '98: Third International Conference on Requirements Engineering, (1998) 148–155.
21. Breitman, K-K., Leite, J., Berry, D.M. Supporting scenario evolution, Requirements Engineering, 10, (2005) 112–131
22. Chung, L., Nixon, B., Yu, E. and Mylopoulos, J. "Non-Functional Requirements in Software Engineering" Kluwer Academic Publishers, (2000).
23. Leite JCSP, Doorn JH., Hadad GDS, Kaplan GN., Scenario inspections, Requirements Engineering, 10, (2005) 1–21.
24. Olson, J. S., Moran, T. P., Mapping the method muddle: Guidance in using methods for user interface design. In HCI design: Success stories, emerging methods, and real-world context, edited by Rudisill, M., Lewis, C., Polson, P. B., & McKay, T. D., (San Francisco, CA: Morgan Kaufmann Publishers), (1996) 101-121.
25. Carroll, J. M. and Rosson, M. B., Getting around the task-artifact cycle: How to make claims and design by scenario. ACM Trans. Inf. Syst. 10, 2 (Apr.), (1992) 181–212.
26. MacLean, A., Young, R., Bellotti, V., Moran, T., Questions, options, and criteria: elements of design space analysis. Human-Computer Interaction, 6, (3&4), (1991) 201-250.
27. Nielsen. J., Usability Engineering, Morgan Kaufmann, San Francisco, (1993).
28. Yakemovic, B., Conklin, J. Report on a development project use of an issue-based information system, Proceedings of the 1990 ACM conference on Computer-supported cooperative work, Los Angeles, California, October 07-10 (1990) 105-118.
29. Beynon-Davies, P., Holmes, S. Design breakdowns, scenarios and rapid application development, Information and Software Technology 44, (2002) 579–592.

Requirements Elicitation and Elaboration in Task-Based Design Needs More Than Task Modelling: A Case Study

Anke Dittmar, Andreas Gellendin, and Peter Forbrig

Rostock University, 18055 Rostock, Germany
ad@informatik.uni-rostock.de, andreas-gellendin@gmx.de,
pforbrig@informatik.uni-rostock.de

Abstract. In this paper, a small case study is presented to illustrate our conceptual understanding of a task-based requirements process. We argue that sub-models as known in model-based design (e.g. task models, dialog models) support the reflection about an existing work situation at a conceptual level and allow a formal specification of requirements. However, it is also shown that the integration of complementary analysis approaches facilitates a richer consideration of social as well as technical aspects. An intertwined creation of models differing in their focus and in the degree of abstraction and formality supports a more effective requirements elicitation and elaboration.

In addition, the paper discusses some crucial issues in task- and model-based design such as the 'myth' of generalised task models, the different roles of task and dialog models, or the influence of intentions on models of current situations. We hope to contribute to a further clarification of the problem space.

Keywords: Task models in user-centered software design, Early requirements, elicitation and elaboration for task-based design, Task-based design, User-task elicitation.

1 Introduction

A main assumption in model-based design (MBD) is that part of the task knowledge of users can be described explicitly. It is claimed that task models are useful during the whole development process to come to interactive systems which really support users in performing their tasks. However, most of the existing work concentrates on the exploitation of task models for deriving system specifications, and particularly, user interface specifications (e.g. [1,2]). Although it is widely accepted that models of the current and the envisioned working situation help to elicitate appropriate requirements on the envisioned system [3,4,5], relatively few works exist exploring how to integrate task-based design practices with those of requirements engineering.

The number of publications and discussions about the limitations of either 'pure technical' or 'pure social' approaches to design interactive systems should

K. Coninx, K. Luyten, and K.A. Schneider (Eds.): TAMODIA 2006, LNCS 4385, pp. 275–291, 2007.

suggest a common understanding of an appropriate development process. Both social aspects as well as technical possibilities and constraints have to be reflected in formal systems specifications. Even if there is such a common understanding - we also have to live it, but this is a learning process.

In this paper, we want to show how a 'combination' of qualitatively different approaches stimulating the creation of models with different focus and at different levels of abstraction can help to see deficiencies in current practices and tools which are not necessarily evident 'at first glance'. We use a small case study to present our conceptual understanding of early requirements elicitation and elaboration for task-based design. It is examined how conference programs can be organised by using the conference tool MyReview. The formal specification language TaOSpec (Tasks and Objects, [6,7]) was applied to develop conceptual models of the existing situation (task models, dialog and application models). Additionally, the communication between the program organisers of a small conference was analysed. The resulting set of models and descriptions served to identify new requirements on the conference tool which were specified using TaOSpec again. We neither claim that the techniques applied in the case study could not be improved nor that the analysis is sufficient.

We further use the case study to address several crucial issues in task- and model-based design (see particularly Sect. 3.4, 4). We argue, for example, that there is no clear separation between models describing an existing task situation and models describing an envisioned one. It makes sense to separate them conceptually. So, a detailed analysis of the current situation can also help to identify what is worth to maintain. However, we should be aware that we rather deal with a set of models and model fragments and every model of an existing situation is already affected by the intention of its developers to change this situation.

A description mechanism like TaOSpec allowing the specification of tasks including task domain objects as well as the specification of the dialog and the application part of an interactive system with the same means supports the reuse of descriptions. For example, current task model fragments can be reused in the specification of the envisioned software system. In addition, formal requirements specifications facilitate a smooth transition from requirements analysis steps to design steps and vice versa. As pointed out, e.g. in [8], both processes are deeply intertwined.

It is sometimes criticized that using the same description formalism can blur the roles different models play in the development process. (In fact, there are, for instance, few software tools which really support an intertwined development of object-oriented analysis and design models.) We think the problem is not so much the specification formalism, but rather a weak conceptual understanding. We hope the case study can also help to bring some clarity to this issue.

The paper is organised as follows. Sect. 2 relates task modelling and requirements engineering. In Sect. 3, the case study is introduced by describing the general modelling approach and TaOSpec as well as models of the current situation. Sect. 4 is a reflection of the task-based approach so far. In Sect. 5, an integration of complementary analysis approaches is recommended and illustrated by using the case study again. The last section gives some conclusions.

2 Task Modelling and Requirements Engineering

"Traditionally, the role of requirements engineering is to establish a complete, consistent, and unambiguous requirements specification which defines the requirements of the derived system at a conceptual level" [9]. However, it is also common ground that we deal with two types of models in RE: - models describing the state of the current system, and - models defining the requirements for a future system [9].

The description of current and desired states generally makes sense for at least two reasons. First, designers are encouraged to think about maintainance goals by creating models of existing situations[1]. Second, software development is an iterative process. That is to say, envisioned models of one iteration step could be used for relating or developing current models in the next step.

Task analysis is one of the oldest methods in Human-Computer Interaction. In the context of interactive system design, it can be used for "providing an idealised, normative model of the task that any computer system should support if it is to be of any use in the given domain"[11]. It is distinguished between *task analysis* (involving steps of extracting, organising, and describing task-related data [12]) and *task design*. "Task modelling can be applied to both tasks that have, and tasks that have not been brought into existence. A task model is a hypothesis of how a task is or might be carried out"[11]. It describes task knowledge in terms of task decomposition, goals, actions, temporal constraints, task domain objects etc. (a survey of concepts in common task modelling approaches is given in [13]). Lim and Long [3] and many others argue that the development of interactive systems has to be embedded into task analysis and task design. One reason why this is not common practice so far might be the historical separation of software engineering and HCI as pointed out in [12]. "Many task analysis methods were developed by researchers with a psychological background, and these methods and their outputs often do not integrate well with those of software engineering."

According to Davis "all requirements, regardless of language, notation, or technique used: (1) define an object, a function, or a state, (2) limit or control the actions associated with an object, a function, or a state, or (3) define relationships between objects, functions and states" [14]. Although task modelling emphasizes the exploration of human behaviour and requirements reflect a "technological focus" we think that (formal) requirements specifications and task models have a similar level of abstraction and contain similar modelling elements or at least elements which can be related. In addition, the common underlying assumption is a goal-oriented behaviour. Humans apply tools to manipulate their environment in a purposeful way. Hence, task domain objects can be mapped to elements in models of interactive systems, tasks and their temporal

[1] In [10], requirements are divided into *maintainance goals* and *achievement goals*.

relations have to be reflected in a dialog specification, functions are automated tasks and so on. This is shown in more detail in the following sections.

3 Case Study - Part I

3.1 General Modelling Approach and TaOSpec

The case study analysed how people organise the program of workshops or small conferences by using the conference tool MyReview [15]. Three kinds of models were created.

- *Task models* which describe normative knowledge about the task domain and actions of users in different roles.
- *Dialog models* which specify the user interface of the conference tool at a conceptual level.
- *Application models* for specifying the functional core of interactive systems.

Fig. 1 gives an overview of the modelling approach. The model of the envisioned tool is the 'classical' requirements specification. All other models support its development and reasonable embedding in a possibly reorganised task environment.

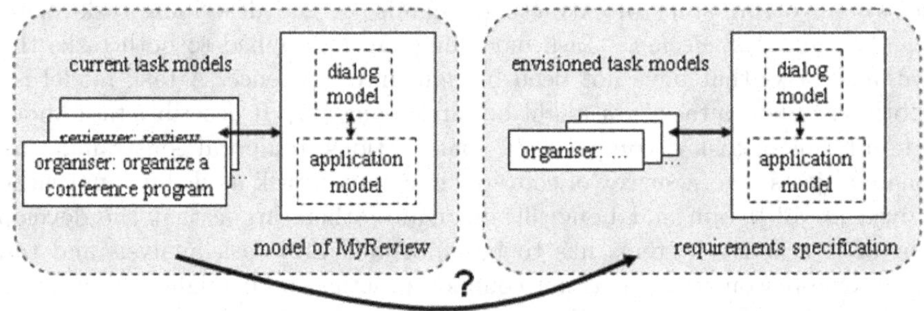

Fig. 1. Models used in the case study

TaOSpec is a specification formalism we originally designed for task modelling in the context of MBD [6]. In the case study, it is used for creating all three kinds of models (see also [7,16]). In short, TaOSpec allows e.g. an abstract description of tasks by specifying possible sequences of sub-tasks and the effect of their execution on the appropriate domain objects. In contrast to other task-modeling approaches all concepts are structured along identical modelling principles and expressed by *elements*. The inner structure of an element (intensional description) is determined by a finite set of attributes describing properties and by *partial descriptions*. It is distinguished between *basic* and *additional attributes*. The extensional description of an element E refers to a finite, possibly empty set of elements $\{E_1, \ldots, E_n\}$ which are at least similar with respect to the basic attributes of E. $E_1, \ldots, E_n$ are called *instances* of E, which is their *pattern element*. Partial descriptions referring to subsets of instances of a pattern element are expressed by partial equations. The left hand side of an equation consists of the identifier of the appropriate partial description. On the right hand side the designer specifies an expression whose operands can be identifiers of other partial descriptions, restrictions of attribute values and introduced additional attributes. TaOSpec offers a set of predefined state and temporal operators. Partial descriptions facilitate, for example, action decomposition and the description of states.

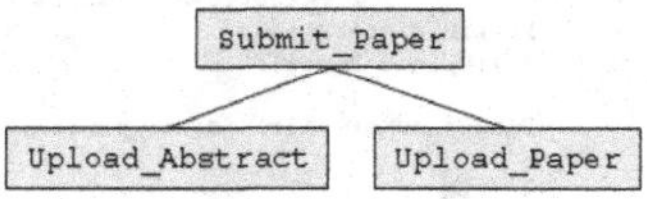

```
OPERATION Submit_Paper
USES Paper                                                    Submit_Paper            (1)
DECL
  Submit_Paper ($p),                              Upload_Abstract    Upload_Paper
    Upload_Abstract ($p),
    Upload_Paper ($p)
EQU
  Submit_Paper ($p) = [Upload_Abstract ($p)] >> Upload_Paper ($p),                    (2)
  Upload_Abstract ($p) = setAttr ($p,"title",read_string ("title: "))
                         >> setAttr ($p,"abstract",read_string ("abstract: ")),        (3)
  Upload_Paper ($p) [PRE $p.HasAbstract] = setAttr ($p,"content",read_string ("file: ")), (4)
  Upload_Paper ($p)[PRE not ($p.HasAbstract)] = setAttr ($p,"title",read_string ("title: "))
  ...
--------------------------------------------------------------------------------
ELEMENT Paper
ATTR
  $title: string,
  $abstract: string,
  $content: string      // file
ADDATTR
  $accepted: bool,
  $camera_ready_file: string
STATES
  HasAbstract = $abstract != "",                                                      (5)
  ForProceedings = $accepted==true and $camera_ready_file!=nil
  ...
```

Fig. 2. Example specification in TaOSpec

This is illustrated in the small example in Fig. 2. Action `Submit_Paper` is decomposed into `Upload_Abstract` and `Upload_Paper`. This and temporal constraints between both sub-tasks are to be seen in equation (2) ([...] and `>>` are temporal operators for option and sequence). The example also shows how a domain object (an instance of `Paper`, (1)) is manipulated by the action. TaOSpec provides a set of basic operations for creating an object, setting attribute values (3), creating additional attributes etc. Furthermore, preconditions - as state descriptions of domain objects - can influence the way tasks are performed. So, equation (4) is applicable if an abstract is assigned to the paper. This state is specified by the partial description `HasAbstract` in object `Paper` (5).

The used TaOSpec implementation separates between procedural and state descriptions. Therefore it is not possible, for instance, to consider action models as task domain objects as suggested in [17,16]. The interpreter enables users to animate models interactively. Fig. 3 demonstrates how ⟨`Upload_Abstract`, `Upload_Paper`⟩ as one possible sequence of basic sub-tasks of Fig. 2 modifies an appropriate paper.

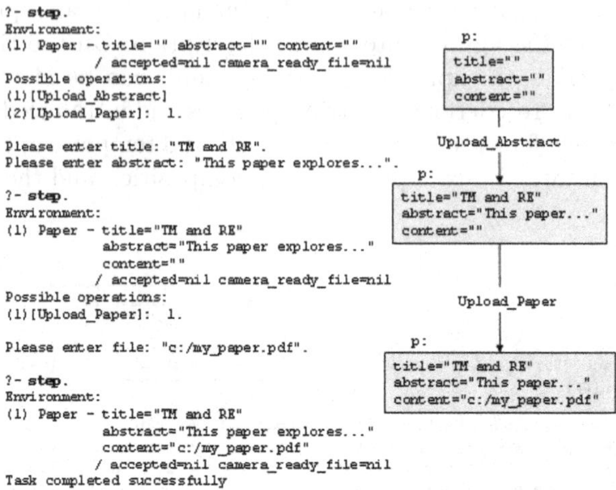

?- step.
Environment:
(1) Paper - title="" abstract="" content=""
/ accepted=nil camera_ready_file=nil
Possible operations:
(1)[Upload_Abstract]
(2)[Upload_Paper]: 1.
Please enter title: "TM and RE".
Please enter abstract: "This paper explores...".
?- step.
Environment:
(1) Paper - title="TM and RE"
abstract="This paper explores..."
content=""
/ accepted=nil camera_ready_file=nil
Possible operations:
(1)[Upload_Paper]: 1.
Please enter file: "c:/my_paper.pdf".
?- step.
Environment:
(1) Paper - title="TM and RE"
abstract="This paper explores..."
content="c:/my_paper.pdf"
/ accepted=nil camera_ready_file=nil
Task completed successfully
p:
title=""
abstract=""
content=""
Upload_Abstract
p:
title="TM and RE"
abstract="This paper..."
content=""
Upload_Paper
p:
title="TM and RE"
abstract="This paper..."
content="c:/my_paper.pdf"

Fig. 3. An animation of the model in Fig. 2

3.2 Description of Current Tasks

People who organise a conference program act in the role of organisers, reviewers, or authors. Here, we concentrate on the tasks of an organiser who is responsible for finding the program committee (PC), distributing the call for paper (CfP), organising the reviewing process... In the following 'first approximation' of a task model the hierarchical decomposition into some sub-tasks and temporal constraints between them are given (as partial equations). This structure is similar to CTT-models [1] or task models in TKS [11].

```
OrganiseConference = ((( Find_PC | Announce_Conf | Install_ConfTool ) >>
      >> Accept_Papers ) | Find_Keynotes ) >>
   >> (Edit_Proceedings | Compose_Program) >> [Edit_Final_Proceedings],
Announce_Conf = Edit_CfP >> Distribute_CfP,
Install_ConfSystem = Install >> Configure,
Accept_Papers = ( Organise_Submission | Organise_Reviewing ) >>
   >> Decide_Finally >> Announce_Results,
Organise_Submission = [Organise_Abstract_Submission] >>
   >> Organise_Paper_Submission,
Organise_Reviewing = [Ask_Reviewers_For_Preferences] >>
   >> Assign_Papers_to_Reviewers >> Organise_Discussion,
Edit_Proceedings  = Organise_CameraReadySubmission >> Edit,
Edit_Cfp = done, ...
```

The model would express the actual execution of the task more precisely if sub-tasks in the leaf nodes were refined and task domain objects considered. For example, `Find_PC` and `Announce_Conf` are combined by the parallel temporal operator (`|`) although there are dependencies. If we added elements specifying

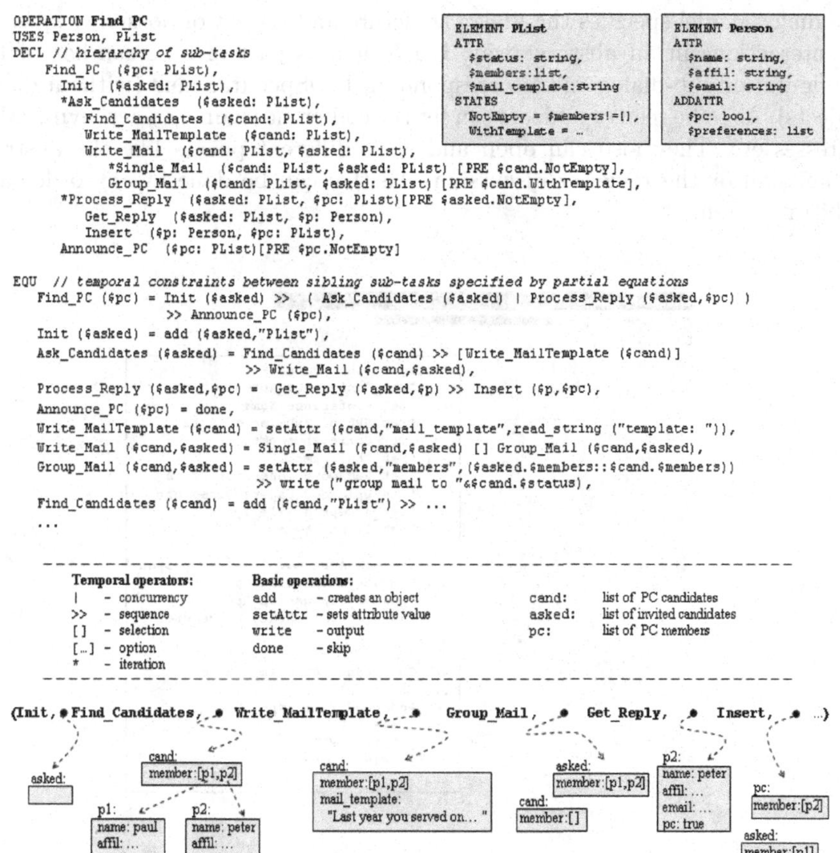

OPERATION Find_PC
USES Person, PList
DECL // hierarchy of sub-tasks
Find_PC ($pc: PList),
Init ($asked: PList),
*Ask_Candidates ($asked: PList),
Find_Candidates ($cand: PList),
Write_MailTemplate ($cand: PList),
Write_Mail ($cand: PList, $asked: PList),
*Single_Mail ($cand: PList, $asked: PList) [PRE $cand.NotEmpty],
Group_Mail ($cand: PList, $asked: PList) [PRE $cand.WithTemplate],
*Process_Reply ($asked: PList, $pc: PList)[PRE $asked.NotEmpty],
Get_Reply ($asked: PList, $p: Person),
Insert ($p: Person, $pc: PList),
Announce_PC ($pc: PList)[PRE $pc.NotEmpty]
ELEMENT PList
ATTR
$status: string,
$members:list,
$mail_template:string
STATES
NotEmpty = $members!=[],
WithTemplate = ...
ELEMENT Person
ATTR
$name: string,
$affil: string,
$email: string
ADDATTR
$pc: bool,
$preferences: list
EQU // temporal constraints between sibling sub-tasks specified by partial equations
Find_PC ($pc) = Init ($asked) >> (Ask_Candidates ($asked) | Process_Reply ($asked,$pc))
>> Announce_PC ($pc),
Init ($asked) = add ($asked,"PList"),
Ask_Candidates ($asked) = Find_Candidates ($cand) >> [Write_MailTemplate ($cand)]
>> Write_Mail ($cand,$asked),
Process_Reply ($asked,$pc) = Get_Reply ($asked,$p) >> Insert ($p,$pc),
Announce_PC ($pc) = done,
Write_MailTemplate ($cand) = setAttr ($cand,"mail_template",read_string ("template: ")),
Write_Mail ($cand,$asked) = Single_Mail ($cand,$asked) [] Group_Mail ($cand,$asked),
Group_Mail ($cand,$asked) = setAttr ($asked,"members",($asked.$members::$cand.$members))
>> write ("group mail to "&$cand.$status),
Find_Candidates ($cand) = add ($cand,"PList") >> ...
...
Temporal operators:
| - concurrency
>> - sequence
[] - selection
[...] - option
* - iteration
Basic operations:
add - creates an object
setAttr - sets attribute value
write - output
done - skip
cand: list of PC candidates
asked: list of invited candidates
pc: list of PC members
(Init, Find_Candidates, Write_MailTemplate, Group_Mail, Get_Reply, Insert, ...)
asked:
cand:
member:[p1,p2]
p1:
name: paul
affil: ...
email: ...
p2:
name: peter
affil: ...
email: ...
cand:
member:[p1,p2]
mail_template:
"Last year you served on... "
asked:
member:[p1,p2]
cand:
member:[]
p2:
name: peter
affil: ...
email: ...
pc: true
pc:
member:[p2]
asked:
member:[p1]

Fig. 4. Part of 'Find_PC' task model and illustration of some effects of a valid sequence of basic sub-tasks on domain objects (below)

CfP-objects and lists of PC members we could assign e.g. a precondition to sub-task `Distribute_CfP` saying that the CfP has to contain the final PC. In Fig. 4, a more detailed description of finding PC members is to be found. Additionally, a possible task scenario fragment illustrates the model granularity.

3.3 Description of the Current Tool

MyReview is a web-based conference tool. It allows authors to submit abstracts and papers. Reviewers can give their preferences with respect to topics. They can download papers assigned to them, submit reviews, and discuss about papers. For reasons of brevity, we concentrate on organisers again and explore how they are supported by the system. The analysis of the user interface resulted in a *dialog model* written in TaOSpec. Partial descriptions reflect sub-dialogs and the corresponding equations reflect temporal constraints between them. Hence, the dialog model specifies the dialog structure and the set of possible sequences of interactions in an abstract way. Fig. 5 depicts part of a screenshot of the configuration sub-dialog and a corresponding TaOSpec-fragment (without dialog objects). As to be seen organizers can set the conference name, an acronym, eMail adresses etc. They also can open and close different phases like the abstract submission or the reviewer discussion. All this can be done in any order and arbitrary often.

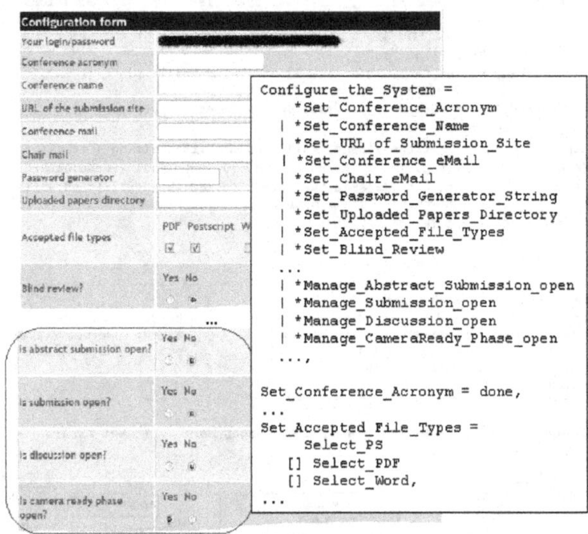

Fig. 5. Configuration dialog: Screenshot and dialog model fragment

While Fig. 6,7 represent two more screenshots and corresponding fragments of the dialog model concerning the registration of PC members and the acceptance of papers the part of the *application model* describing the 'life cycle' of a paper object is shown below.

```
Appl_Paper($paper) =
  [Submit_Abstract($paper)]
  >> Submit($paper)
  >> Review($paper)
  >> ( ( Accept($paper) >> Revised($paper)
          >> Published($paper) )
      [] Reject($paper) ),
Submit_Abstract($paper) = setAttr($paper,"abstract",
  read_string("Please enter abstract: ")),
Accept($paper) = setAttr($paper,"status","accept"),
Reject($paper) = setAttr($paper,"status","reject"), ...
```

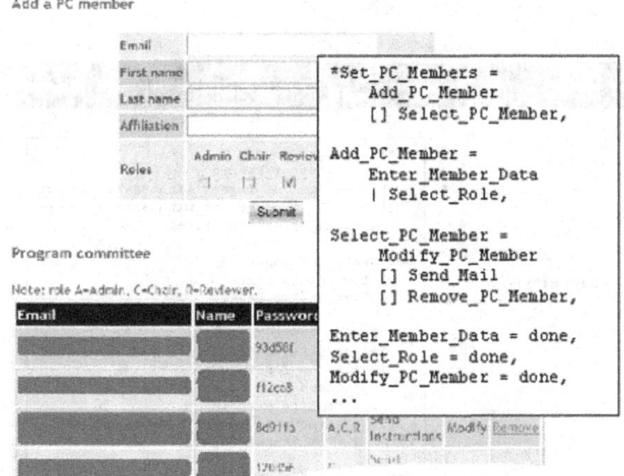

Fig. 6. Model fragment: `Set_PC_Members`

3.4 Relating Current Situation Models

One of the advantages of model-based approaches is that different models represent different perspectives on the same domain. That is to say, elements can be related across models because they refer to the same thing or process in the domain. For example, operations on application objects can be mapped to interactions offered in a dialog model which in turn should refer somehow to tasks in a task model. Hence, a comparison between models can help e.g. to identify 'inconsistencies' or to refine model parts. Of course, task knowledge of people is deeply influenced by the tools they use. Humans perceive the world through the lenses of their (physical and cognitive) tools and tasks are performed under specific conditions by applying a variety of tools. On the other hand, an interactive system has generally to support many different users in accomplishing several tasks. This difference finds expression in corresponding task models and systems specifications. As for our small case study, sub-tasks `Find_Keynotes` as well as `Announce_Conf`, `Edit_Proceedings`, and `Compose_Program` are not supported by MyReview[2]. There are no sub-dialogs or sequences of interactions across sub-dialogs which can be related. A closer look at the TaOSpec description of `Find_PC` in Fig. 4 and the dialog part in Fig. 6 reveals that the system supports sub-task `Insert` (the insertion of new PC members into the list) but not the other ones.

Another aspect are temporal relations between model elements. At first sight one could think that all temporal constraints occurring in task models and application models have to be considered by corresponding dialog models. On a closer inspection, this is not always advisable. Sometimes it is a good decision to allow

[2] MyReview, version 1.8.1 (published in December 2005) supports the production of proceedings, booklets of abstracts, and conference programs.

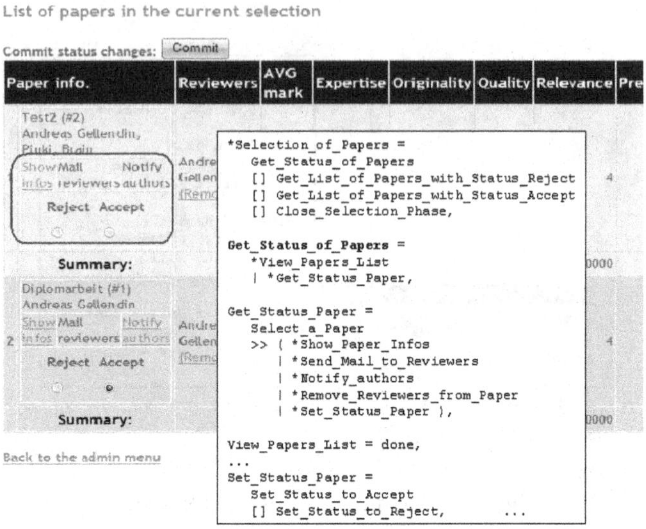

```
*Selection_of_Papers =
   Get_Status_of_Papers
   [] Get_List_of_Papers_with_Status_Reject
   [] Get_List_of_Papers_with_Status_Accept
   [] Close_Selection_Phase,

Get_Status_of_Papers =
   *View_Papers_List
   | *Get_Status_Paper,

Get_Status_Paper =
   Select_a_Paper
   >> ( *Show_Paper_Infos
      | *Send_Mail_to_Reviewers
      | *Notify_authors
      | *Remove_Reviewers_from_Paper
      | *Set_Status_Paper ),

View_Papers_List = done,
...
Set_Status_Paper =
   Set_Status_to_Accept
   [] Set_Status_to_Reject,      ...
```

Fig. 7. Model fragment: `Get_Status_of_Papers`

less constrained dialogs in order to 'serve' different tasks. In these cases users are 'more responsible'. The task model in the example prescribes a more rigid order of submission and reviewing phases than realized in the dialog part of MyReview (Fig. 5). For instance, a user could close the 'camera ready phase' and then open the abstract submission again. However, this design decision could perhaps be reconsidered.

Another point concerns the mapping of task structures to dialog structures. Often, a mixture of two 'strategies' can be found. First, sub-tasks are mapped to sub-dialogs. Second, tasks associated to a task domain object are grouped in the same sub-dialog. An example for an inconvenient dialog design is the following. MyReview offers the opportunity to close the submission and the selection phase within the sub-dialog presented by the main administrator form, but in order to open them and to open/close other phases users have to go to the configuration sub-dialog (Fig. 5, in the rounded box).

4 Reflecting the Approach

Completeness of models

Most approaches which recommend an explicit modelling of current and envisioned task situations assume generalised models, e.g. (Extant) Generalised Task Model and (Target) Composite Task Model in [3], Existing Task Model and Envisioned Task Model in [4], or task model 1 and 2 in [5]. According to [11], such models represent task knowledge of a specific domain independently of the detail of the individual tasks analysed (or imagined). Diaper [12] and others note that "only a small number of tasks can be selected for analysis" and "only a small part of a system can ever be observed". Hence, "task analysis always deals with simulations." Furthermore, Diaper refers to the problem of task combination by stating "almost all task analysis methods claim to be able to combine descriptions of a task performed by different people in different ways. Quite a few methods are able to combine different tasks into a single task representation" [12]. Indeed, this is true. Therefore, it is not possible to create one complete task specification with respect to current practices. Instead, we deal with a set of rather fragmentary task models. Their development is intertwined with the development of other models describing a current situation and with the creation of envisioned models. In other words, (fragments of) models are developed "on demand". Often, analysts look for 'inconsistencies' between different models to come to new insights. So, it is their decision which model parts are explored and elaborated in more detail. However, a 'final' requirements specification should ideally have properties such as completeness or consistency because it describes a computer artifact and "a computer is the most formal artifact possible; all it does is interpret meaningless symbols according to formal rules" [18].

Modelling means designing

In MBD, a current task situation is analysed with the intention to change. Although there is never a total separation between current descriptions and visions, analysts who put more energy into describing a situation 'as it is' can find improvements (and express them as requirements) which otherwise might not be obvious. To give a small example, a 'Call for Paper'-object was specified in a first attempt as an element with an attribute referring directly to the list of PC members which is a result of sub-task `Find_PC` (Sect. 3.2 and Fig. 4). However, a more realistic description of the current practice would distinguish between two lists because the PC members have to insert 'manually' into a Call for Paper - a process which can be error-prone. Additionally, a task analysis encourages stakeholders to reflect (and hence change) their own practices. "[T]here is nearly always a Heisenberg effect: the act of collecting the data alters what is being studied" [12].

Some further aspects deserve to be mentioned though often discussed elsewhere.

- It can be difficult to change the focus during modelling activities. However, a task model which describes e.g. user tasks from the 'user interface perspective' of an interactive system is too similar to a corresponding dialog model as if it would really help to elicitate requirements.
- (Formal) modelling languages and corresponding tool support are means by themselves. They support the description of some phenomena, but are also limited in their expressiveness. Additionally, analysts could be persuaded to 'reuse old solutions' (models) meaning that they have a too narrow view on real working practices.
- As already mentioned, task models are idealised and normative. They are criticized e.g. as "treating tasks as discrete, isolated chunks of behaviour as if they were representations of how the work is actually done" [19].

5 Case Study - Part II

5.1 Complementary Analysis Approaches

In the following, part of the email communication between the organisers of a small conference which we call RETM (Requirements Engineering and Task Modelling), an author whom we call Lucy (L.) and reviewers is presented. The organisers are called Stephen (S.) and Paul (P.).

> P. to S.: *I've had mail from L. asking if she can be late. She's asking for 10th and I'm inclined to be a little generous even though we have said everything is hard deadlines. If a substantial number were late this would be difficult for reviewing, but a few probably won't be too bad.*
> L. to S.: *Is it possible to have a deadline extension for submitting a paper to RETM to October 13?*
> S. to P.: *Look at this mail - now she's asking for 13th! But I think it's ok.*
> L. to S.: *Our submission for RETM is ready. We tried to upload it through the conference tool but it was closed. How can we submit it?*
> S. to L.: *You can send a mail to me with your paper attached.*
> . to reviewers: *paper #45 is submitted now and you can download it for reviewing...*

Alone this tiny piece of 'communication' reveals something about practices, activities, and attitudes concerning the submission of papers which we probably cannot find in 'a first approximation' of a corresponding task model (and even more unlikely in a 'classical' requirements specification) although techniques such as interviews, questionnaires, workshops, direct observation, concurrent or retrospective protocol (are recommended to) inform the modelling process (e.g. [11]). Of course, all data aquisition techniques have their pros and cons. Questionnaires hinder subjects and interviewers in establishing a shared meaning, open ended interviews are "vulnerable to distortion by interviewer bias",... and most above mentioned techniques are faced with the problem that they rely on the explanations of users. This enables an elicitation of conceptual knowledge but is not suitable for exploring tacit knowledge (see [20] for a good survey).

Often, the use of rich media such as video is proposed "for recording and discussing current system usage" because it "leads to a better understanding of the usage domain, enforces focused observation of (temporally and/or spatial) distributed aspects, avoids presumptuous abstractions, enables repeatability of results and late reflections" [9]. Haumer et al. interrelate concrete usage scenarios and conceptual current-state models in an 'instance-type way' to refine conceptual models and detect conflicts. Furthermore, scenarios facilitate a common understanding among stakeholders. In the case study, the above presented scenario could be used to refine sub-task `Organise_Submission` (Sect. 3.2) and to discuss how MyReview supports the completion of the different organisation phases which are also characterized by late submissions (of papers and reviews, see also Fig. 8). Scenario-based approaches like [21] but also some use-case approaches exploit both conceptual task knowledge and 'concrete' knowledge to

P to S:
... make sure I read all the potentially difficult ones...so that this can help resolve any boundary cases.

P to S:
I suggest we do something like 'kick' reviewers to discuss if reviews differ by 2 or more and are either side of the neutral point, so 3,4,5 would get a 'kick'... We seem to be getting a reasonable spread so far, so we may be able to have a fairly simple rule if all reviews are 5 and above accept if all are 3 and below reject, and then we look ourselves in detail at the ones which, after discussion are in the middle.

P to S:
...from rank 28 look like definite rejects unless ... papers above rank 8 look like definitely in... hopefully discussion will bring some...into definite yes or no.

S to P:
... definitely accept:...
I think definite rejects are: #26,...
We should look in detail at papers #35,...
according to the discussion #13,... should be rejected.

P to S:
#35 - ??? - POSSIBLE because ...
#7 - YES - I WANT IT IN! ...
...

S to P:
I refer to the reviews. Do you have access now?...from my point of view:
accepted: #4 because...,...
not sure but tend to accept:...(#35 as short)...
not sure:...
not sure but tend to reject:...
reject:...

P to S:
DEFINITE ACCEPTS - #2,...
PROBABLE ACCEPTS - #5,...
BORDERLINE - but we have room in the program ...
PROBABLE REJECT ...
DEFINITE REJECT ...

S to P:
I set the status of the above papers to 'accept'... removed all reviewers who didn't submit their reviews - otherwise we cannot inform the authors. ...

P to S:
#35 will need a special email as we are asking to chop it down to a short.

Fig. 8. Part of the email conversation between the organisers during the final decision phase

construct stories which evoke a more or less well-directed reflection and discussion about current working practices among stakeholders. Basically, the communication fragment at the beginning is already a construct because it is an intentional selection of 'statements' extracted from a sequence of emails.

However, complementary approaches are not only characterized by a possibly different choice of elicitation and elaboration techniques which can result in models of lower levels of abstraction[3] but also, and this is perhaps more important, by different underlying assumptions and perspectives. While scenario-based approaches use a similar conceptual task understanding as task-based methods participative and ethnographic approaches "try to gain access to and knowledge of the social practices, knowledge, beliefs, attitudes and activities, as they are exhibited by participants" [19].

In our case study, the communication between the organisers of RETM was analysed. This was possible because Stephen and Paul organised the program exclusively via email and by using the conference tool. Fig. 8 shows a part of the email conversation concerning the final decision about the acceptance of papers. It first illustrates how Paul and Stephen establish a common understanding about how to proceed at the beginning of the discussion phase between reviewers. Then, it reveals how the organisers create and use 'labels' in order to find a shared view on papers which are 'boundary cases'. However, these 'labels' have a temporary character - papers are finally accepted or rejected.

It is pointed out in [20] that practices are developed by the participants in their moment by moment activities. Instead of imposing their own orders analysts should try to find out "what categories the members themselves use to organise their interaction". In the example, Stephen and Paul followed generally accepted procedures. However, they also decided to send emails to reviewers of 'boundary cases' to encourage a discussion and to read these papers by themselves. By the way, Stephen discovered that he had to remove all reviewers assigned to a paper who didn't supply a review to be able to send notification mails to the authors. So, the original assignment of reviewers were lost (see also Fig. 7).

Techniques like field studies or conversation analysis support the exploration of social settings and tacit knowledge. As indicated in the previous section, we do not think that all models we are dealing with have to be (or can be) 'complete', 'consistent' or whatever. They are means to support an intertwined process of analysing current situations and creating visions, of developing abstract and conceptual models and exploring social settings and usage scenarios... and to come finally to a requirements specification which takes into consideration social understanding, values, and practices as demanded e.g. in [22].

5.2 Modelling the Envisioned Situation

Perhaps, five typical situations for using models and descriptions can be identified.

- The current system does not support a certain sub-task. However, the corresponding task model can help to develop a systems specification for envisioned tool support. An example is the model of sub-task `Find_PC` (Fig. 4).
- Parts of current task, dialog, or application models can be reused in corresponding envisioned models if they describe what is worth to maintain. An

[3] Every (textual) representation even if it is called 'concrete scenario' is an abstraction of the real world.

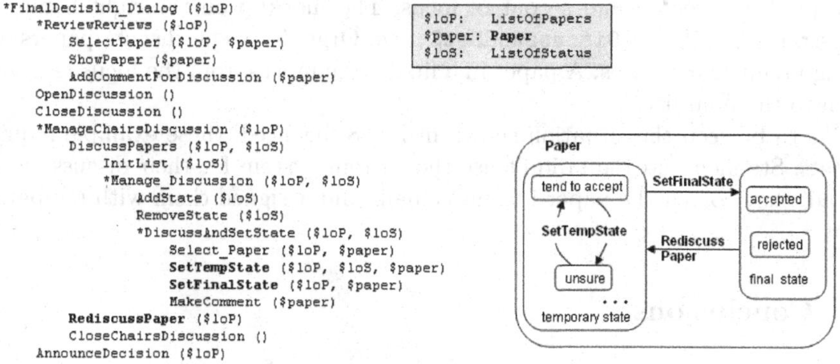

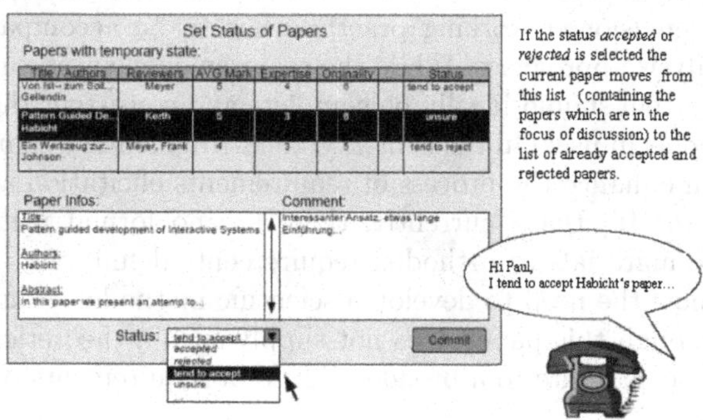

Fig. 9. Envisioned support for task `Decide_Finally`: Dialog structure, state chart for object `Paper` and a mockup for sub-dialog `DiscussAndSetState` (below)

example could be the login-dialog for authors, reviewers, and administrators which is not described in this paper.

- A model-based analysis can help to elicit 'inconsistencies' between models at the same level of abstraction in a deeper way (e.g. between task and dialog models).
- Models at a different level of abstraction are used to refine or revise a model referring to the same situation. In the case study, the email conversation between Paul and Stephen concerning the organisation of the program committee was used to inform the current task model (Fig. 4).
- Models are used for 'inspiration'.

The example depicted in Fig. 9 could stand for the last mentioned situation. It describes that a future system has to support the organisers during the final decision *process*. Organisers can create temporary states. In Fig. 9 `'tend to accept'` and `'unsure'` were created. Corresponding dialog model parts are `AddState` and `RemoveState`. Additionally, two lists of papers are distinguished. The first list contains those papers which are in the focus of discussion (temporary state), the second those which are, at this stage, considered as being accepted or rejected and so out of focus. The mockup on the right hand side illustrates sub-dialog `DiscussAndSetState`. Organisers can discuss papers and assign temporary states. A paper in a final state moves from the focus of discussion to the final list.

As to be seen the situation shown in Fig. 8 'inspired' these example requirements. Stephen and Paul didn't use the current system for their discussion. Instead, they copied the paper-id's into emails and assigned them with temporary states.

6 Conclusions

A small case study was used to illustrate our idea of a task-based requirements process. We argue that the development of several conceptual models describing current and envisioned working practices has to be accompanied by complementary analysis approaches. While the requirements specification of the future interactive system should ideally be complete and consistent this is not required for other models in use. On the contrary, their fragmentary character and inconsistencies can enhance the process of requirements elicitation and elaboration. It is stated in [19] that "currently, there are no formal methods of relating ethnographic materials to orthodox requirements definitions". In [20], Goguen and Linde show the need to develop a scientific methodology for systems development. Although this paper does not supply such a theoretical foundation we hope that we contribute to a broader view of a requirements process in MBD.

References

1. Paterno, F.: Model-Based Design and Evaluation of Interactive Applcations. Springer-Verlag (2000)
2. Luyten, K., Clerckx, T., Coninx, K., Vanderdonckt, J.: Derivation of a dialog model from a task model by activity chain extraction. In Jorge, J., Nunes, N., e Cunha, J., eds.: DSV-IS 2003, LNCS 2844, Springer (2003)
3. Lim, K., J.Long: The MUSE Method for Usability Engineering. Cambridge University Press (1994)
4. Johnson, P., Wilson, S.: Bridging the Generation Gap: From Work Tasks to User Interface Designs. In Vanderdonckt, J., ed.: CADUI'96. (1996)
5. Veer, G., Lenting, B., Bergevoet, B.: GTA: Groupware Task Analysis - Modeling Complexity. In: Acta Psychologica 91. (1996) 297–322
6. Dittmar, A., Forbrig, P., Heftberger, S., Stary, C.: Tool Support for Task Modelling - A Constructive Exploration. In: EHCI-DSVIS'04. (2004)
7. Dittmar, A., Forbrig, P.: Models and Patterns for the Specification of Context of Use. In: HCII'05. (2005)
8. Siddiqi, J.: Challenging Universal Truths of Requirements Engineering. IEEE Software **11**(2) (1994) 18–19
9. Haumer, P., Pohl, K., Weidenhaupt, K.: Requirements Elicitation and Validation with Real World Scenes. IEEE Transaction on Software Engineering **24** (12 1998)
10. Antón, A.I.: Goal-Based Requirements Analysis. In: Second Int. Conference on Requirements Engineering, IEEE Computer Society Press (1996)

11. Johnson, P.: Human computer interaction: psychology, task analysis, and software engineering. McGraw-Hill Book Company (1992)
12. Diaper, D.: Understanding Task Analysis for Human-Computer Interaction. In: [23]. (2004)
13. Limbourg, Q., Vanderdonckt, J.: Comparing Task Models for User Interface Design. In: [23]. (2004)
14. Davis, A.: Software Requirements: Objects, Functions and States. Prentice-Hall, Englewood Cliffs, NJ. (1993)
15. Rigaux, P.: The MyReview System Version 1.7.3. Laboratoire de Recherche en Informatique Universite Paris-Sud. (jul 2005) http://myreview.lri.fr/.
16. Dittmar, A., Forbrig, P.: A unified description formalism for complex HCI-systems. In: Software Engineering and Formal Methods, SEFM 2005. (2005)
17. Dittmar, A., Forbrig, P.: Higher-Order Task Models. In Jorge, J., Nunes, N., e Cunha, J., eds.: DSV-IS 2003, LNCS 2844, Springer (2003)
18. Dix, A.: Upside-Down ∀s and Algorithms - Computational Formalisms and Theory. In Carroll, J., ed.: HCI Models, Theories, and Frameworks - Toward a Multidisciplinary Science. Morgan Kaufmann Publishers (2003)
19. Randall, D., Hughes, J., Shapiro, D.: Steps towards a partnership: Ethnography and system design. In Jirotka, M., Gougen, J., eds.: Requirements Engineering: Social and Technical Issues. San Diego, Ca, Academic Press (1994)
20. Goguen, J., Linde, C.: Techniques for Requirements Elimination. In: Int. Symp. Requirements Eng., IEEE CS Press, Los Alamitos (1993) 152–164
21. Rosson, M., Carroll, J.M.: Scenario Based Developement of Human-Computer Interaction. Morgan Kaufmann (2002)
22. Nardi, B.A., O'Day, V.L.: Information ecologies: using technology with heart. MIT Press (1999)
23. Diaper, D., Stanton, N., eds.: The handbook of task analysis for human-computer interaction, Lawrence Erlbaum Associates (2004)

Discovering Multitasking Behavior at Work: A Context-Based Ontology

Marielba Zacarias[1,2,3], H. Sofia Pinto[1,2,4], and José Tribolet[1,2]

[1] Department of Information Systems and Computer Science,
Instituto Superior Técnico, Technical University of Lisbon.
[2] Organizational Engineering Center, INESC.
[3] University of Algarve
[4] ALGOS, INESC-ID
Surface mail address: INESC, Rua Alves Redol 9, 1000-029 Lisboa, Portugal.
mzacaria@ualg.pt

Abstract. Despite the availability of several task and personal information management tools, an appropriate support to human multitasking at work is still lacking. Supporting multitasking behavior entails capturing and modeling this behavior. In this paper, we refine an approach to model multitasking behavior in organizations, through an ontology based on two interrelated primitives; *action* and *interaction contexts.* The main contributions of the proposed ontology are: (1) enable the discovery of scheduling heuristics combining personal and inter-personal elements, (2) enable bottom-up discovery of tasks and (3) suggest a flexible system architecture for multitasking support. The first two contributions are illustrated through a case study.

Keywords: multi-tasking, context modeling, task discovery, ontology.

1 Introduction and Motivation

The reality of multitasking at work is undeniable. Evidence can be observed through several case studies [1]. Furthermore, task interleaving is constantly increasing due to the improvement of personal and group information technologies. A diary study of task switching and interruptions of eleven experienced Microsoft Windows users, reported a 50 task switch average during a week, when performing their computer-assisted tasks [2]. Human multitasking capabilities and limitations have been studied in Cognitive Sciences and Experimental Psychology. The literature in multiple-task performance is extensive [3,4,5]. However, there is no consensus around multitasking benefits and costs for businesses. Whereas some view it as an opportunity to draw on human capabilities, build their skills and enhance their productivity [6], others consider multitasking counterproductive [9] due to switching costs, showed by several psychological experiments [10].

In any case, it is a fact that people at work typically handle several, independent and unrelated tasks. Due to scarce resources such as attention and short-term memory [15], it is necessary to focus on a single task at a time. Thus, current work dynamics

K. Coninx, K. Luyten, and K.A. Schneider (Eds.): TAMODIA 2006, LNCS 4385, pp. 292–307, 2007.

force individuals to 'break' tasks and 'switch' among them according to criteria encompassing not only task-related factors, but also to resource availability or personal scheduling heuristics. Task-switching at work complicates information provision to workers -already a challenge due to information overload issues- because it requires *personalized* and *timely* mechanisms. Despite the availability of several task and personal information management tools, an appropriate support to human multitasking at work is still lacking [11].

To support multitasking behavior we must capture and model this behavior. In this paper, we propose an ontology to discover multitasking behavior in organizations and illustrate its benefits through a case study. Ontologies are specifications of a conceptualization [34]. Ontologies are means for the definition of a set of concepts and their inter-relationships. The proposed ontology is based on a model defined in [7], which addresses multitasking in terms of two different but interrelated concepts; *action* and *interaction contexts*. At a particular moment, the specific set of resources used by an individual depend on a combination of personal, task, role, location or time-related factors that define specific *action contexts*. Modeling multitasking entails acknowledging (1) the several action contexts handled by a single individual and (2) how he or she handles these action contexts. Since we rarely work in isolation, multitasking behavior is also influenced by interactions. The importance of interactions on task switching is acknowledged in [2,16]. Drawing from speech act theory [13], interactions produce commitments that are handled according to inter-personal and social rules. We approach interaction contexts as sets of *commitments* between two or more personal action contexts. Commitments are a fundamental factor of action context switching. The relationship of action and interaction contexts with other common modeling primitives is also defined.

The main contributions of this ontology are: (1) enable the discovery of scheduling heuristics combining personal and inter-personal elements, (2) enable bottom-up discovery of tasks and (3) suggest a flexible system architecture for multitasking support. The present work illustrates benefits related to the first two contributions through a case study. The case study results show first, that the action context primitive enables to handle sets of resources as single entities. This approach facilitates the detection of context switches and context switching patterns. Moreover, the analysis of context switching patterns reveals some generic personal heuristics and underlying interpersonal rules. Second, it illustrates that grouping actions and interactions in their corresponding contexts facilitates the detection of recurrent personal action and interaction patterns and a bottom-up discovery of tasks.

The remaining of this paper is structured as follows; section 2 summarizes work on tools for multitasking support; sections 3 and 4 summarize theories and models supporting this approach. Section 5 defines action and interaction contexts and illustrates these definitions with examples drawn from a case study, section 6 summarizes case study results on personal action contexts and section 7 summarizes related work on modeling approaches for user interface design addressing multitasking. Section 8 gives our conclusions and future directions.

2 Multitasking Support

There are several research prototype tools intended to enhance user support regarding multitasking issues. GroupBar [27] enables to organize project-related documents, e-mails and other windows together in the windows XP toolbar. GroupBar allows users to drag and drop taskbar "tile" on top of each other, forming groups of items in the bar that can then be operated on as a unit. Also, once the user lays out their work in a preferred configuration, GroupBar saves and restores these layouts. ROOMS is another project-oriented tool [28], which allows the user to set up specialized workspaces or "rooms" containing the resources necessary to carry out different types of activities. The use of dedicated work spaces has been limited due to the configuration overhead posed on their users [29]. The system UMEA aims at overcoming these limitations through a systems design which (a) organizes resources into project-related pools consisting of documents, folders, URLs and contacts, (b) monitors user activities and tracks resource usage in each project, (c) automatically organizes and updates these resources to make them easily available to the user when he or she resumes each project. Communication-based environments tools (such as e-mail applications) organize resources around contacts, communication threads or messages. E-mail conduit's function has lead to exploit inboxes for task management [16]. Moreover, its inter-personal nature poses interesting challenges for task management which have not been addressed. Reported limitations of current tools are (1) lack of more intelligent and flexible means for associating user actions and interactions with tasks or projects and enabling an automatic switching between them and (2) exclusion of inter-personal elements. The value of context identification heuristics in overcoming the first limitation has been acknowledged in [29].

From our point of view, the discovery of scheduling heuristics including personal and inter-personal factors are another valuable aid in enhancing current capabilities of associating individual actions and interactions with their respective contexts. Another limitation of most current tools is their inflexible design, which forces to organize actions, interactions or resources according to single pre-defined schemes (e.g. tasks, projects or communication threads). We argue that limitation is due to the lack of an underlying theoretical model of human multitasking. These models may suggest systems architectures capable of providing a more adequate multitasking support.

3 Human Multitasking Models

This section summarizes two representative cognitive models described in [10]: the attention-to-action (ATA) model and the frontal-lobe executive (FLE) model. These theories show how multitasking may be modeled through a three-layered model were task execution is separated from executive control processes that handle task interleaving and from processes that handle new situations or complex situations.

Attention-to-Action Model: The ATA model has three subcomponents: *action schemas*, *contention scheduling*, and a *supervisory attentional system)*. **Action schemas** are specialized routines for performing individual tasks that involve well-learned perceptual-motor and cognitive skills. Each action schema has a current degree of activation that may be increased by either specific perceptual 'trigger' stimuli or outputs from other related schemas. When its activation exceeds a preset threshold, an action schema may direct a person's behavior toward performing some task. Moreover, on occasion, multiple schemas may be activated simultaneously by different trigger stimuli, creating error-prone conflicts if they entail mutually exclusive responses (e.g., typing on a keyboard and answering a telephone concurrently). To help resolve such conflicts, the ATA model uses **contention scheduling**. Contention scheduling allows task priorities and environmental cues to be assessed on a decentralized basis without explicit top-down executive control. However, this may not always suffice to handle conflicts when new tasks, unusual task combinations, or complex behaviors are involved. Consequently, the ATA model also has a **Supervisory Attentional System (SAS)**. The SAS guides behavior in a top-down manner. It helps organize complex actions and perform novel tasks by activating or inhibiting particular action schemas, superseding the bottom-up influences of contention scheduling and better accommodating a person's overall capacities and goals. Figure 1 illustrates the ATA model.

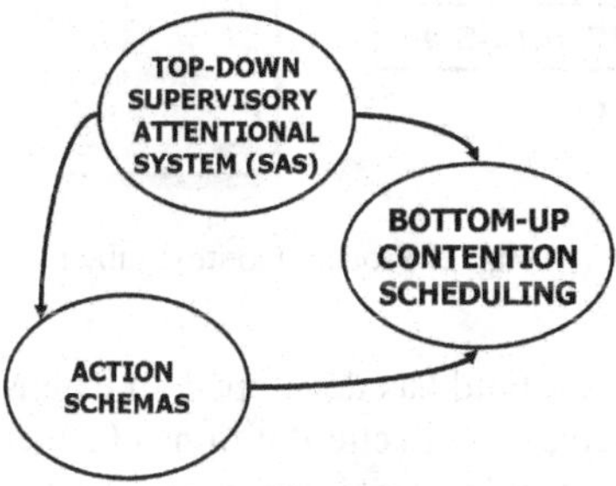

Fig. 1. ATA model

Frontal-Lobe Executive Model : Assumptions similar to those of the ATA model have been embodied in the Frontal Lobe Executive (FLE) model. It has three main components: *goal lists, means-ends analysis procedures*, and *action structures*. **Goal lists** represent a person's current set of prioritized intentions. **Means-ends analysis**, like the SAS, updates the contents and order of goals in working memory, considering of how well they are being achieved over time. Supplementing such functions, the **action structures** of the FLE model constitute a large store of procedural knowledge for goal-directed behaviors embodied as sets of condition-action production rules. The conditions of these rules refer to goals and perceptual stimuli; the actions involve responses to achieve the goals (e.g., *"if the goal is to do task a and the stimulus is s, then produce response r"*). Action structures are analogous to the ATA model's action schemas.

4 Context Models and Approaches

The concept of context is essential to our modeling approach. The notion and models of context vary according to the area of application. This section briefly summarizes computer sciences, cognitive and sociological approaches to context.

Computer Sciences approaches

Context in the *Operating Systems* field refer to the context of processes [13]. Contexts are regarded as a *state* and are implemented with tables maintained by the operating system that have an entry for each process (fig. 2). This entry contains information about the process' state (running, blocked or waiting), its program counter, stack pointer, memory allocation, the status of its open files, its accounting and scheduling information and everything that must be saved when the process is switched back from running to ready or blocked state so it can be restarted later as if it had never been stopped.

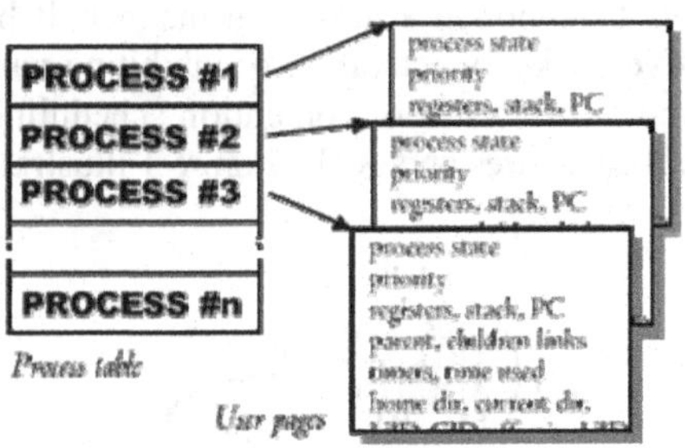

Fig. 2. Process Context tables

The *Artificial Intelligence* field has developed an extensive research on context. In this field, context is viewed as a collection of things (sentences, propositions, assumptions, properties, procedures, rules, facts, concepts, constraints, sentences, etc) associated to some specific situation (environment, domain, task, agents, interactions, conversations, etc). This consensus is reflected in the "box metaphor" [20] (fig.3). The intuition is that context can then be seen as a container where its content depends on some set of situational parameters or dimensions. Dimensions such as time, location, culture, topic, granularity and modality have been proposed as defining elements of context space [22]. A proposal for a workflow context space in [23] includes function, behavior, causality, organization, information, operation and history parameters.

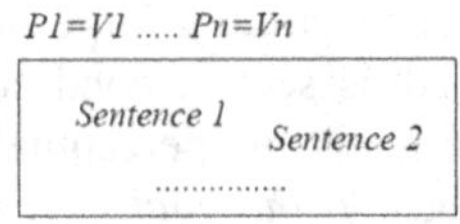

Fig. 3. The box metaphor

Context-aware applications have also modeled contexts as a function of localization, user identity, activity and time parameters [24]. However, more recently this field and the CSCW field are acknowledging the need of developing richer context models providing other information than time and location [14, 26]. The need to model user contexts and interaction contexts for improving user support is also acknowledged in [25].

A Cognitive Approach
B. Kokinov [17] developed a dynamic approach to context modeling to understand how human cognitive processes are influenced by context and how to model this influence in computer simulations. This work defines context as *the set of all entities that influence human (or system's) behavior on a particular occasion.* This context model assumes that mental representations involved in the current context are being formed by the interaction between at least three processes: *perception* that builds new representations of the current environment; *memory* that reactivates or builds representations of old experiences; and *reasoning* that constructs representations of generated goals, inferred facts, induced rules, etc. It is also assumed that context in turn influences perception, memory, and reasoning processes. The main principles of the dynamic theory of context are: (1) context is a state of the mind, (2) context has no clear-cut boundaries, (3) context consists of all associatively relevant elements and (4) context is dynamic.

Sociological Approaches
Sociological approaches typically regard context as networks of interacting entities (people, agents or actors and artifacts). These approaches focus on the structural properties of contexts, resulting from recurrent interactions among entities. Whereas some focus on the network elements, others focus on its emergent properties. In the latter case, the context itself is regarded as an entity which both supports and regulates interactions among its members [19]. Activity Theory (AT) [30] and Actor-Network Theory (ANT) [21] have been widely used in modeling social contexts. Both theories approach contexts as networks. Whereas ANT has been mostly used for a 'macro-modeling' of contexts, AT has been used in addressing finer-grained context models.

5 A Context-Based Ontology

Organizational activities have been modeled with a variety of concepts such as tasks, actions, interactions, roles, actors, goals, events, time and resources (e.g. tools, information, skills or people). We agree with [11] in the need of different primitives, capable of tying together other sets of common primitives used in modeling user behavior. In [7] we proposed *action* and *interaction contexts* as basic primitives to capture and model multitasking. However, these primitives need refinement.

In this section, we provide a description of the structure and state variables of action and interaction contexts. In terms of its structure, we follow sociological and cognitive approaches and regard contexts as networks of people and/or artifacts. In terms of its state, we use the operating systems notion and regard contexts as a set of state variables. These variables describe not only the state of individual network elements, but also of the state of the network emergent properties.

i) Actions and Interactions: To capture and model multitasking we must identify "broken" tasks. This entails looking inside tasks and working on the basis of smaller execution units. We define **actions** as atomic acts that change the state of some information or application resource (e.g. document is finished, sent, etc.). Unlike tasks, actions do not have clearly identified goals (e.g. update, print

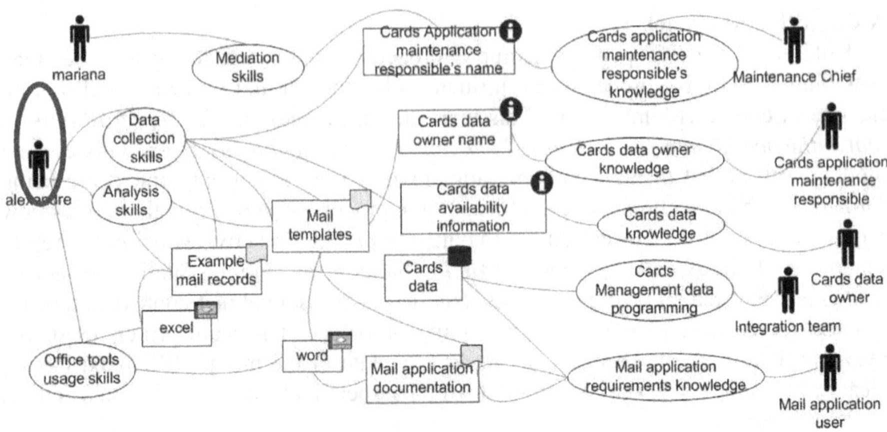

Fig. 4. The "Cards and Mail Data Collection" Action Context of Alexandre

document). Tasks are composed of several actions. **Interactions** are actions involving two kinds of actors (persons); a **sender** and a **receiver** (e.g. request meeting, ask questions). An interaction is performed by one person and intends to change the state of another person.

ii) Personal Action Contexts: Each individual at work uses some particular set of resources. These resources may be related to task (procedures, practices or routines), information, application or technological items. Resources may also include personal competencies, habits, preferences or rules. Cognitive limitations force individuals to focus on one sub-set at a time, forcing to a continuous suspension and reactivation of concurrent sub-sets. **Personal action contexts** define the *sub-sets* of relevant resources (along with its state) and the relationships among them (and the state of this relationship) for an individual *during particular time intervals*. Each person handles several *action contexts* that assemble together task, domain, tool and personal-related knowledge.

Figure 4 shows an example of an action context that belongs to an individual (Alexandre), which is a programmer from our case study. This action context shows the network of relevant resources for Alexandre, when collecting data required for an application to manage the correspondence with clients (Mail Application). As depicted in figure 4, this action context encompasses the following resources; *formal information items* (yellow folders and blue database symbol): *mail records* and *template* and *mail application documentation cards database*; informal information items (white i's in blue circle): name of responsible of cards application maintenance; *cards data owner name* and *cards data availability information;* application items (red and gray boxes): *MS outlook, Word* and *Excel* and *human resources* (names in figure 5), which provide two kinds of competencies (depicted with ellipsis): skills *–data collection, analysis, mediation and MS office usage skills-* and knowledge about cards data and mail applications. There are two fundamental aspects to be considered in the relation between resources and contexts; first, they may belong to several contexts. Second, context resources are not equally relevant. Resource relevance is reflected through a *membership degree.*

Personal action contexts are created and continually updated by actions and interactions. Hence, actions and interactions are also part of action contexts. Moreover, they reflect their past (action/interaction history), present (on-going actions/interactions) and future (actions/interactions to-do). Personal action contexts have also global variables that reflect emergent properties such as its general state, i.e. they may be active, suspended (due to lack of a resource) or interrupted by another action context. They also have a priority attributed by their owner and they may be triggered by some specific events i.e. they may have activation rules. Figure 5 summarizes action context state variables. Thus, action contexts become 'entities' that are created, activated, modified, suspended, resumed or terminated according to criteria that may encompass task or resource-related factors, as well as **personal scheduling heuristics**. related to time, location and individual preferences or habits. Personal scheduling heuristics also resolve potential conflicts when two or more action contexts with equal priority are activated at the same time.

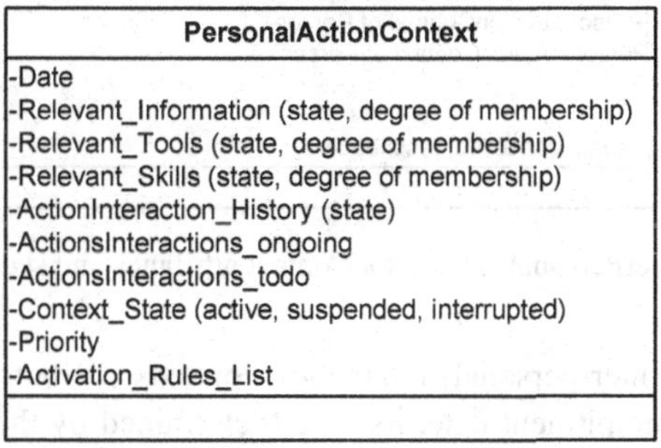

PersonalActionContext
-Date -Relevant_Information (state, degree of membership) -Relevant_Tools (state, degree of membership) -Relevant_Skills (state, degree of membership) -ActionInteraction_History (state) -ActionsInteractions_ongoing -ActionsInteractions_todo -Context_State (active, suspended, interrupted) -Priority -Activation_Rules_List

Fig. 5. Personal Action Context Attributes and State Variables

iii) Inter-personal Interaction Contexts: Inter-personal relations and interactions are important influencing factors of multitasking behavior. Task interleaving not only depends on the kind of messages, but also on the nature of the interaction context shared by message sender(s) and receiver(s). Interaction contexts may refer to inter-personal, group, organizational or even societal levels. This work addresses interaction contexts at an inter-personal level. **Inter-personal relations** emerge from successive interactions between any two individuals and define the **interaction rules** between them [31]. Drawing from speech act theory [13], commitments are created, changed or cancelled through communicative acts or interactions. At the inter-personal level, commitments refer to answering to questions, accepting or rejecting proposals, performing requested actions, delivering information items, etc. Interactions and commitments are related to specific tasks or roles and consequently, to particular action contexts of the individuals involved. Whereas any two individuals share a single inter-personal relationship, they may share several interaction contexts: This idea is depicted in figure 6.

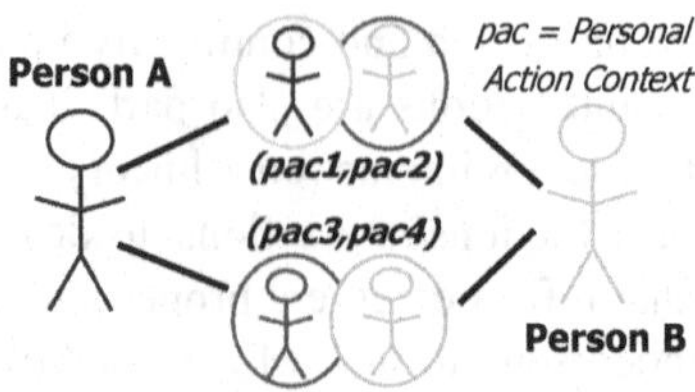

Fig. 6. Context-based (inter-personal)interaction contexts

We define (inter-personal) **interaction contexts** as the *relevant commitments* (and their state) produced by interactions between specific *personal action context*s of two different individuals.

InterPersonalInteractionContext
-Date -Type-of-Commitment (to-do task, answer questions, provide information, solution, etc.) -Commited-by (PersonalActionContext of Person) -Commited-to (PersonalActionContext of Person) -Original-Date -Actual-Date -State (pending, done, cancelled, rescheduled)

Fig. 7. (InterPersonal)InteractionContext attributes and state variables

Figure 7 depicts (inter-personal) interaction contexts attributes and state variables. These include the commitment date, its type (determined by the speech act type e.g. promises, requests, proposals, etc.), the original and actual date of accomplishmente and its state (pending, done, cancelled or re-scheduled). Figure 8. Illustrates an example of two (inter-personal) interaction context entries of our case study

- ***Date:*** 06-12
  - ***Commited-by:*** Mariana (pac10)
  - ***Commited-to:*** Catarina (pac5)
  - ***Type:*** ACCEPT/REJECT PROPOSAL
  - ***Description:*** solution to the automatic table update problem
  - ***Original date of accomplishment:*** 06-12
  - ***Actual date of accomplishment:*** 09-12

- ***Date:*** 06-12
  - ***Commited-by:*** Catarina (pac5)
  - ***Commited-to:*** Mariana (pac10)
  - ***Type:*** PROPOSE
  - ***Description:*** solution to the automatic table update problem
  - ***Original date of accomplishment:*** 06-12
  - ***Actual date of accomplishment:*** 06-12

Fig. 8. Two (interpersonal) interaction context entries

iv) Relation with other modeling primitives: Figure 9 shows the relationship between the proposed primitives and most common modeling primitives. Some of these primitives are based on the human multitasking models of section 2.1. Action contexts draw on action structures or schemas and personal scheduling rules draw on the contention scheduling component. Inter-personal relation and interaction context primitives draw on sociological approaches of context. Fig. 9 depicts first, the relation of action contexts with task, actor or role, or resource primitives. Second, it illustrates that interacting individuals share a set of interaction rules defined by their inter-personal relation. Third, the same two individuals may interact from different action contexts, creating several interaction contexts. These interaction contexts are supported and regulated by the inter-personal rules shared by the two individuals. Finally, figure 9 suggests a system architecture that integrated with proper clustering and classification techniques, enables more flexible association of actions and interactions with tasks, actors or resources through action and interaction contexts. This architecture is proposed and described in [33].

Acquiring the Context Models

Acquiring action and interaction contexts require a combination of manual and automatic mechanisms to capture, analyze, group and classify actions and interactions. Whereas computer-mediated actions and interactions may be automatically captured, future actions (actions to-do) and actions in the physical world require manual mechanisms. Due to their personalized nature, action contexts are ultimately defined by their owners. Thus, although its acquisition can be aided with the use of automatic clustering and classification techniques, some degree of user intervention is always required.

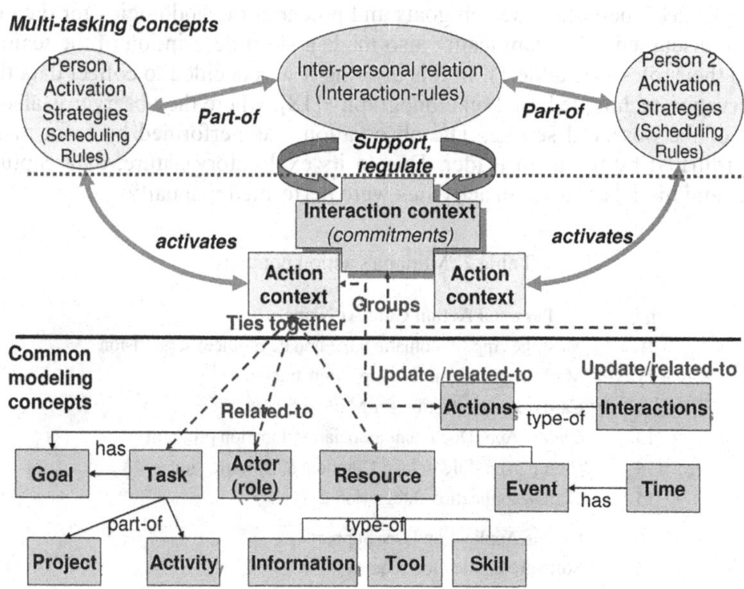

Fig. 9. Multitasking vs. common modeling concepts

6 Case Study

Some benefits of the proposed model are illustrated in this section through a case study in a real organizational environment. The case study involved a 3 week observation of a software development team of 4 programmers and the project leader. The team develops web applications for a commercial bank. Team members perform systems analysis, design, programming, test and maintenance activities. They also provide user support for the applications developed by them. During the observation period, the team performed tasks on the following applications; (1) *Suppliers,* (2) *Claims,* (3) *Clients' Correspondence (called Mail application),* (4) *Evictions* and (5) *Marketing Campaigns.* The team leader performed both system developing and *project management* tasks.

Table 1. Subject actors and personal action contexts

Team member	*Role(s)*	*pac*
Mariana	Group leader, Programmer	13
Gonçalo	Programmer	2
Catarina	Programmer	4
Alexandre	Programmer	4
Carla	Programmer	2

i) Method and techniques employed: The work started with a briefing session with the team leader where the research goals and potential methodologies for data collection were discussed. The team leader also made a short description of the team members and their roles (see table 1). In this briefing it was decided to collect data through an observation technique based on ethnography [18], where the observer is also a participant of the observed setting. The observation was performed by team members, and coordinated by the team leader. Due to its exploratory nature, data capture and analysis, and model acquisition activities were performed manually.

Table 2. Mariana's action contexts

pac	Personal Action Context Name
10	Message App. Automatic table update problem supervision
11	Marketing Campaings App. Adjustments
12	Cards Data Collection for Mail App.
13	Claims App. Document association function program
14	Claims App. File upload Component Modification
15	Claims application integration tests
16	Claims Application User Support
17	Software publication request
18	Message Maintenance
19a	Management Report Elaboration
19b	Management-related interactions
19c	Technical interactions with Microsoft consultant
20	Suppliers App. programming (web components).

Computer and non-computer mediated actions and interactions of the team members were registered in a chronological order. Each action or interaction was described with a separate sentence. Three weeks of actions and interactions were registered, encompassing 534 sentences. Registered sentences were first parsed using grammatical rules to separate the subject and predicate (verb and its complements). Synonym verbs were replaced by a single verb to avoid inconsistencies. Each action and interaction description was complemented with the set of application, information and human (competencies) resources involved. Parsed interactions were further structured using speech theory (for more details see [8]). We acquired action context models in a bottom-up fashion. First, actions and interactions were grouped according first, to their description and second, to the resources used. Second, a list of used resources was elaborated, separating them in three types (information, tools and human), according to the personal action context resource composition (fig. 9).

ii) Identifying Personal Action Contexts: As a result, 25 personal action contexts were identified and described. Table 1 depicts the number of personal action contexts associated to each team member during the three week period. While in some cases a personal action context encompassed several tasks, in others one task encompassed several personal action contexts. One example of the first case is the personal action context of Alexandre; the mail data collection action context (fig. 5). This context is related to a single task; the Mail Application Programming task. In fact, this task is related to several action contexts. The second case is illustrated in Mariana's *management report elaboration action context* (pac 19a in table 2). This action context is related to the *project plan, annual budget* and *project status report elaboration* tasks.

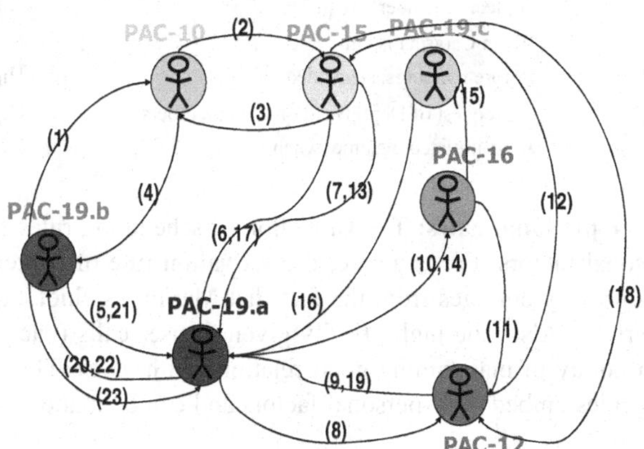

Fig. 10. Mariana's context switches on first day

Capturing Action Context Switches: Grouping actions and interactions in action contexts allows for context switch detection. Mariana (the group leader) handled a greater number of contexts. Thus, we selected her to analyze context switches and discovering scheduling rules. Table 2 shows Mariana's action contexts. During the observation, she handled 13 different action contexts. Data was registered in a chronological order. Hence, once actions and interactions were associated to a particular action context, it was easy to detect if a following action (or interaction) belonged to the same or to a different action context. In that case, a switch was registered. Figure 10 depicts the context switches of Mariana (group leader) on the first day of observation. On this day, Mariana handled seven different action contexts (colored circles) and performed 23 context switches, (numbered lines). Switching causes were also registered for each context switch. Due to space limitations, the whole list of causes identified is not included.

Discovering Scheduling Rules: Other personal action context state variables (fig. 5) are action context *activation (scheduling) rules* and *priority*. Registering switching causes enabled the discovery of these scheduling rules. Table 3 shows the scheduling rules discovered from Mariana's recurrent context switches and causes along the whole observation period. Action context priority was inferred from the number of times a particular action context interrupted active action contexts. These rules were rapidly and easily validated with the team members.

Table 3. Some Scheduling rules

pac	(Personal Action Context) Scheduling Rule	Priority
10	On user or Catarina's request	Normal
13	Auto-initiated, resume when free.	Normal
15	On team CG feedback reception	Normal
16	When Claims Application user calls	High
17	On team member's request	Normal
18	When Catarina is out	Normal
19.a	Before meetings, scheduled	High
19.b	On request of Dept. Head or team members	High
20	Auto-initiated, resume when free	Normal

Underlying inter-personal rules: The validation of scheduling rules revealed underlying inter-personal factors. For example, the activation rule of context (pac 19.b in table 3) and its priority emerges from the fact that Mariana's chief expects rapid answers from Mariana. Also, the high priority given to user calls (pac 16) has to with Mariana's own policy of maintaining good relations with users. Thus, personal context scheduling rules embed inter-personal factors and can be made explicit analyzing these rules.

Bottom-up task discovery: The observation of recurring action and interaction patterns also enabled the discovery of some tasks. These tasks were discovered during the process of grouping actions and interactions in their corresponding personal action contexts. Its correctness was validated by the team leader. Fig. 11 shows an example of the tasks discovered; the software publication procedure. Task specifications are personalized i.e. they reflect recurren*t* patterns of particular *individuals*.

- **Team members:**
  - Upon completion of a software component, request Mariana its publication in quality environment
  - Upon publication in quality or production environments, test component
  - If tests in quality environment succeed, request Mariana its publication in production environment
  - If tests in production succeed, request user to perform tests
- **Team leader (Mariana):**
  - Upon component publication request from team member, request the component publication in quality to publication team
  - When informed by publication team, informs team member that the component is in quality or production
  - Inform systems developer about user test results
- **Publication team:**
  - When requested, perform software publication in quality or production
- **Users:**
  - When requested by systems developer, test software in production

Fig. 11. Software Publication Procedure

7 Related Work

Traditional task modeling approaches such as GOMS and CCT [15] are limited to modeling user behavior within tasks. Dix work on Trigger Analysis [32] defines several types of triggers and complements task models by including the triggers for each task. This modeling approach enables to capture not only how things are done, but by whom when and where they are done. However, trigger analysis is proposed as an enrichment of task models and thus, it is a task-based approach. Consequently, it does not provide straightforward means to discover generic personal scheduling heuristics (e.g. dispatching short task first).

A composed approach to model multitasking behavior (CMM) is proposed in [11]. CMM combines task, goal, event and time-based-models in an integrated model. CMM allows to define triggers for task groupings. Although more generic, these triggers are also directly related to tasks. Moreover, this work argues the need of modeling multitasking behavior through a different set of primitives, capable of tying together other sets of already defined primitives. Nevertheless, no new primitives are defined. None of these two modeling approaches address the bottom-up discovery of tasks from actions and interactions.

8 Conclusions and Future Work

This work proposes a context-based ontology to discover multitasking behavior. The proposed ontology defines a set of primitives for modeling multitasking and associates them with other modeling primitives used in user interface design. Some of its benefits are illustrated through a case study.

The identification and modeling of personal action contexts provides groupings of actions, interactions around related resources. This kind of grouping exhibits higher resemblance with models of cognitive structures than other grouping criteria such as tasks or projects. Moreover, regarding action contexts as entities allowed identifying context-related emergent properties such as its priority and activation rules. Action contexts may be related to several tasks. Conversely, a task may be related to several action contexts. This enabled the discovery of personal scheduling heuristics not related to specific tasks, as well as some underlying inter-personal rules. Through context action and interaction history it was also possible to find action and interaction patterns and to discover tasks in a bottom-up fashion. Although not addressed in this work, the defined interaction context model aims at facilitating the provision of proactive and timely reminders of the commitments associated to each individual, organized according to priority of the corresponding action context. It also aims at enabling the inference of other inter-personal factors influencing multitasking behavior.

The observation technique employed proved to be feasible, with participant collaboration. Nonetheless, analyzing the data through manual means has several limitations, particularly in finding and analyzing interaction contexts, due to the level of detail and volume of this data. We are presently aiming to capture actions and interactions and acquiring action and interaction context models through semi-automatic means. A prototype system for the observation and grouping of user actions and interactions is being developed. Clustering algorithms are being explored for this end. The prototype will include an interface for the display and manual capture and modification of action and interaction contexts. This prototype will also allow testing the suggested system architecture in supporting multitasking.

References

1. Parama C., Multitasking and the returns to experience, [online] gsbwww.uchicago.edu/labor/parama.pdf, April 2002
2. Czerwinski M., Horvitz E., Wilhite S., A diary study of task switching and interruptions. *Proceedings of the SIGCHI conference on Human Factors in Computing Systems*, pp. 175–182, 2004. ACM Press.
3. Sohn M. et al., The role of prefrontal cortex and posterior parietal cortex in task switching. *In PNAS Proceedings of the National Academy of Sciences of the United States of America*, 97:13448–13453, 2000.
4. Altmann E., Functional decay of memory for tasks. Psychological Research, 66:287297, 2002.
5. Sohn M. and Anderson J., Task preparation and task repetition: Two component model of task switching. Journal of Experimental Psychology: General, 130(4):764–778, 2001.
6. Red L., A multitasking fish story , [online] http://www.bizwatchonline.com/archive/august2001/index.asp, 2001.
7. Zacarias M., Caetano. A., Pinto H.S., and Tribolet J., Modeling contexts for a business process oriented support. LNAI 3782, pages 431–442.Springer-Verlag, 2005.
8. Zacarias M., Marques A.R., Pinto H.S., and Tribolet J. Enhancing collaboration services with business context models. *CEUR Proceedings of the Workshops on Cooperative Systems and Context*, volume 133, July 2005
9. Porter A., Study: Multitasking is counterproductive. [online] http://cnn.com/career, Dec. 2001.
10. Rubinstein J., Meyer D., and Evans J. Executive control of cognitive processes in task switching. *Journal of Experimental Psychology: Human Perception and Performance*, 27(4):763–797, 2001.

11. Wild P. J., Johnson P. and Johnson H., Towards A Composite Modelling Approach for Multitasking, *Proceedings of the Task Models & Diagrams for UI Design, TAMODIA'04*, pp. 17-24, ACM Press, 2004
12. Searle J., Austin on locutionary and illocutionary acts. The Philosophical Review, 77:405–42, 1978.
13. Tannenbaum A. S., Modern Operating Systems. Prentice Hall, 2nd ed., 2001.
14. Riss U., Ricksayzen A., and Maus H., Challenges for business process and task management. Proceedings of the 5th International Conference on Knowledge Management I-KNOW '05, June 2005.
15. Dix A. et al., *Human–Computer Interaction*. Prentice–Hall, 1998.
16. Whittaker S., Bellotti V., Jacek G., E-Mail In Personal Information Management, *Acm Communications*, 49(1):68-73, 2004
17. Kokinov B., A dynamic approach to context modeling. In Proceedings of the IJCAI Workshop on Modeling Context in Knowledge Representation and Reasoning, pp., London, UK, 1995. Springer-Verlag.
18. Beynon-Davis P., *Information Systems*. Palgrave, Great Britain, 2002.
19. Reassembling the Social : An Introduction to Actor-Network, Oxford University Press, 2005
20. Benerecetti M., Bouquet P., Ghidini C., On the dimensions of context dependence: partiality, approximation, and perspective, *CONTEXT'03 Conference,* Springer-Verlag, LNAI 2116: 59-72, 2001
21. Giddens A., The Constitution of Society, University of California Press, 1984
22. Lenat D., *The Dimensions of Context-Space*, CycCorp, http://casbah.org/resources/cyccontextspace.shtml
23. Maus H., Workflow Context as a Means for Intelligent Information Support, *CONTEXT'03 Conference,*, Springer-Verlag LNAI 2116: 261–274, 2001.
24. Dey A., Abowd G., Towards a Better Understanding of Context and Context-Awareness,. *GVU Technical Report*, ftp://ftp.cc.gatech.edu/pu b/gvu/tr/1999/99-22.pdf
25. Brézillon P., Using context for supporting users efficiently. In 36th Annual Hawaii International Conference on System Sciences (HICSS'03) , Track 5, IEEE Computer Society, pp. 127- 2003.
26. Brézillon P., Role of context in social networks. FLAIRS Conference, pp. 20–25, 2005.
27. Smith, G., Baudisch, P., Robertson, G. G., Czerwinski, M., Meyers, B., Robbins, D., and Andrews, D., GroupBar: The TaskBar evolved. *Proceedings of OZCHI 2003*.
28. Henderson, A., Card and S. K., Rooms: The use of virtual workspaces to reduce space contention in a windowbased graphical user interface. *ACM Transactions on Graphics*, 5 (3), 1986.
29. Kaptelinin V., UMEA: Translating Interaction Histories into Project Contexts,., *Proceedings of the CHI'2003 Conference*, 5(1):353-360, 2003
30. Engeström Y., Miettinen R. and Punamäki R.L. Perspectives on Activity Theory, Cambride University Press, 2005
31. Magalhães R., Organizational Knowledge and Technology, Edward Elgar Publishing , 2004
32. Dix A., Ramduny-Ellis D., and Wilkinson J., Handbook of Task Analysis for Human–Computer Interaction, Trigger Analysis – understanding broken tasks, pp. 381–400. Lawrence Erlbaum Associates, 2004.
33. Zacarias M., Gomes R., Coimbra J. Pinto H.S., Tribolet J., Discovering Personal Action Contexts with SQL Server Analysis and Integration Services, *accepted for the IVNET '06 Conference*, Brazil, 2006
34. Gruber T., A translation approach to portable ontologies. *Knowledge Acquisition*, 5(2):199-220, 1993.

The Tacit Dimension of User Tasks: Elicitation and Contextual Representation

Jeannette Hemmecke and Chris Stary

University of Linz, Department of Business Information Systems – Communications Engineering, Linz Austria
{Jeannette.Hemmecke, Christian.Stary}@JKU.AT

Abstract. Traditional task-elicitation techniques provide prepared structures for acquiring and representing knowledge about user tasks. As different users might perceive work tasks quite differently, normative elicitation and representation schemes do not necessarily lead to accurate support of individual users. If the individual perception of tasks should guide the development of user interfaces personal constructs have to be taken into account. They can be elicited through repertory grids: Personal work content and task-relevant information emerge in the course of structured interviews and can be transformed to conventional representation schemes, even for execution and prototyping. In this paper we introduce an elicitation procedure based on repertory grids and its embodiment in a working user-centered and task-based design approach.

Keywords: User-task elicitation, repertory grids, mental constructs, design-knowledge acquisition, user-interface specification, model-based design, task context, task awareness, externalization.

1 Introduction

User-centered system design in its current dominant implementation requires developers to gain some familiarity with user activities ([25], p. 91ff). Methodological support for developers to achieve that objective is provided either through guidelines [25], model structures, conceptual modeling or specification languages, such as the Unified Modeling Language (UML) [34]. On the level of elicitation, these support instruments have two major drawbacks: First, they do not allow developers to capture user tasks beyond their (inherent) representational capability, and secondly, they are limited to the user's explicit knowledge of the tasks.

Most of the representation schemes for elicitation are intertwined with tools for further processing. Therefore, they only allow to address user-task information that can be captured by the representation scheme, rather than those aspects not inherent in the representation scheme, but nevertheless relevant for task accomplishment. To avoid such a representational bias of user-task elicitation, we argue for a pre-representational technique of user-task elicitation. Such techniques have to be open for inputs structured along individual mental models rather than driven by elements of knowledge-representation schemes.

K. Coninx, K. Luyten, and K.A. Schneider (Eds.): TAMODIA 2006, LNCS 4385, pp. 308–323, 2007.

From work and cognitive psychology it is known that an essential part of the user's task-relevant knowledge is tacit (i.e. unconscious). Knowledge either becomes tacit through automation of work procedures, i.e. formerly explicit knowledge lapses into the unconscious and, by that, becomes tacit [14], or the tacit knowledge is acquired through implicit learning, i.e. task-relevant knowledge is learned without awareness through personal experience and practical examples like in a master-apprentice relationship [24]. In a variety of professions that rely on complex problem solving capabilities and creativity like law, medicine, sales, teaching, or management, tacit knowledge is seen as a crucial factor for success [35]. In particular, it plays a central role in dealing with critical, i.e. non-routine situations at work [3, 4]. The main characteristic of the tacit dimension of knowledge is that it is difficult to communicate and formalize [26, 28]. Consequently, tacit knowledge is difficult to capture with traditional task elicitation methods like questionnaires, surveys, structured interviews, or analyses of existing documentations, because the task analyst simply does not know what kind of questions to ask [1]. When eliciting user-task information we, therefore, have to deal with the tacit dimension that indwells work procedures.

Herrmann et al. [17] have shown that workers should not only be able to describe their *particular* view on the assigned work tasks, but also co-construct a common understanding of collaborative work tasks. Such type of participation facilitates technology development, even when different paths to accomplish a certain task are followed by individual workers. Empirical results from work psychology, too, give evidence that there are many alternative efficient and effective procedures when users have freedom in their task accomplishment procedure [39, 40]. Hence, when dealing with different users and different individual perception of tasks and task accomplishment procedures, elicitation techniques should support the elicitation of both, idiographic (i.e. the individual user's perception of the task) and co-constructive (i.e. common aspects of user groups in task perception) user-task information. In order to achieve this objective, the elicitation as well as the representation of user-tasks has to be context-sensitive [23].

From the method perspective elicitation techniques should 1) avoid the influence of representational structures and 2) be capable of capturing the tacit dimension of user-tasks in a context-sensitive way, and 3) value individual differences as well as commonalties of user-task information.

With respect to processing Herrmann et al. [18] have also found out that diagrammatic representations should be linked directly to software functionality for task execution. Through activating those links users should immediately be provided with interactive hands-on-experience and provide developers with task-specific feedback. As we will demonstrate model-based prototyping tools can meet this requirement based on proper representations.

We introduce an elicitation technique that does not impose representational restrictions through dedicated representation structures, but rather let structures emerge according to the individual mental models of the users (see section 2). The elicitation procedure we suggest is based on the repertory grid technique. It is domain-independent and provides a structured procedure for eliciting individual mental models with respect to the dedicated range of convenience (cf. [21]; see section 2.1). Repertory grids have been suggested and successfully applied in various software-development domains, most of all in expert system development [2, 11], but also in requirements engineering [27], and instructional design [20].

After giving an overview of the elicitation procedure in section 2.2 and exemplifying its use in the field of customer-relationship knowledge management (see section 2.3), we address the transformation of externalized user knowledge to a model-based scheme (see section 3). We show which elements and relationships of a multi-dimensional scheme have to be utilized for the representation and processing of user-task knowledge. Section 4 concludes the paper.

2 Elicitation

We first give some background on the traditional repertory grid method and the personal construct theory forming its foundation. Then, we introduce and exemplify the elicitation procedure.

2.1 The Repertory Grid Method

The repertory grid technique is a special interview technique developed by George A. Kelly [21]. Its purpose is the elicitation of personal constructs, i.e. individuals' mental models.

Kelly used the term personal construct to describe the basic cognitive dimensions individuals develop while interacting with the world. Personal constructs constitute the way individuals perceive, think about and make sense of the world. "A construct is like a reference axis, a basic dimension of appraisal, often unverbalized, frequently unsymbolized, and occasionally unsignified in any manner except by the elemental processes it governs. Behaviorally it can be regarded as an open channel of movement, and the system of constructs provides each man with his own personal network of action pathways, serving both to limit his movements and to open up to him passages of freedom which otherwise would be psychologically non-existent" (Kelly, 1969 in [12], p. 3). This definition shows that personal constructs can be seen as tacit dimension of behavior, as already demonstrated by others, e.g. [3, 16].

The repertory grid method has to be understood in the frame of Kelly's comprehensive psychology of personal constructs (PPC) and his philosophical position of constructive alternativism [21]. Kelly assumed that there are always several viable alternatives in construing the world and that neither of them is right or wrong. All construing serves the anticipation of future events and, by that, helps individuals in reducing the complexity of the "real" world and in getting a sense of control in life. In the context of user-task analysis it means that each individual has a particular view on organizations and task systems and, most important, that all these particular views are equally valid.

To demonstrate how personal constructs develop, Kelly has used the metaphor of "the man as a scientist". Scientists develop hypotheses and test them against "real-world" events. From the position of PPC, every person behaves like a scientist in order to orient him/herself within the complex world: he/she develops constructs, relates them mutually in hierarchical structures, and uses them to anticipate future events. In case the prediction of an event is not adequate, parts of the construct system (the construct itself or the realm to which constructs are applied) have to be revised. In case the prediction is successful, the construct system will be strengthened. For the elicitation of user-tasks it means that individual perceptions of tasks are valid in its particular context, and that perceptions of tasks change over time, i.e. user task information has to be considered as a dynamic entity.

Repertory grids have especially been used as a means to make individual or collective changes in knowledge transparent. Empirical evidence for the application of repertory grids as a tool for the measurement of change can be found in psychotherapy research, e.g., in [6, 42].

Understanding knowledge as personal constructs should enable developers to recognize how individuals 'construct' their work activities. Since the same activity might be 'constructed' differently by different workers, it makes sense to elicit partly overlapping, partly conflicting knowledge. "No two people can play precisely the same role in the same event, no matter how closely they are associated" ([21], p. 38). This even holds, when – from an observer's perspective – two persons seem to have made the same experience. To know about differences in perception of activities facilitates inter-individual transfer of elicited codified knowledge, especially between users and system developers.

Although the repertory grid technique has been developed for psychotherapy as a means for understanding the client's way of construing and for facilitating the therapist-client dialog and possible interventions, in a software-development setting, repertory grids might be used in the same way. They might help to elicit various points of view on organizational entities or tasks, and following that, they might be the starting point for designing user interfaces and organizational changes. In this paper we focus on the first type of application and demonstrate the utility of our procedure.

The repertory grid technique consists of four steps [13,19, 31, 32]: (1) choice of elements, (2) construct elicitation, (3) rating, and (4) analysis.

(1) Choice of Elements. Elements are the basic items upon which construing takes place. The choice of elements, therefore, determines the range of convenience of the elicited constructs. As a consequence of that, the chosen elements constitute the subject of investigation of the grid itself [13]. An element can be every "item of meaning" [38] in human life, such as persons, situations, or artifacts. Elements should have certain properties in order to support the elicitation of meaningful constructs [36]. They should be

- *Discrete*: the element choice should contain elements on the same level of hierarchy, and should not contain sub-elements
- *Homogeneous*: the elements should be comparable
- *Comprehensible:* the person whose constructs are elicited should know the elements, otherwise the results will turn out meaningless
- *Representative:* the elicited construct system will reflect the individually perceived reality, once the element choice is representative for the domain of investigation

When using the repertory grid technique for a new purpose – like user task elicitation in our case – the researcher's crucial conceptual task lies in adapting the technique to the new field by choosing one or more appropriate element types (see section 2.2).

(2) Construct Elicitation. The construct elicitation is based on comparative questions. The triad method is the original and still most common form of construct elicitation [21, 32]; for a description of further techniques see also [31]. In the triad method, three elements are mutually compared according to their similarities and differences. The person is asked to specify "*some important way in which two of them are alike and thereby different from the third*" ([12], p. 27). The elicited similarity between the two elements is termed and documented as the construct. Subsequently, the person is asked to detail the contrast using the following question: *In what way differs the third element from the other two*? The construct elicitation continues as long as new constructs can be elicited.

(3) Rating. The third phase of a repertory grid interview is the rating of the elements according to the elicited constructs. The mutual relations of elements and constructs can be explored by using a rating procedure. According to Kelly [21], the rating is dichotomous, i.e. each element can be described either by the construct *or* by the contrast (0/1). Today the rating primarily ranges on a 5 to 7 point scale [31].

(4) Analysis. The goal of the analysis of a repertory grid is to represent the construct system in a way that both, the interviewer and the interviewee get new insights about the interviewee's view on the corresponding elements. Finally, other individuals should come to an understanding about the interviewee's way of thinking. The most common forms of visualization are bi-plots (derived from principal component analysis) and dendrograms (derived from cluster analysis). In bi-plots the relations of elements *and* constructs can be displayed whereas in dendrograms only the relations of elements *or* the relations of constructs can be visualized. It is not necessary to use computer programs for analysis, especially when the results of a single person are subject to analysis. Applying content analysis [13, 19], the constructs can be clustered according to a category system.

2.2 The Task-Elicitation Procedure

In this section we describe the elicitation procedure qualifying repertory grids for user task elicitation. Our procedure consists of three steps:

(1) activity-theory based interview
(2) repertory grid interview
(3) repertory-grid based group co-construction

The first step serves for getting a systematic overview of the task-related activities and their context, in order to prepare the repertory grid interview. The second step is the elicitation of the tacit dimension of task knowledge. The third step consolidates the individual results within a user group, i.e. commonalties should be found and differences should become transparent.

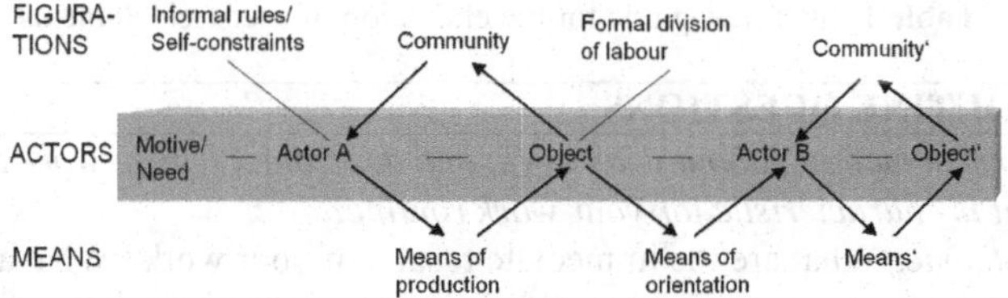

Fig. 1. Three process levels of activity of two interacting activity systems (based on [30], p. 407 and [7], p. 43)

Activity-theory based interview. Since the choice of elements in repertory grids determines the subject of investigation and since neither the theory of personal constructs nor the repertory grid technique itself provide means to elicit appropriate elements in contexts other than psychotherapy, the crucial task is to support that process of element choice for work contexts [15]. Organizational applications of repertory grids in general and user-task elicitation in particular require flexibility in the element choice, because each user task including its environment has its specific characteristics. Consequently, the elements have to represent a specific task and its specific environment.

In order to provide such a flexibility, we consider activity theory [8, 22, 30] to be a valuable framework for the element choice in work contexts [16]. Instead of concentrating on bits of individual behavior detached of its embodiment in the work, activity theory focuses on an activity system, i.e. a (work) activity seen in its broader cultural, social, individual, and physical context ('means', 'community', 'division of labor', 'rules'; see Figure 1). Moreover, activity theory provides a process view on work. It considers logically sequenced and intertwined tasks that are performed by 'actors' working on certain 'objects' and, by that, producing intended and unintended outcomes. The latter are being passed from one actor to another as a result of a work step. We consider activity systems as a "lens" for analyzing user-tasks in their context [8, 9, 33].

Since activity theory merely provides the framework but no concrete methods for analysis, we suggest the following procedure for finding appropriate elements for the elicitation of a specific user task. In that procedure, we combine and adapt psychological methods that have been validated seperately in many areas of application (for an overview on applications of the critical incident technique cf. [5]). We have developed a semi-structured interview guide based on the critical incident technique [10] and work routine questions to elicit salient items of meaning that represent the work task in its organizational, individual and physical context (see Table 1).

The interviewer starts questioning users about daily or weekly work routines (depending on what the users consider more significant for their work), and continues questioning critical events along these routines. The interview guide consist of one major question and several adjacent questions (see Table 1). The latter and the scheme of analysis have been derived from activity theory.

The interview has to be conducted either with all users or with representatives of user groups for whom user-task-centered design is intended.

Table 1. Interview guide for the elicitation of user-task elements

WORK ROUTINE QUESTIONS
Please tell me something about your work, and describe a typical work day or week? What is characteristic for your work routine? *Objects/Outcome:* What are the immediate results of your work? What are the products/services of your organization? What are their mutual relations? *Goals/Tasks:* Overall, what are the tasks you have/want to accomplish, what are the goals you have/want to achieve? *Motive:* Why do you do this job/perform this activity? What is your personal motive for that? *Conditions:* Are there special conditions for your work, such as physical (sounds, light etc.), technical (Characteristics of machines, tools etc.), organizational (time constraints etc.), social (professional status, relationships between colleagues etc), and financial conditions (salary etc.)? *Community:* With whom do you work more or less closely? Think of your colleagues, supervisors, colleagues from other departments, suppliers, customers etc.. *Division of Labor:* Are there intra- or extra-organizational departments that your task/product/service obliges you to co-operate? Where do structural boundaries limit or open up possibilities for your activity? *Social Rules:* How are processes and relationships in your work regulated? Thinking about the way you collaborate with A, B,... (based on answers to the questions above), what formal or informal rules you can think of mediate that collaboration? *Means:* Which tools, instruments, symbols, technical language, etc. do you use to accomplish your task? What about the availability and applicability of those means for transforming the object of your work into the desired outcome?
CRITICAL INCIDENT ELICITATION
Please remember a situation concerning ... [include the task at hand] which you experienced to be very challenging and which resulted in extreme positive (negative) outcomes! Please tell me about… *Conditions:* …the general circumstances that have led to the situation! Where and when did the incident happen? *Activity, actions, operations:* ...the concrete chains of actions in the situation! What exactly did you do? What exactly have your interaction partners done? *Community*: …the persons who were involved? Were there persons that helped or hindered you in your actions? Who? *Means:* ...the resources, tools, and aids which you have been using in the situation? Which means would you have used if they had been available in the situation? *Rules:* ...formal and informal rules, that supported or hindered your actions? Could you prepare yourself for the situation? *Division of Labor:* …about the history and expected future consequences of the event! Who has worked on the task/request before the incident occurred, who was

Table 2. (*continued*)

the person/department that you expected to deal with the task/request in succession? What kind of division of labor did you experience (according to personal interests/strength, according to clearly defined rules,...)? *Summary:* Did the event occur under any particular circumstances we did not talk about so far? Overall, which factors did you find particularly critical during the situation and for the situation's outcome?

Shifting from explicit to tacit task knowledge. By analyzing the activity-theory based interviews the elements of a repertory grid can be determined. Appropriate elements are those items (instances of the categories of the activity system) that can be identified as meaningful and relevant for the task. When more than one user is involved, it is especially interesting to focus on those aspects where users show divergence.

Since elements in a repertory grid have to be homogeneous (i.e. comparable to each other), we suggest choosing elements that belong to the same category of the activity system (i.e. either actors or means or objects etc.). The selection of category depends on the kind of deeper knowledge to be elicited using the repertory grid: (1) The interviewer could ask for similarities and differences between all *actors* who act in the same role in a work process in order to understand the variety of task accomplishment procedures used. (2) The interviewer could compare available and non-available *means* for task accomplishment in order to understand how the means are used and what their explicit and implicit impact on the outcome is or is not. (3) The interviewer could use intended and unintended *outcomes* as elements in order to understand the interrelation of different outcomes and the intertwined ways how those outcomes are achieved (in terms of means, rules, roles and individual knowledge that lead to the transformation of an object of work into the outcome). (4) Rules are difficult to choose as elements for a grid because most of them are tacit and therefore difficult to elicit by the activity-theory based interview. To get a deeper understanding of the tacit social rules that are applied during task accomplishment, elements have to be used that are mediated by those social rules, i.e. the interviewee him/herself and his/her *relation to other persons* fulfilling several roles related to the task accomplishment (co-workers, supervisors, colleagues from related departments, customers, suppliers). (5) If the activity-theory based interview suggests that organizational structure impedes the task accomplishment in certain ways, elements could be *structural units* with regard to its impact on the task accomplishment procedure and the desired outcome.

Despite the quest for homogenous elements for a grid, there might be complex tasks depending on intertwined factors which hinder to focus on one category at a time. Therefore, we show two ways of element choice that help integrate several of the five perspectives in one grid. (6) The positive and negative *incidents* as well as the routine events elicited during the activity-theory based interview might be chosen as 'holistic' elements in the sense of compact items. Events or situations meet the criteria of homogeneity. Even if they are complex in nature, i.e. all categories of the activity system are inherent in situations, they are of the same quality and thus, can be compared mutually. The comparison of events leads to insights in the interrelation of several task-related factors (rules, roles, means, objects, involved actors). However, it is up to the interviewee which factors and interrelations she/he focuses on. (7) A final possibility of element choice is the use of element rewording – Wright and Lam [43] showed that rewording elements into "doing-words" might help to enable mutual comparisons of elements of different categories. For user-task elicitation we can reword items of meaning being part of different categories into *activities*. For example, if one wants to mutually compare the influence of actors involved and aspects of organizational structure, one could define elements such as "talking with my team supervisor" and "compensate the missing role Y".

Given a certain element type repertory grid interview(s) can be conducted as described in the section 2.1. As a result of the grid interview the tacit dimension of a user-task is elicited. A sample grid is shown in Table 3 and discussed in detail in the section 3.

Group Co-construction. In many cases of user-task elicitation, more than one user is involved. Step 1 and 2 of the elicitation procedure provide individual task-related knowledge. The group co-construction in step 3 puts a common understanding of the work task on trial. In that process commonalties and differences in the way of dealing with the task and perceiving task context are made transparent.

The concept of co-construction has been formulated by Wehner et al. in their model of co-operation at work [41]. Co-construction is considered as the highest form of communication: Roles, rules, work objectives, or patterns of interaction are subject to discussion and common re-definition. In order to implement such a group co-construction, we revert to focused group discussion (or focus group), a well known qualitative method for knowledge elicitation in software development [29]. The results of the analysis of the individual repertory grids serve as the input for the focus group. After a moderated discussion on the similarities and differences in task perception, a joint repertory-grid on the common 'co-constructed' understanding of the user task is generated as the output of the focus group discussion.

2.3 Example

Case. In order to demonstrate the accuracy and contextual richness of the technique we describe the elicitation of customer-relationship management knowledge. The case is taken from a large insurance company. Customer service is crucial due to the high competitiveness of this business sector. The company is the result of the merger with different cultures, as reflected by the differences in handling work tasks.

Procedure. First, individual interviews based on the critical incident technique and daily routines with representatives from customer service have been conducted. The answers have been structured with the help of activity theory, and conflicting perceptions in behavior have been identified for further elicitation. Using these results, the element type for the repertory grid for further elicitation has been determined in terms of customer service members. 7 interviews have been performed involving the same interviewees we started with. The construct elicitation has been conducted with the help of the triad method.

Results. The results of the repertory grids have been analyzed individually (cf. Table 3) with the help of principal component analysis (by SPSS, Statistical Software Package for Social Sciences). The principal component analysis helps to reduce the dimensions of variables and to span a two dimensional space enabling the visualization of all constructs and elements.

The results have been consolidated in a single co-construction session involving all interviewed parties. The data have been enriched and could be used for generating user-interface prototypes (based on a contextual representation) for the intended customer relationship management-software system. The most prominent result was the variety of ways to accomplish customer-service related tasks.

Table 3. Rated grid for approaching customers and handling requests

		Elements (employees)						
No.	**Constructs (1 2 3)**	**A**	**B**	**C**	**D**	**E**	**F**	**Contrasts (4 5 6)**
1	Service description and customer briefing	1	6	2	2	3	1	Recognizing barriers for customer service advice
2	Customer binding	2	6	2	2	1	1	'One-shot' customer treatment
3	Email presorting before reply to customer request	1	6	1	1	1	1	First-come-first-serve handling of incoming emails
4	Read and listen first (reactive customer approach)	1	5	1	6	3	4	Immediate service application (pro-active approach)
5	Rephrase requests to ensure mutual understanding of request when answering	2	4	3	4	4	4	Never rephrase
6	Consult colleague in case of complex cases	1	5	2	6	3	4	Detail request to reduce complexity

3 Contextual Representation

In this section we show how a concrete grid representing user-task knowledge that has been elicited through co-construction and analyzed as shown above can be successively transformed to model-based user-interface specifications.

3.1 Codified Work Intelligence

Table 2 shows a typical grid that has been elicited from users with respect to customer contact. After getting an overview of the individual perspectives on the activity system (step 1 of the procedure – see previous section), the elements of repertory grids have been determined for approaching customers and handling email customer requests. The elements (middle part of the table) were employees who have identified the structure of approaching customers (task description) and the organization of tasks.

The table contains task-relevant constructs, such as service description and briefing. Note that these constructs have emerged in the course of user interviews and co-construction and have neither been biased by the interviewer nor a representation scheme. Interestingly, the contrasts do not necessarily correspond to negations of constructs, as can be seen for the first entry. The first construct/contrast pair shows two ways to approach customers, either describing services and briefing, or recognizing that customers do not want to be briefed on the offered services. The second entry (Customer binding) reveals that customer contact can either be understood as an activity within a customer-relationship program or as an unrelated event to that type of activities. As we will see this information is essential for putting tasks into mutual contexts.

Request handling (entry 3) might be handled in sequence or after presorting incoming emails. Finally, services might either be applied in a push-oriented or pull-oriented way (entry 4).

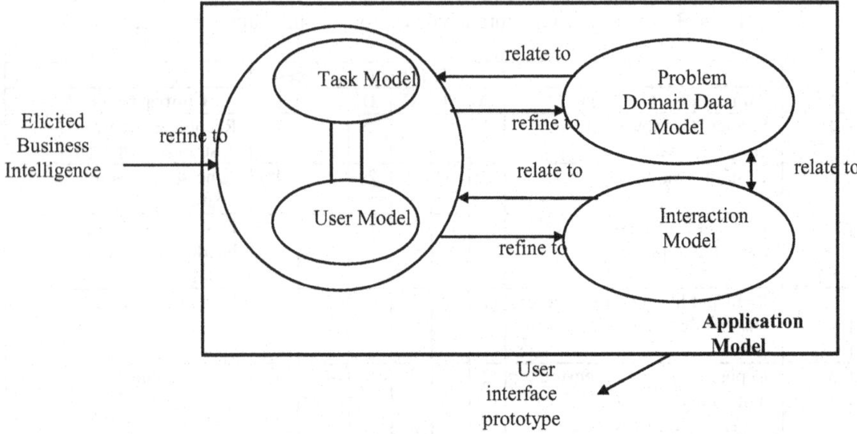

Fig. 2. Model-based representation and design using ProcessLens, cf. [34, 37]

For the sample part of the grid the ratings for each of the elements are also shown. They are the result of individual sessions using the triad method described in the sub section 2.1 (step 2 of our procedure) and a co-construction session, in order to consolidate the results (step 3). Some patterns indicate a common organization of tasks, e.g., when dealing with emails (entry 3), however, also different ways of dealing with work tasks and customers. That information has to become part of the model-based representation for design and prototyping.

3.2 Model-Based Representation

ProcessLens is a third-generation model-based design-support tool. It guides the task- und role-sensitive development of interactive software through providing an ontology that captures the essentials of work processes [34, 37]. It captures the structural and dynamic linking of executable (UML-)models. It supports a model-based design procedure –

Figure 2 relates the different models with respect to design tasks:

- The *user model* represents a role model by defining specific views on tasks and data (according to the functional roles of users).
- The *task model* comprises the decomposition of user tasks according to the economic and the social organization of work as well as the different activities that users have to perform to accomplish their tasks.

- The *(problem domain) data model* describes the data required for work-taskaccomplishment, including their life cycles.

The *ProcessLens* ontology supports the modeling activities in a process-oriented way. Figure 3 depicts a sample task model (composed of diagrammatic elements for <<Task>>, <<Activity>> and ''is part of' and 'before'-relationships), the user model and its fundamental relation 'handles', for the running example. Interaction elements have to be assigned in the course of design to represent the presentation of data and the navigation capabilities. Activity diagrams assigned to interactive tasks have to be synchronized – in ProcessLens a dedicated transition makes the models operational (in our case for user-interface prototyping) as illustrated in Figure 3 (linking a task- and user model diagram). Note that the distinction between user model and task model allows to represent the overall organization of work tasks (see activity chain in Figure 4), as well as the part of the activity chain that is assigned to a particular functional role. It is the set of activity chains for each of the role definitions that has to capture the individual differences in task-accomplishment as elicited.

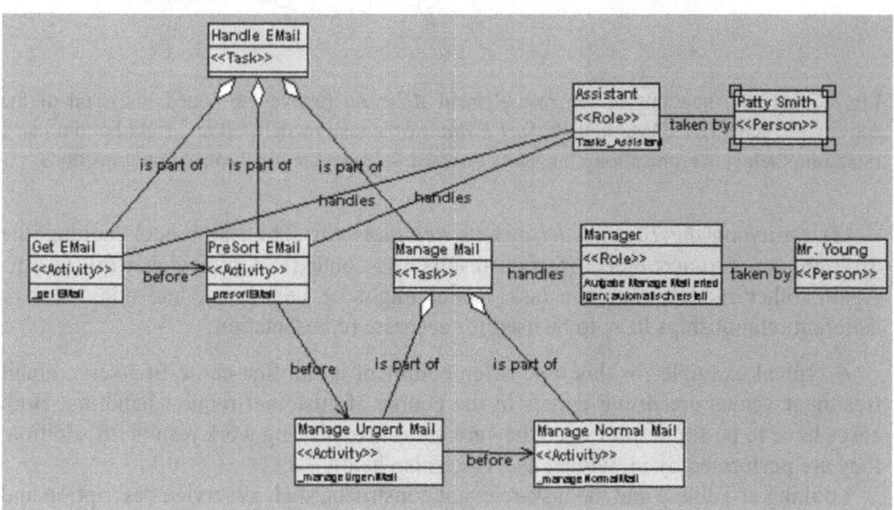

Fig. 3. Sample Integrated Task/Role Representation in ProcessLens

3.3 Embodiment of Task Context

Given the individual perception of user tasks and the elicitation results, indicating not only individual flavors of accomplishing work tasks, but also significant social differences (as shown through the results of the analysis), the question remains, how this type of knowledge can be embedded into traditional representation schemes. Overall there are two different ways for embodiment, i.e. explicit representation:

(1) *Enriching the User Model and its Relationships*: As soon as particular skills and constellations of social parameters occur they can be assigned to persons or role specifications. The relationships to other models, namely the task, interaction, and

data model have to be revisited, since this information might change interaction styles, the access to functionality for cooperation and others.

A typical example of this sort is given when embedding the results of the elicitation shown in Table 2. Social skills can be represented and valued in the user model, either with respect to particular tasks or independently (note, the 'handle'-relationship captures that context). The same holds for data on loyality, and behavior when an employee is in contact to customers or makes decisions.

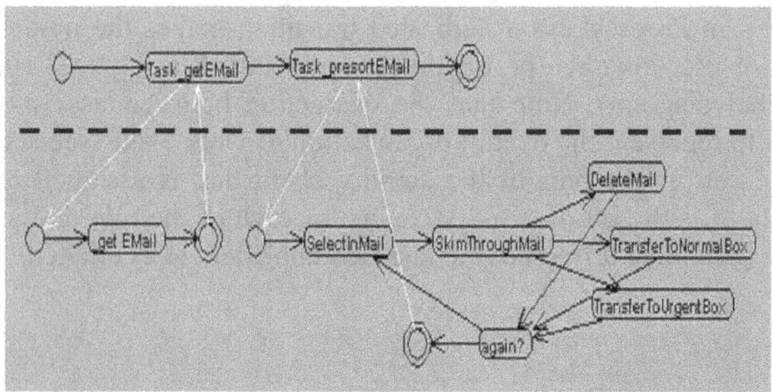

Fig. 4. Activity diagrams of the role element *Assistant* (above the dotted line) and of the activity elements *Get EMail* and *PreSort EMail* of the task model (left and right bottom part), including their synchronization - the white directed links denote synchronization transitions

(2) *Enriching the Task Model and its Relationships*: The task model captures the different ways to accomplish certain results and contexts of achieving work results. Again, other models than the task model might be concerned, and additional or different relationships have to be used for accurate representation.

A typical example for this type of embodiment is the first-come-first-serve email treatment versus presorting emails in the course of customer request handling. Both cases have to be supported, since they are valid in achieving work results. In addition, they are performed by individual users (see also below).

Looking at Table 2 and the task-relevant constructs, such as service description and briefing, we can assign this context information as follows: The first construct/contrast pair indicates through its rating rather diverse service handling procedures, either due to customer data or personal profiles. In that case the task model should at least contain activity descriptions for customer briefing. As a case 2 approach it also has to capture the non-use of briefing functionality. This is expressed through the lack of before-relationships as well as optional paths through the activity diagrams of that task.

The second entry (Customer binding) is again a task modeling issue: When customer contact is understood as an activity within a customer-relationship program there have to be relationships to that sort of tasks. A typical example is a relationship between customer-relationship management (CRM) tasks, such as 'identify customer knowledge' and email handling. Certain activities will be linked through a 'part of'-relationship or another type of association. Again, it has to be noted that data from either task model part (CRM or emailing) might become accessible to roles or persons that did not have access before. Any access restriction or permission might require further tuning of activity information in the task model. For the other case, considering customer contact as an unrelated event to CRM activities, the task model does not need be modified. Note, that both cases have to be considered due to the consolidated rating of the elements.

According to entry 3 of Table 2 a typical request for diversified task handling is revealed. Emails might either be answered on a first-come-first-serve basis or in a sorted approach. In order to meet the request the task model in Figure 3 has to be enriched with the possibility to manage emails without presorting, eventually assigning a responsible person (as indicated through the 'is taken by'-relationship in Figure 3) to that case. Technically, standard email tools provide that type of access.

The matter of push- versus or pull-oriented service provision to customers seems to depend heavily on the individual personality of users (entry 4 in Table 3). The respective data could be stored in the user model (case 1) and trigger the mailing of service data according to the user-model entries. In case the designer decides to permanently allow push-functionality, any user might push customers or deactivate the permanent availability of that function. In order to represent that, the relationship between the task model and the interaction model (presentation part of tasks, e.g., permanent display of the functionality as an icon), has to be adjusted.

4 Conclusion

Conventional task elicitation techniques provide fundamental structures for acquiring and representing task knowledge, whereas user-centered elicitation focusing on the emergence of structure rather than on pre-defined representational elements, deliver a more accurate picture of human tasks and their accomplishment. Taking into account personal constructs repertory grids reveal not only different perceptions of activities but also hidden contexts that direct human work. The challenging task in design is, then, to transform explicit constructs into software specifications, in order to enable their execution and in this way, user-interface prototyping. Mutually tuned approaches for elicitation and representation are promising candidates to implement user-centered design.

References

1. H. Beyer and K. Holtzblatt. *Contextual Design: Defining Customer-Centered Systems*. Morgan Kaufmann Publishers, San Francisco, 1998.
2. J. Boose. Uses of Repertory Grid-centred Knowledge Acquisition Tools for Knowledge-Based Systems. *International Journal of Man-Machine Studies*, 29:287-310, 1988.
3. Büssing, B. Herbig, and T. Ewert. Implizites Wissen und erfahrungsgeleitetes Arbeitshandeln. *Zeitschrift für Arbeits- und Organisationspsychologie*, 46(1):2-21, 2002.
4. Büssing, B. Herbig, and A. Latzel. *Das Zusammenspiel zwischen Erfahrung, implizitem und explizitem Wissen beim Handeln in kritischen Situationen*. Report No. 66 (Berichte aus dem Lehrstuhl für Psychologie). Technische Universität München, Lehrstuhl für Psychologie, München, 2002.
5. L. Butterfield, W. Borgen, N. Amudson, and A.-S. Maglio. Fifty Years of the Critical Incident Technique: 1954-2004 and beyond. *Qualitative Research*, 5(4):475-497, 2005.

6. Catina. Erfolgs- und Prozessforschung in der Gruppentherapie. In J. W. Scheer and A. Catina, editors, *Einführung in die Repertory Grid-Technik. Band 2: Klinische Forschung und Praxis,* pages 115-127. Huber, Bern, 1993.
7. Clases and T. Wehner. Steps across the Border – Cooperation, Knowledge Production and Systems Design. *Computer Supported Cooperative Work*, 11:39-54, 2002.
8. Y. Engeström. *Learning by Expanding: An Activity-theoretical Approach to Developmental Research*. Orienta-Konsulit, Helsinki, 1987.
9. Y. Engeström. Expansive Learning at Work: Toward an Activity Theoretical Reconceptualization. *Journal of Education and Work*, 14(1):133-156, 2001.
10. J. C. Flanagan. The Critical Incident Technique. *Psychological Bulletin*, 51(4):327-359, 1954.
11. K. Ford, F. Perty, J. Adams-Webber, and P. Chang. An Approach to Knowledge Acquisition Based on the Structure of Personal Construct Systems. *IEEE Trans. Knowledge and Data Engineering*, 4(1):78-88, 1991.
12. F. Fransella, R. Bell, and D. Bannister. *A Manual for Repertory Grid Technique*, second edition. Wiley, Chichester, 2004.
13. M. Fromm. *Repertory Grid Methodik: Ein Lehrbuch*. Deutscher Studienverlag, Weinheim, 1995.
14. W. Hacker. *Allgemeine Arbeitspsychologie: Psychische Regulation von Arbeitstätigkeiten*. Hans Huber, Bern, 1998.
15. J. Hemmecke. Repertory Grids in Organisational Practice: How to Choose Elements. Paper presented at the *8th Conference of the European Personal Construct Association*, Kristianstad, Sweden, 8-11 April 2006.
16. J. Hemmecke and Ch. Stary. A Framework for the Externalization of Tacit Knowledge Embedding Repertory Grids. *Proceedings OKLC-2004, 5th European Conference on 'Organizational Knowledge, Learning and Capabilities'*, Innsbruck, April 2004.
17. T. Herrmann, M. Hoffmann, G. Kunau, and K. U. Loser. Modelling Cooperative Work: Chances and Risks of Structuring". In M. Blay-Fornarino et al., editors, *Cooperative Systems Design, A Challenge of the Mobility Age (Coop 2002)*, pages 53-70. IOS Press, 2002.
18. T. Herrmann, G. Kunau, K. Loser, and N. Menold. Sociotechnical Walkthrough: Designing Technology along Work Processes. In *Proceedings of the 8th Participatory Design Conference 2004*, pages 132-141. ACM, New York, 2004.
19. D. Jankowicz. *The Easy Guide to Repertory Grids*. Wiley, Chichester, 2004.
20. D. H. Jonassen, M. Tessmer, and W. H. Hannum. *Task Analysis Methods for Instructional Design*. Lawrence Erlbaum Associates, Mahwah, New Jersey, 1999.
21. G. A. Kelly. *The Psychology of Personal Constructs*. London; Routledge, New York, 1991. (Reprint, Norton, New York, 1955)
22. N. Leontjew. *Tätigkeit, Bewußtsein, Persönlichkeit*. Pahl-Rugenstein, Köln, 1982. (English Translation: *Activity, Consciousness, and Personality*. Prentice Hall, Englewood Cliffs/NJ, 1978)
23. Mirel. *Interaction Design for Complex Problem Solving*. Morgan Kaufmann, San Francisco, 2004.
24. G. H. Neuweg. Tacit Knowing and Implicit Learning. In M. Fischer and N. Boreham, editors, *European Perspectives on Learning at Work. The Acquisition of Work Process Knowledge*. Cedefop Reference Series. Office for Official Publication fot the European Communities, Luxembourg, 2004.
25. W. M. Newman and M. G. Lamming. *Interactive System Design*. Addison Wesley, Wokingham, England, 1995.

26. Nonaka. A Dynamic Theory of Organizational Knowledge Creation. *Organization Science*, 5(1):14-37, 1994.
27. N. Nui and S. Easterbrook. Discovering aspects in requirements with repertory grid. In *Proceedings of the 2006 international workshop on Early aspects at ICSE*, pages 35-42. ACM Press, New York, Mai 2006.
28. M. Polanyi. *The Tacit Dimension*. Peter Smith, Glouchester, 1983. (Reprint 1966)
29. J. Preece, Y. Rogers, and H. Sharp. *Interaction Design: Beyond Human-Computer Interaction*. Wiley, New York, 2002.
30. Raeithel. Activity Theory as a Foundation for Design. In C. Floyd, H. Züllighoven, R. Budde, and R. Keil-Slawik, editors, *Software Development and Reality Construction*, pages 391-415). Springer, Berlin, 2002.
31. R. Riemann. *Repertory Grid Technik: Handanweisung*. Hogrefe Verlag für Psychologie, Göttingen, 1991.
32. W. Scheer. Planung und Durchführung von Repertory Grid-Untersuchungen. In J. W. Scheer and A. Catina, editors, *Einführung in die Repertory Grid-Technik. Band 1: Grundlagen und Methoden*, pages 24-40. Huber, Bern, 1993.
33. Ch. Stary. Activity Theory and Task-Based User-Interface Development. Model-based and Task-complete Embodiment. *Journal of Human-Machine Interaction (R.I.H.M. - Revue d'Interaction Homme-Machine)*, 5(1):65-87, 2004.
34. Ch. Stary. TADEUS: Seamless Development of Task-Based and User-Oriented Interfaces". *IEEE Transactions on Systems, Man, and Cybernetics*, 30:509-525, 2000.
35. R. J. Sternberg and J. A. Horvath, editors. *Tacit Knowledge in Professional Practice: Researcher and Practitioner Perspectives*. Lawrence Erlbaum Associates, Mahwah, New Jersey, 1999.
36. V. Stewart, A. Stewart, A., and N. Fonda. *Business Applications of Repertory Grid*. McGraw-Hill, Maidenhead, Berkshire, England, 1981.
37. S. Stoiber and Ch. Stary. Model-Based Electronic Performance Support. In *Interactive Systems, Design, Specification and Verification: 10th International Workshop, DSV-IS 2003*, Madeira, June 2003, Springer Lecture Notes in Computer Science LNCS, Vol. 2844, pages 259-274.
38. F. Thomas and E. S. Harri-Augstein. *Self-organised learning:Foundations of a conversational science for psychology*. Routledge, London, 1985.
39. J. K. Triebe. Untersuchungen zum Lernprozess während des Erwerbs der Grundqualifikation (Montage eines kompletten Motors). In *Arbeits- und sozialpsychologische Untersuchungen von Arbeitsstrukturen im Bereich der Aggregatefertigung der Volkswagen AG*, vol. 3 (HA 80-019). Bundesministerium f. Forschung und Technologie, Bonn, 1980.
40. E. Ulich. *Arbeitspsychologie*. Schäffer-Poeschel, Stuttgart, 1994.
41. T. Wehner, A. Raeithel, C. Clases, and E. Endres. Von der Mühe und den Wegen der Zusammenarbeit: Theorie und Empirie eines arbeitspsychologischen Kooperationsmodells. In E. Endres and T. Wehner, editors, *Zwischenbetriebliche Kooperation: Die Gestaltung von Lieferbeziehungen*, pages 31-58. Beltz Psychologie Verlags Union, Weinheim, 1996.
42. U. Willutzki. Veränderungsmessung in der Einzeltherapie. In J. W. Scheer and A. Catina, editors, *Einführung in die Repertory Grid-Technik. Band 2: Klinische Forschung und Praxis*, pages 97-114. Huber, Bern, 1993.
43. R. P. Wright and S. S. K. Lam. Comparing Apples with Apples: The Importance of Element Wording in Grid Applications. *Journal of Constructivist Psychology*, 15:109-119, 2002

The COMETs Inspector: Towards Run Time Plasticity Control Based on a Semantic Network

Alexandre Demeure[1], Gaëlle Calvary[1], Joëlle Coutaz[1], and Jean Vanderdonckt[1,2]

[1] Université Joseph-Fourier
CLIPS-IMAG, BP 53
F-38041 Grenoble Cedex 9, France
{Alexandre.Demeure, Gaelle.Calvary, Joelle.Coutaz}@imag.fr
[2] Louvain School of Management,
Université catholique de Louvain
Place des Doyens, 1
B-1348 Louvain-la-Neuve, Belgium
jean.vanderdonckt@uclouvain.be

Abstract. In this paper, we describe the COMETs Inspector, a software tool providing user interface designers and developers with a semantic network in order to control the plasticity of their User Interfaces (UI) at run-time. Thanks to a set of predefined relationships, the semantic network links together various concepts ranging from the final UI (i.e., the UI described in terms of technological spaces) to the concrete and abstract UIs (i.e., the UI respectively described in terms of concrete interaction objects independently of any technological space, and abstract individual components and containers independently of any interaction modality) up to the tasks and concepts of the interactive system. In this way, plasticity can be addressed at four levels of abstraction (task and concepts, abstract, concrete, and final user interface) for forward, reverse, and lateral engineering. The end user exploits the semantic network at run time to adapt his/her UI to another context of use by identifying, selecting, and applying plasticity suitable operations.

Keywords: Abstract user interface, Active model, Ambient intelligence, COMET, Concrete user interface, Model-based approach, Plasticity, Semantic network, Task modeling, User interface eXtensible Markup Language.

1 Introduction

In an ever-changing world, end users of interactive systems are constantly demanding a higher level of adaptation of their User Interfaces (UI) to fit their purpose and better address their needs and wishes. The wide availability of different computing platforms makes this desire even stronger as the aspiration for executing the same interactive system on these different platforms is expressed, while minimizing the changes in the UI across these platforms. In these circumstances, the notion of plasticity plays a fundamental role as it denotes the "capacity of a UI to withstand

K. Coninx, K. Luyten, and K.A. Schneider (Eds.): TAMODIA 2006, LNCS 4385, pp. 324–338, 2007.

variations of context of use while preserving predefined usability properties" [2]. Supporting plasticity is more sophisticated than merely ensuring UI adaptation. Any kind of UI adaptation always induces some disruption from the end user's point of view as parts or whole of the UI may change during adaptation. Simple adaptation does not necessarily guarantee any level of quality. In contrast, plasticity aims at maintaining a certain level of usability by explicitly addressing the evolving context of use in which the user is carrying out his/her interactive task. By context of use [2], we hereby refer to the combination C of a user U working with a platform P in a given physical environment E: $C = <U,P,E>$. Although the adaptation in general and the plasticity in particular both consider the three aspects of this context definition, it is noteworthy to observe that the P aspect is the most frequently and extensively researched area (among them are [3], [4], [6], [8], [9], [11], [14-18], [20]): the platform is probably the facet which affects the UI the most immediately and concretely. This is challenging since a UI which was designed for a given platform in mind may no longer fit another one with extended or reduced interaction capabilities if they were not considered before.

The premises for supporting any form of plasticity are twofold: first, the availability of any valuable *information on the context of use* that may influence the UI adaptation, and secondly, the relationships between this contextual information and the reshuffled UI (remolded and/or redistributed) for that context. The Model-Based UI Development (MB-UIDE) community typically addresses the former aspect by context modeling [2], [4], [14], [17], [20] enriching task and system modeling [6], [15], whereas for the latter, the problem is often characterized as a *mapping problem* between the models [3], [10], [12], [19]. Thanks to the combination of context modeling and a technique for solving the mapping problem, it is possible to adapt the UI presentation, dialog and/or deployment after a context of use variation [13].

The literature identifies three significant instants when this combination occurs depending on the time when the models and their relationships are used: *at design time* to foresee future plastic UI, *at installation time* to take into account the current context of use (especially the platform that is foreseen at that time), and *at run time* to take into account contextual information which is known only at that time. Most recent works are devoted to design and installation time. The few works dedicated to run time are mostly addressing plasticity at the concrete UI level where only the UI look and feel is changed.

In this paper, we present a software tool which goes beyond this situation by supporting plasticity at run time at any level of abstraction (ranging from the final UI to the task and the domain) thanks to a semantic network that solves the mapping problem in a more elaborated way than existing techniques. To prove this, Section 2 summarizes the current trends in design- and installation-time plasticity, and identifies the most recent advances in run-time plasticity so as to locate this work as a next step in the progress. Section 3 provides a general definition of the semantic network that is used throughout this paper and illustrates it with an excerpt centered on the task type of choice. It exemplifies the case study along with a series of *plasticity questions* which can be addressed thanks to this network, and that cannot be addressed by existing systems. Section 4 presents the COMETs Inspector, a software that exploits this network at run time. Section 5 concludes the paper by highlighting the strengths and the shortcomings of the current version of the system and introduces new families of UIs with even a higher level of plasticity to be researched in the future.

2 Related Work

FormsVBT [1] pioneered the field of *plasticity at design time* by providing the UI designer with three views: a view on TeX-based UI specifications, a view on the UI presentation and dialog, and a view on the final UI. These three views are coordinated: any change brought in one view is automatically reflected in the others, thus providing the end user with a mean to directly validate or invalidate a UI crafted for a specific platform. The Graceful Degradation plug-in [8] for GrafiXML editor (www.usixml.org) provides UI designers with a series of transformations to be manually applied on a UI tailored for an initial platform. The resulting UI should be adapted to a computing platform exhibiting reduced interaction capabilities, especially a smaller resolution or reduced widgets set. The Context Toolkit [4] embeds multiple widgets compositions in one single widget with plasticity capabilities. This system is still design time: although the appropriate UI composition is selected at run time, the available compositions are pre-computed at design time. The system only switches from one composition to another depending on the changes of the context of use. This observation is similar for the Ubiquitous Interactor [16], the vocabulary of Generic Widgets found in [18], and the ADUS system [14].

For *plasticity at installation time*, in AUI [20], the UI is also shipped with different compositions which are selected when the interactive application is installed on a particular platform. In the same vein, TERESA [17] automatically generates multiple UIs for multiple platforms, but one UI is used at a time for each considered platform. TERESA also supports some plasticity by achieving transmodality, i.e. a change of modality after a platform change.

For *plasticity at run time*, Keränen and Plomp [11] present an algorithm for repurposing a UI layout depending on its container dimensions. An interesting feature consists in its animation of the adaptation process. ARNAULD [9] is relying on games theory for eliciting the most preferred UI at run time. It is based on SUPPLE, a system which automatically generates a UI layout based on weights of its contents. ARNAULD shows very interesting plasticity questions such as widget substitution, layout reshuffling and re-portraiting. In this paper, we will show that the COMETs Inspector supports more sophisticated forms of what we will define as *plasticity questions*.

Puerta & Eisenstein [19] defined a computational framework for managing relationships within and across the various models (e.g., the task, the domain, the abstract UI, the concrete UI, the system, the context) to solve the mapping problem. Teallach [10] is probably the first implementation of this framework, although it is not targeted at plasticity, but merely UI development. Since then, several attempts have been made to expand this form of plasticity, as in [3] for ambient intelligence and in [12] for multi-platform UIs. The predefined usability involved in the plasticity in [3] is the consistency, while it is the UI guidance in [12].

All the aforementioned efforts to support plasticity involve some form of information on the context of use (usually in a context model) and some ways to infer a UI from this context (typically as a system of inference rules, as a knowledge base, as a set of transformations). Next section introduces our semantic network, our new approach to condensate UI design knowledge captured at design-time, but to be exploited at run time.

3 A Semantic Network for Run Time Plasticity

This section provides a general definition of a semantic network (3.1). It is then applied to plasticity (3.4) based on concepts and relationships (3.3) defined in the CAMELEON reference framework (3.2). The section concludes with plasticity questions that are covered by the approach (3.5).

3.1 General Definition

Sowa [21] defines a semantic network as "a graphic notation for representing knowledge in patterns of interconnected nodes and arcs. Computer implementations of semantic networks were first developed for artificial intelligence and machine translation, but earlier versions have long been used in philosophy, psychology, and linguistics". Each semantic network may exhibit one or many of the following dimensions [21]:

- *Definitional networks* emphasize the subtype or "is-a" relation between a concept type and a newly defined subtype. The resulting network, also called a generalization or subsumption hierarchy, supports the rule of inheritance for copying properties defined for a supertype to all of its subtypes.
- *Assertional networks* are designed to assert propositions. Unlike definitional networks, the information in an assertional network is assumed to be contingently true, unless it is explicitly marked with a modal operator.
- *Implicational networks* use implication as the primary relation for connecting nodes.
- *Executable networks* include some mechanisms, such as marker passing or attached procedures, which can perform inferences, pass messages, or search for patterns.
- *Learning networks* build or extend their representations by acquiring knowledge from examples.

By defining the concepts and relationships appropriate for UI plasticity (3.3), we argue that our semantic network combines the five above dimensions. Concepts and relationships for plasticity are based on the CAMELEON reference framework.

3.2 CAMELEON Reference Framework

The CAMELEON Reference Framework (www.plasticity.org) structures the development life cycle of multi-target UIs according to four levels: (1) the *Final UI* (FUI) is the operational UI, i.e. any UI running on a particular platform either by interpretation (e.g. through a Web browser) or by execution (e.g., after the compilation of code in an interactive development environment); (2) the *Concrete UI* (CUI) expresses any FUI independently of any term related to a peculiar rendering engine, that is independently of any markup or programming language; (3) the *Abstract UI* (AUI) expresses any CUI independently of any interaction modality (e.g., graphical, vocal, tactile) via the mechanisms of Abstract Interaction Objects (AIO) [22] as opposed to Concrete Interaction Objects (CIO) for the CUI; and (4) the *Task & Concept* level, which describes the various interactive tasks to be carried out by the end user and the domain objects that are manipulated by these tasks. We refer to [11] and to www.usixml.org for its translation into models uniformly expressed in the same User Interface Description Language (UIDL), selected to be UsiXML (which stands for User Interface eXtensible Markup Language). In Figure 1, two contexts of use are represented with the possibility of moving from one context to another one through three relationships: *abstraction*, *reification* and *translation* for respectively reverse, forward and lateral engineering.

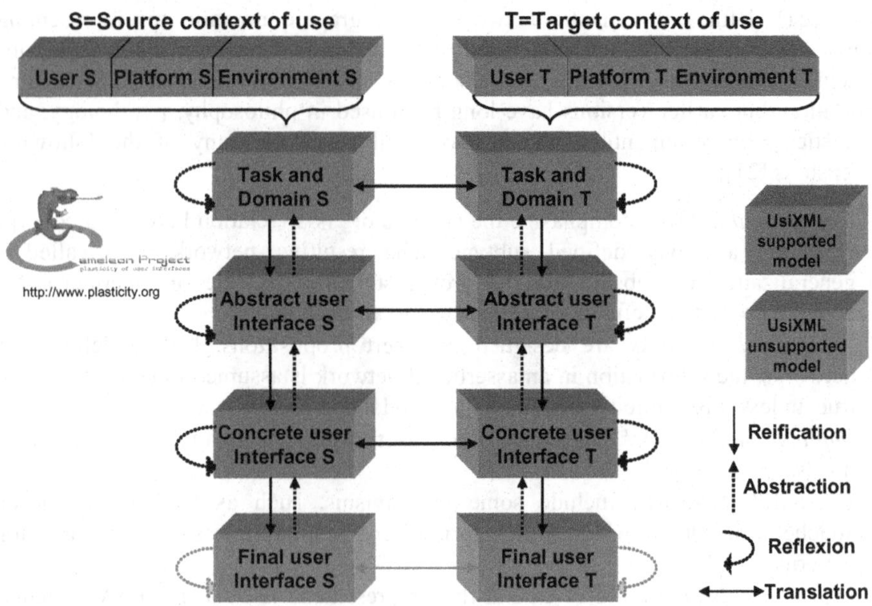

Fig. 1. The four levels of the CAMELEON framework

3.3 Concepts and Relationships for Plasticity

The concepts are those that are involved at each level of the CAMELEON reference framework (Fig. 1), which can be found in UsiXML (www.usixml.org): the "task & domain" level manipulates a task model (which consists of a recursive decomposition of a task into sub-tasks ordered with temporal relationships) and a domain model (which consists of a UML class diagram). In UsiXML, each task is associated with a task type: acquire, convey, select, navigate, compute, print, publish, etc. The task type is associated to an attribute, a group of attributes, or a class in the domain model. Therefore, the data type and the definition of the domain and co-domains are inferred from the domain model.

At the AUI level, any AUI consists of a decomposition of Abstract Containers into Abstract Individual Components (AIC). Each AIC exhibits one or many facets among input, output, control, etc. For instance, a task "select the value of an attribute" could be mapped onto an AIC "input an element from a collection".

At the CUI level, the AUI is reified into Concrete Containers and Concrete Interaction Objects satisfying the constraints imposed by the AUI. In our example ("input an element from a collection"), any CIO matching the AIC could work, such as a list box, a combo box, a radio box.

The concepts of the network are structured with multiple types of relationships such as inheritance, aggregation, composition, etc. The relationships themselves are arranged in an inheritance hierarchy, as presented in Fig. 2. Therefore, the semantic network is represented as a graph (i.e. a set of nodes and edges between the nodes), whose nodes represent fragments of models appearing at any level of abstraction and edges consist of transformation between nodes. The transformations represent a key aspect of exploiting UI design knowledge [19].

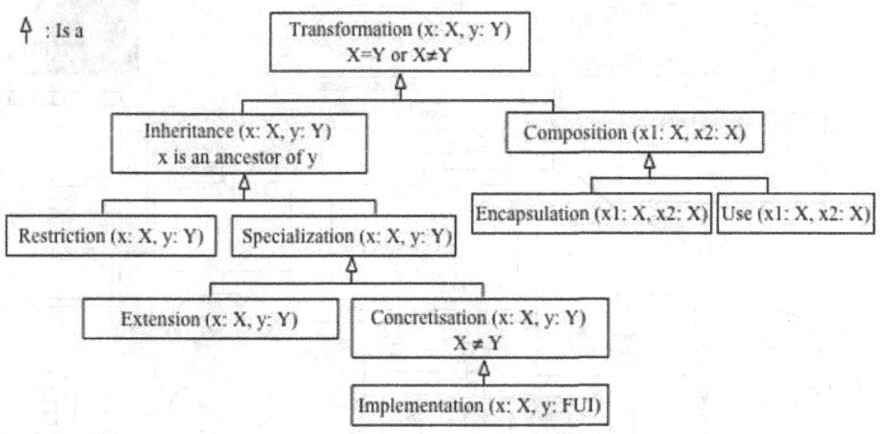

Fig. 2. Inheritance hierarchy between the relationships

The transformations are the following ones:

- *Inheritance.* *y* inherits from *x* if *y* refines *x*. The relation can be *total* versus *partial*, *exclusive* versus *non exclusive*. *Total* means that *x* cannot be instantiated as is: only *y* can exist. *Exclusive* means that there can be no *t* inheriting from both *y* and *z* if *y* and *z* refine *x* in an exclusive way.
- *Restriction.* Restriction refers to cuts that make of *y* a sub-case of *x*. As a result, *y* and *x* are no more substitutable. One example is the type restriction.
- *Specialization.* Specialization refers to inheritance that preserves properties. If *y* specializes *x* then *y* satisfies all the properties of *x*. As a result, *y* can be seen as an *x* making it substitutable to *x*.
- *Extension.* *y* extends *x* if *y* adds new descriptions to *x*, but *x* is still an *X*. This kind of inheritance is always partial.

- *Concretisation*. Concretisation refers to reification (Fig. 1). *y* concretises *x* if *y* adds concrete descriptions to *x* but *x* is not changed.
- *Implementation*. Whatever *x* is except an FUI, *y* is an FUI corresponding to *x*.
- *Composition*. *y* is part of *x* if *y* is included as is in *x*. *y* can be seen as a subsystem of *x*. Mappings between *x* and *y* are weaved.
- *Encapsulation*. Encapsulation means that *y* is embedded in *x*. *y* is consumed. It does no more exist as is.
- *Use*. Conversely to encapsulation, if *y* is used in *x*, then *y* still exists.
- *Abstraction* and *reification* are two other kinds of transformations. They are defined accordingly to Fig. 1.

Based on these concepts and relationships, next section presents a semantic network for plasticity.

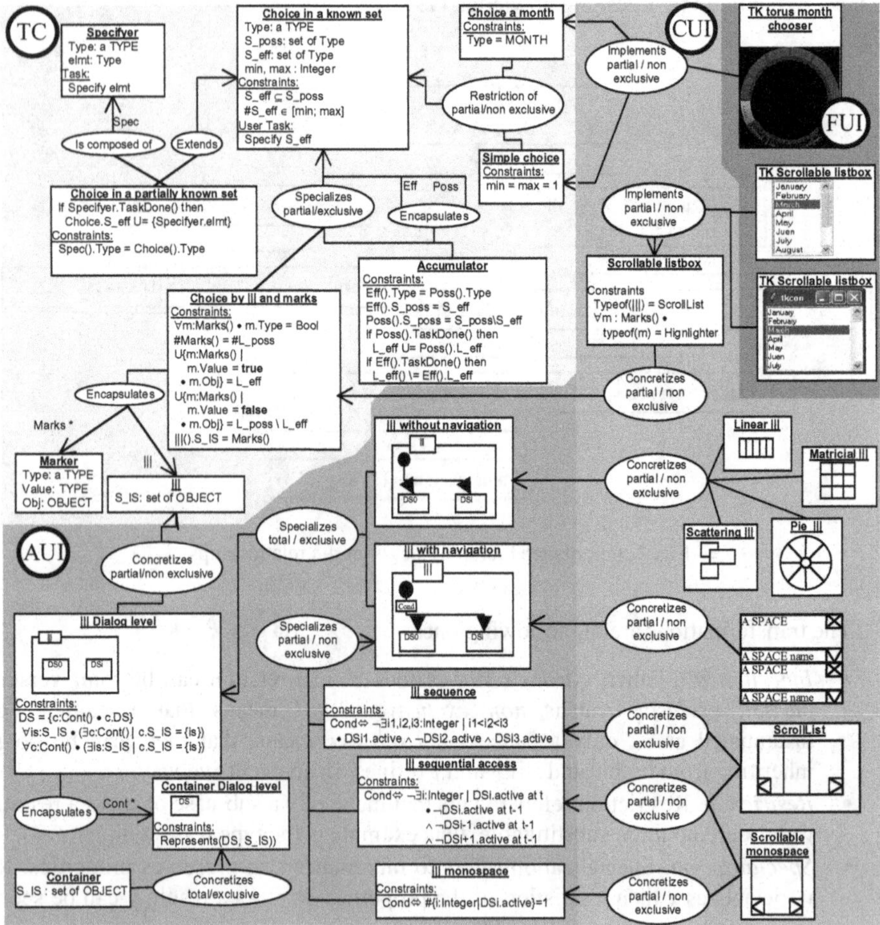

Fig. 3. Excerpt of the semantic network for the "Choice" case study

3.4 The Semantic Network for Plasticity

For legibility, this subsection focuses on an excerpt of the entire semantic network: the portion related to the "Choice" task type (Fig. 3). We have selected this portion because many interactive systems involve some form of choice among items, objects, menus, actions, etc. In addition, the available widget set for implementing a choice is wide: list box, drop-down list, combination box, drop-down combination box, radio button, check box, etc. In addition to these typical widgets, specialized widgets exist too: fast scrolling list box, accumulator, pie menu, season selector, calendar, etc. Usually, usability guidelines convey information to the designer on how to choose, format, and implement a choice widget in a UI. But this knowledge remains always subject to human interpretation and is never provided in an explicit, exploitable way. Our semantic network tackles this problem.

As illustrated in Fig. 3, the semantic network collects descriptions of a same entity (here the "Choice") in a same schema and makes explicit the relationships between them. The concepts and relationships are those that have been elicited in subsection 3.3. For legibility, the level of abstraction to which the descriptions belong is indicated by colors and labels: TC for Task & Concepts, AUI, CUI, FUI.

A description is provided for each node. For instance, at the TC level, the task "Choice in a known set" (of elements) makes explicit that:

- It manipulates elements of a given type TYPE.
- Elements can be chosen in a set of possible elements (S_poss).
- The selected elements are stored in a set of effective elements (S_eff).
- The number of selected elements can vary between a minimum (min) and a maximum (max).
- And of course (constraints part), S_eff is a subset of S_poss, and the number of effective elements is comprised between the min and max values.

The task "Choice a month" is a restriction of "Choice in a known set" as the type of the elements is constrained to be a month (see the constraint "Type=MONTH" in Fig. 3). A round FUI is provided as an example of implementation ("TK torus month chooser"). It is interesting to note that this FUI is an implementation of both "Choice a month" and "Simple choice" tasks. They are both restrictions of "Choice in a known set" (of elements). "Choice a month" is a restriction along the type of elements, whereas "Simple choice" restricts the number of selectable elements (see the constraint min=max=1).

"Choice in a known set" of elements can be specialized in many ways: for instance accumulators ("Accumulator"), and interleaving and markers ("Choice by ||| and marks"). For legibility, accumulators are not described in Fig. 3. They are typically concretized as two lists exchanging elements according to the user's selection. Fig. 3 elaborates further on the interleaving and markers specialization. A marker is a Boolean that indicates whether the corresponding element is selected (true) or not (false). Markers are managed by interleaving. Scrollable list boxes are typical concretizations (Fig. 3): the scrollbar corresponds to the interleaving, whereas the highlighting color corresponds to the marker (true). Two TK implementations are provided in Fig. 3. Check boxes are another option, whereas radio buttons would concretize both "Choice by ||| and marks" and "Simple choice".

At the AUI level, interleaving ("|||") is concretized as a dialog space ("||| dialog level") managing the elements that are interleaved. One dialog space is associated per element. They are nested in the interleaving dialog space. Two specializations are mentioned whether there is or not a navigation between the interleaved dialog spaces ("||| with navigation", "||| without navigation"). By navigation, we mean articulatory user's actions that do not directly contribute to the user's task but that are necessarily to access to the dialog spaces in which the user will perform his/her task. For instance, opening a menu is an articulatory task. One CUI with navigation is provided (Fig. 3): the user has to deploy the menu before achieving his/her task. This CUI contrasts with a linear, grid, scattering or pie interleaving that directly makes observable all the dialog spaces: no navigation is required (Fig. 3).

As pointed out in Fig. 3, interleaving with navigation ("||| with navigation") can be specialized in many ways. Three variants are mentioned:

- *Sequence* ("||| sequence"): the possible elements are browsed in a sequential way. The scroll list is a typical CUI example;
- *Sequential access* ("||| sequential access"): the possible elements are browsed in sequential way, parcel by parcel, whatever the size of the parcel is (i.e., the number of elements that are browsed step by step). Roughly speaking, it is not possible to switch from X to X+2 without first displaying X+1. The scroll list is another implementation;
- *Monospace* ("||| monospace"): only one dialog space is observable at a time. An example of FUI is provided in Fig. 3.

Besides this organized capitalization of knowledge, the semantic network promotes creation through composition. Composition is supported as a Cartesian product. It is for instance possible to combine any specialization of interleaving with any specialization of marker to create new interactors that had never been seen in the past. This is powerful for exploring new possibilities at design and/or run time: for instance, what about a monospace multiple choice with highlighters?

Now that the principles of the semantic network have been roughly introduced, let us examine how it can help in designing or plastifying UIs. Exploitation may be driven by strategies, such as:

- "Select the existing FUI that is the most compliant with the functional requirements". That means that producing FUIs manually or automatically is not an option. An existing FUI has to be selected. In that case, only three FUIs are available: the TK torus month chooser and the two TK scrollable list boxes. Again, for legibility, all the existing widgets supporting the "Choice" task have not been mentioned on Fig. 3.
- "Identify the element that map the best with all the functional and non functional requirements and if necessary generate an FUI from that point". Of course, the new FUI will be inserted in the network at the right place to enrich the knowledge for further designs and/or adaptations.
- "Prefer general purpose widgets" such as list box, combo box, pie menu that serve the simple choice with no restriction. As they are less exotic, they will probably be more familiar to the user.

Next section elaborates on the relevance of the semantic network for solving plasticity questions.

3.5 Covered Plasticity Questions

Since plasticity is a particular form of adaptation, it is equally submitted to the problems to be solved by adaptation. The main goal of performing some adaptation consists in defining an adaptation goal, identifying and executing adaptation rules in order to reach the adaptation goal. The literature abounds in providing adaptation rules, but seems more silent in defining properly adaptation goals by linking them to adaptation rules which could be executed for this purpose. Similarly, it is expected here to uncouple the adaptation goals from the adaptation rules. Therefore, we define a *plasticity question* Q as a couple $Q = (G, S)$ where G denotes a *plasticity goal* to reach when performing plasticity and S denotes a set of *plasticity solutions* which are potential actions to be executed to reach the plasticity goal. Let us assume that a plasticity goal G would be "migrate a graphical UI from a desktop to a PDA". The reduced screen real estate of the PDA stems for trying to reduce the surface of the UI widgets, a possible solution among others. For instance, "a list box could be turned into a drop-down list", "a radio box of radio items could be transformed into a drop-down list" are two possible plasticity solutions. The main shortcoming observed in the state of the art is that the set S is usually defined in extension by hard-coding opportunistic plasticity solutions in the adaptation engine, thus leaving little or no room for flexibility and modifiability. In this paper, the definition of S is given in comprehension so that the definition of plasticity questions remains unchanged: any extension of the semantic network will be automatically incorporated in the related plasticity questions.

A plasticity question is said to be *simple*, respectively *composite*, if and only if its goal G involves concepts and relationships of at most, respectively at least, one level of the CAMELEON reference framework (Fig. 1).

Since a FUI plasticity question only refers to elements of technological spaces, a restriction of the questions to be addressed is imposed. For instance, the plasticity goal "transcode a form from HTML to Java" is decomposed into similar sub-goals for all constituents of the form, such as "transcode a SELECT element from HTML into its counterpart in Java". If XUL is the target language, the goal becomes "transcode a SELECT element from HTML into its counterpart in XUL". To solve this question, the mappings between counterpart elements in various technological spaces are required. In terms of the semantic network, the plasticity solution consists of an abstraction of the SELECT element followed by a reification in the target platform, which is expressed as:

$$S = \{\ rei_{c\text{-}f}\,(abs_{f\text{-}c}\,(\text{SELECT, HTML}),\ \text{Java})\ \}$$

where $rei_{c\text{-}f}$ denotes the reification from CUI to FUI, $abs_{f\text{-}c}$ denotes the abstraction from FUI to CUI. If the previous plasticity goal is extended up to the CUI level, it would give "abstract a SELECT element from HTML into a CUI", a platform agnostic goal which is expressed as:

$$S = \{\ abs_{f\text{-}c}\,(\text{SELECT, HTML})\ \}$$

If the previous plasticity goal is extended up to the AUI level, it would give "abstract a SELECT element from HTML into a AUI", a modality agnostic goal which is expressed as:

$$S = \{ abs_{c\text{-}a} (abs_{f\text{-}c} (\text{SELECT, HTML})) \}$$

where $abs_{c\text{-}a}$ denotes the abstraction from CUI to AUI. If the previous plasticity goal is extended up to the TC level, it gives "abstract a SELECT element from HTML into a task and domain", a computing independent goal which is expressed as:

$$S = \{ abs_{a\text{-}tc} (abs_{c\text{-}a} (abs_{f\text{-}c} (\text{SELECT, HTML}))) \}$$

where $abs_{a\text{-}tc}$ denotes the abstraction from AUI to TC.

The original plasticity question in natural language could be generalized as "Give me all the widgets that are equivalent to this HTML widget" ($S = \{rei_{c\text{-}f} (abs_{f\text{-}c}$ (SELECT, HTML), $X)\}$) where X denotes any technological space. If this widget is itself composed of other sub-widgets, the plasticity solution is recursively addressed. For instance, if a group box is composed of a group and a series of radio items, the plasticity solution is queried on the semantic network on the sub-nodes.

Other typical plasticity questions involve: "Give me all the possible reifications of this CIO for any technological space", or "for the X technological space", "Give me the abstraction of this CIO", "Give me the possible reifications of this AIO satisfying this property", "Give me the behaviorally-equivalent widgets in the same technological space corresponding to a given widget", "Give me a modality-equivalent CIO of this CIO", "Give me any equivalent CIO of this CIO independently of any modality", "Give me a browsable version of this observable interaction component", "Give me all the possibilities for implementing a simple choice".

Next section introduces a small case study that takes benefit from the semantic network at run time to solve few of these questions under the control of the end user.

4 A Case Study: The COMETs Inspector

The Home Heating Control System (HHCS) allows the user to manage the temperature at home depending on the month. In an interleaving way, the user selects the month and controls the temperature of the different rooms. They are here limited to the living room and the wine cellar (Fig. 4). HHCS has been implemented in COMETs (COntext Mouldable widgETs). COMETs are interactors specially fashioned for plasticity [2]. A COMET is "a self descriptive interactor that publishes the quality in use it guarantees for a set of contexts of use. It is able to either self-adapt to the current context of use, or be adapted by a tier-component. It can be dynamically discarded, respectively *recruited*, when it is unable, respectively *able*, to cover the current context of use" [2].

HHCS is made of four major COMETS:

- One for each user's task ("choose a month", "control living-room" and "control wine cellar"). Each COMET recursively embeds (encapsulates) other COMETs for both guiding the task (e.g., the label "Select a month") and sustaining interaction (e.g., the list boxes and sliders on Fig. 4a).

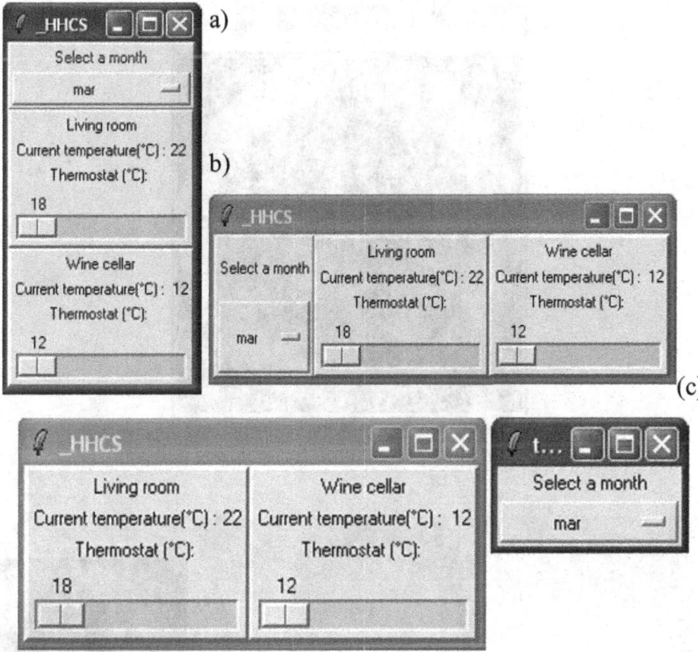

Fig. 4. A set of FUIs obtained by tuning the interleaving comet. Detachable windows are easily implemented thanks to COMETs.

- One for the interleaving. This comet is in charge of managing the three previous ones (they are nested in this COMET). Depending on the layout (Fig. 4 a and b) and whether the embedded containers are displayed as frames (Fig. 4 a and b) or windows (Fig. 4c), the rendering is updated, possibly implementing detachable/(re-)attachable windows (Fig. 4c).

In our approach, adaptation is placed under the control of the end user (yet the designer only, because of a too poor quality of the tool's UI). A COMETS inspector [5] supports the inspection of the UI and its modification thanks to the support of the semantic network. The TK torus month chooser has been selected in Fig. 5.

Only basic operations (i.e., Add, Remove and Substitute) are supported yet, for instance enabling the end-user to substitute one FUI with another one. Fig. 6 shows the inspector (the left window). It displays the hierarchy of comets (left part). A zoom in the selected one is provided (central part). The performable operations are listed in the right part according to the freedoms leveraged by the semantic network. On Fig. 6, the user is being to switch from a window-based to a frame-based presentation for the "control living room" COMET. This will have the effect of re-attaching the living-room window to the main HHCS window. Actually, the semantic network is outside the COMETs. We envision embedding local semantic networks in the COMETs to support a mix of open and close adaptations.

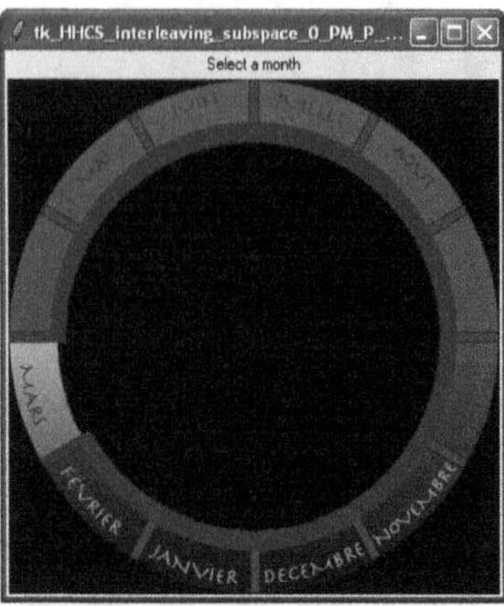

Fig. 5. The torus presentation for selecting a month

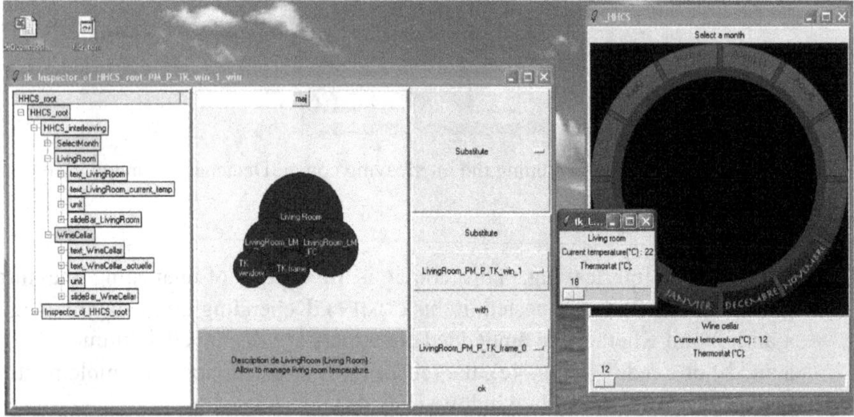

Fig. 6. Based on the semantic network, the comets inspector (left window) provides the user (yet, the designer; in the future, the end-user) with a set of operations (right part of the left window) that can be applied to the interactive system (the two right windows) for its design and/or adaptation. Here, the substitute operation will replace the living room window (the small middle window) with a frame that will be attached to the main window (right window).

5 Conclusion

First of all, it is important to emphasize that the semantic network defined in this paper is independent from its exploitation through the COMETs Inspector: whether you are using a COMET-compliant system [2] or not, it does not matter and it does not change the structure of concepts. The network structures the concepts throughout the four levels of the CAMELEON Reference Framework, thus enabling us to address plasticity questions at run time with an unprecedented level of flexibility and exploitation. Plasticity can now be based on the task and the concepts models. Since the network is exploited at run time to address the plasticity questions requested by the end user, genuine run time plasticity could be achieved. The COMETs Inspector is just one implementation of a software which accesses this network and performs the desired operations. In the provided example, the task type was predefined (here, a choice). We could even imagine that this task type is provided at run time by the end user by asking "what task do you want to carry out on this object?". The user could then be presented by a series of options like "Insert an object, delete an object, list existing objects, select an object among several (our example)". This is compliant with the CRUD pattern (Create-Read-Update-Delete) design pattern usually found in the UML method and notation. Therefore, the design knowledge that is contained in the semantic network remains stable over time since the plasticity questions do not change. If, for instance, another widget should be added, it could be added only where it is required and the rest is re-composed straightforwardly. Changing the network is a matter of adapting the internal representation (a graph) of the network and exploiting it therefore becomes a problem of graph exploration according to predefined semantic relationships. Of course, the quality of the results heavily depends on the network quality.

Acknowledgments. We gratefully acknowledge the support of the SIMILAR network of excellence (http://www.similar.cc), the European research task force creating human-machine interfaces similar to human-human communication of the European Sixth Framework Programme (FP6-2002-IST1-507609). Jean Vanderdonckt would like to thank Université Joseph Fourier for supporting his position as invited professor for two months since May 2006.

References

1. Avrahami, G., Brooks, K.P., Brown, M.H. A Two-view Approach to Constructing User Interfaces. In *Proc. of SIGGRAPH'89* (Boston, July 31-August 4, 1989), Computer Graphics, *23, 3* (July 1989), 137-146
2. Calvary, G., Coutaz, J., Dâassi, O., Balme, L., Demeure, A. Towards a new Generation of Widgets for Supporting Software Plasticity: the "Comet". In *Proc. of 9th IFIP Working Conf. on Engineering for Human-Computer Interaction EHCI-DSVIS'2004* (Hamburg, July 11-13, 2004). Lecture Notes in Computer Science, Vol. 3425. Springer-Verlag, Berlin, (2005), 306-324
3. Clerckx, T., Luyten, K., Coninx, K. The Mapping Problem Back and Forth: Customizing Dynamic Models while Preserving Consistency. In *Proc. of the 3rd Int. Workshop on Task Models and Diagrams for User Interface Design TAMODIA'2004* (Prague, November 15-16, 2004). ACM Press, New York, (2004), 33-42
4. Crease, M., Gray, P.D., Brewster, S.A. A Toolkit of Mechanism and Context Independent Widgets. In *Proc. Of Int. Workshop on Design, Specification, and Verification of Interactive Systems DSVIS'2000* (Limerick, June 5-6, 2000). Lecture Notes in Computer Science, Vol. 1946. Springer-Verlag, Berlin, (2000), 121-133
5. Demeure, A., Calvary, G., Coutaz, J., Vanderdonckt, J. The Comets Inspector, Manipulating Multiple Interface Representations Simultaneously, In *Proc. of 6th Int. Conf. on Computer-Aided Design of User Interfaces CADUI'06* (Bucarest, June 3-5, 2006). Springer-Verlag, Berlin, (2006), 167-174
6. Dittmar, A., Forbrig, P. Methodological and Tool Support for a Task-Oriented Development of Interactive Systems. In *Proc. of 3rd Int. Conf. on Computer-Aided Design of User Interfaces CADUI'99* (Louvain-la-Neuve, Oct. 21-23, 1999). Kluwer Academics Pub., Dordrecht, (1999), 271-274

7. Fensel, D., Benjamins, V., Motta, E., Wielinga, B. UPML: A Framework for Knowledge System Reuse. In *Proc. of the 16th Int. Joint Conf. on Artificial Intelligence IJCAI'99* (Stockholm, July 31-August 6, 1999). Morgan Kaufmann, San Francisco, (1999), 16-23
8. Florins, M., Montero, F., Vanderdonckt, J., Michotte, B. User Interface Graceful Degradation for Small Platforms. In *Proc. of 8th Int. Working Conference on Advanced Visual Interfaces AVI'2006* (Venezia, May 23-26, 2006). ACM Press, New York, (2006)
9. Gajos, K., Weld, D.S. Preference Elicitation for Interface Optimization. In *Proc. of the 18th Annual ACM Symp. on User Interface Software and Technology UIST'2005* (Seattle, Oct. 23-26, 2005). ACM Press, New York, (2005), 173-182
10. Griffiths, T., Barclay, P.J., Paton, N.W., McKirdy, J., Kennedy, J.B., Gray, P.D., Cooper, R., Goble, C.A., da Silva, P. Teallach: a Model-Based User Interface Development Environment for Object Databases. *Interacting with Computers 14, 1* (2001), 31-68
11. Keränen, H., Plomp, J. Adaptive Runtime Layout of Hierarchical UI Components. In *Proc. of the 2nd Nordic Conf. on Human-Computer Interaction NordiCHI'02* (Aarhus, October 19-23, 2002). ACM Press New York, (2002), 251-254
12. Limbourg, Q., Vanderdonckt, J. Addressing the Mapping Problem in User Interface Design with UsiXML. In *Proc. of the 3rd Int. Workshop on Task Models and Diagrams for User Interface Design TAMODIA'2004* (Prague, November 15-16, 2004). ACM Press, New York, (2004), 155-163
13. McKinley, P.K., Sadjadi, S.M., Kasten, K.P., Cheng, B.H.C. Composing Adaptive Software. *IEEE Computer 37*, 7 (July 2004), 56-64
14. Mitrovi , N., Royo, J.A., Mena, E. ADUS: Indirect Generation of User Interfaces on Wireless Devices. In *Proc. of 7th Int. Workshop Mobility in Databases and Distributed Systems MDDS'2004* (Zaragoza, August 30-September 3, 2004). IEEE Computer Society, Los Alamitos, (2004), 662-666
15. Navarre, D., Palanque, P., Paternò, F., Santoro, C., Bastide, R. A Tool Suite for Integrating Task and System Models through Scenarios. In *Proc. of 8th Int. Workshop on Design, Specification, and Verification of Interactive Systems DSV-IS'2001* (Glasgow, June 13-15, 2001). Lecture Notes in Comp. Science, Vol 2220. Springer-Verlag, Berlin, 88-113
16. Nylander, S., Bylund, M., Waern, A. The Ubiquitous Interactor – Device Independent Access to Mobile Services. In *Proc. of 5th Int. Conf. of Computer-Aided Design of User Interfaces CADUI'2004* (Funchal, January 13-16, 2004). Kluwer Academics, Dordrecht, (2005), 271-282
17. Paternò, F., Santoro, C. One Model, Many Interfaces. In *Proc. of 4th Int. Conf. on Computer-Aided Design of User Interfaces CADUI'2002* (Valenciennes, May 15-17, 2002). Kluwer Academics Pub., Dordrecht, (2002), 143-154
18. Plomp, C.J., Mayora-Ibarra, O. A Generic Widget Vocabulary for the Generation of Graphical and Speech-Driven UIs. *Int. J. of Speech Technology 5* (2002), 39-47
19. Puerta, A.R., Eisenstein, J. Towards a General Computational Framework for Model-based Interface Development Systems. *Knowledge-Based Systems 12,* 8 (1999), 433-442
20. Schneider, K.A., Cordy, J.R. Abstract User Interfaces: A Model and Notation to Support Plasticity in Interactive Systems. In *Proc. of 8th Int. Workshop on Design, Specification, and Verification of Interactive Systems DSV-IS'2001* (Glasgow, June 13-15, 2001). Lecture Notes in Comp. Science, Vol. 2220. Springer-Verlag, Berlin, (2001), 28-48
21. Sowa, J.F. *Knowledge Representation: Logical, Philosophical, and Computational Foundations*. Brooks/Cole Publishing Co., Pacific Grove, (2000)
22. Vanderdonckt, J., Bodart, F. Encapsulating Knowledge for Intelligent Automatic Interaction Objects Selection. In *Proc. of ACM Conf. on Human Aspects in Computing Systems INTERCHI'93* (Amsterdam, April 24-29, 1993). ACM Press, New York, (1993), 424-429

A Prototype-Driven Development Process for Context-Aware User Interfaces

Tim Clerckx, Chris Vandervelpen, Kris Luyten, and Karin Coninx

Hasselt University, Expertise Centre for Digital Media (EDM)
and transnationale Universiteit Limburg
Wetenschapspark 2, B-3590 Diepenbeek, Belgium
{tim.clerckx,chris.vandervelpen,kris.luyten,
karin.coninx}@uhasselt.be

Abstract. This paper describes a model-based development process for context-aware user interfaces. The development process consists of the specification and updates of several models followed by the generation and evaluation of a prototype. A generic runtime architecture will be presented supporting distinct prototyping renderers at different abstraction levels in order to support prototyped development during the whole design cycle of the context-aware user interface. To clarify the functioning of the architecture, a case study will be presented, demonstrating the possibilities of this prototype-driven development approach.

1 Introduction

The shift to the increasing use of context-aware systems brings along the question whether traditional methodologies still result in systems that are sufficiently usable. Context-aware systems are more unpredictable than static systems because external context information can change both the system's and the user interface's state. This is why context-aware systems require a better insight in what may happen with the user interface in the near future in order to keep the system usable when a significant change of context occurs. We believe these problems can be reduced by taking two measurements: (1) restricting the possible influence of context on the user interface and (2) testing and evaluating context-changes causing changes in the user interface at early design stages until the actual deployment of the system.

In previous work, we have been concentrating on how we could restrict the influence of context on the user interface. We developed a task-centered design approach to model the interaction of a context-aware system [7,6]. Furthermore, we developed a runtime architecture, supporting the early prototyping of the specified user interface models [8]. In this work we will show how we generalized this runtime architecture to a generic one, in order to build prototypes of context-aware user interfaces during the whole development cycle of a context-aware system with little application specific code to be written in the user interface part of the system. We will show that this was made possible by using a modular architecture where loosely coupled models communicate

K. Coninx, K. Luyten, and K.A. Schneider (Eds.): TAMODIA 2006, LNCS 4385, pp. 339–354, 2007.

asynchronously in order to test several aspects of the user interface solitarily or all at the same time.

The paper is structured as followed. First we will elaborate on which types of context are relevant for the user interface and how relevant context can be modelled. In section 3 we will discuss our prototype-driven development process. Afterwards, a case study will be discussed in section 4. Finally we will compare our approach to related work and we will give a conclusion and further research directions.

2 Context-Aware User Interfaces

In the development of context-aware user interfaces it is important to define under which circumstances context can have an influence on the user interface. In this section we first define and describe several levels where context is relevant to request adaptation of the user interface. Afterwards, we will discuss some modelling techniques we have developed to support context influencing distinct levels of the user interface.

2.1 Relevance of Context in User Interface Design

We make a distinction between five levels of the user interface where context can have an influence [5]:

Task Level User's can perform different tasks in different contexts of use [11,23,7]. Detecting a context change relevant to a different task can initiate a major change to the user interface. For example, when a user who is using a car navigation system runs out of gas, his task will switch from reaching the destination to finding a gas station.

Data Level Context can have an impact on the data to be presented to the user. For example, in a tourist guide a map of the visited area can be shown to the user, where the user's current location is indicated with a triangle. The user's location is a constantly changing context and requires updates of the data (the user's coordinates on the displayed map) shown in the user interface.

Dialog Level Context can invoke a transition to a different state of the user interface (implying another dialog with the system). For example, when an employee enters his company while wearing his badge, access to the intranet might be enabled without any additional authentication dialog. Another example can be that specific information about a statue in a museum is shown when a visitor approaches it within a certain range.

Service Level Services accessible to the user and the user's system (e.g. embedded systems providing a communication interface with the system embedding the CPU) may require user interaction (e.g. remote controlling a system with the mobile device). When this is the case, a user interface needs to be presented to the user without disturbing her current task.

Presentation Level Context can influence the way the user interface is presented to the user. When a user is using a desktop computer, keyboard and mouse input is possible, but when a mobile user wants to enter text on a small portable device, speech interaction may be more useful. Another type of context influence at the presentation level is distribution of user interfaces.

2.2 Modelling Context for Context-Aware User Interfaces

The acquisition of context information is not a case of user interface developers. While designing a context-aware user interface, developers would like to make an abstraction of context information in order to concentrate on the development and usability of the user interface. This is why considering context information from the perspective of a context-aware user interface developer is a bit different from the perspective of a context-aware application designer. For these reasons we have introduced a distinction between different types of reusable components providing context information to applications. On the one hand Concrete Context Objects (CCOs) gather fine-grained context information acquired by sensors,... These CCOs are interpreted by a Context Management System (CMS) where historical data is stored and used to make assumptions about context in order to obtain more abstract context information. Abstract Context Objects (ACOs), on the other hand, encapsulate fine-grained context information from UI Designers in order to stimulate reuse of ACOs and hide information about how decisions about context are made.

Figure 4 shows how this works at runtime. The CMS provides other components of the application logic of the system with this context information or new information that can be deduced from lower level context data. The user interface however, is provided with the abstract information of ACOs. ACOs will deliver a discrete context state to the Context Control Unit (CCU) in order to notify the dialog controller when a significant (according to the specified models) change of context has occurred.

This approach has several advantages. User interface designers do not have to worry about how context information is gathered. Furthermore the working of ACOs can be simulated in order to test the influence of context on the user interface without the need of a module taking care of context acquisition. This is important because context-aware user interfaces can be tested *during* the development process without actual context acquisition in place. ACO simulators can then be dynamically constructed from ontological information and context simulators can be replaced by real context data from a Context Management System without applying any changes.

The description of an ACO (figure 1) consists of an `id` referring to the ontology we use [22]. In this way, the link to a CMS using this ontology is implicitly made when the ACOs are linked to the the CMS instead of a simulator. Next a `description` is given to explain the purpose of this ACO. Furthermore, the different states are provided in the XML in order to provide the designer with the information about which state an ACO can be in so that messages from the CMS can be interpreted by the ACO.

As a result, the XML description of the ACO can be used by the design tool, to provide the user interface developer with a set of possible ACOs and which states the ACOs can be in. Furthermore, the description can be used at runtime to dynamically generate a context simulator (e.g. figure 2) and to link the ACOs with the CMS as explained above.

In the following sections, we will discuss how this approach of modelling context is useful in our development process.

```
<ACOs>
 <aco>
  <id>Environment.Location.Relative.MuseumBE0002</id>
  <description>Location of the
              User in Museum BE0002</description>
  <states>
   <state>Start</state>
   <state>Artifact1</state>
   <state>Artifact2</state>
   <state>Artifact3</state>
  </states>
 </aco>
</ACOs>
```

Fig. 1. XML describing an ACO

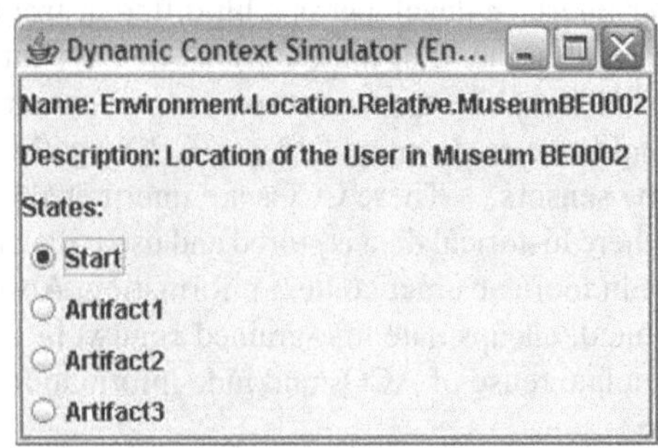

Fig. 2. Dynamically generated context simulator

3 The DynaMo-AID Development Approach

3.1 Overview of the DynaMo-AID Approach

In this section, we describe the DynaMo-AID development process supporting the development cycle of context-aware user interfaces in providing methodologies and tool support in the design, prototyping and deployment phase of the production of context-aware user interfaces.

The development process is prototype-driven consisting of several iterations over a prototype until a final iteration results in a deployable user interface. The process is presented in figure 3, inspired by the spiral model introduced by Boehm [4].

The process consists of four iterations which on their turn consist of four phases. Each iteration starts with the specification of an artefact, i.e. specification of models or code implementation (Artefact Construction). Subsequently a prototype is derived from this artefact and test runs are performed with this prototype (Prototyping). Afterwards this prototype is evaluated (Evaluation) in order to apply some changes to the basic artefact of the current iteration (Artefact Reconsideration). The updated artefacts are brought along to the next iteration.

The first iteration starts with the specification of models defining a user interface. Firstly, abstract models are specified describing the interaction at a high level, such as user tasks (task model). Afterwards, tools assist the user interface developer in transforming these abstract models into more concrete models (dialog and abstract presentation model) in order to make the models suitable for automated prototype generation. Next a static prototype is generated by the supporting design tool to perceive how the

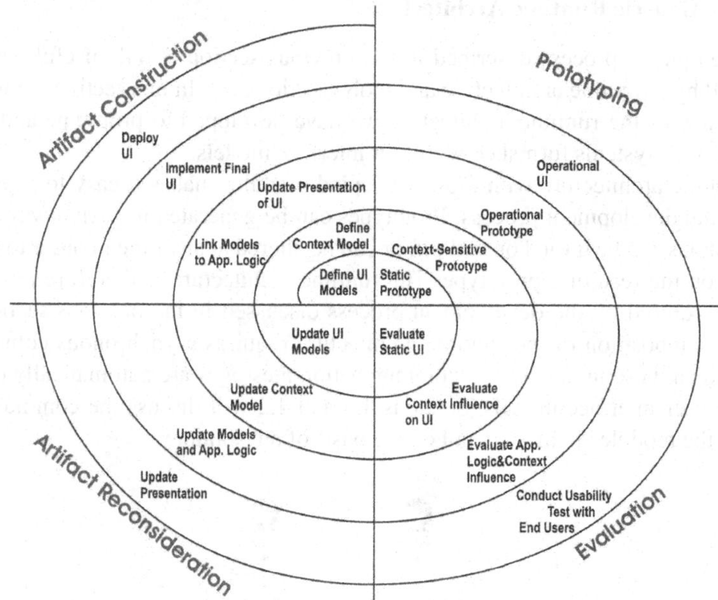

Fig. 3. Overview of the DynaMo-AID development process

modelled user interface actually works. Finally, the prototype is evaluated and possible changes to the modelled UI can be carried out.

The next iteration is meant to introduce context-awareness in the user interface. Because context is only relevant when it has a direct influence on the user's task [11], we chose to attach the context model, existing of ACOs (section 2.2), to a task model [6]. Next a new prototype is automatically generated by the design tool. This prototype is linked to the dynamically constructed context simulators that are discussed in section 2.2. Afterwards the prototype is evaluated by the user interface developer and possible changes to the context and user interface models are allowed until the developer is satisfied with the resulting prototype.

In the third iteration the user interface models are linked to the functional core of the system. Furthermore the presentation of the user interface is altered in order to present the data provided by the functional core of the system. Next a prototype can be rendered. This prototype is now operational and can be used to test the user interface on top of a working functional core and influenced by external context information. The prototype is evaluated, and changes can be applied.

The final iteration includes the actual implementation of the final presentation layer of the user interface. This layer can be very thin due to the architecture's modular characteristic as discussed in the following section so that more attention can be paid to the design of the presentation of the user interface. The resulting operational user interface can then be tested by means of a usability test with end users in order to update the presentation layer. Afterwards the user interface is ready for deployment.

3.2 The Generic Runtime Architecture

The development process described in the previous section is only useful when it is supported by a runtime architecture and tools (section 3.3). In this section we will give an overview of the runtime architecture we have developed to prototype and deploy context-aware systems furnished with user interface models.

A runtime architecture with loosely coupled modules makes it easy to support the incremental development process. Prototypes can be generated in such a way the distinct modules can be turned on and off, or can be altered at any time in order to observe changes on the resulting prototype. The runtime architecture is therefore more flexible than required by the development process discussed in the previous section. The modular composition of the runtime architecture requires asynchronous communication between these modules. The communication messages are automatically deduced from the user interface models. Sections 4.3 and 4.2 will discuss the communication between the modules in more detail on the basis of an example.

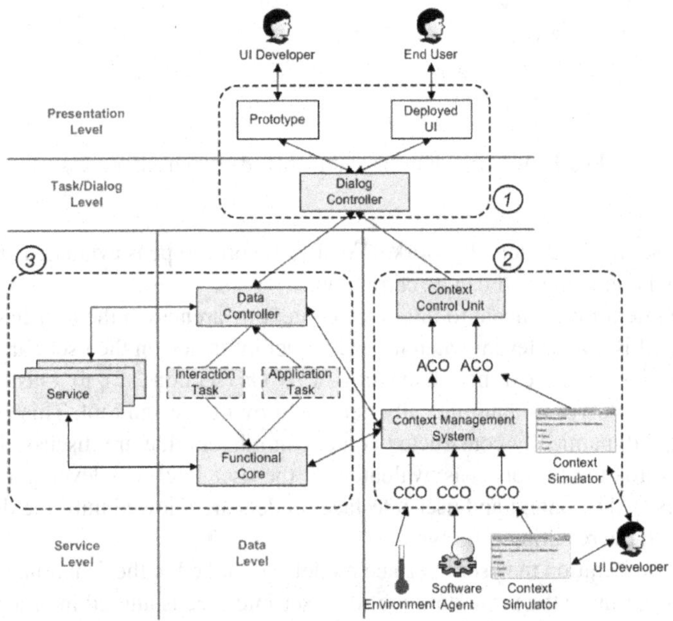

Fig. 4. Overview of the Runtime Architecture

The architecture (figure 4) consists of three main modules (user interface (1), context (2), and functional core (3)) each composed of several other modules. The first module (1) takes care of controlling and presenting the user interface of the system. The dialog controller keeps track of the current state of the user interface and takes care of communication with the other main modules. Apart from that, the module consists of renderers either for the presentation of a prototype or the deployed user interface. When the dialog controller receives a message from the functional core module or the context module notifying an update of the presentation is required, the state of the user interface will change and the current renderer will receive another presentation model to render. Notice that the division between dialog controller and presentation layer implies that a thin presentation layer can be rendered on a device separate from the rest of the system. This is convenient to test a prototype rendered on a certain device used by a test person, while the user interface designer can monitor what happens and what is going to happen on another device.

The context module (2) takes care of the context influence on both the user interface and the application. At the lowest level Concrete Context Objects (CCOs) will harvest low-level context information and provide it to the Context Management System (CMS). The CMS in the environment can be ad hoc implemented for the application or existing CMSs like [12,13,21,14] can be used. The Abstract Context Objects (ACOs) necessary for the current application will send context messages to the Context Control Unit (CCU). Information from the ACOs are aggregated and a message to the dialog controller will be sent if necessary. The dialog controller then can anticipate on the abstract context message. The functional core on the other hand acquires context information directly from the CMS because it is possible the functional core needs more fine-grained context information than the ACOs provide to the user interface.

The third main module of the architecture is the functional core module (3). The communication between the functional core and the user interface is maintained by the Data Controller. The data controller consists of three parts: (1) a data model which is a repository containing the data to be presented by the user interface, (2) interaction task functions which are functions invoked by the user interface in order to send a message to the functional core, and (3) application task functions which are functions invoked by the functional core in order to send a message to the user interface. In section 4.2 we will show an example of a data model and functions controlling the communication between the functional core and the user interface. The data model can be modified by the functional core (with the help of application task functions) and the user interface itself (with the help of the dialog controller). The example will show that the construction and interpretation of the data model is the only part of the architecture where application specific code has to be written to obtain a working user interface.

Figure 4 also pictures how the different modules take care of context information at the distinct levels defined in section 2.1. The user interface module takes care of the presentation, dialog and task level. The functional core module takes care of the service and data level.

3.3 Tool Support

In this subsection, we elaborate on a tool we have implemented to support the design of the user interface models and on the implementation of the generic runtime architecture.

First of all, in the modelling phase the designer has to specify the models (user interface and context models) in a clear environment where models can be constructed, tested, and edited through direct manipulation and multiple views on the models. We discussed a design tool supporting these features to specify the models in previous work [9].

As discussed earlier in this paper, the models specified in the design process are passed on to the runtime architecture when another prototype or the deployed user interface has to be produced. Except for the presentation layer, all components are written in Java (J2SE). We chose to use Java because of its support for communication and language reflection capabilities. Each square in figure 4 works as a separate process. This makes possible to have asynchronous communication between the components. Figure 5 shows a screenshot of the control panel where the designer can load models, launch and abolish controllers to observe changes on the prototype, launch context simulators,...

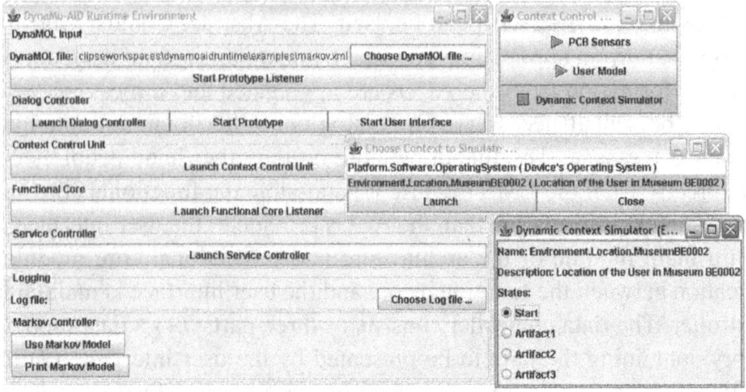

Fig. 5. Control Panel of the Runtime Architecture with a Dynamic Context Simulator

The presentation level is implemented using distinct renderers in distinct programming languages for distinct purposes. First the Dygimes user interface renderer [10] is used for early prototyping. Because Dygimes supports specifications at an abstract level (abstract widgets are used instead of concrete platform-dependent widgets) which makes it easy to map abstract presentation components deduced from the user interface models on a Dygimes user interface specification. The Dygimes renderer supports prototypes for Java (J2SE and J2ME) and HTML. The second renderer is the UIML renderer written on the .net and compact .net-framework [17] supporting more complex user interfaces than Dygimes but UIML-specifications are less abstract than a Dygimes user interface specification. The UIML renderer is used for prototypes linked to the application logic. In this way, the operational prototype can be tested with a more concrete user interface, but still needs no hard-coded user interface implementation (UIML is an XML-based language [1,2]). The final user interface can be implemented in any language/toolkit. The use of asynchronous communication between the dialog controller and the presentation layer makes it possible to use this kind of variety of user interface "back ends" in order to support the incremental design and evaluation of user interface prototypes in the development of context-aware systems.

4 Case Study: Context-Aware Museum Visit

In order to clarify the generic characteristic of the architecture and how the asynchronous communication between the distinct modules is generically constructed from the models, we present a case study in this section. The notation we use to model the tasks is an extension of the ConcurTaskTree notation [20].

Suppose we want to develop an application where museum visitors are supported by a mobile guide displayed on a mobile device. Figure 6 shows the most abstract tasks of the system. When a user enters the museum, he/she will receive an electronic ticket providing his/her device with the necessary software to have a guided visit. Next the visitor can walk around the museum. The task marked with the **D** describes tasks influenced by context at the task level (section 2.1). In this case tasks differ whether location-awareness in the museum visit is currently enabled or not (either because of an option set by the user or the failure of detecting the location). From this point in the task model, a distinction is made between the tasks:

- when location-awareness is disabled, the user can search for an artefact and ask for some information about the selected artefact (figure 7);
- when location-awareness is enabled, the interface can be updated implicitly when the user walks by a certain artefact or the user can select any other artefact to gather some additional information (figure 8).

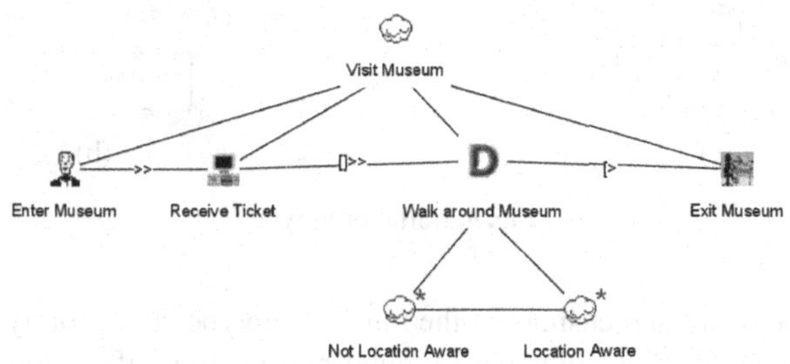

Fig. 6. Abstract task model of the museum visit case study

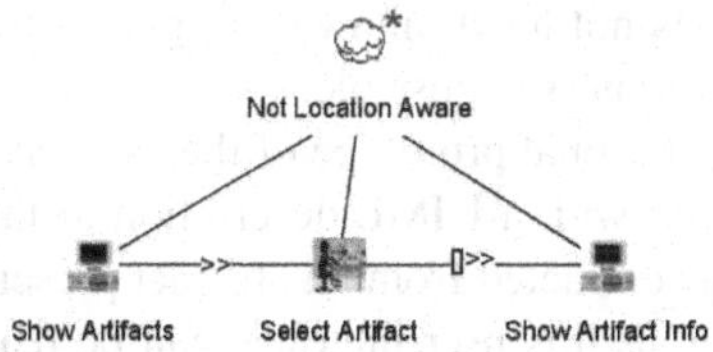

Fig. 7. Tasks without location awareness

In the following sections, we will show some prototypes we have generated in the process of developing the user interface for the abovementioned tasks. Furthermore we will use this case study to elaborate on the communication between the distinct modules of our runtime architecture.

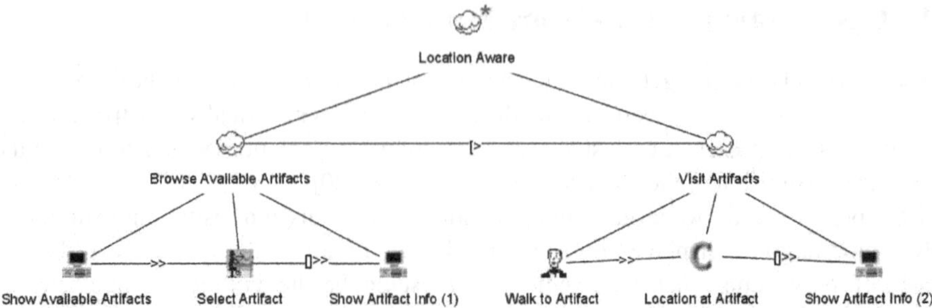

Fig. 8. Tasks with location awareness

4.1 Prototypes

In this section we will elaborate on the several prototypes generated in order to test the user interface at distinct milestones of the development process of our case scenario. We will also show the resulting user interface.

Fig. 9. Initial prototype

Figure 9 shows two screenshots of the initial prototype. The prototype is generated from user interface models containing limited presentation information. The purpose of this prototype is to provide the designer with a brief visualization of the possible tasks when the system is in a certain state and to test the influence of context on the user interface at the task and dialog level. Figure 9(a) shows a prototype with the tasks available when the system is not location-aware. Figure 9(b) on the other hand shows the tasks when location-awareness is possible.

Figure 10 shows the operational prototype of the same system. The presentation of the user interface is replaced with a UIML description of the dialogs instead of automatically generated dialogs extracted from an abstract presentation model. Notice that by the use UIML-descriptions this user interface can be realized without actual code programming. Furthermore, the user interface is bound to the functional core of the system as will be described in section 4.2.

The final step in our process of developing context-aware user interface is the realization and evaluation of the final user interface. The final user interface of the system is shown in figure 11. This user interface can contain custom widgets and interaction techniques. For instance the historical characters are shown on a timeline and moving in front of an artefact enables a shift to the corresponding place in the timeline. In the

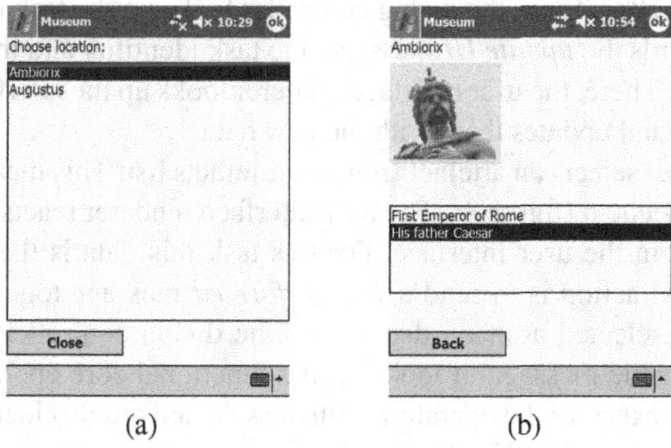

Fig. 10. Operational prototype

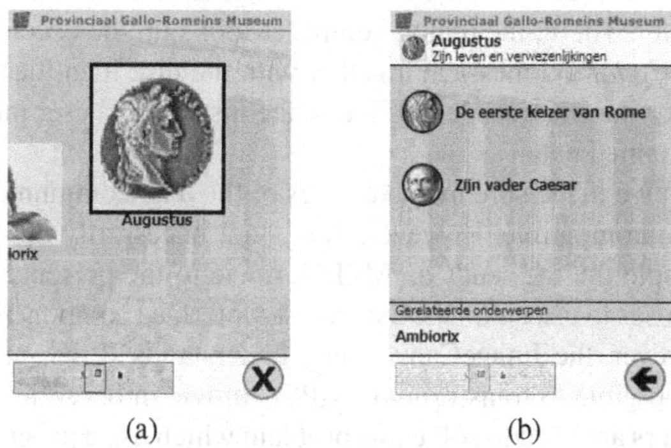

Fig. 11. The final user interface

rest of this section we will discuss how the communication works between the user interface and the other modules.

4.2 Communication Between Functional Core and User Interface

Once a dialog is activated, a connection between the functional core (FC) and the rendered user interface (UI) is maintained through the dialog controller and the user interface renderer which maintains the presentation layer. This connection is used to forward user interface updates to the renderer and to send events, thrown as a result of user interactions, back to the dialog controller. Figure 12 shows this two-way communication. When a user interacts with the instantiated user interface, this interaction is mapped on an executed task. As a result a *TaskPerformed* message together with the task identifier and the parameters needed to execute the task are sent to the dialog controller. The dialog controller then maps this task to an operation. Subsequently this operation is executed and the state of the application updated. However, when the state of the application is updated, the corresponding user interface needs to be synchronized. To accomplish this, the data controller sends an *UpdateUI* message together with the data to the dialog controller. Then, the dialog controller looks up the task that has been performed and forwards the *update UI* message, the task identifier and the data to the user interface renderer. There, the user interface renderer looks up the interface elements that represent the task and updates them with the new data.

Suppose the user selects an artefact from the artefacts list. This means that the *Select Artefact* task is executed (figure 8). The user interface renderer reacts by extracting the necessary data from the user interface. For this task this data is the selected artefact identifier. The next action is to send a *TaskPerformed* message together with the task identifier and the selected artefact identifier to the dialog controller. Once the dialog controller receives the message, it looks up the functional core operation upon which this task maps and executes the operation with the selected artefact identifier as a parameter upon the data controller. Finally, the data controller calls the necessary functional core operation. The task tree in figure 8 shows that the execution of the *Select Artefact* task enables the execution of the *Show Artefact* task. This means the data controller sends an *UpdateUI* message together with the information about the selected artefact to the dialog controller. There, the dialog controller looks up the executed task identifier and forwards the *UpdateUI* message together with the task identifier and the information data to the user interface renderer. Finally the instantiated user interface is updated with the newly obtained data.

At this moment we made sure the data types of the data communicated between the FC and the UI are compatible. However, this is not necessarily the case all the time. Suppose for example the FC sends an MPEG movie to the presentation layer and the user interface chooses to use an ImageCanvas user interface component to represent that information. However, the ImageCanvas only understands JPEG images. This means that it should be possible to transform the MPEG movie into a series of JPEG images. In [19] type handlers are used to solve this problem which use a programmatic interface that is known by both the source and the receiver. This interface is used to encapsulate data. Even if the receiver does not understand the encapsulated data, the interface makes sure it can extract the data in a known format. It is in our intention to further investigate the usefulness of such an approach in our implementation.

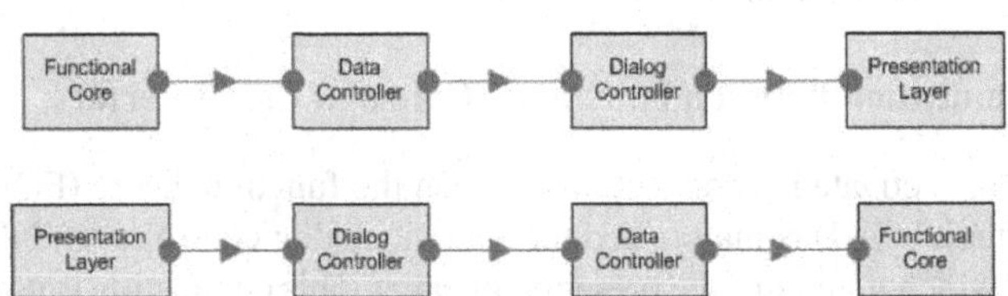

Fig. 12. Functional core communicating with the user interface

4.3 Communication Between Context Management and User Interface

The system makes use of two Abstract Context Objects (ACOs): one for notifying the user interface whether or not location-awareness is enabled, and one for providing abstract information about the user's current location (figure 13). The Context Management System (CMS) will (re)set the state of these ACOs when a change occurs. The

Context Control Unit (CCU) observes these ACOs and will notify the dialog controller when a change occurs at task or dialog level. Afterwards the dialog controller will communicate an updated interface to the presentation layer. For example, suppose location-awareness is enabled and the user walks to a certain artefact. The CMS will change the ACO's state to "location at a certain artefact" when the user is located close enough to the artefact. The CCU will interpret this as the completion of the "Location at Artefact" task and will notify the dialog controller this task has been performed. As a result the dialog model's state will move to the next one and the dialog controller will provide the presentation layer with an interface update.

Meanwhile, the CMS can also update the data model, possibly through the functional core for additional processing. The updated data will be passed on to the dialog controller in order to update the presentation.

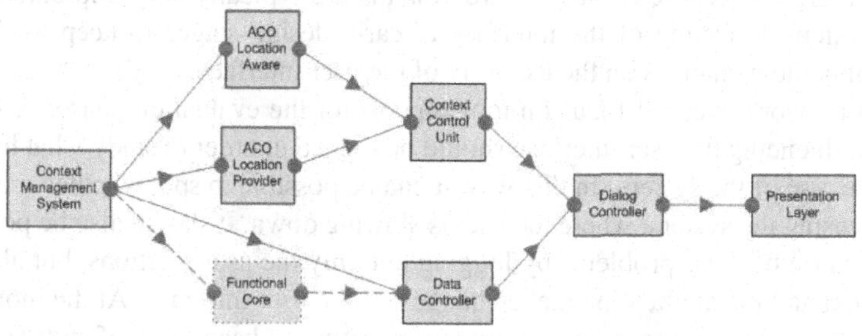

Fig. 13. Context affecting the user interface

5 Related Work

In this section we will discuss some work related to the research efforts described in this paper.

[3] defines the problem space of the domain of our approach. Cameleon-RT is a reference model defining a way runtime architectures can be built addressing the problems we outlined in this paper. The paper presents a conceptual middleware on which context-aware interactive systems can be developed. Also, a distinction is made between several distinct layers to structure a runtime: a platform layer, representing the hardware and operating system, a middleware layer, taking care of the adaptation of the user interface, and an interactive systems layer that can be compared to our presentation layer. However, their framework is more focussed on distributed and migratable user interface, where our approach focuses on the development process and tool support for context-aware applications on mobile devices.

iCAP [24] also supports rapid prototyping of context-aware applications. Their focus, however, is supporting end users in quickly designing prototypes of a context-aware application without the production of source code. The iCAP tool is informal with the purpose of making it easy for end users to interact with. Our approach is meant to support user interface developers in designing context-aware user interface with a formal model-based approach, and providing a solution to integrate context in user interface development in a more explicit way.

Topiary [16] is a special purpose tool for developing prototypes for location-aware applications. The tool provides the possibility of introducing location-based context in the generation of prototypes. Topiary also supports test runs to let designers as well as end users work with the prototype in order to get some feedback about the prototype.

6 Conclusions and Future Work

In this work, we have presented a prototype-based development cycle to construct user interfaces for context-aware systems. In order to accomplish a useful process, we have implemented both design tools and a generic runtime architecture driven by models to support the generation of prototypes during the process without implementing too much application specific code. We chose to make our user interface development process prototype-driven because context-aware systems are typically very unpredictable and require extensive testing of the interface at early design stages to keep track of the effects of context changes on the usability of the user interface.

In future work, we will focus on tool support for the evaluation phase. First of all, actions influencing the user interface should be logged in order to study what happened during the use of the system. In this way, it can be possible to spot whether users make errors in using the system, where the user is slowing down. It should also be possible to find the cause of these problems by logging not only the user's actions, but also when the context and the application make changes on the user interface. At the moment we are implementing logging in the runtime architecture to keep track of statistics where users make errors in performing tasks in the context-aware system.

As aforementioned, the data types of the information communicated between the functional core and the user interface renderer are not always compatible. In the near future it should be possible for entities that do not understand data of a particular data type thrown at them, to transform the data to a type they know or to access the data through a predefined known programmatic interface.

Acknowledgments

The authors would like to thank Jo Vermeulen, Daniël Teunkens, and Frederik Winters for their contributions to this work. Part of the research at EDM is funded by EFRO (European Fund for Regional Development), the Flemish Government and the Flemish Interdisciplinary institute for Broadband Technology (IBBT). The CoDAMoS (Context-Driven Adaptation of Mobile Services) project IWT 030320 is directly funded by the IWT (Flemish subsidy organization). The Archie project (1.2.15./D2/713) is funded by the European Regional Development Fund.

References

1. Marc Abrams, Constantinos Phanouriou, Alan L. Batongbacal, Stephen M. Williams, and Jonathan E. Shuster. *UIML: An Appliance-Independent XML User Interface Language*. World Wide Web, `http://www8.org/w8-papers/5b-hypertext-media/uiml/uiml.html`, 1998.

2. Marc Abrams, Constantinos Phanouriou, Alan L. Batongbacal, Stephen M. Williams, and Jonathan E. Shuster. UIML: An Appliance-Independent XML User Interface Language. *WWW8 / Computer Networks*, 31(11-16):1695–1708, 1999.
3. Lionel Balme, Alexandre Demeure, Nicolas Barralon, Joëlle Coutaz, and Gaelle Calvary. Cameleon-rt: A software architecture reference model for distributed, migratable, and plastic user interfaces. In Markopoulos et al. [18], pages 291–302.
4. Barry W. Boehm. A spiral model of software development and enhancement. *IEEE Computer*, 21(5):61–72, 1988.
5. Tim Clerckx, Jan Van den Bergh, and Karin Coninx. Modeling Multi-Level Context Influence on the User Interface. In *3rd Workshop on Context Modeling and Reasoning (CoMoRea'06) at the 4th IEEE International Conference on Pervasive Computing and Communication (PerCom'06), March 13–17 2006, Pisa, Italy*, 2006. Accepted for publication.
6. Tim Clerckx, Kris Luyten, and Karin Coninx. Dynamo-aid: A design process and a runtime architecture for dynamic model-based user interface development. In Rémi Bastide, Philippe A. Palanque, and Jörg Roth, editors, *EHCI/DSV-IS*, volume 3425 of *Lecture Notes in Computer Science*, pages 77–95. Springer, 2004.
7. Tim Clerckx, Kris Luyten, and Karin Coninx. Generating context-sensitive multiple device interfaces from design. In Jacob et al. [15], pages 281–294.
8. Tim Clerckx, Kris Luyten, and Karin Coninx. Designing interactive systems in context: From prototype to deployment. In *People and Computers XIX - The Bigger Picture, Proceedings of HCI 2005: The 19th British HCI Group Annual Conference, September 5-9 2005, Napier University, Edinburgh, UK*, pages 85–100. Springer, 2005.
9. Tim Clerckx, Frederik Winters, and Karin Coninx. Tool Support for Designing Context-Sensitive User Interfaces using a Model-Based Approach. In Alan Dix and Anke Dittmar, editors, *International Workshop on Task Models and Diagrams for user interface design 2005 (TAMODIA 2005)*, pages 11–18, Gdansk, Poland, Sep 26–27 2005.
10. Karin Coninx, Kris Luyten, Chris Vandervelpen, Jan Van den Bergh, and Bert Creemers. Dygimes: Dynamically Generating Interfaces for Mobile Computing Devices and Embedded Systems. In Luca Chittaro, editor, *Mobile HCI*, volume 2795 of *Lecture Notes in Computer Science*, pages 256–270. Springer, 2003.
11. Anind K. Dey. *Providing Architectural Support for Building Context-Aware Applications*. PhD thesis, College of Computing, Georgia Institute of Technology, December 2000.
12. Anind K. Dey and Gregory D. Abowd. Support for the Adaptation and Interfaces to Context. In Ahmed Seffah and Homa Javahery, editors, *Multiple User Interfaces, Cross-Platform Applications and Context-Aware Interfaces*, pages 261–296. John Wiley and Sons, 2004.
13. Karen Henricksen and Jadwiga Indulska. A Software Engineering Framework for Context-Aware Pervasive Computing. In *Second IEEE International Conference on Pervasive Computing and Communications, 14-17 March 2004, Orlando, Florida*, pages 77–86, 2004.
14. Jason I. Hong. The context fabric: An infrastructure for context-aware computing. In *CHI '02 extended abstracts on Human factors in computer systems, Minneapolis, Minnesota, USA*, pages 554–555. ACM Press, 2002.
15. Robert J. K. Jacob, Quentin Limbourg, and Jean Vanderdonckt, editors. *Computer-Aided Design of User Interfaces IV, Proceedings of Fourth International Conference on Computer-Aided Design of User Interfaces, January 14-16, 2004, Funchal, Portugal*. Kluwer, 2005.
16. Yang Li, Jason I. Hong, and James A. Landay. Topiary: a tool for prototyping location-enhanced applications. In Steven Feiner and James A. Landay, editors, *UIST*, pages 217–226. ACM, 2004.
17. Kris Luyten and Karin Coninx. Uiml.net: an open uiml renderer for the .net framework. In Jacob et al. [15], pages 257–268.

18. Panos Markopoulos, Berry Eggen, Emile H. L. Aarts, and James L. Crowley, editors. *Ambient Intelligence: Second European Symposium, EUSAI 2004, Eindhoven, The Netherlands, November 8-11, 2004. Proceedings*, volume 3295 of *Lecture Notes in Computer Science*. Springer, 2004.
19. Mark W. Newman, Shahram Izadi, W. Keith Edwards, Jana Z. Sedivy, and Trevor F. Smith. User interfaces when and where they are needed: an infrastructure for recombinant computing. In *UIST '02: Proceedings of the 15th annual ACM symposium on User interface software and technology*, pages 171–180, New York, NY, USA, 2002. ACM Press.
20. Fabio Paternò. *Model-Based Design and Evaluation of Interactive Applications*. Springer Verlag, ISBN: 1-85233-155-0, 1999.
21. Davy Preuveneers and Yolande Berbers. Adaptive context management using a component-based approach. In Lazaros Merakos, Nancy Alonistioti, and Lea Kutvonen, editors, *LNCS 3543: Proceedings of 5th IFIP International Conference on Distributed Applications and Interoperable Systems (DAIS2005)*, volume 3543 of *Lecture Notes in Computer Science (LNCS)*, pages 1–12, Athens/Greece, June 2005. Springer Verlag.
22. Davy Preuveneers, Jan Van den Bergh, Dennis Wagelaar, Andy Georges, Peter Rigole, Tim Clerckx, Yolande Berbers, Karin Coninx, Viviane Jonckers, and Koen De Bosschere. Towards an extensible context ontology for ambient intelligence. In Markopoulos et al. [18], pages 148–159.
23. Costin Pribeanu, Quentin Limbourg, and Jean Vanderdonckt. Task Modelling for Context-Sensitive User Interfaces. In Chris Johnson, editor, *Interactive Systems: Design, Specification, and Verification*, volume 2220 of *Lecture Notes in Computer Science*, pages 60–76. Springer, 2001.
24. Timothy Sohn and Anind K. Dey. icap: an informal tool for interactive prototyping of context-aware applications. In *CHI Extended Abstracts*, pages 974–975, 2003.

Author Index

Lecture Notes in Computer Science

For information about Vols. 1–4284

please contact your bookseller or Springer

Vol. 4385: K. Coninx, K. Luyten, K.A. Schneider (Eds.), Task Models and Diagrams for Users Interface Design. XI, 355 pages. 2007.

Vol. 4384: T. Washio, K. Satoh, H. Takeda, A. Inokuchi (Eds.), New Frontiers in Artificial Intelligence. IX, 401 pages. 2007. (Sublibrary LNAI).

Vol. 4381: J. Akiyama, W.Y.C. Chen, M. Kano, X. Li, Q. Yu (Eds.), Discrete Geometry, Combinatorics and Graph Theory. XI, 289 pages. 2007.

Vol. 4380: S. Spaccapietra, P. Atzeni, F. Fages, M.-S. Hacid, M. Kifer, J. Mylopoulos, B. Pernici, P. Shvaiko, J. Trujillo, I. Zaihrayeu (Eds.), Journal on Data Semantics VIII. XV, 219 pages. 2007.

Vol. 4377: M. Abe (Ed.), Topics in Cryptology – CT-RSA 2007. XI, 403 pages. 2006.

Vol. 4373: K. Langendoen, T. Voigt (Eds.), Wireless Sensor Networks. XIII, 358 pages. 2007.

Vol. 4371: K. Inoue, K. Satoh, F. Toni (Eds.), Computational Logic in Multi-Agent Systems. X, 315 pages. 2007. (Sublibrary LNAI).

Vol. 4369: M. Umeda, A. Wolf, O. Bartenstein, U. Geske, D. Seipel, O. Takata (Eds.), Declarative Programming for Knowledge Management. X, 229 pages. 2006. (Sublibrary LNAI).

Vol. 4368: T. Erlebach, C. Kaklamanis (Eds.), Approximation and Online Algorithms. X, 345 pages. 2007.

Vol. 4367: K. De Bosschere, D. Kaeli, P. Stenström, D. Whalley, T. Ungerer (Eds.), High Performance Embedded Architectures and Compilers. XI, 307 pages. 2007.

Vol. 4364: T. Kühne (Ed.), Models in Software Engineering. XI, 332 pages. 2007.

Vol. 4362: J. van Leeuwen, G.F. Italiano, W. van der Hoek, C. Meinel, H. Sack, F. Plášil (Eds.), SOFSEM 2007: Theory and Practice of Computer Science. XXI, 937 pages. 2007.

Vol. 4361: H.J. Hoogeboom, G. Păun, G. Rozenberg, A. Salomaa (Eds.), Membrane Computing. IX, 555 pages. 2006.

Vol. 4360: W. Dubitzky, A. Schuster, P.M.A. Sloot, M. Schroeder, M. Romberg (Eds.), Distributed, High-Performance and Grid Computing in Computational Biology. X, 192 pages. 2007. (Sublibrary LNBI).

Vol. 4357: L. Buttyán, V. Gligor, D. Westhoff (Eds.), Security and Privacy in Ad-Hoc and Sensor Networks. X, 193 pages. 2006.

Vol. 4355: J. Julliand, O. Kouchnarenko (Eds.), B 2007: Formal Specification and Development in B. XIII, 293 pages. 2006.

Vol. 4354: M. Hanus (Ed.), Practical Aspects of Declarative Languages. X, 335 pages. 2006.

Vol. 4353: T. Schwentick, D. Suciu (Eds.), Database Theory – ICDT 2007. XI, 419 pages. 2006.

Vol. 4352: T.-J. Cham, J. Cai, C. Dorai, D. Rajan, T.-S. Chua, L.-T. Chia (Eds.), Advances in Multimedia Modeling, Part II. XVIII, 743 pages. 2006.

Vol. 4351: T.-J. Cham, J. Cai, C. Dorai, D. Rajan, T.-S. Chua, L.-T. Chia (Eds.), Advances in Multimedia Modeling, Part I. XIX, 797 pages. 2006.

Vol. 4349: B. Cook, A. Podelski (Eds.), Verification, Model Checking, and Abstract Interpretation. XI, 395 pages. 2007.

Vol. 4348: S.T. Taft, R.A. Duff, R.L. Brukardt, E. Ploedereder, P. Leroy (Eds.), Ada 2005 Reference Manual. XXII, 765 pages. 2006.

Vol. 4347: J. Lopez (Ed.), Critical Information Infrastructures Security. X, 286 pages. 2006.

Vol. 4345: N. Maglaveras, I. Chouvarda, V. Koutkias, R. Brause (Eds.), Biological and Medical Data Analysis. XIII, 496 pages. 2006. (Sublibrary LNBI).

Vol. 4344: V. Gruhn, F. Oquendo (Eds.), Software Architecture. X, 245 pages. 2006.

Vol. 4342: H. de Swart, E. Orłowska, G. Schmidt, M. Roubens (Eds.), Theory and Applications of Relational Structures as Knowledge Instruments II. X, 373 pages. 2006. (Sublibrary LNAI).

Vol. 4341: P.Q. Nguyen (Ed.), Progress in Cryptology - VIETCRYPT 2006. XI, 385 pages. 2006.

Vol. 4340: R. Prodan, T. Fahringer, Grid Computing. XXIII, 317 pages. 2007.

Vol. 4339: E. Ayguadé, G. Baumgartner, J. Ramanujam, P. Sadayappan (Eds.), Languages and Compilers for Parallel Computing. XI, 476 pages. 2006.

Vol. 4338: P. Kalra, S. Peleg (Eds.), Computer Vision, Graphics and Image Processing. XV, 965 pages. 2006.

Vol. 4337: S. Arun-Kumar, N. Garg (Eds.), FSTTCS 2006: Foundations of Software Technology and Theoretical Computer Science. XIII, 430 pages. 2006.

Vol. 4335: S.A. Brueckner, S. Hassas, M. Jelasity, D. Yamins (Eds.), Engineering Self-Organising Systems. XII, 212 pages. 2007. (Sublibrary LNAI).

Vol. 4334: B. Beckert, R. Hähnle, P.H. Schmitt (Eds.), Verification of Object-Oriented Software. XXIX, 658 pages. 2007. (Sublibrary LNAI).

Vol. 4333: U. Reimer, D. Karagiannis (Eds.), Practical Aspects of Knowledge Management. XII, 338 pages. 2006. (Sublibrary LNAI).

Vol. 4332: A. Bagchi, V. Atluri (Eds.), Information Systems Security. XV, 382 pages. 2006.

Vol. 4331: G. Min, B. Di Martino, L.T. Yang, M. Guo, G. Ruenger (Eds.), Frontiers of High Performance Computing and Networking – ISPA 2006 Workshops. XXXVII, 1141 pages. 2006.

Vol. 4330: M. Guo, L.T. Yang, B. Di Martino, H.P. Zima, J. Dongarra, F. Tang (Eds.), Parallel and Distributed Processing and Applications. XVIII, 953 pages. 2006.

Vol. 4329: R. Barua, T. Lange (Eds.), Progress in Cryptology - INDOCRYPT 2006. X, 454 pages. 2006.

Vol. 4328: D. Penkler, M. Reitenspiess, F. Tam (Eds.), Service Availability. X, 289 pages. 2006.

Vol. 4327: M. Baldoni, U. Endriss (Eds.), Declarative Agent Languages and Technologies IV. VIII, 257 pages. 2006. (Sublibrary LNAI).

Vol. 4326: S. Göbel, R. Malkewitz, I. Iurgel (Eds.), Technologies for Interactive Digital Storytelling and Entertainment. X, 384 pages. 2006.

Vol. 4325: J. Cao, I. Stojmenovic, X. Jia, S.K. Das (Eds.), Mobile Ad-hoc and Sensor Networks. XIX, 887 pages. 2006.

Vol. 4323: G. Doherty, A. Blandford (Eds.), Interactive Systems. XI, 269 pages. 2007.

Vol. 4320: R. Gotzhein, R. Reed (Eds.), System Analysis and Modeling: Language Profiles. X, 229 pages. 2006.

Vol. 4319: L.-W. Chang, W.-N. Lie (Eds.), Advances in Image and Video Technology. XXVI, 1347 pages. 2006.

Vol. 4318: H. Lipmaa, M. Yung, D. Lin (Eds.), Information Security and Cryptology. XI, 305 pages. 2006.

Vol. 4317: S.K. Madria, K.T. Claypool, R. Kannan, P. Uppuluri, M.M. Gore (Eds.), Distributed Computing and Internet Technology. XIX, 466 pages. 2006.

Vol. 4316: M.M. Dalkilic, S. Kim, J. Yang (Eds.), Data Mining and Bioinformatics. VIII, 197 pages. 2006. (Sublibrary LNBI).

Vol. 4314: C. Freksa, M. Kohlhase, K. Schill (Eds.), KI 2006: Advances in Artificial Intelligence. XII, 458 pages. 2007. (Sublibrary LNAI).

Vol. 4313: T. Margaria, B. Steffen (Eds.), Leveraging Applications of Formal Methods. IX, 197 pages. 2006.

Vol. 4312: S. Sugimoto, J. Hunter, A. Rauber, A. Morishima (Eds.), Digital Libraries: Achievements, Challenges and Opportunities. XVIII, 571 pages. 2006.

Vol. 4311: K. Cho, P. Jacquet (Eds.), Technologies for Advanced Heterogeneous Networks II. XI, 253 pages. 2006.

Vol. 4309: P. Inverardi, M. Jazayeri (Eds.), Software Engineering Education in the Modern Age. VIII, 207 pages. 2006.

Vol. 4308: S. Chaudhuri, S.R. Das, H.S. Paul, S. Tirthapura (Eds.), Distributed Computing and Networking. XIX, 608 pages. 2006.

Vol. 4307: P. Ning, S. Qing, N. Li (Eds.), Information and Communications Security. XIV, 558 pages. 2006.

Vol. 4306: Y. Avrithis, Y. Kompatsiaris, S. Staab, N.E. O'Connor (Eds.), Semantic Multimedia. XII, 241 pages. 2006.

Vol. 4305: A.A. Shvartsman (Ed.), Principles of Distributed Systems. XIII, 441 pages. 2006.

Vol. 4304: A. Sattar, B.-H. Kang (Eds.), AI 2006: Advances in Artificial Intelligence. XXVII, 1303 pages. 2006. (Sublibrary LNAI).

Vol. 4303: A. Hoffmann, B.-H. Kang, D. Richards, S. Tsumoto (Eds.), Advances in Knowledge Acquisition and Management. XI, 259 pages. 2006. (Sublibrary LNAI).

Vol. 4302: J. Domingo-Ferrer, L. Franconi (Eds.), Privacy in Statistical Databases. XI, 383 pages. 2006.

Vol. 4301: D. Pointcheval, Y. Mu, K. Chen (Eds.), Cryptology and Network Security. XIII, 381 pages. 2006.

Vol. 4300: Y.Q. Shi (Ed.), Transactions on Data Hiding and Multimedia Security I. IX, 139 pages. 2006.

Vol. 4299: S. Renals, S. Bengio, J.G. Fiscus (Eds.), Machine Learning for Multimodal Interaction. XII, 470 pages. 2006.

Vol. 4297: Y. Robert, M. Parashar, R. Badrinath, V.K. Prasanna (Eds.), High Performance Computing - HiPC 2006. XXIV, 642 pages. 2006.

Vol. 4296: M.S. Rhee, B. Lee (Eds.), Information Security and Cryptology – ICISC 2006. XIII, 358 pages. 2006.

Vol. 4295: J.D. Carswell, T. Tezuka (Eds.), Web and Wireless Geographical Information Systems. XI, 269 pages. 2006.

Vol. 4294: A. Dan, W. Lamersdorf (Eds.), Service-Oriented Computing – ICSOC 2006. XIX, 653 pages. 2006.

Vol. 4293: A. Gelbukh, C.A. Reyes-Garcia (Eds.), MICAI 2006: Advances in Artificial Intelligence. XXVIII, 1232 pages. 2006. (Sublibrary LNAI).

Vol. 4292: G. Bebis, R. Boyle, B. Parvin, D. Koracin, P. Remagnino, A. Nefian, G. Meenakshisundaram, V. Pascucci, J. Zara, J. Molineros, H. Theisel, T. Malzbender (Eds.), Advances in Visual Computing, Part II. XXXII, 906 pages. 2006.

Vol. 4291: G. Bebis, R. Boyle, B. Parvin, D. Koracin, P. Remagnino, A. Nefian, G. Meenakshisundaram, V. Pascucci, J. Zara, J. Molineros, H. Theisel, T. Malzbender (Eds.), Advances in Visual Computing, Part I. XXXI, 916 pages. 2006.

Vol. 4290: M. van Steen, M. Henning (Eds.), Middleware 2006. XIII, 425 pages. 2006.

Vol. 4289: M. Ackermann, B. Berendt, M. Grobelnik, A. Hotho, D. Mladenič, G. Semeraro, M. Spiliopoulou, G. Stumme, V. Svátek, M. van Someren (Eds.), Semantics, Web and Mining. X, 197 pages. 2006. (Sublibrary LNAI).

Vol. 4288: T. Asano (Ed.), Algorithms and Computation. XX, 766 pages. 2006.

Vol. 4287: C. Mao, T. Yokomori (Eds.), DNA Computing. XII, 440 pages. 2006.

Vol. 4286: P.G. Spirakis, M. Mavronicolas, S.C. Kontogiannis (Eds.), Internet and Network Economics. XI, 401 pages. 2006.

Vol. 4285: Y. Matsumoto, R.W. Sproat, K.-F. Wong, M. Zhang (Eds.), Computer Processing of Oriental Languages. XVII, 544 pages. 2006. (Sublibrary LNAI).